Words Preview

Unit 01 주제 파악하기

Reading 01

familiar 친숙한, 익숙한
reflection 반사, (거울 등에 비친) 모습
be used to ~에 익숙하다
reverse 뒤집다, 거꾸로 하다
seem ~으로 보이다
confident 자신감 있는
awkward 어색한, 서투른
tend to ~하는 경향이 있다
factor 요인, 요소

Reading 02

be familiar with ~에 익숙하다
probably 아마, 대개는
sensitive 민감한
temperature 온도, 기온
conduct 전달하다
expose 노출시키다
pressure 압력
process 과정
property 특성, 속성
browning 갈변
proper 적절한
facility 시설, 설비

Reading 03

vegetarian 채식주의(의)
diet 식단
nutritious 영양가 있는
prevent 방지하다
concern 걱정, 염려, 관심
statistics 통계
majority 대부분, 대다수
protest 저항하다, 항의하다
pollution 오염

Unit 02 제목 파악하기

Reading 04

dust 먼지
shrink 수축하다, 줄어들다
gravity 중력
force 힘을 가하다
squeeze 압축하다, 짜다

enable 가능하게 하다
run out 고갈되다
gather 모이다, 모으다
fade away 사라지다
use up 다 써버리다

Reading 05

take place 발생하다, 일어나다
subject (영화, 사진 등의) 피사체, 대상
attract (이목, 관심 등을) 끌다
minimize 최소화하다
atmosphere 분위기
contrast 대조, 대비
emphasize 강조하다
tension 긴장감
position 위치
holiness 신성함
technique 기술

Reading 06

end up 결국 ~하게 되다
electronic equipment 전자기기
estimate 추산하다
billion 10억
roughly 대략, 약
goods 물건, 제품, 상품
government 정부
waste 낭비, 쓰레기
pure 순전한, 순수한
rubbish 쓰레기
observe (발언·의견을) 말하다

Unit 03 목적·주장 파악하기

Reading 07

in response to ~에 답하여
serve 제공하다
nutrient 영양소, 영양분
oppose 반대하다
allergic 알레르기의
unfair 불공정한, 부당한
well-balanced 균형 잡힌
protein 단백질
remove 제거하다
limit 제한하다
hinder 방해하다

label 라벨[표]을 붙이다
contain 포함하다

Reading 08

expert 전문가
nonverbal 비언어적인
significant 상당한, 중요한
relationship 관계
be aware of ~를 인식하다
encouraging 격려하는
empower 힘을 실어 주다
require 요구하다
climate 분위기
be at work 일하고 있다, 가동 중이다

Unit 04 요지 파악하기

Reading 09

coral reef 산호초
marine 바다의, 해양의
species 종
environmental 환경의
result in ~를 초래하다
industrial 산업의
immediate 즉시의, 즉각의
combination 결합, 조합
reduce 줄이다
emission 배출
uncertain 불확실한

Reading 10

comfortable 편안한
discomfort 불편함
succeed 성공하다
benefit (~에게) 유익하다
valuable 귀중한
opportunity 기회
unfamiliarity 생소함, 익숙하지 않음
expand 확장하다
achieve 성취하다

Unit 05 요약하기

Reading 11

advertisement 광고

melt away 녹아서 없어지다
partnership 동반자 관계
bless 축복하다

Reading 22

explore 탐험하다
numerous 수많은
dinosaur 공룡
fossil 화석
amateur 아마추어
bone-hunter 뼈 발굴자
anticipation 기대
rare 희귀한
eagerly 열심히
search for ~을 찾다
wander 헤매고 다니다
deserted 인적이 드문
darken 어두워지다
sigh 한숨을 쉬며 말하다

Unit 09 글의 순서 파악하기

Reading 23

resolution 결심
psychologist 심리학자
suggest 시사하다
unrealistic 비현실적인
expectation 기대
underestimate 과소평가하다
dramatic 극적인
rapid 빠른
false 거짓의, 틀린
syndrome 증후군, 신드롬
involve 포함하다
overconfidence 지나친 자신감
visible 눈에 보이는
give up ~을 포기하다
attempt 시도

Reading 24

distraction 집중을 방해하는 것, 주의산만
come up with ~을 생각해 내다
dealing 행위, 관계
annoying 짜증나게 하는
legend 전해오는 이야기, 전설
constantly 끊임없이

interrupt 방해하다
demand 요구
suffer 시달리다, 고통받다
emotional 감정적인
knock over 쳐서 넘어뜨리다
candle 초, 양초

Reading 25

interact 상호 작용하다, 소통하다
critical 중요한
examine 검토하다
misinformation 잘못된 정보
raise 제기하다
well-known 잘 알려진
weakness 약점
youth 젊은이, 청년
tech platform 기술 플랫폼
certainly 분명히, 확실히
responsibility 책임
combat 싸우다
threat 위협

Unit 10 주어진 문장 넣기

Reading 26

typically 전형적으로
improve 향상시키다
cue 신호, 단서
recall 기억, 회상
function 기능
come out on top 1등을 차지하다
additionally 게다가
cautious 주의 깊은
detail-oriented 세부적인 것을 지향하는
pay attention 집중하다
object 물건, 사물

Reading 27

decision 결정
factual 사실적인
knowledge 지식
despite ~에도 불구하고
remain 남아 있다
accurately 정확하게
identify 식별하다
spot 찾아내다

awareness 인식
workforce 노동자, 노동력
self-knowledge 자기 이해
mastery 숙달

Reading 28

observation 관찰
transfer 이동, 옮기다, 이동하다
potential 잠재적인
source 원천, 근원
a series of 일련의
organism 유기체
grassland 초원, 목초지
hence 이런 이유로
available 이용 가능한
intake 섭취(량)

Unit 11 무관한 문장 찾기

Reading 29

muscle 근육
overtrain 과도하게 훈련하다
musical instrument 악기
memorization 암기
practical 실용적인
complex 복잡한
concept 개념
along with ~와 함께
concentration 집중(력)
observation 관찰(력)

Reading 30

spread 확산
disease 질병
operate 운영되다
advance 발전하다
century 세기
destructive 파괴적인
outbreak 발생, 발발
replanning 재계획
rebuilding 재건
in spite of ~에도 불구하고
reconstruction 재건, 복원
decline 쇠퇴하다
pioneering 선구적인
cholera 콜레라

Words Preview

Unit 12 빈칸 완성하기1(단어)

Reading 31

fiction 소설, 허구
mystery 미스터리
creativity 창의성
effective 효과적인
nonfiction 논픽션(소설이 아닌 산문)
react 반응하다
set aside ~을 제쳐두다

Reading 32

consistently 일관되게
predictably 예측 가능하게
distress 고통, 괴로움
ensure 반드시 ~하게 하다, 보장하다
hold ~ in ~을 참다
companion 친구, 동반자
display 보이다, 나타내다
withhold (~을) 주지 않다

Unit 13 빈칸 완성하기2(구·절)

Reading 33

look back at ~을 돌아보다
statement 발언, 말
charismatic 카리스마 있는
entire 전체의
sit up and take notice 주목하다
faith 신념
emotion 감정
strength 힘
wholly 전적으로
be convinced of ~을 확신하다
amazement 놀람

Reading 34

ancestor 조상
water-dwelling 물에 사는
relative 동족, 동류
shelter 거처, 은신처
lung 폐
take a dip (몸을) 잠깐 담그다
dry out 건조해지다
lay (알을) 낳다
creature 생물

land-dwelling 육지에 사는
adult 성체

Unit 14 밑줄 친 부분 파악하기

Reading 35

religion 종교
tradition 전통
perceive 인식하다
pressure 압박
remain 머무르다
internalize 내면화하다
identity 정체성
define 정의하다

Reading 36

interpret 해석하다
selectively 선택적으로
stack 쌓다
arrange 배열하다
evidence 증거
support 뒷받침하다
viewpoint 관점
perception 지각, 인식
stand out 두드러지다, 눈에 띄다
expectation 기대, 예상
current 현재의
quote 인용(문)
highlight 강조하다
phenomenon 현상

Unit 15 장문 독해하기

Reading 37

inherent 타고난, 고유한
physical 신체적인, 물리적인
mental 정신적인
limitation 한계
independently 독립적으로
brilliant 뛰어난, 훌륭한
means 수단
community 공동체
commodity 상품
conceptual 개념적인
irrespective of ~에 상관없이

willingly 기꺼이
essentially 본질적으로

Reading 38

fall off 넘어지다
second nature 습관, 제2의 천성
judge 판단하다, 판정하다
shame 애석한 일, 수치
repetition 반복
central 핵심적인
rewire 재연결하다, 전선을 다시 배치하다
neuron 뉴런, 신경 세포
reliable 신뢰할 만한
involve 연관시키다

Unit 16 복합 문단 독해하기

Reading 39

pedal 페달을 밟다
side by side 나란히, 함께
rescue 구조하다
scrape 긁다
dorm 기숙사
encouragement 격려
breeze 산들바람
incident 사건
housemother 여자 사감
swollen 부은
edge 모퉁이
fork 갈라지다
run into ~와 충돌하다

Reading 40

organize 정리하다
paper clip 종이 클립[집게]
rust 녹, 녹슬다
hand 건네주다
permission 허락, 허가
face 직면하다, 마주보다
generation 세대, (비슷한 연령의) 사람들
equality 평등, 균등
marvel 놀라다, 경탄하다
separate 분리하다, 나누다
deliver (연설을) 하다
audience 청중

Reading master 중등
수능 plus 내신
Level 2

WRITERS

송현우 이승옥 이혜은 류은정 신성원 홍미정

STAFF

발행인 정선욱
퍼블리싱 총괄 남형주
개발 · 기획 김태원 박하영
디자인 김정인 차혜린
유통 · 마케팅 서준성 김지희
제작 김한길 김경수

Reading master 중등 Level 2 202306 제2판 1쇄 202507 제2판 6쇄

펴낸곳 이투스에듀(주) 서울시 서초구 남부순환로 2547
고객센터 1599-3225
등록번호 제2007-000035호
ISBN 979-11-389-1411-6 [53740]
· 이 책은 저작권법에 따라 보호받는 저작물이므로 무단전재와 무단복제를 금합니다.
· 잘못 만들어진 책은 구입처에서 교환해 드립니다.

기본 독해부터 수능 독해까지 한번에 완성

Reading master 중등

수능+내신

"한 권의 독해서로 독해 기본기도 쌓고,
수능식 영어 지문 독해까지 할 수는 없을까?"

Reading master 중등은 이와 같은 고민으로 태어났습니다.

수능 경향을 담되,
어휘 및 문장 구조는 중등 수준에 맞는 지문으로 구성하였습니다.

Level별로 단어 수와 렉사일 지수로 중등 난이도를 적용하며
수능 영어식 지문과 문제로 구성하여
Reading master 중등 한 권으로
'영어 독해'를 완성하도록 담아냈습니다.

Level 1	Level 2	Level 3
Words: 120-140 Lexile: 500-700	Words: 140-150 Lexile: 700-900	Words: 150-160 Lexile: 800-1000

* LEXILE® measures(렉사일 지수)는 MetaMetrics®라는 미국 교육연구소에서 개발한 가장 공신력 있는 읽기 지수입니다.

How to Study

독해의 기본을 위한
Reading Key

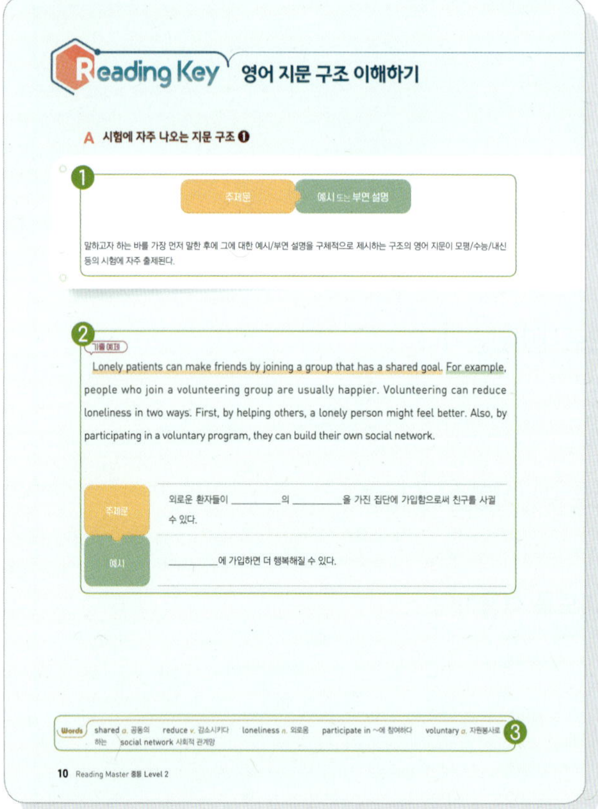

수능 유형의 대표 문제 + 내신형 문제로
독해 실력 완성

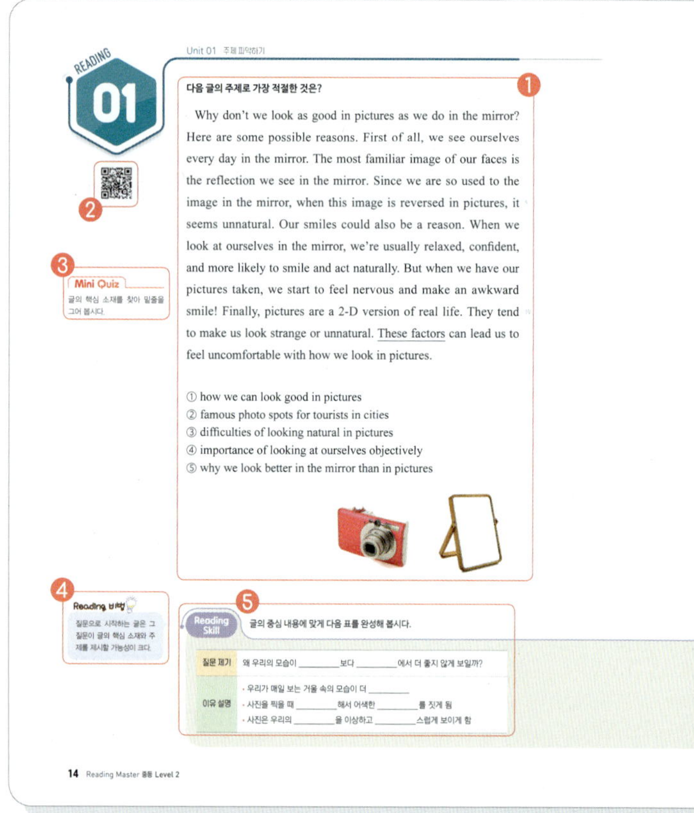

① 도식화로 확인하고 간략한 설명으로 이해하는 독해 비법

② 각 레벨 수준에 맞게 응용된 교육청·평가원 모의평가 및 수능 기출 문제로 핵심 독해 스킬 습득

③ 독해 지문 속 어휘 실력 강화

① 수능 유형의 대표 문제 제시

② 원어민의 지문 음원 QR 코드 제시

③ 어떤 부분에 지문 이해의 중점을 두어야 하는지 Mini Quiz를 통해 가이드

④ 문제 해결을 위한 다양한 독해 전략과 Reading 비법을 제공

⑤ 독해 유형별 지문에 적용되는 Reading Skill 연습으로 글의 구조 분석

Workbook으로
내신 대비 및 직독직해 연습

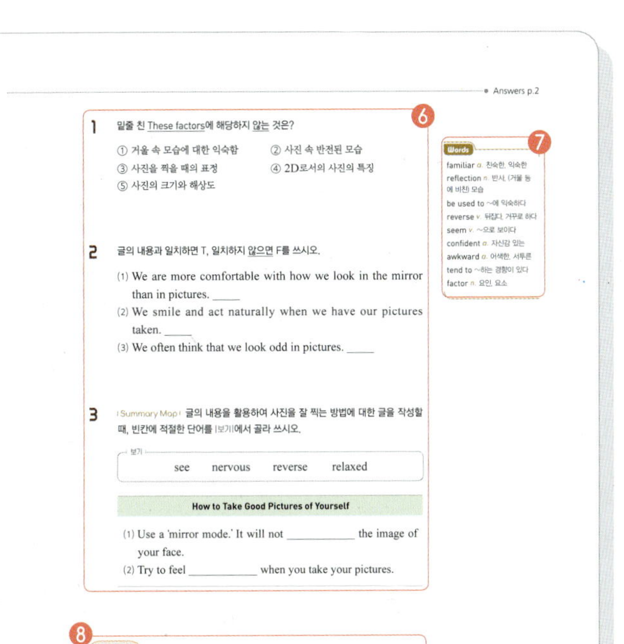

6 지문의 완벽한 이해를 돕는 다양한 독해 내신 문제 및 지문 구조화 연습

7 독해 지문 속 어휘 실력 강화

8 의미 단위 끊어 읽기 방식의 직독직해와 주어와 동사 찾기를 통해 정확한 문장 해석 연습

1 Review Test 지문별 내신 문제 및 서술형 문제 완벽 대비

2 핵심 직독직해 지문별 주요 문장의 직독직해 및 주어와 동사 찾기를 통해 정확한 문장 해석과 독해 속도를 높이는 연습

Contents

○ 책속의 책 | 내신대비 워크북

중심 내용 파악하기

 영어 지문 구조 이해하기

A 시험에 자주 나오는 지문 구조 ❶

주제문 → 예시 또는 부연 설명

말하고자 하는 바를 가장 먼저 말한 후에 그에 대한 예시/부연 설명을 구체적으로 제시하는 구조의 영어 지문이 모평/수능/내신 등의 시험에 자주 출제된다.

기출 예제

Lonely patients can make friends by joining a group that has a shared goal. For example, people who join a volunteering group are usually happier. Volunteering can reduce loneliness in two ways. First, by helping others, a lonely person might feel better. Also, by participating in a voluntary program, they can build their own social network.

주제문	외로운 환자들이 __________의 __________을 가진 집단에 가입함으로써 친구를 사귈 수 있다.
예시	__________에 가입하면 더 행복해질 수 있다.

 시험에 자주 나오는 지문 구조 ❷

예시 또는 소재 소개   주제문

주제와 관련 있는 소재를 소개하거나 사례를 먼저 말한 후에 글쓴이가 말하고자 하는 주제를 마지막에 결론처럼 제시하는 구조의 영어 지문이 모평/수능/내신 등의 시험에 자주 출제된다.

기출 예제

  If you walk into a room that smells like fresh bread, you quickly detect the pleasant smell. But after you stay in the room for a few minutes, the smell seems to disappear. This can happen with happiness, too. We all have things that make us happy, such as a loving partner, good health, a satisfying job, or enough food to eat. But over time, we get used to these things and forget how lucky we are.

예시

처음 방에 들어갔을 때 갓 구운 빵 냄새를 __________ 알아차리지만 그 냄새에 __________지면 냄새가 나지 않는 것 같다.

주제문

우리를 __________하게 해 주는 것들에 __________지면 우리는 그 소중함을 잊어버린다.

Words detect *v.* 알아차리다, 감지하다   pleasant *a.* 기분 좋은, 즐거운   disappear *v.* 사라지다   satisfying *a.* 만족스러운
get used to ~에 익숙해지다   forget *v.* 잊다

C 시험에 자주 나오는 지문 구조 ❸

일반적인 이야기　반론(주제문)

일반적인 상식, 당연하게 생각되는 사실로 글을 시작한 후, '그렇지만 더 중요한 것이 있다'는 반론을 통해 글을 읽는 사람들의 주의를 집중시키는 구조의 영어 지문이 모평/수능/내신 등의 시험에 자주 출제된다.

기출 예제

Many people think of what might happen in the future based on past failures and get trapped by them. For example, if you have failed at something before, you might be scared to try again in case you fail again. But your future is not your past, and you can have a better future. You must decide to forget about your mistakes. If you let your past control you, you won't be able to achieve your dreams.

일반적인 이야기
많은 사람들이 과거의 __________ 에 근거하여 __________ 의 일을 생각한다.

반론(주제문)
__________ 에 얽매이면 __________ 을 이룰 수 없다.

| 주제문 | 예시나 근거 | 주제문 |

말하고자 하는 바를 앞에서 화두를 던지듯이 얘기하고 나서 소재를 소개하거나 사례를 먼저 말한 후에 글쓴이가 말하고자 하는 주제를 마지막에 결론처럼 제시하는 구조의 글도 있다. 주제문이 겉으로 드러나지 않지만 주제를 함의하고 있는 단락도 있으니 이 점도 유의해야 한다.

기출 예제

In colleges across the United States and other countries, pets are being used to help students who are feeling depressed or anxious. To help students feel less stressed, school officials organize pet therapy events, especially during exams. Research shows that spending time with pets can lower blood pressure and stress levels while increasing happiness. Pet visits on campus can be a great way to support students.

주제문 ___________은 우울한 ___________에게 도움이 된다.

예시/근거
1. 학교에서는 학생들을 위한 ___________ 행사를 마련하기도 한다.
2. 연구 결과 ___________ 과 ___________ 수치를 낮추고 행복감을 증가시킨다고 한다.

주제문 학교 내 ___________은 학생들을 도와주는 훌륭한 방법이다.

Words college *n.* 대학 depressed *a.* 우울한, 의기소침한 anxious *a.* 불안해하는 official *n.* 관계자 therapy *n.* 치료 especially *ad.* 특히 lower *v.* 낮추다 blood pressure 혈압 support *v.* 도와주다

READING 01

다음 글의 주제로 가장 적절한 것은?

Why don't we look as good in pictures as we do in the mirror? Here are some possible reasons. First of all, we see ourselves every day in the mirror. The most familiar image of our faces is the reflection we see in the mirror. Since we are so used to the image in the mirror, when this image is reversed in pictures, it seems unnatural. Our smiles could also be a reason. When we look at ourselves in the mirror, we're usually relaxed, confident, and more likely to smile and act naturally. But when we have our pictures taken, we start to feel nervous and make an awkward smile! Finally, pictures are a 2-D version of real life. They tend to make us look strange or unnatural. <u>These factors</u> can lead us to feel uncomfortable with how we look in pictures.

① how we can look good in pictures
② famous photo spots for tourists in cities
③ difficulties of looking natural in pictures
④ importance of looking at ourselves objectively
⑤ why we look better in the mirror than in pictures

Mini Quiz

글의 핵심 소재를 찾아 밑줄을 그어 봅시다.

Reading 비법

질문으로 시작하는 글은 그 질문이 글의 핵심 소재와 주제를 제시할 가능성이 크다.

Reading Skill 글의 중심 내용에 맞게 다음 표를 완성해 봅시다.

질문 제기	왜 우리의 모습이 __________보다 __________에서 더 좋지 않게 보일까?
이유 설명	• 우리가 매일 보는 거울 속의 모습이 더 __________ • 사진을 찍을 때 __________해서 어색한 __________를 짓게 됨 • 사진은 우리의 __________을 이상하고 __________스럽게 보이게 함

1 밑줄 친 These factors에 해당하지 <u>않는</u> 것은?

① 거울 속 모습에 대한 익숙함   ② 사진 속 반전된 모습
③ 사진을 찍을 때의 표정   ④ 2D로서의 사진의 특징
⑤ 사진의 크기와 해상도

familiar *a.* 친숙한, 익숙한
reflection *n.* 반사, (거울 등에 비친) 모습
be used to ~에 익숙하다
reverse *v.* 뒤집다, 거꾸로 하다
seem *v.* ~으로 보이다
confident *a.* 자신감 있는
awkward *a.* 어색한, 서투른
tend to ~하는 경향이 있다
factor *n.* 요인, 요소

2 글의 내용과 일치하면 T, 일치하지 <u>않으면</u> F를 쓰시오.

(1) We are more comfortable with how we look in the mirror than in pictures. ______

(2) We smile and act naturally when we have our pictures taken. ______

(3) We often think that we look odd in pictures. ______

3 |Summary Map| 글의 내용을 활용하여 사진을 잘 찍는 방법에 대한 글을 작성할 때, 빈칸에 적절한 단어를 |보기|에서 골라 쓰시오.

┤ 보기 ├

| see | nervous | reverse | relaxed |

How to Take Good Pictures of Yourself

(1) Use a 'mirror mode.' It will not ___________ the image of your face.

(2) Try to feel ___________ when you take your pictures.

직독직해 Skill

다음을 의미 단위로 끊어 읽고(/), 주어(S)와 동사(V)에 표시해 봅시다.

· But when we have our pictures taken, we start to feel nervous and make an awkward smile!

READING 02

Mini Quiz

글을 읽으면서 구체적인 이유가
처음 제시되는 문장을 찾아 밑줄
을 그어 봅시다.

다음 글의 주제로 가장 적절한 것은?

Have you ever seen milk in a can? While you may be familiar with milk in cartons or plastic bottles, you probably haven't seen it in cans. There are interesting reasons for this. Milk is very sensitive to temperature and must be stored at temperatures between 0 and 4 degrees Celsius. Unfortunately, cans can make milk go bad quickly because they conduct heat well. Furthermore, many canned foods are heated at high temperatures and exposed to high pressures. But when milk goes through this process, it can change the taste and properties of the milk due to browning. Additionally, cans are more expensive to produce than cartons or plastic bottles. Although milk producers could produce canned milk, the reasons mentioned above and a lack of proper packaging facilities make it a less attractive option.

*carton: (우유 포장에 사용되는) 종이 팩

① difficulties in producing canned milk
② the role of milk in improving our health
③ temperature as an important factor for milk
④ differences between milk and canned drinks
⑤ disadvantages of drinking canned milk every day

Reading 비법

주제는 글 전체의 내용을 포
괄해야 한다.

Reading Skill 글의 중심 내용에 맞게 다음 표를 완성해 봅시다.

주제	우리가 __________ 된 우유를 __________ 이유
근거	• 캔은 __________ 을 잘 전달하여 우유를 쉽게 __________ 함 • 캔 제품이 되는 과정은 __________ 으로 인해 우유의 __________ 과 __________ 을 변하게 함 • 캔이 다른 포장재에 비해 가격이 __________

1 글을 읽고 답할 수 있는 질문은?

① How much milk is produced in a day?
② Why does milk in cans go bad easily?
③ Why are cans more expensive to make?
④ Where can we buy milk in cans?
⑤ When will milk in cans be popular?

2 글의 제목을 아래와 같이 쓸 때, 빈칸에 적절한 단어를 글에서 찾아 쓰시오.

Milk in Cans: Not a(n) _____________ Choice in Milk Production

3 | Summary Map | 글의 내용을 활용하여 다음 중 캔을 포장재로 사용하기에 적합한 음료를 고르시오.

Checklist	A	B	C	D
Is it very sensitive to heat?	Yes	No	No	No
Can it be heated at high temperatures and exposed to high pressures?	Yes	Yes	Yes	No
Is it necessary to reduce packaging costs?	No	No	Yes	Yes

Words

be familiar with ~에 익숙하다
probably *ad.* 아마, 대개는
sensitive *a.* 민감한
temperature *n.* 온도, 기온
conduct *v.* 전달하다
expose *v.* 노출시키다
pressure *n.* 압력
process *n.* 과정
property *n.* 특성, 속성
browning *n.* 갈변
proper *a.* 적절한
facility *n.* 시설, 설비

직독직해 Skill 다음을 의미 단위로 끊어 읽고(/), 주어(S)와 동사(V)에 표시해 봅시다.

· Unfortunately. cans can make milk go bad quickly because they conduct heat well.

READING 03

다음 글의 주제로 가장 적절한 것은?　　　　　기출 응용

　Vegetarian eating is becoming more popular as more and more young adults say no to eating meat and fish. According to the American Dietetic Association, planned vegetarian diets are healthful and nutritious. They also provide health benefits in preventing and treating certain diseases. However, young adults don't decide to change their diets only out of concern for their health. Some make the choice out of concern for animal rights. Many statistics show that the majority of the animals raised for food are kept in small cages. So, many teens give up meat to protest those conditions. Others turn to vegetarianism to support the environment. Meat production uses large amounts of water, land, grain, and energy. It also creates problems with animal waste resulting in pollution. <u>These trends</u> show that today's youth are more aware of and sensitive to animal rights and environmental problems.

① reasons why young people go for vegetarian diets
② ways to build healthy eating habits for teenagers
③ vegetables that help lower your risk of cancer
④ importance of maintaining a balanced diet
⑤ disadvantages of plant-based diets

Mini Quiz

글의 흐름이 바뀌는 문장을 찾아 밑줄을 그어 봅시다.

Reading 비법

표현이나 문장 구조만 다르며 의미가 같은 문장은 주제문일 가능성이 크다.

Reading Skill

주제문과 근거문을 찾아 다음 표를 완성해 봅시다.

주제문	젊은이들은 단순히 __________을 신경 쓰기 때문에 __________을 바꾸는 것이 아니다.
근거문	• 식용으로 길러지는 __________들의 열악한 환경과 그들의 __________를 생각한다. • 고기를 생산하며 사용되는 수많은 양의 __________과 발생하는 __________을 고려한다.

1 밑줄 친 <u>These trends</u>가 의미하는 것은?

① 젊은이들이 건강 문제를 신경 쓰는 것
② 젊은이들이 체계적인 식단을 계획하는 것
③ 젊은이들이 동물들의 권리를 보호하는 것
④ 젊은이들이 환경 문제에 관심을 가지는 것
⑤ 젊은이들이 다양한 이유로 채식을 결심하는 것

2 글의 내용과 일치하도록 **틀린** 부분을 고쳐 문장을 다시 쓰시오.

Many teens choose vegetarian eating to support the poor conditions of the animals raised for food.

→ ________________________________

3 | Complete a Poster | 다음은 채식을 장려하는 포스터이다. 글의 내용과 일치하도록 빈칸에 적절한 단어를 글에서 찾아 쓰시오.

Words
vegetarian *a.* 채식주의(의)
diet *n.* 식단
nutritious *a.* 영양가 있는
prevent *v.* 방지하다
concern *n.* 걱정, 염려, 관심
statistics *n.* 통계
majority *n.* 대부분, 대다수
cage *n.* 우리
protest *v.* 저항하다, 항의하다
pollution *n.* 오염

직독직해 Skill 다음을 의미 단위로 끊어 읽고(/), 주어(S)와 동사(V)에 표시해 봅시다.

· Vegetarian eating is becoming more popular as more and more young adults say no to eating meat and fish.

____

다음 글의 제목으로 가장 적절한 것은?

Stars start out as clouds of gas and dust. After millions of years, these clouds begin to shrink because gravity forces the gas and dust together. As it is squeezed, the cloud heats up to form a young star. If this reaches 27 million degrees Fahrenheit, it is hot enough to start nuclear fusion. This reaction is needed for a new star to form. The energy enables a star to keep its shape and shine. What happens when the fuel runs out and the star dies? It depends on how much dust gathered in the first place. For example, stars with less than half the mass of the sun fade away very slowly. But most stars use up their fuel and finally return to clouds of gas and dust after a series of steps.

*nuclear fusion: 핵융합

① Stars: Shining Jewels in the Sky
② The Life Cycle of a Star: Its Start and End
③ The Darker the Night, the Brighter the Stars
④ Look Up at the Stars, Not Down at Your Feet
⑤ The Magical Power behind the Growth of Stars

Mini Quiz

글의 핵심 소재를 찾아 밑줄을 그어 봅시다.

Reading 비법

제목은 글의 주제를 함축적 혹은 비유적으로 나타낸 문장이다.

Reading Skill

글의 중심 내용에 맞게 다음 표를 완성해 봅시다.

주제	별의 __________부터 __________에 이르는 __________
세부 내용	• 별이 만들어지기 이전 __________의 __________ • __________ 별이 __________하기 위한 조건 • 별이 __________를 다 __________하고 겪는 소멸의 과정

1 글을 읽고 답할 수 <u>없는</u> 질문은?

① Why do clouds of gas and dust start to shrink?
② What is necessary for nuclear fusion to happen?
③ What makes a star keep shining?
④ What is the mass of the sun?
⑤ When does a star return to clouds of gas and dust?

2 다음 영영 풀이에 해당하는 단어를 글에서 찾아 쓰시오.

> the force that attracts a body toward the center of the earth

→ ___________

Words

dust *n.* 먼지
shrink *v.* 수축하다, 줄어들다
gravity *n.* 중력
force *v.* 힘을 가하다
squeeze *v.* 압축하다, 짜다
enable *v.* 가능하게 하다
run out 고갈되다
gather *v.* 모이다, 모으다
fade away 사라지다
use up 다 써버리다

3 ⌐Summary⌐ 다음은 별의 일생을 정리한 표이다. 빈칸에 적절한 단어를 글에서 찾아 쓰시오. (단, 어형 변화 가능)

The Life of a Star	
Before a Star	· There are clouds of gas and dust. · They start to (1)___________ due to gravity, and this produces (2)___________.
A New Star	After nuclear (3)___________, a new star (4)___________ brightly.
After Using Up Fuel	It (5)___________ to a cloud of gas and dust after a series of steps.

직독직해 Skill 다음을 의미 단위로 끊어 읽고(/), 주어(S)와 동사(V)에 표시해 봅시다.

· If this reaches 27 million degrees Fahrenheit, it is hot enough to start nuclear fusion.

____

05

다음 글의 제목으로 가장 적절한 것은?

In a movie, lighting does more than just allow us to see what is taking place. Brightly lit subjects naturally attract people's attention. On the other hand, dimly lit subjects can create curiosity and fear. How shadows are used is also an important part of lighting. If a bright light is used to minimize shadows, it creates a bright and cheerful atmosphere. This effect is usually used in comedies and action movies. Light can also make dark shadows for a strong contrast between bright and dark scenes. This can emphasize the subject and create tension. So, it is used in horror movies or films with a dark atmosphere. The position of the light source can produce various dramatic effects as well. For example, a light shining directly down on the subject creates a feeling of holiness and mystery. Understanding these lighting techniques and their effects makes watching movies even more exciting.

① Light: The Best Way to Show Subjects
② Lighting in Movies: Its Roles and Effects
③ Successful Movies Come from Creativity
④ How to Find Hidden Messages in Movies
⑤ The Brighter the Lighting, the Better the Movie

Mini Quiz

밝기 이외에 조명의 효과를 결정 짓는 중요한 요소 2가지를 찾아 밑줄을 그어 봅시다.

Reading 비법

글의 도입부는 글의 핵심 소재와 주제를 제시할 가능성이 크다.

Reading Skill 주제문과 근거문을 찾아 다음 표를 완성해 봅시다.

주제문	__________은 영화에서 대상을 __________ 것 이상의 것을 한다.
근거문	• 조명을 __________ 또는 __________ 비춤에 따라 사람들의 __________을 끌거나 __________과 두려움을 유발한다. • 어떻게 __________를 활용하는지는 조명의 쓰임에서 중요하다. • 광원의 __________는 다양한 극적인 __________를 만들어낸다.

1 글에서 언급된 것은?

① 조명의 기원
② 영화에서 흔히 쓰이는 조명의 색
③ 코미디 영화에서 활용하는 조명의 크기
④ 공포 영화에서 조명을 잘 쓰지 않는 이유
⑤ 신성함과 신비감을 만드는 광원의 위치

2 글의 내용과 일치하도록 빈칸에 적절한 단어를 글에서 찾아 쓰시오.

When a bright light shines on a subject, people naturally pay ____________ to it.

3 | Summary | 다음 표의 빈칸에 적절한 단어를 글에서 찾아 쓰시오.

	Light/Few Shadows	Dark Shadows
Use What?	(1) ____________ light	strong (4) ____________
Effect	to create a bright and cheerful (2) ____________	to (5) ____________ the subject and create (6) ____________
Genre	(3) ____________ or action movies	(7) ____________ movies or films with a (8) ____________ mood

직독직해 Skill 다음을 의미 단위로 끊어 읽고(/), 주어(S)와 동사(V)에 표시해 봅시다.

· The position of the light source can produce various dramatic effects as well.

____

READING 06

다음 글의 제목으로 가장 적절한 것은?　　　　기출 응용

　Think, for a moment, about when you bought something and you never ended up using it. An item of clothing you never ended up wearing? A book you never read? Some piece of electronic equipment that never even came out of the box? It is estimated that Australians alone spend on average $10.8 billion AUD 5 (roughly $9.99 billion USD) every year on goods they do not use. That is more than the total government spending on universities and roads. That is an average of $1,250 AUD (roughly $1,156 USD) for each household. All the things we buy and then never use are waste — a waste of money, a waste of time, and waste in 10 the sense of pure rubbish. As the author Clive Hamilton observes, 'The difference between the stuff we buy and what we use is waste.'

① Spending Enables the Economy
② Money Management: Dos and Don'ts
③ What You Buy Is Waste Unless You Use It
④ Too Much Shopping: A Sign of Loneliness
⑤ 3R's of Waste: Reduce, Reuse, and Recycle

Mini Quiz

글을 읽으면서 예시가 끝나고 주제가 시작되는 부분에 / 표시를 해 봅시다.

Reading 비법

다양한 예시가 나오는 글은 그 공통점을 통해 글쓴이가 말하고자 하는 바가 무엇인지를 생각해 본다.

Reading Skill　글의 중심 내용에 맞게 다음 표를 완성해 봅시다.

도입	우리는 __________하고 한 번도 __________하지 않는 경우가 많음
예시 품목	__________, __________, __________
주제	우리가 __________ 후 __________하지 않는 __________들은 시간과 돈의 __________임

1 글에서 낭비의 예로 언급되지 <u>않은</u> 것을 <u>모두</u> 고르면?

① 한 번도 입지 않은 옷

② 요리하지 않고 버려진 식료품

③ 한 번도 읽지 않은 책

④ 충동 구매한 가방

⑤ 사용한 적 없는 전자기기

2 글의 내용과 일치하면 T, 일치하지 <u>않으면</u> F를 쓰시오.

(1) Australians spend on average more than $10 billion AUD every year on products they never use. ______

(2) Australians' yearly spending on unused goods is less than the total government spending on universities and roads. ______

3 | Complete a Poster | 글의 내용을 활용하여 올바른 소비 방법을 홍보하는 포스터를 만들려고 할 때, 빈칸에 적절한 단어를 글에서 찾아 쓰시오.

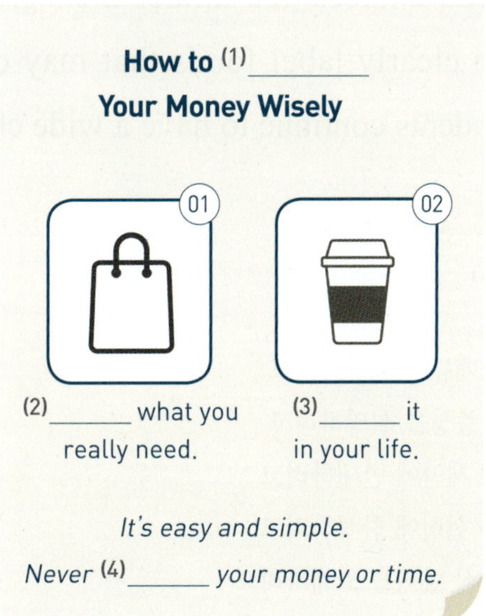

직독직해 Skill 다음을 의미 단위로 끊어 읽고(/), 주어(S)와 동사(V)에 표시해 봅시다.

· Think, for a moment, about when you bought something and you never ended up using it.

Words

end up 결국 ～하게 되다
electronic equipment 전자기기
estimate *v.* 추산하다
billion *n.* 10억
roughly *ad.* 대략, 약
goods *n.* 물건, 제품, 상품
government *n.* 정부
waste *n.* 낭비, 쓰레기
pure *a.* 순전한, 순수한
rubbish *n.* 쓰레기
observe *v.* (발언·의견을) 말하다

READING 07

다음 글의 목적으로 가장 적절한 것은?

To the Principal of Alcanse Middle School,

  My name is Cathy Brown. My daughter, Amy, is a student at your school. I'm writing this email in response to the message I received from her homeroom teacher. He is suggesting that the school stop serving food made with eggs. As the mother of a girl who needs a lot of nutrients, I strongly oppose the suggestion. I understand that some students are allergic to eggs. However, his suggestion is unfair to the other students. Our children need a well-balanced diet. Eggs have lots of nutrients such as protein and are widely used in so many types of food. Removing them from the menu would limit our children's food choices and hinder their growth. Instead, the school could clearly label foods that may contain eggs. It is important students continue to have a wide choice of foods.

Sincerely,

Cathy Brown

① 창의적인 급식 메뉴를 제안하려고
② 달걀 알레르기 증상을 설명하려고
③ 학교 급식 정책 제안에 반대하려고
④ 학교 급식 메뉴 선정에 찬성하려고
⑤ 새로운 학교 급식 방식을 소개하려고

Mini Quiz

글쓴이가 이메일을 쓰는 목적이 가장 잘 드러난 문장을 찾아 밑줄을 그어 봅시다.

Reading 비법

글의 목적 유형은 편지, 공고문 등 다양한 형태의 지문이며 목적은 주로 글의 초반부에 등장한다.

Reading Skill

글의 중심 내용에 맞게 다음 표를 완성해 봅시다.

글쓴이의 주장	__________이 들어간 __________을 __________ 것을 __________함
근거	• 아이들은 __________ 식단이 필요함 • 아이들의 선택을 __________하고 __________을 __________하게 됨

1 글쓴이가 대안으로서 제안한 방법은?

① 달걀이 든 음식에 라벨을 붙이기
② 다른 영양소가 풍부한 음식 제공하기
③ 알레르기가 있는 학생들의 명단 파악하기
④ 달걀이 든 음식을 찾고 피하는 법 가르치기
⑤ 학생들에게 급식 메뉴에 대해 설문조사하기

2 주어진 질문에 대한 답을 영어로 쓸 때, 빈칸에 들어갈 말을 글에서 찾아 쓰시오.

Q: Why are eggs good for our health?
A: They ______________________________________.

3 |Summary| 다음은 글쓴이가 이메일을 쓰기 전 학교 선생님에게 받은 문자메시지이다. 빈칸에 적절한 단어를 글에서 찾아 쓰시오.

> "Good afternoon, parents. This is Mr. Smith from Alcanse Middle School. I just wanted to suggest that we should not offer food with (1)______________ at our school. As you know, some of our students are (2)______________ to them. It is important that we keep these students safe and offer them a well-balanced (3)______________ without eggs. If you have any concerns or questions, please feel free to reach out to me. Have a great day."

Words

in response to ~에 답하여
serve *v.* 제공하다
nutrient *n.* 영양소, 영양분
oppose *v.* 반대하다
allergic *a.* 알레르기의
unfair *a.* 불공정한, 부당한
well-balanced *a.* 균형 잡힌
protein *n.* 단백질
remove *v.* 제거하다
limit *v.* 제한하다
hinder *v.* 방해하다
label *v.* 라벨[표]을 붙이다
contain *v.* 포함하다

직독직해 Skill 다음을 의미 단위로 끊어 읽고(/), 주어(S)와 동사(V)에 표시해 봅시다.

· He is suggesting that the school stop serving food made with eggs.

____

READING 08

다음 글에서 필자가 주장하는 바로 가장 적절한 것은? 기출응용

Some experts say that we communicate by moving our bodies. This means we use 'body language'. Let's pay attention to the nonverbal messages you teachers send to your students. It can make a significant difference in your relationship with students. In general, most students are often very aware of their teacher's body language. For example, when students first enter the classroom, they look for their teacher. Imagine that the teacher has a friendly greeting and a welcoming smile. It must be encouraging and empowering for a student. The teacher smiles at students to let them know that he or she is glad to see them. It does not require a great deal of time or effort. But it can make a significant difference in the classroom climate right from the start of class. Teachers should remember that their body language is always at work when they are with their students.

① 교사는 학생 안전을 위해 교실 환경을 개선해야 한다.
② 교사는 학생 간의 상호 작용을 주의 깊게 관찰해야 한다.
③ 학교는 학생에게 다양한 역할을 경험하게 해 주어야 한다.
④ 수업 시 교사는 학생의 수준에 맞는 언어를 사용해야 한다.
⑤ 학생과의 관계에서 교사는 비언어적 표현에 유의해야 한다.

Mini Quiz

글의 핵심 소재를 찾아 밑줄을 그어 봅시다.

Reading 비법

주장을 파악할 때는 명령문이나 필요성을 말하는 표현 등 필자의 의견을 직접적으로 드러내는 표현에 주목해서 읽어야 한다.

Reading Skill 글의 중심 내용에 맞게 다음 표를 완성해 봅시다.

주제	__________과의 관계에서 __________의 중요성
근거	• 학생들은 교사의 __________를 매우 __________하고 있음 • 학생들에게 __________ 것이 교실 __________에 큰 차이를 가져올 수 있음

1 글의 제목으로 가장 적절한 것은?

① Be Honest with Your Students
② Teacher's Guide: Dos and Don'ts
③ Kindness: The Best Way to Teach
④ Body Language: What Matters in Class
⑤ What We Need for Better Communication

2 다음 빈칸에 적절한 단어를 글에서 찾아 쓰시오.

> ______________ communication is the act of sending or receiving information without the use of words. It includes using facial expressions and gestures.

3 |Summary| 빈칸에 적절한 단어를 글에서 찾아 써서 요약문을 완성하시오.

> Teachers can use their body language to build a good (1)______________ with their students. For example, if they show a(n) (2)______________ gesture like smiling at the students, it will make a(n) (3)______________ change in their class.

직독직해 Skill 다음을 의미 단위로 끊어 읽고(/), 주어(S)와 동사(V)에 표시해 봅시다.

·In general, most students are often very aware of their teacher's body language.

READING 09

글을 읽으면서 글의 요지가 가장 잘 드러난 문장을 찾아 밑줄을 그어 봅시다.

다음 글의 요지로 가장 적절한 것은?

The Great Barrier Reef in Australia is one of the largest coral reef systems in the world. ⓐIt is home to various marine species including over 1,500 different types of fish. However, in recent years, ⓑit has been facing numerous environmental challenges. Global warming has caused an increase in ocean temperatures, resulting in coral bleaching. This causes the coral to lose its color and even die. Furthermore, water pollution from water used for agriculture and industrial waste makes the water quality poor. We must take immediate action to protect the Great Barrier Reef and ⓒits marine life. This requires a combination of efforts, such as reducing the amount of greenhouse gas emissions and improving water quality. The future of the Great Barrier Reef and the millions of species that call ⓓit home depends on ⓔit. Without action, the future of this incredible ecosystem is uncertain.

*coral bleaching: 산호 탈색

① 온난화는 산호초 지대의 생태계에 커다란 위협을 가한다.
② 환경친화적인 소재를 사용하면 해양 생태계를 지킬 수 있다.
③ 자연을 보호하기 위해 수많은 연구와 실험이 진행되고 있다.
④ 산호초 지대의 생태계를 보호하기 위한 노력과 실천이 필요하다.
⑤ Great Barrier Reef는 호주의 아름답고 웅장한 자연을 보여준다.

Reading 비법

글의 요지는 글의 핵심이 되는 중요한 내용으로 글쓴이가 결국 하고 싶어 하는 말이 무엇인지를 생각하며 읽는 것이 중요하다.

Reading Skill 글의 중심 내용에 맞게 다음 표를 완성해 봅시다.

현 상황	____________에 직면한 Great Barrier Reef
원인	• ________로 인해 물의 ________ 상승 • ________ 용수와 산업 ________로 인한 ________
해결 방안	• ________ 배출량 줄이기 • ________ 개선하기

1 글의 밑줄 친 ⓐ ~ ⓔ 중, 가리키는 대상이 나머지 넷과 <u>다른</u> 것은?

① ⓐ　　　② ⓑ　　　③ ⓒ　　　④ ⓓ　　　⑤ ⓔ

2 글의 내용과 일치하면 T, 일치하지 <u>않으면</u> F를 쓰시오.

(1) A lot of marine species live in the Great Barrier Reef. ______
(2) Ocean temperatures have decreased in recent years. ______

3 |Summary| 빈칸에 적절한 단어를 |보기|에서 골라 넣어 요약문을 완성하시오.

> 보기
>
> protect　　choices　　understand　　threats　　efforts

> The Great Barrier Reef in Australia is under pressure from multiple (1)____________. To (2)____________ its marine ecosystem, it is time to make (3)____________ and take action immediately.

직독직해 Skill 다음을 의미 단위로 끊어 읽고(/), 주어(S)와 동사(V)에 표시해 봅시다.

· It is home to various marine species including over 1,500 different types of fish.

____

Words

coral reef 산호초
marine *a.* 바다의, 해양의
species *n.* 종
environmental *a.* 환경의
result in ∼를 초래하다
industrial *a.* 산업의
immediate *a.* 즉시의, 즉각의
combination *n.* 결합, 조합
reduce *v.* 줄이다
emission *n.* 배출
uncertain *a.* 불확실한

READING 10

다음 글의 요지로 가장 적절한 것은?

  You need to get comfortable with discomfort if you want to succeed. In other words, you should step out of your comfort zone. Trying new things outside of your comfort zone will greatly benefit you in many ways. First, you can gain valuable opportunities to grow. Challenging yourself provides opportunities [5] for new experiences and unexpected changes, which can lead to personal growth. Furthermore, you will learn about yourself. As you try new things, you will discover your talents, interests, strengths and weaknesses. Finally, you can also build new relationships. If you try something new, you can meet new people [10] who you otherwise would never have had the chance to meet. It can make your life more exciting. And you will learn from them, too. The unfamiliarity will feel very uncomfortable. However, you will be able to expand your horizons and achieve success.

Mini Quiz

글을 읽으면서 주제를 가장 잘 드러내는 8단어의 어구를 찾아 밑줄을 그어 봅시다.

① 우리는 삶의 익숙한 것에서 다양한 가치를 발견할 수 있다.
② 자기 자신에 대한 탐색과 공부는 성공적인 삶의 밑거름이다.
③ 많은 사람을 만나는 것은 변화에 익숙해지는 데 도움이 된다.
④ 안주하는 삶에서 벗어나 새로운 것에 도전할 때 성공할 수 있다.
⑤ 불편함의 원인을 찾아 개선함으로써 성장의 기회를 마련할 수 있다.

Reading 비법

글에 비슷한 의미의 어구가 반복된다면 그 어구를 통해 글의 주제를 추론할 수 있다.

Reading Skill 글의 중심 내용에 맞게 다음 표를 완성해 봅시다.

글쓴이의 주장	__________ 하기 위해서는 __________ 을 __________ 것이 필요함
근거	__________ 에서 __________ 것은 다양한 __________ 을 제공함
결론	이를 통해 결국 우리의 __________ 를 넓히고 __________ 을 이룰 수 있음

1 글을 읽고 답할 수 <u>없는</u> 질문은?

① What should we be comfortable with in order to succeed?
② What are some benefits of going outside our comfort zone?
③ When can we learn about ourselves?
④ How can we meet new people who we otherwise would not have met?
⑤ Why do we need familiar things in our lives?

2 글의 내용과 일치하도록 <u>틀린</u> 부분을 고쳐 문장을 다시 쓰시오.

Stepping out of your comfort zone means to be comfortable with trying to do new and comfortable things.

→ ____

Words

comfortable *a.* 편안한
discomfort *n.* 불편함
succeed *v.* 성공하다
benefit *v.* (~에게) 유익하다
valuable *a.* 귀중한
opportunity *n.* 기회
unfamiliarity *n.* 생소함, 익숙하지 않음
expand *v.* 확장하다
achieve *v.* 성취하다

3 | Summary | 빈칸에 적절한 단어를 |보기|에서 골라 넣어 요약문을 완성하시오.

| 보기 |

aware   think   grow   establish   proud   destroy

Getting out of Our Comfort Zone	
Advantage 1	It can provide us with new experiences and help us (1)______________ as a better person.
Advantage 2	It can encourage us to be more (2)______________ of ourselves.
Advantage 3	It can help us to (3)______________ new relationships with new people.

직독직해 Skill 다음을 의미 단위로 끊어 읽고(/), 주어(S)와 동사(V)에 표시해 봅시다.

· It can make your life more exciting.

____

다음 글의 내용을 한 문장으로 요약하고자 한다. 빈칸 (A), (B)에 들어갈 말로 가장 적절한 것은?

It is important for advertisements to grab people's attention. They need to reach people on an emotional level. That is, the advertisement needs to show how the product can help them. Every good product or service can help people live, work, or enjoy their lives more. For example, imagine an advertisement for a new smartphone that just talks about its amazing features. That advertisement feels like an explanation. Unfortunately, it would not be a very effective advertisement. Now imagine an advertisement showing people taking beautiful photos in their daily lives or watching movies on their new smartphone. It would be far more memorable and people would be interested in it. Advertisements sell benefits, not features. Therefore, a successful advertisement must show people how its product can make their lives richer and more convenient.

⬇

> Effective advertisements target people's ______(A)______ by showing how the products will ______(B)______ their lives.

	(A)		(B)			(A)		(B)
①	feelings	⋯⋯	describe		②	knowledge	⋯⋯	describe
③	feelings	⋯⋯	improve		④	knowledge	⋯⋯	change
⑤	prejudice	⋯⋯	improve					

Mini Quiz

첫 문장에서 글의 핵심 소재를 찾아 밑줄을 그어 봅시다.

Reading 비법

요약은 글의 소재와 내용을 간추려서 주제를 정리해야 한다.

Reading Skill 글의 주제와 예시를 찾아 다음 표를 완성해 봅시다.

주제문	사람들에게 제품이 어떻게 그들을 __________지 __________ 차원에서 설명하는 것이 중요하다.
예시문	새로운 __________에 대한 두 가지 다른 광고를 __________해봐라.
주제문	성공적인 광고는 어떻게 사람들의 삶을 더 __________ 편리하게 만드는지를 보여줘야 한다.

1 글의 주제로 가장 적절한 것은?

① difficulties of coming up with new items
② how advertisements can attract consumers
③ roles of advertisements in selling products
④ why people are not interested in new products
⑤ effects of people's knowledge on advertisements

2 글의 내용과 일치하도록 <u>틀린</u> 부분을 고쳐 문장을 다시 쓰시오.

Effective advertisements will show consumers how the products make their lives inconvenient.

→ ____

3 | Choose the Ad | 다음 중 글쓴이가 생각하는 좋은 광고로 적절한 것을 고르시오.

(A)   (B)

Words
advertisement *n.* 광고
grab *v.* 끌다
reach *v.* ~에 다가가다
feature *n.* 기능
explanation *n.* 설명
unfortunately *ad.* 불행하게도
far *ad.* (비교급 앞에 쓰여) 훨씬
memorable *a.* 기억할 만한
benefit *n.* 혜택, 이점
convenient *a.* 편리한

직독직해 Skill 다음을 의미 단위로 끊어 읽고(/), 주어(S)와 동사(V)에 표시해 봅시다.

· It is important for advertisements to grab people's attention.

____

READING 12

다음 글의 내용을 한 문장으로 요약하고자 한다. 빈칸 (A), (B)에 들어갈 말로 가장 적절한 것은?

  Artificial intelligence (AI) is rapidly changing the job market. Some experts predict that AI will lead to job loss in certain industries by automating many simple tasks. However, other experts believe that AI will create new job opportunities. The truth likely lies somewhere in between. But it is clear that AI is changing the nature of work. Workers in various industries will need to adapt to new technologies and acquire new skills. For example, the use of AI in customer service requires workers to improve their interpersonal skills. They also need to be familiar and comfortable with human-centered technology. In addition, AI will likely lead to the development of new job categories, such as AI ethics officers. Their job would be to make sure that AI systems are used in a responsible and ethical manner. As AI continues to have an impact on the job market, it is necessary for workers and organizations to adapt to the changes.

> As the job market is _____(A)_____ by AI, we should _____(B)_____ our abilities to be successful workers.

	(A)		(B)			(A)		(B)
①	transformed	……	access		②	attacked	……	limit
③	transformed	……	develop		④	attacked	……	create
⑤	transformed	……	ignore					

Mini Quiz

글을 읽으면서 요약문의 내용을 가장 잘 나타내는 문장을 찾아 밑줄을 그어 봅시다.

Reading 비법

요약문을 먼저 읽으면 글의 대략적인 소재와 주제를 쉽게 파악할 수 있다.

Reading Skill 글의 중심 내용에 맞게 다음 표를 완성해 봅시다.

주제	__________이 __________에 미치는 __________
세부 내용	다양한 분야에서 사람들에게 새로운 __________과 __________을 갖추도록 요구함

1 글을 읽고 답할 수 있는 질문은?

① Who first invented AI?
② What does AI ask workers to do?
③ What jobs will AI never change?
④ Where can we learn AI technologies?
⑤ When did AI appear in the job market?

2 글의 제목을 다음과 같이 쓸 때, 빈칸에 적절한 단어를 글에서 찾아 쓰시오.

Artificial Intelligence: Its ______________ on the Job Market

3 | Complete the Ad | 다음은 인공지능이 발달한 미래 사회의 직업 공고문이다. 빈칸에 적절한 단어를 |보기|에서 골라 쓰시오.

| 보기 |

human-centered   study   interact   aggressive

Job Title: Customer Service Manager
  We are looking for new customer service managers. The successful candidate will do a variety of tasks in our company like (1)______________ing with customers and offering solutions to their inquiries.
Responsibilities:
  Respond to customer questions through phone, email, and chat.
Requirements:
• Familiar with a(n) (2)______________ technology
• Excellent verbal and written communication skills

Words

artificial intelligence *n.* 인공지능
rapidly *ad.* 빠르게
predict *v.* 예상하다
industry *n.* 산업
nature *n.* 특성, 본질
adapt *v.* 적응하다
acquire *v.* 습득하다
interpersonal *a.* 개인 간의
human-centered 인간 중심의
ethics *n.* 윤리, 윤리학
manner *n.* 방식

직독직해 Skill 다음을 의미 단위로 끊어 읽고(/), 주어(S)와 동사(V)에 표시해 봅시다.

· Workers in various industries will need to adapt to new technologies and acquire new skills.

____

다음 글의 내용을 한 문장으로 요약하고자 한다. 빈칸 (A), (B)에 들어갈 말로 가장 적절한 것은?

기출 응용

In one study, researchers asked pairs of strangers to sit down in a room and chat. In half of the rooms, a cell phone was placed on a nearby table; in the other half, no phone was present. After the conversations ended, the researchers asked the participants what they thought of each other. When a cell phone was present in the room, the participants reported the quality of their relationship was worse than those who talked in a cell phone-free room. The pairs who talked in the rooms with cell phones thought their partners showed less empathy. Imagine you sit down to have lunch with a friend and set your phone on the table. You might feel good about yourself because you don't pick it up to check your messages. But your unchecked messages are still hurting your connection with the person sitting across from you.

> The presence of a cell phone ______(A)______ the connection between people involved in conversations, even when the phone is being ______(B)______ .

	(A)		(B)		(A)		(B)
①	maintains	……	ignored	②	weakens	……	ignored
③	maintains	……	updated	④	weakens	……	answered
⑤	renews	……	answered				

Mini Quiz

글을 읽으면서 실험 조건의 차이를 설명하는 문장을 찾아 밑줄을 그어 봅시다.

Reading 비법

실험을 다룬 지문은 실험의 결과가 글의 주제일 가능성이 크다.

Reading Skill

글의 중심 내용에 맞게 다음 표를 완성해 봅시다.

주제	__________의 존재 유무가 __________의 질에 영향을 미침
근거	실험 결과: __________의 존재 유무에 따라 참가자들이 서로에 대해 __________ 점이 __________

1 글의 제목으로 가장 적절한 것은?

① Empathy: What Makes a Better Conversation
② Cell Phones as an Amazing Tool for Communication
③ Too Much Use of Your Phone Hurts Others' Feelings
④ The Cell Phone: Its Negative Impact on Conversations
⑤ Are Cell Phones Really Bad for Relationships with Others?

2 빈칸에 공통으로 들어갈 단어를 글에서 찾아 쓰시오.

> · I will give a special ____________ to you!
> · Trying other things is not easy in the ____________ situation.
> · There were 300 people ____________ at the meeting.

3 |Summary| 글의 내용을 다음과 같이 표로 정리할 때, 빈칸에 적절한 단어를 글에서 찾아 쓰시오.

Study	Researchers asked pairs of (1)____________ to sit down and (2)____________ in a room with or without a cell phone.
Result	Participants reported that the quality of the relationship was (3)____________ and they received less (4)____________ from their partner when a cell phone was present.
Example	A phone on the table during lunch with a friend can (5)____________ your connection.

직독직해 Skill 다음을 의미 단위로 끊어 읽고(/), 주어(S)와 동사(V)에 표시해 봅시다.

· After the conversations ended, the researchers asked the participants what they thought of each other.

Words

researcher *n.* 연구자
place *v.* 두다, 놓다
present *a.* 있는, 존재하는
participant *n.* 참가자
report *v.* 보고하다, 말하다
quality *n.* 질
empathy *n.* 공감
connection *n.* 관계, 연결
maintain *v.* 유지하다
ignore *v.* 무시하다
weaken *v.* 약화시키다

정보 파악하기

A 정보 중심의 빠른 독해가 필요한 지문 ❶

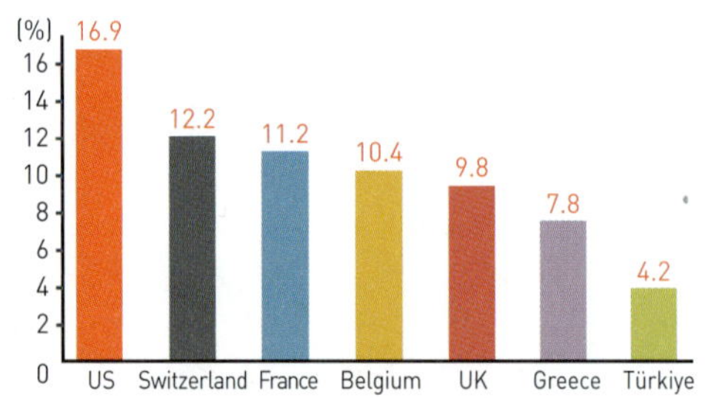

The Percentage of GDP Spent on Health Care in 2018

'할인 안내,' '여행 서비스' 등의 **광고**나 **안내문**, 또는 **도표**에서 주제를 찾는 것은 무의미하며, 내신/수능/모평에서도 이와 같은 글은 주제를 묻는 문제로 출제되지 않는다. 따라서 광고/안내문/도표와 같은 글에서는 글의 주제를 파악하기보다는, '무엇을, 언제 할인하는지', '어떤 여행 서비스를 제공하는지', '무엇이 증가/감소했는지' 등의 핵심 정보를 빠르게 파악하는 것이 중요하다.

[기출 예제]

Waverly High School

Friendly Chess Tournament

Saturday, March 23, 10 a.m.

- <u>Where</u>: Waverly High School auditorium

- <u>Entry Deadline</u>: March 22, 4 p.m.

- <u>Age Categories</u>: 7-12, 13-15, 16-18

- <u>Prizes</u>: Gold, Silver, and Bronze for each category

If you are interested, enter online at www.waverly.org.

친선 __________ 토너먼트를 안내/홍보하는 글

경기 일정, __________, 등록 마감일, __________, __________, 웹사이트를 안내함

Words friendly *a.* 친선의   auditorium *n.* 강당   entry *n.* 참가 (신청)   category *n.* 부문   enter *v.* 들어가다

B 정보 중심의 빠른 독해가 필요한 지문 ❷

어떤 인물의 일대기나 사물/동물에 대한 글 역시 다양한 정보로 이루어진 글로, 주제를 찾기보다는 주요 정보 중심으로 빠르게 독해하는 것이 좋다.

기출 예제

James Van Der Zee was born on June 29, 1886, in Lenox, Massachusetts. The second of six children, James grew up in a family of creative people. In 1907, he moved to Phoetus, Virginia, and there he worked in the dining room of the Hotel Chamberlin. During this time he also worked as a photographer on a part-time basis. He opened his own studio in 1916. In 1969, he gained international recognition due to his exhibition, *Harlem On My Mind*. He died in 1983.

________________의 일대기

1886년: 6남매 중 __________로 출생

1907년: 호텔 식당 종업원 및 __________로 일함

1916년: 자신의 __________를 엶

1969년: 전시회로 __________인 __________을 받음

1983년: 사망

Words photographer *n.* 사진사   on a part-time basis 시간제로   recognition *n.* 인정   exhibition *n.* 전시회

READING 14

A Day with an Author 행사에 관한 다음 안내문의 내용과 일치하지 <u>않는</u> 것은?

A Day with an Author

Amelia Tylor, the award-winning author of children's books, invites you to her new book, *Tommy's Adventure Under the Sea*. Join her at a special story time for kids!

- When: Saturday, May 18th 11 a.m. ~ 1 p.m.
- Where: Neilson Hall in the City Library
- For whom: from 9 to 11-year-old kids
- Event Includes: · The author's reading session (*Tommy's Adventure Under the Sea*, Chapter 1)
  · Acting performance of scenes in the book
  · Book signing by the author

※ Please register at www.citylibrary.org/events to attend the event.

※ Children should come with a parent/parents or guardian.

※ Please arrive on time. After the author's reading session begins, you cannot enter the hall until the session ends.

※ You can buy all of the author's books, including her new one, at a discount of 30% after the session.

① Amelia Tylor 작가의 새 책을 만날 수 있다.
② 5월 18일 토요일에 열린다.
③ 9살에서 11살까지의 아이들을 위한 행사이다.
④ 책에 작가의 서명을 받을 수 있다.
⑤ 새 책을 제외한 기존 책들을 할인 가격에 구입할 수 있다.

Mini Quiz

안내문의 제목만 먼저 읽고, 어떤 행사에 관한 안내문인지 추측하여 두세 단어의 우리말로 적어 봅시다.

Reading 비법

안내문이 무엇에 관한 것인지, 주요 정보가 무엇인지를 파악하는 것이 좋다.

Reading Skill

글에서 안내된 행사의 주요 정보를 찾아 빈칸을 완성해 봅시다.

일시	__________월 __________일 __________요일
참가 대상	__________살에서 __________살까지의 아이들
포함된 활동	작가가 __________, 책 장면으로 __________, 작가의 책 __________

1 A Day with an Author 행사에 관해 글에서 언급되지 <u>않은</u> 것은?

① 소개할 책 제목 ② 행사 장소

③ 참여 등록 방법 ④ 기념품 추첨 방법

⑤ 보호자 동반 여부

2 글의 내용과 일치하면 T, 일치하지 <u>않으면</u> F를 쓰시오.

(1) Amelia Tylor won an award for her books in the past. _____

(2) You can visit the event without a reservation. _____

(3) If you arrive after the author starts her book reading, you cannot enter the hall until it ends. _____

Words

author *n.* 작가
award-winning 상을 받은
invite *v.* 초대하다
include *v.* 포함하다
session *n.* (특정한 활동을 위한) 시간
performance *n.* 공연
scene *n.* 장면
sign *v.* 서명하다 *n.* 서명
register *v.* 등록하다
attend *v.* 참석하다
guardian *n.* 보호자
discount *n.* 할인

3 | Complete a Diary | 다음은 행사에 참석한 아이의 일기이다. 글의 내용과 일치하도록 빈칸에 적절한 단어를 글에서 찾아 쓰시오.

> After I read *Tommy's Adventure in Toy World*, Amelia Tylor has become my favorite (1)_____________. Luckily, the (2)_____________ _____________ held an author reading event with her. I asked my father to (3)_____________ us on the library site and to take me there because every child had to come with a(n) (4)_____________ or guardian. At the event, I especially enjoyed the (5)_____________ _____________ of the scene where Tommy swims with dolphins. I had a really great time.

직독직해 Skill 다음을 의미 단위로 끊어 읽고(/), 주어(S)와 동사(V)에 표시해 봅시다.

· Amelia Tylor, the award-winning author of children's books, invites you to her new book, *Tommy's Adventure Under the Sea*.

Unit 06 **45**

READING 15

Dream Company Cruise에 관한 다음 안내문의 내용과 일치하는 것은?

Dream Company Cruise

Are you looking for something special for your family?
A Dream Company cruise creates memories that bring families together.

Our ship, the Magic Dream, is your dream holiday itself. This cruise ship is famous for its classical design and modern facilities. It also has the biggest pool of any cruise ship.

* Date of Departure: April 1 — 5 (4 nights sailing)
* Departing from / Returning to: Port of Miami, Florida
* Sailing to: Three islands in the Caribbean
* Facilities: 4 pools, 3 restaurants, 3 snack bars, 2 gyms
* Onboard Activities: magic shows, musicals, fireworks at night
* Meals: free breakfast, lunch, and dinner
      (additional charge for snacks and drinks)
* Room Description: 2 king beds, bathroom with shower, refrigerator, wireless Internet access, TV with recent movies
* Price: $4,500 ~ $5,000
• For more information and reservation, please call (122) 341-1234.

① 현대적인 디자인의 배로 유명하다.　② 4월 1일에 출발하여 5박을 배에서 보낸다.
③ 출발지와 도착지가 다르다.　　　④ 간식과 음료수는 추가 비용을 내야 한다.
⑤ 추가 정보와 예약은 이메일로 가능하다.

Mini Quiz

선택지 ①~⑤를 먼저 읽으면서 중요 내용 또는 key word에 밑줄을 그어 봅시다. 그 후 글을 읽으면서 밑줄 그은 내용이 나오는지 확인해 봅시다.

Reading 비법

선택지를 먼저 읽으면 찾아야 할 내용을 미리 알 수 있어서 독해 속도가 빨라진다.

Reading Skill　선택지의 중요 단어와 관련된 해당 정보를 찾아 빈칸을 채우고 비교해 봅시다.

선택지의 중요 단어	안내문 속 관련 내용
① 현대적 디자인의 배	＿＿＿＿＿ 디자인으로 유명
② 4월 1일, 5박	4월 1일부터 ＿＿＿＿＿일까지 ＿＿＿＿＿박
③ 출발지와 도착지	출발지/도착지: ＿＿＿＿＿＿, 플로리다
④ 간식과 음료수	간식과 음료수는 ＿＿＿＿＿ 지불
⑤ 정보, 예약, 이메일	정보와 예약을 위해 ＿＿＿＿＿로 연락

1   Dream Company Cruise에 관해 알 수 <u>없는</u> 내용은?

① 돌아오는 날짜   ② 방문하는 섬의 개수
③ 마술 쇼 시간   ④ 식사 비용
⑤ 객실 내 인터넷 가능 여부

2   안내문을 읽은 후의 반응으로 알맞지 <u>않은</u> 것은?

① I've always wanted to visit the islands of the Caribbean.
② I can't wait to swim in the biggest pool of any cruise ship!
③ I will enjoy the food in all three restaurants and snack bars!
④ I am happy to know that the cruise has orchestra concerts.
⑤ I will watch some recent movies in my room on the ship.

3   ❘ Complete a Travel Essay ❘ 다음은 Dream Company Cruise를 다녀온 아이의 소감문이다. 글의 내용과 일치하도록 빈칸에 적절한 단어를 글에서 찾아 쓰시오.

> My mom and dad had prepared something really
> (1) ___________ for our family vacation. A Dream
> Company Cruise! I had really wanted to spend some time
> on a big cruise ship and my dream came true! On
> (2) ___________ first, we boarded the cruise ship at the
> (3) ___________ of Miami. Everything was perfect. I
> enjoyed so much delicious food for (4) ___________! I
> mean, at no extra charge! I also enjoyed watching the
> (5) ___________ at night while on the sea. But the most
> amazing thing was that the ship has (6) ___________ pools,
> and one of them is the (7) ___________ pool of any cruise
> ship! I enjoyed every moment on the ship and on my cruise.

직독직해 Skill   다음을 의미 단위로 끊어 읽고(/), 주어(S)와 동사(V)에 표시해 봅시다.

· A Dream Company cruise creates memories that bring families together.

Words

cruise *n.* 유람선 여행
memory *n.* 기억, 추억
classical *a.* 고전적인
facility *n.* 시설
sailing *n.* 항해
port *n.* 항구
onboard *a.* 선상의, 배 위의
additional *a.* 추가적인
charge *n.* 비용, 요금
recent *a.* 최근의

READING 16

도표의 제목, 가로축과 세로축을
먼저 확인해 봅시다.

다음 도표의 내용과 일치하지 <u>않는</u> 것은?   기출 응용

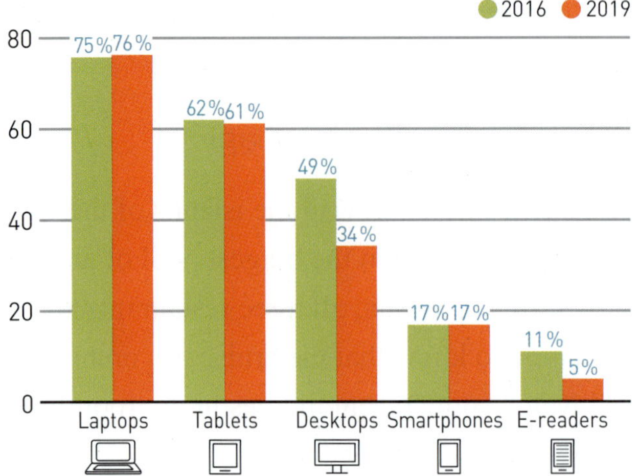

The above graph shows us what devices students used to access digital educational content. The survey was done in both 2016 and 2019. Students from kindergarten to the 12th grade participated in the survey, and they used many kinds of digital devices. ① Laptops were the most popular device to access digital content in both years. ② Both in 2016 and in 2019, more than 60 percent of the students used tablets for digital content. ③ More than half the students used desktops for digital content in 2016, and more than 30 percent used desktops for digital content in 2019. ④ The percentage of students who used smartphones in 2016 was the same as that in 2019. ⑤ The percentages of students who used E-readers were the lowest in both years.

Reading 비법

문장 ① 앞까지는 도표에 대한 전체적인 설명이므로 무엇에 관한 도표인지 파악한 후, ①~⑤는 한 문장씩 읽으면서 바로 도표와 비교한다.

Reading Skill   도표의 제목과 항목을 살펴보고 다음 질문의 답을 적어 봅시다.

무엇을 조사한 도표인가?	___________ ___________ 에 접근하기 위해 학생들이 사용한 ___________
조사한 시기는 언제인가?	___________ 년, ___________ 년
막대 그래프는 무엇을 나타내는가?	___________ 를 사용한 학생들의 ___________

1 도표를 보고 답할 수 <u>없는</u> 질문은?

① What percentage of students used E-readers in 2019?
② What's the device that students used more in 2019 than in 2016?
③ How many devices show the same percentage of use, both in 2016 and 2019?
④ What are the devices that more than 50 percent of the students used in both years?
⑤ What is the most popular device for high school students in 2019?

2 도표의 내용과 일치하도록 다음 문장에서 <u>틀린</u> 부분을 찾아 고쳐 쓰시오.

The percentage of students who used E-readers in 2016 was less than twice of that in 2019.

___________ → ___________

3 | Summary | 도표의 내용과 일치하도록 빈칸에 알맞은 단어를 |보기|에서 골라 쓰시오.

| 보기 |

> up　down　most　least　twice　third

(1) The second ___________ used device was a tablet, both in 2016 and in 2019.
(2) The percentage of students who used desktops in 2019 was ___________ that of the students who used smartphones in the same year.
(3) The percentage of students who used desktops went ___________ as time passed from 2016 to 2019.

직독직해 Skill 다음을 의미 단위로 끊어 읽고(/), 주어(S)와 동사(V)에 표시해 봅시다.

· The percentage of students who used smartphones in 2016 was the same as that in 2019.

____

Words

device　*n.* 기기, 장치
access　*v.* 접근하다
content　*n.* 콘텐츠, 내용물
laptop　*n.* 노트북 (컴퓨터)
e-reader *n.* 전자책 단말기
educational *a.* 교육의
survey　*n.* (설문)조사
kindergarten　*n.* 유치원
participate in ～에 참여하다

June Almeida에 관한 다음 글의 내용과 일치하지 <u>않는</u> 것은?

June Almeida was born in 1930 in Scotland. Almeida excelled in school, and won the top science prize at her school. She wanted to continue her studies in science after high school, but there was no money for her college education. So, at the age of 16, Almeida took a job as a lab technician. After that, she moved to London, then to Canada in 1954. There, she took a job detecting viruses and making detailed pictures of them using a microscope. She became one of the best experts in that job. Then, in London in 1964, she created a sharp, clear picture of a mysterious virus and named it coronavirus. It was the first identified human coronavirus. Due to her contributions in the field of biology, the University of London awarded her university degrees in 1970 and 1971. She finally received the degrees that she had wanted since high school.

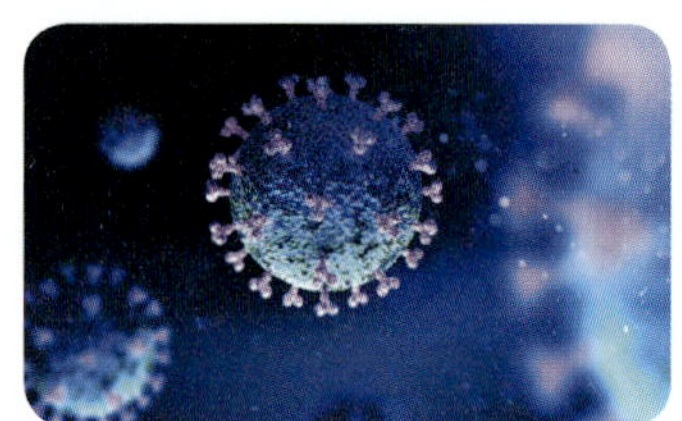

Mini Quiz

June Almeida의 업적이 드러난 두 문장을 찾아 밑줄을 그어 봅시다.

① 학교에서 과학 최고상을 받았다.
② 16살부터 실험실에서 일하기 시작했다.
③ 캐나다에서 바이러스를 찾아 촬영하는 일을 했다.
④ 처음으로 코로나 바이러스의 사진을 찍어 이름을 붙였다.
⑤ 학위를 받기 위해 늦은 나이에 대학에 입학했다.

Reading 비법

인물의 일대기에 관한 글은 주로 시간 순서에 따라 인물의 삶을 설명한다.

Reading Skill 글에 소개된 June Almeida의 일대기에 관한 표를 완성해 봅시다.

인물 이름	June Almeida
시간 순서에 따른 인물 정보	출생년도 및 출생지 → __________ → __________ → 업적

1 글을 읽고 답할 수 <u>없는</u> 질문은?

① Where was she born?

② What kinds of work did she do as a lab technician?

③ How did she make detailed pictures of viruses?

④ Where did she move from Canada?

⑤ When did she get degrees from the University of London?

2 글을 읽은 후의 소감으로 알맞지 <u>않은</u> 것은?

① She must have been good at science because she won the top prize in it.

② I felt sorry because she couldn't go to college due to money.

③ It was impressive that she became an expert at making vaccine for a virus.

④ I am surprised to know that she named it coronavirus.

⑤ I think she was happy to get the degrees she had wanted.

3 | Summary Map | 다음 인물 카드의 빈칸에 적절한 단어를 글에서 찾아 쓰시오.

June Almeida	
Birth	where: (1) _______________
Education	· excelled in school, especially in the subject of (2) _______________ · the University of London awarded her (3) _______________ _______________
Job	started to work as a(n) (4) _______________ _______________ at the age of (5) _______________
Achievement	made a clear picture of a mysterious (6) _______________ and named it (7) _______________

직독직해 Skill 다음을 의미 단위로 끊어 읽고(/), 주어(S)와 동사(V)에 표시해 봅시다.

· Then, in London in 1964, she created a sharp, clear picture of a mysterious virus and named it coronavirus.

____

Words

excel *v.* 뛰어나다

lab *n.* 실험실

technician *n.* 기술자

detect *v.* 찾아내다

detailed *a.* 자세한

microscope *n.* 현미경

expert *n.* 전문가

identify *v.* 확인하다

due to ~ 때문에

contribution *n.* 기여, 도움

award *v.* 수여하다

degree *n.* 학위

18

READING

선택지 ①~⑤를 먼저 읽은 후 관련 내용이 나오는 부분에 밑줄을 그어 봅시다.

The Secret: A Treasure Hunt에 관한 다음 글의 내용과 일치하지 <u>않는</u> 것은?

The Secret: A Treasure Hunt is a book created by Byron Preiss in 1982. Before the book was published, Preiss buried 12 small treasure boxes across the United States and Canada. Each box had a small key that could be exchanged for one of 12 jewels in a safe deposit box in New York. The book has 12 mysterious paintings 5 and poems. They contain the information that indicates the location of the buried treasures. For example, a flower and a bell in one image stand for Bellflower Road in Cleveland. Up to the year of 2023, only three of the twelve boxes have been found. One was discovered in 1983 in Grant Park in Chicago, the next one 10 in 2004 in the Greek Cultural Garden in Cleveland, and the most recent one was found in 2019 in Langone Park in Boston. Preiss didn't leave any record of the treasures' exact locations before his sudden death in a car accident in 2005. Many people are still out there looking for those treasures. 15

① Byron Preiss에 의해 창작되었다.
② 보물 상자의 위치를 가리키는 12개의 그림과 시가 실려 있다.
③ 2023년까지 3개의 상자가 발견되었다.
④ 가장 최근의 상자는 Chicago에서 발견되었다.
⑤ 저자인 Preiss는 자동차 사고로 갑작스럽게 사망했다.

Reading 비법

어떤 사물이나 작품에 관해 설명하는 글은 선택지를 먼저 읽으면 글에 소개될 주요 정보를 쉽게 추측할 수 있다.

Reading Skill 선택지를 통해 추론할 수 있는 *The Secret: A Treasure Hunt*를 완성해 봅시다.

The Secret: A Treasure Hunt	
선택지 ①, ②	Byron Preiss에 의해 창작된 __________으로, __________과 __________가 실려 있음
선택지 ③, ④	최근까지도 __________들이 발견되고 있음
선택지 ⑤	저자의 사망 원인은 __________임

1 글에서 언급되지 <u>않은</u> 것은?

① the author who wrote the book
② the countries where the treasure boxes were buried
③ the thing that is inside a treasure box
④ the kinds of jewels in the safe deposit box
⑤ the name of the garden where the second box was found

2 다음 빈칸에 공통으로 알맞은 단어를 글에서 찾아 쓰시오.

> · If you bring this coupon to the ABC cafeteria, it can be ____________ for a free coffee.
> · The students ____________ phone numbers so they could keep in touch with each other.

3 | Complete a Poster | 도서관 게시판에 붙일 책 소개 포스터의 빈칸에 적절한 정보를 글에서 찾아 쓰시오.

You should check out this book!

book title	*The Secret: A Treasure Hunt*
author	(1)____________________
special feature	The author buried 12 treasure boxes in the (2)____________ and (3)____________, and this book contains hints to the (4)____________ of those boxes. Of the boxes, only (5)____________ have been found. You can be the person who finds the next one!

직독직해 Skill 다음을 의미 단위로 끊어 읽고(/), 주어(S)와 동사(V)에 표시해 봅시다.

· Each box has a small key that could be exchanged for one of 12 jewels in a safe deposit box in New York.

____

Words

publish *v.* 출판하다
bury *v.* (땅에) 묻다
exchange *v.* 교환하다
poem *n.* 시
contain *v.* ~이 들어 있다
indicate *v.* 나타내다
location *n.* 위치
stand for ~을 상징하다
discover *v.* 발견하다
recent *a.* 최근의
sudden *a.* 갑작스러운

Ellen Church에 관한 다음 글의 내용과 일치하지 <u>않는</u> 것은?   기출 응용

Ellen Church was born in Cresco, Iowa, in 1904. After graduating from high school, she studied nursing. She worked as a nurse in San Francisco. One day Ellen stopped in at the Boeing office. She asked if she could get a job as a nurse on their airplanes. Ellen suggested that nurses take care of frightened passengers during flights. In 1930, she became the world's first female flight attendant. She worked on a Boeing 80A airplane, flying from Oakland to Chicago. Ellen, however, was forced to quit flying after eighteen months, due to an injury from a car accident. She started her nursing career again at Milwaukee County Hospital. During World War II, Ellen joined the Army Nurse Corps. She helped evacuate wounded soldiers by airplane. She received an Air Medal for <u>this</u>. The Ellen Church Field Airport in Cresco was named after her. She died in a horseback riding accident in 1965.

① San Francisco에서 간호사로 일했다.
② 간호사가 비행 중에 승객을 돌봐야 한다고 제안했다.
③ 세계 최초의 여성 비행기 승무원이 되었다.
④ 자동차 사고로 다쳤지만 비행기 승무원 생활을 계속했다.
⑤ 고향에 그녀의 이름을 따서 이름을 붙인 공항이 있다.

Mini Quiz

글을 읽으면서 인물의 직업에 있어서 특별한 점을 알 수 있는 문장을 찾아 밑줄을 그어 봅시다.

Reading 비법

인물에 대한 정보를 드러내는 장소나 시간, 사건 등을 표시하면서 읽는다.

Reading Skill 글의 내용에 맞게 다음 표를 완성해 봅시다.

인물	Ellen Church
정보	• 출생년도: ___________ 년 • 출생지: ___________, ___________ • 직업: ___________, ___________ • 업적: 세계 최초의 ___________ 비행 승무원 ___________을 받았음 고향에 그녀의 이름을 따서 이름 붙인 ___________이 있음

1 글의 밑줄 친 this가 가리키는 것은?

① 고등학교를 졸업하고 간호학을 공부하여 간호사가 되었던 것

② 18개월 동안 Boeing 항공사에서 비행 승무원으로 근무했던 것

③ Oakland에서 Chicago까지 Boeing 80A를 타고 근무했던 것

④ 2차 세계대전 중 간호 부대에 입대하여 부상당한 병사들을 비행기로 대피시켰던 것

⑤ 그녀의 이름을 따서 Ellen Church Field Airport라고 불리는 공항이 있는 것

2 글의 내용과 일치하도록 빈칸에 들어갈 말을 글에서 찾아 쓰시오.

Before 1930, there was no ____________ ____________ ____________ in the world.

3 | Summary | 다음 독서록의 빈칸에 적절한 단어를 글에서 찾아 쓰시오.

I read a book about a special woman. Her name is Ellen Church. She worked as a (1)____________ and as a flight (2)____________. She is well-known for being the world's (3)____________ woman flight attendant. Also, she is famous for receiving an Air Medal. During World War II, she joined the Army Nurse Corps and helped to (4)____________ injured soldiers by (5)____________.

Words

graduate from ~를 졸업하다

nursing *n.* 간호학

take care of ~를 돌보다

frightened *a.* 겁에 질린

passenger *n.* 승객

flight *n.* 비행

female *a.* 여성의

flight attendant 비행 승무원

be forced to ~할 수밖에 없다

due to ~ 때문에

injury *n.* 부상

career *n.* 경력, 이력

evacuate *v.* 대피시키다

wounded *a.* 부상당한

name after ~의 이름을 따서 이름 짓다

직독직해 Skill 다음을 의미 단위로 끊어 읽고(/), 주어(S)와 동사(V)에 표시해 봅시다.

· Ellen, however, was forced to quit flying after eighteen months, due to an injury from a car accident.

묘사된 분위기나 심경 파악하기

 인물과 사건 중심으로 빠르게 읽기

 분위기·심경 파악하기

Reading Key 인물과 사건 중심으로 빠르게 읽기

A 사건/일화나 상황을 묘사하는 글

즐겁고(joyful) 축제 분위기인(festive)

평화롭고(peaceful) 차분한(calm)

바쁘고(busy) 혼잡한(crowded)

사건이나 상황을 묘사하는 글은 나열식 구조이다. 주제가 있는 글이 아니므로, 한 가지 주제문을 찾기보다는 전반적인 글의 분위기를 빠르게 파악하며 읽어야 한다. 예를 들어, 즐거운 운동회를 묘사하는 글은 활기찬 분위기를 전달한다.

기출 예제

One night, I opened the door to go to the second floor and noted that the hallway light was off. When I put my foot down on the first step, I felt a movement under the stairs. Once I realized something strange was happening, my heart started beating fast. Suddenly, I saw a hand reach out from between the steps and grab my ankle. I screamed loudly, but nobody answered!

상황 묘사
- 복도의 전등이 __________ 있고, 계단 아래에서 어떤 __________을 감지함
- 어떤 손이 계단 사이에서 내 __________을 잡아서, 나는 __________을 지름

➡ **글 전반의 분위기:** ☐ 활기찬 분위기 vs ☐ 무서운 분위기

Words hallway *n.* 복도   movement *n.* 움직임   stair *n.* 계단   beat *v.* (심장 등이) 뛰다   reach out (손 등을) 뻗다   grab *v.* 붙잡다
ankle *n.* 발목   scream *v.* 비명을 지르다

+

wonderful smile the best
friendly better
beautiful cannot wait to

−

exhausted pale
uneasy terribly wrong
grief terrible

사건이나 일화를 설명하는 글 중에서도 사건보다는 등장인물의 마음 상태, 즉 심경에 초점을 맞춘 글들이 있다. 이런 글 역시 주제를 찾기보다는 등장인물이 처한 상황과 그때 느꼈을 심경을 파악하며 읽어야 한다.

기출 예제

Norm and his friend Jason went on a winter camping trip. During the night, Norm woke up and was surprised to see the stove was glowing red! Norm woke up Jason and found out that Jason had put too much wood in the stove. Norm thought the cabin was going to catch fire. He pulled Jason out of his bed. Norm yelled out in anger, "Look what you've done! How careless you were!"

상황 묘사
- 캠핑 중 Norm은 밤에 __________가 붉게 타고 있는 것을 발견함
- Jason이 난로에 __________을 너무 많이 넣은 것을 알게 됨
- Norm이 Jason을 침대에서 끌어내며 __________

➡ **Norm의 심경:** ☐ surprised and angry vs ☐ pleased and thankful

Words wake up 깨다, 깨우다   glow *v.* 불타다   cabin *n.* 오두막   catch fire 불이 나다   yell out 소리치다   careless *a.* 부주의한

다음 글의 상황에 나타난 분위기로 가장 적절한 것은?

  Alex and Angie looked around their new little house and immediately felt at home. The kitchen was delightful, with plenty of space for cooking. The family room had a large window and offered a comfortable place to relax. Upstairs, the bedrooms were cozy and promised sweet dreams, while a family room downstairs awaited movie nights and games. They were satisfied and went out to the small yard. The fenced-in yard was perfect for their needs and provided a sense of safety and privacy. Alex and Angie were excited to start planting a garden in the coming spring and even discussed getting a small dog. Suddenly, children's laughter came from the neighborhood and created a warm and friendly atmosphere. Great! Sarah, their daughter, would have many playmates. This was the home of their dreams, and they knew they belonged here.

① calm and silent
② sad and gloomy
③ noisy and funny
④ warm and happy
⑤ tense and urgent

Mini Quiz

글을 읽으면서 글의 분위기를 나타내는 표현을 찾아 밑줄을 그어 봅시다.

Reading 비법

글의 분위기를 알기 위해서는 글의 상황을 묘사하는 표현과 인물의 감정을 나타내는 표현 등을 종합적으로 파악해야 한다.

Reading Skill 주요 상황과 세부 내용을 찾아 다음 표를 완성해 봅시다.

주요 상황	Alex와 Angie가 __________을 둘러보는 상황
세부 내용	• 집을 둘러보고 __________을 느낌 • 집안의 주방, 거실, __________의 특징 묘사 • 작은 마당의 특징 묘사 • 밖에서 들려오는 아이들의 __________

1 글에서 새집에 관해 언급되지 <u>않은</u> 것은?

① 주방의 모습   ② 위층 침실의 분위기

③ 마당의 특징   ④ 정원에 심은 꽃의 종류

⑤ 동네의 분위기

2 글의 내용과 일치하지 <u>않는</u> 부분을 찾아 바르게 고쳐 쓰시오.

(1) Alex and Angie were disappointed with their new house.

______________ → ______________

(2) Alex and Angie discussed getting a large dog.

______________ → ______________

3 ｜Summary｜ 다음은 집의 각 부분에 대해 설명한 표이다. 빈칸에 적절한 말을 글에서 찾아 쓰시오.

kitchen	· looking (1)______________ · having plenty of (2)______________ for cooking
family room	· having a large (3)______________ · offering a comfortable place to relax
bedrooms	· being (4)______________ · promising sweet dreams
yard	· being fenced in · being (5)______________ for their needs · providing a sense of safety and (6)______________

직독직해 Skill 다음을 의미 단위로 끊어 읽고(/), 주어(S)와 동사(V)에 표시해 봅시다.

· The family room had a large window and offered a comfortable place to relax.

____

Words

immediately *ad.* 즉시
delightful *a.* 마음에 드는
family room 거실, 가족실
upstairs *ad.* 위층에
cozy *a.* 아늑한
downstairs *ad.* 아래층에
await *v.* 기다리다
fence *v.* 울타리를 치다
privacy *n.* 사생활
discuss *v.* 논의하다
laughter *n.* 웃음
atmosphere *n.* 분위기
playmate *n.* 놀이 친구
belong *v.* 속하다

READING 21

다음 글에 드러난 Emily의 심경으로 가장 적절한 것은?

Emily had a tough week at work, with long hours and tight deadlines. So, when her husband surprised her with beautiful roses after lunch, she was overjoyed. The vibrant colors and delicate petals were refreshing. She could tell that her husband had put a lot of thought into the gift, and it made her feel appreciated 5 and loved. As they stood there chatting and admiring the roses, Emily felt her stress and worries melt away. She thought that even on the toughest of days, there are always reasons to smile and find joy in the world. The roses served as a symbol of their love and partnership, and Emily felt lucky to have such a wonderful 10 person by her side. She hugged her husband and thanked him for the surprise. It was moments like this that made Emily feel truly blessed.

① relieved and proud
② scared and worried
③ uneasy and nervous
④ angry and frustrated
⑤ pleased and satisfied

Mini Quiz

글을 읽으면서 Emily의 심경을 잘 나타내 주는 말을 찾아 밑줄을 그어 봅시다.

Reading 비법

등장인물의 심경을 파악하기 위해서는 인물이 처한 상황과 감정을 나타내는 표현에 주목한다.

Reading Skill

주요 상황과 세부 내용을 찾아 다음 표를 완성해 봅시다.

주요 상황	남편에게서 __________ 을 선물받은 Emily
세부 내용	• 점심 식사 후에 남편으로부터 아름다운 장미를 받아 놀랐음 • 장미는 Emily와 남편의 사랑과 __________ 관계의 상징 역할을 함 • Emily는 남편을 안고 뜻밖의 선물에 대해 __________

1 Emily에 대한 설명으로 글의 내용과 일치하는 것은?

① She spent an easy week at work.
② She got roses from her husband before lunch.
③ She got stressed while chatting with her husband.
④ She was frustrated because she couldn't find any joy.
⑤ She felt that she was a lucky person.

2 다음 질문에 대한 답을 글에서 찾아 쓰시오.

(1) What was a symbol of Emily and her husband's love and partnership? → ___________________________

(2) How did Emily feel when she understood her husband's thoughtfulness? → ___________________________

3 | Summary | Emily에게 있었던 일을 정리한 다음 표의 빈칸에 적절한 말을 글에서 찾아 쓰시오.

her week at work	tough, with long hours and tight (1)___________
the present from her husband	beautiful roses with vibrant colors and delicate (2)___________
the things Emily and her husband did	standing while chatting and (3)___________ the roses
the things Emily did for her husband	(4)___________ and thanked him

Words

tough *a.* 힘든
tight *a.* 빠듯한
deadline *n.* 마감일
overjoy *v.* 매우 기쁘게 하다
vibrant *a.* 선명한, 강렬한
delicate *a.* 섬세한
petal *n.* 꽃잎
refreshing *a.* 상쾌한
appreciate *v.* 감사하다
admire *v.* 감탄하다
melt away 녹아서 없어지다
partnership *n.* 동반자 관계
bless *v.* 축복하다

직독직해 Skill 다음을 의미 단위로 끊어 읽고(/), 주어(S)와 동사(V)에 표시해 봅시다.

· She thought that even on the toughest of days, there are always reasons to smile and find joy in the world.

____

READING 22

다음 글에 드러난 Evelyn의 심경 변화로 가장 적절한 것은? 기출 응용

It was Evelyn's first time exploring the Badlands of Alberta, famous across Canada for its numerous dinosaur fossils. As a young amateur bone-hunter, she was filled with anticipation. She had not travelled this far for the bones of common dinosaur species. Her life-long dream to find rare fossils of dinosaurs was about to come true. She began eagerly searching for them. After many hours of wandering throughout the deserted lands, however, she was unsuccessful. Now, the sun was beginning to set, and her goal was still far beyond her reach. She was looking at the slowly darkening ground before her. She sighed to herself, "I can't believe I came all this way for nothing. What a waste of time!"

① confused   → scared
② discouraged → confident
③ relaxed   → annoyed
④ indifferent → depressed
⑤ hopeful   → disappointed

Mini Quiz

글을 읽으면서 Evelyn의 심경을 추측할 수 있는 표현들을 찾아 밑줄을 그어 봅시다.

Reading 비법

심경 변화가 생길 정도로 상황이 급변하는 내용을 다룬 글에서는 어떤 상황의 변화가 생겼는지에 주목한다.

Reading Skill 주요 상황과 세부 내용을 찾아 다음 표를 완성해 봅시다.

주요 상황	희귀한 __________ 을 찾고 있는 Evelyn
세부 내용	• __________ 으로 유명한 Alberta의 Badlands를 처음으로 탐험하는 중이었음 • Evelyn은 젊은 아마추어 __________ 임 • __________ 을 해가 저물 때까지 열심히 찾아다님

1 글을 읽고 답할 수 <u>없는</u> 질문은?

① What are the Badlands of Alberta famous for?
② What was Evelyn's life-long dream?
③ How long did Evelyn wander through the deserted lands?
④ What was Evelyn looking at when the sun was beginning to set?
⑤ How many times did Evelyn find fossils of dinosaurs?

Words

explore *v.* 탐험하다
numerous *a.* 수많은
dinosaur *n.* 공룡
fossil *n.* 화석
amateur *n.* 아마추어
bone-hunter *n.* 뼈 발굴자
anticipation *n.* 기대
species *n.* 종
rare *a.* 희귀한
eagerly *ad.* 열심히
search for ~을 찾다
wander *v.* 헤매고 다니다
deserted *a.* 인적이 드문
darken *v.* 어두워지다
sigh *v.* 한숨을 쉬며 말하다

2 다음 영영풀이에 해당하는 단어를 글에서 찾아 쓰시오.

(1) not happening very often → _____________
(2) to move about without a fixed course, aim, or goal
   → _____________

3 |Summary| 빈칸에 적절한 어구를 글에서 찾아 써서 요약문을 완성하시오.

> Evelyn, a young amateur bone-hunter, was exploring the Badlands of Alberta to (1)_____________________. Even though she eagerly searched for rare fossils of dinosaurs, she failed to find them before (2)_____________________.

직독직해 Skill 다음을 의미 단위로 끊어 읽고(/), 주어(S)와 동사(V)에 표시해 봅시다.

· Her life-long dream to find rare fossils of dinosaurs was about to come true.

____

Chapter 04

글의 흐름 파악하기

Reading Key 글의 흐름을 파악하고 이어질 내용 예측하기

A 글의 흐름 파악하기

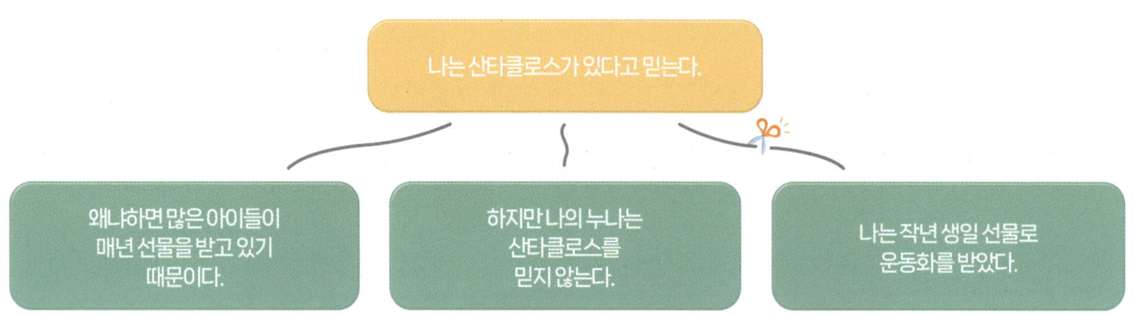

시험에 출제되는 지문은 짜임새가 잘 갖추어진 글들이다. 다양한 글이 있기에 첫 문장이 나온 후 그에 대한 이유가 이어질 수도, 예시가 이어질 수도, 반론이 이어질 수도 있지만 무관한 내용이 나올 수는 없다.

(기출 예제)

Training and conditioning for baseball focuses on developing strength, power, speed, quickness and flexibility. Before the 1980s, strength training was not an important part of conditioning for a baseball player.

> **흐름상 이어지기에 어색한 내용 고르기**
> ☐ 근력 운동을 중요시하지 않았던 이유
> ☐ 보디빌딩 운동과 야구선수용 운동의 차이
> ☐ 근력 운동의 중요성에 대한 이해와 적용

Words conditioning *n.* 몸만들기   focus on ~에 초점을 두다   develop *v.* 발전시키다, 성장하다   flexibility *n.* 유연성

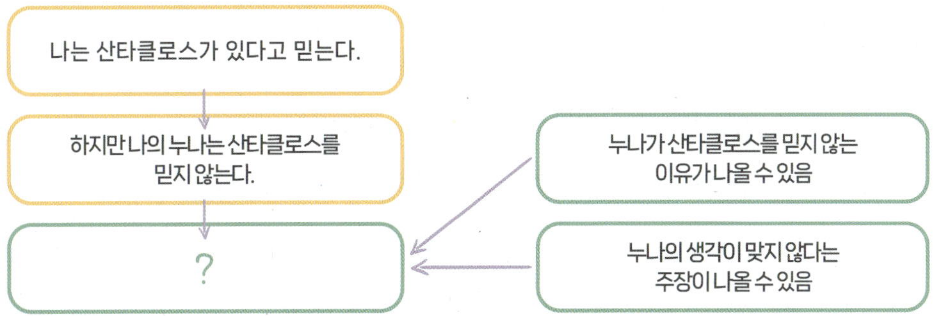

글의 흐름을 파악하는 것에 그치지 않고, 이어질 내용을 예측하며 적극적으로 읽는 것이 좋다.

기출 예제

(A) Product displays work the same way. Place bright-colored products higher and dark-colored products lower. This will look more stable and allow customers to comfortably browse the products.

(B) Dark colors look heavy, and bright colors look lighter. Interior designers often use a darker color on the bottom and a brighter color on top to create a calming effect for the viewer.

(A) 상품 전시도 같은 방식임 – 밝은 색을 __________, 어두운 색을 __________ 배치해서 소비자들이 편하게 상품을 보게 함

(B) 어두운 색은 무거워 보이고, 밝은 색은 가벼워 보임 – 실내 디자이너들은 어두운 색을 __________에, 밝은 색을 __________에 사용해서 진정 효과를 만듦

➡ 적절한 흐름:　☐ (A) – (B)의 순서　vs　☐ (B) – (A)의 순서

Words　display *n.* 전시　place *v.* 놓다, 두다　stable *a.* 안정적인　browse *v.* 훑어보다　calming effect 진정 효과
viewer *n.* 보는 사람

READING 23

주어진 글 다음에 이어질 글의 순서로 가장 적절한 것은?

> Why do we so often fail to keep our resolutions? Some psychologists suggest that most of us have unrealistic expectations about our ability to change our behavior (in general, not only at New Year's).

(A) It often begins with an unrealistic goal (e.g., "I will exercise for two hours every day!"). We also underestimate how difficult it will be to change our behavior (e.g., "I'll have no trouble stopping my computer games!"). Finally, we tend to expect dramatic, rapid results (e.g., "I'll probably lose about 10 pounds a week!").

(B) According to them, this produces the *false hope syndrome*. This syndrome involves exaggerated feelings of control and overconfidence about our ability to change our behavior successfully.

(C) Because of these wrong expectations, we usually fail. The new behavior proves to be more difficult than we expected. Visible results turn out to be slow. Then we often give up our attempts to change.

*exaggerated: 과장된

① (A) − (C) − (B) ② (B) − (A) − (C)
③ (B) − (C) − (A) ④ (C) − (A) − (B)
⑤ (C) − (B) − (A)

Mini Quiz

(A), (B), (C) 각각의 첫 문장에서 글의 순서를 파악하는 데 단서가 될 수 있는 바로 앞의 내용을 가리키는 말을 찾아 밑줄을 그어 봅시다.

Reading 비법

글쓴이가 질문으로 글을 시작할 때에는 그에 대한 글쓴이의 생각, 의견이 글의 중심 내용이 되는 경우가 많다.

Reading Skill 주제와 근거를 찾아 다음 표를 완성해 봅시다.

주제	__________ 을 지키지 못하는 이유
근거	• 행동을 바꿀 수 있는 능력에 대한 __________ 기대 • 비현실적인 목표, 행동을 변화시키는 것의 어려움에 대한 __________ • 극적이고 __________ 결과를 예상하는 경향 • __________ 증후군

1 글의 요지로 가장 적절한 것은?

① 결심을 지키지 못하는 이유는 자기 능력에 대한 과소평가이다.
② 자신의 행동 변화 능력을 믿으면 빠른 결과를 기대할 수 있다.
③ 목표를 구체적이고 뚜렷하게 세워야 행동 변화를 달성할 수 있다.
④ 변화의 실패는 행동 변화 능력에 대한 비현실적인 기대 때문이다.
⑤ 비록 때때로 실패하더라도 변화하려는 시도를 포기해서는 안 된다.

2 글의 내용과 일치하지 <u>않는</u> 부분을 찾아 바르게 고쳐 쓰시오.

The *false hope syndrome* means that we have realistic expectations of self change.

_____________ → _____________

3 |Summary| 행동 변화의 기대와 현실에 대한 다음 표의 빈칸에 적절한 말을 글에서 찾아 쓰시오. (단, 어형 변화 가능)

Why do we so often fail to keep our resolutions?

	Expectation	Reality
goal	(1)_____________	*not mentioned*
ability to change our behavior successfully	exaggerated and (2)_____________	*not mentioned*
degree of difficulty	underestimated	more (3)_____________ than expected
speed of seeing results	dramatic, rapid	(4)_____________

직독직해 Skill 다음을 의미 단위로 끊어 읽고(/), 주어(S)와 동사(V)에 표시해 봅시다.

· Some psychologists suggest that most of us have unrealistic expectations about our ability to change our behavior (in general. not only at New Year's).

____

Words

resolution *n.* 결심
psychologist *n.* 심리학자
suggest *v.* 시사하다
unrealistic *a.* 비현실적인
expectation *n.* 기대
underestimate *v.* 과소평가하다
dramatic *a.* 극적인
rapid *a.* 빠른
false *a.* 거짓의, 틀린
syndrome *n.* 증후군, 신드롬
involve *v.* 포함하다
overconfidence *n.* 지나친 자신감
visible *a.* 눈에 보이는
give up ~을 포기하다
attempt *n.* 시도

READING 24

주어진 글 다음에 이어질 글의 순서로 가장 적절한 것은?

Isaac Newton is one of history's greatest scientists. During his lifetime he made numerous contributions to science. But few people realize that he was also a pet lover — or that sometimes many of his animal friends could drive him to distraction.

(A) So, the scientist was annoyed and quickly came up with a solution — the pet door. The cat could come in and go out of Newton's house without disturbing him. Today, every cat with the ability to enter and leave a room without troubling their human friends has Newton to thank.

(B) However, his dealings with an annoying cat led to a happier result. According to legend, a cat constantly interrupted Newton with its demands to be let in and out of the house.

(C) For instance, he once suffered an emotional breakdown when a favorite dog knocked over a candle on his desk. The dog burned some of his important research notes. *breakdown: 신경쇠약

① (A) − (C) − (B)　　② (B) − (A) − (C)
③ (B) − (C) − (A)　　④ (C) − (A) − (B)
⑤ (C) − (B) − (A)

Mini Quiz

(B) 첫 번째 문장의 However, his dealings with an annoying cat으로 보아 앞에는 어떤 내용이 올 수 있는지 생각해 봅시다.

Reading 비법

However나 On the other hand 뒤에는 앞의 내용과 반대되는 내용, For instance나 For example 뒤에는 앞의 내용에 대한 예시, So나 Therefore 뒤에는 앞의 내용에 대한 결과를 말하는 경우가 많다.

Reading Skill　글의 중심 내용에 맞게 다음 표를 완성해 봅시다.

주제문	뉴턴은 __________ 애호가였고 그들로 인해 산만해질 수 있었다.
부연 설명	• __________을 생각해 냈음 • __________의 끊임없는 방해를 받음 • 가장 좋아하는 개가 ______________를 쳐서 넘어뜨림 • 그 개가 중요한 연구 노트 중 일부를 태웠음

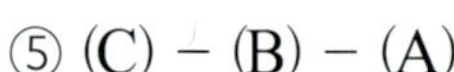

1 글의 밑줄 친 a happier result가 의미하는 바로 가장 적절한 것은?

① a candle
② a pet lover
③ the pet door
④ an emotional breakdown
⑤ the contribution to science

2 글의 내용과 일치하도록 다음 질문에 대한 답을 완전한 문장으로 쓰시오.

(1) Why should all cats thank Newton?

→ _______________________________________

(2) What drove Newton to distraction?

→ _______________________________________

3 | Summary | 다음 표의 빈칸에 적절한 말을 글에서 찾아 쓰시오. (단, 어형 변화 가능)

Distractions Caused by Newton's Animal Friends	
Dog	· burned some of his important research notes by (1) _____________ over a candle on his desk · made him suffer a(n) (2) _____________ breakdown
Cat	· demanded to come in and go out of the house whenever it wanted and constantly (3) _____________ him · made him (4) _____________

직독직해 Skill 다음을 의미 단위로 끊어 읽고(/), 주어(S)와 동사(V)에 표시해 봅시다.

· According to legend, a cat constantly interrupted Newton with its demands to be let in and out of the house.

____

Words

numerous *a.* 수많은
contribution *n.* 공헌
distraction *n.* 집중을 방해하는 것, 주의산만
come up with ~을 생각해내다
dealing *n.* 행위, 관계
annoying *a.* 짜증나게 하는
legend *n.* 전해오는 이야기, 전설
constantly *ad.* 끊임없이
interrupt *v.* 방해하다
demand *n.* 요구
suffer *v.* 시달리다, 고통받다
emotional *a.* 감정적인
knock over 쳐서 넘어뜨리다
candle *n.* 초, 양초

READING 25

주어진 글 다음에 이어질 글의 순서로 가장 적절한 것은? `기출 응용`

> People spend much of their time interacting with media. But that does not mean that people have the critical skills to examine it carefully and understand it.

(A) Research from New York University found that people over 65 shared seven times as much misinformation as younger people. All of this raises a question: What's the solution to the misinformation problem?

(B) There's one well-known study from Stanford University in 2016. The study showed that young people are easily fooled by misinformation, especially when it comes through social media channels. This weakness is not found only in youth, however.

(C) Governments and tech platforms certainly have a role to play in blocking misinformation. However, every individual needs to become more information literate. And they should take responsibility for combating this threat by becoming more information literate.

*information literate: 정보를 이용할 줄 아는

① (A) − (C) − (B)
② (B) − (A) − (C)
③ (B) − (C) − (A)
④ (C) − (A) − (B)
⑤ (C) − (B) − (A)

Mini Quiz

글에서 주제문을 찾아 밑줄을 그어 봅시다.

Reading 비법

주어진 글에는 글의 주제가 드러나 있는 경우가 많기 때문에 주어진 글에서 주제문을 먼저 찾아 보아야 한다.

Reading Skill 글의 주제문과 근거를 찾아 다음 표를 완성해 봅시다.

주제문	사람들은 __________를 주의 깊게 검토하여 이해하는 데 중요한 기술을 가지고 있지 않다.
근거	• __________를 공유하는 것에 대해 연령별로 연구한 뉴욕 대학의 연구 결과 • 소셜 미디어의 잘못된 정보에 대해 __________들을 연구한 스탠퍼드 대학의 연구

1 글의 내용과 일치하지 <u>않는</u> 것은?

① Interacting with media is a way people spend much of their time.
② Young people are not the only ones who are easily fooled by misinformation.
③ Governments and tech platforms must block misinformation.
④ Being information literate is the skill every individual should have.
⑤ Individuals don't need to fight against the threat of misinformation.

2 글에서 필자가 주장하는 바로 가장 적절한 것은?

① 노인들에 대한 미디어 이용 교육을 대폭 늘려야 한다.
② 미디어 사용에 지나치게 많은 시간을 보내지 말아야 한다.
③ 정보를 이용하는 능력을 갖춰 잘못된 정보에 맞서 싸워야 한다.
④ 모든 연령을 대상으로 하는 미디어 교육을 대학이 주도해야 한다.
⑤ 정부와 기술 플랫폼이 잘못된 정보에 대해 더 큰 책임을 져야 한다.

3 |Summary| 인터넷 정보에 대한 뉴욕 대학의 연구와 스탠퍼드 대학의 연구를 비교한 다음 표의 빈칸에 적절한 말을 쓰시오.

	New York University	**Stanford University**
subject	people over 65 and younger people	young people
result	People over 65 shared much (1)__________ misinformation than younger people.	Young people are easily (2)__________ by the misinformation that comes through (3)_____ _____ channels.

직독직해 Skill 다음을 의미 단위로 끊어 읽고(/), 주어(S)와 동사(V)에 표시해 봅시다.

· Research from New York University found that people over 65 shared seven times as much misinformation as younger people.

Words

interact *v.* 상호 작용하다, 소통하다
critical *a.* 중요한
examine *v.* 검토하다
misinformation *n.* 잘못된 정보
raise *v.* 제기하다
well-known *a.* 잘 알려진
especially *ad.* 특히
weakness *n.* 약점
youth *n.* 젊은이, 청년
government *n.* 정부
tech platform 기술 플랫폼
certainly *ad.* 분명히, 확실히
responsibility *n.* 책임
combat *v.* 싸우다
threat *n.* 위협

READING 26

글의 흐름으로 보아, 주어진 문장이 들어가기에 가장 적절한 곳은?

> Red is the color of stop signs and danger, and it is typically the color of pens used by teachers.

Colors can help improve memory. For example, some studies on Alzheimer's patients found that color cues helped improve their recall of certain images. Furthermore, they could not remember black-and-white images, but could remember colored ones. (①) Another study found that red and blue were the best colors for improving brain function. (②) Red came out on top because of its role in society. (③) This means that red is an important color in learning and in the real world, and a person is more likely to remember something red. (④) Additionally, as the color red makes people cautious, they become more detail-oriented and pay better attention. (⑤) This results in people recalling a red-colored object better later.

Mini Quiz

글의 주제문을 찾아 밑줄을 그어 봅시다.

Reading 비법

글에서 어떤 연구가 예시로 제시된다면, 그 연구 결과가 주제를 보여주는 경우가 많다.

Reading Skill

주제와 근거 문장을 찾아 다음 표를 완성해 봅시다.

주제	색과 __________ 사이의 관계
근거	• __________ 환자들에 대한 실험: 컬러로 된 이미지를 기억함 • 빨간색과 파란색에 대한 실험 결과: 빨간색인 사물을 더 잘 기억함 　– 학습과 실제 세상에서 중요한 색임 　– 사람들을 __________ 만듦 　– 사람들이 __________ 것을 지향하게 하고 더 집중하게 함

1 글의 주제로 가장 적절한 것은?

① colors that can help you study
② the necessity of color education
③ the impact of colors on memory
④ how colorful memories enrich life
⑤ two colors that go together really well

2 다음 빈칸에 공통으로 들어갈 단어를 글에서 찾아 쓰시오.

> • I always feel ____________ when I cross the street.
> • Mike is always ____________ when he uses sharp tools.

3 |Summary| 다음 표의 빈칸에 적절한 어구를 글에서 찾아 쓰시오.

Memory can be improved by (1)____________.	
Studies on Alzheimer's patients	**A study on red and blue**
• Their recall of certain images improved with the help of (2)____________. • (3)____________ images cannot be remembered but (4)____________ ones can be remembered.	• The important color in learning and in the real world is (5)____________. • The color red makes people become more detail-oriented and pay better (6)____________.

직독직해 Skill 다음을 의미 단위로 끊어 읽고(/), 주어(S)와 동사(V)에 표시해 봅시다.

• For example, some studies on Alzheimer's patients found that color cues helped improve their recall of certain images.

Words

typically *ad.* 전형적으로
improve *v.* 향상시키다
cue *n.* 신호, 단서
recall *n.* 기억, 회상
function *n.* 기능
come out on top 1등을 차지하다
additionally *ad.* 게다가
cautious *a.* 주의 깊은
detail-oriented *a.* 세부적인 것을 지향하는
pay attention 집중하다
result in (결과적으로) ~을 낳다, 야기하다
object *n.* 물건, 사물

READING 27

글의 흐름으로 보아, 주어진 문장이 들어가기에 가장 적절한 곳은?

> Good decisions require far more than factual knowledge.

Despite the growing focus on EQ, a global lack in understanding and managing emotions still remains. In a test, only 36 percent of the people who were tested were able to accurately identify their emotions as they happened. What does this suggest? It means that two-thirds of us are typically controlled by our emotions. (①) But we are not yet skilled at spotting our emotions and using them to our benefit. (②) Emotional awareness and understanding are not taught in school. (③) We enter the workforce after learning how to read, write, and report on bodies of knowledge. (④) Too often, however, we lack the skills to manage our emotions in the heat of the challenging problems that we face. (⑤) They are made by using our self-knowledge and emotional mastery when they are needed most.

Mini Quiz

글의 첫 문장 Despite ~ remains.를 읽고 이어질 내용을 추론하여 5단어 내외의 우리말로 써 봅시다.

Reading 비법

지시어가 가리키는 것은 대개 바로 앞 문장에 있을 가능성이 높지만 앞 문장에서 찾을 수 없는 경우에는 주어진 문장에서 찾아야 한다.

Reading Skill

주제와 근거 문장을 찾아 다음 표를 완성해 봅시다.

주제	감정에 대한 __________와 __________의 부족
근거	• 감정에 의해 통제되지만 감정을 찾아내어 __________하는 데 능숙하지 않음 • 감정의 인식과 이해는 __________에서 가르치지 않음 • 감정을 관리하는 기술이 __________함

1 글의 제목으로 가장 적절한 것은?

① How Emotions Are Made Through Talk
② Between Us: How Cultures Create Emotions
③ Echoes of the Heart: Revealing Hidden Emotions
④ How Emotions Are Made: The Secret Life of the Brain
⑤ A Long Way to Go in Understanding and Managing Emotions

2 글의 내용과 일치하면 T, 일치하지 <u>않으면</u> F를 쓰시오.

(1) There are few people who are poor at spotting their emotions and using them to their benefit. ______
(2) We learn emotional awareness and understanding in school. ______

3 |Summary| 빈칸에 적절한 단어를 글에서 찾아 알맞은 형태로 써서 요약문을 완성하시오.

> Even though we are mostly (1) ____________ by emotions, we don't fully understand emotions and can't (2) ____________ them at will. But to make good decisions, self-knowledge and emotional mastery are (3) ____________.

Words

decision *n.* 결정
require *v.* 요구하다
factual *a.* 사실적인
knowledge *n.* 지식
despite *prep.* ~에도 불구하고
remain *v.* 남아 있다
accurately *ad.* 정확하게
identify *v.* 식별하다
typically *ad.* 보통, 전형적으로
spot *v.* 찾아내다
benefit *n.* 이익
awareness *n.* 인식
workforce *n.* 노동자, 노동력
self-knowledge *n.* 자기 이해
mastery *n.* 숙달

직독직해 Skill 다음을 의미 단위로 끊어 읽고(/), 주어(S)와 동사(V)에 표시해 봅시다.

· They are made by using our self-knowledge and emotional mastery when they are needed most.

READING 28

글의 흐름으로 보아, 주어진 문장이 들어가기에 가장 적절한 곳은? 기출응용

> According to observations, at each level of transfer, 80—90 percent of the potential energy is lost as heat.

You may have heard of the food chain quite often in science class. What is a food chain? It means the transfer of food energy from its source in plants. The transfer is done through a series of organisms during the repeated process of eating and being eaten. (①) In a grassland, grass is eaten by rabbits, while rabbits in turn are eaten by foxes. (②) This is an example of a simple food chain. (③) In the course of following this food chain, food energy is transferred from the plant to the animal or to a higher trophic level. (④) Hence the number of steps or links in a course is limited, usually to four or five. (⑤) The shorter the food chain, the greater the available energy intake is.

*trophic: 영양의

Mini Quiz

글의 핵심 소재를 찾아 두 단어로 써 봅시다.

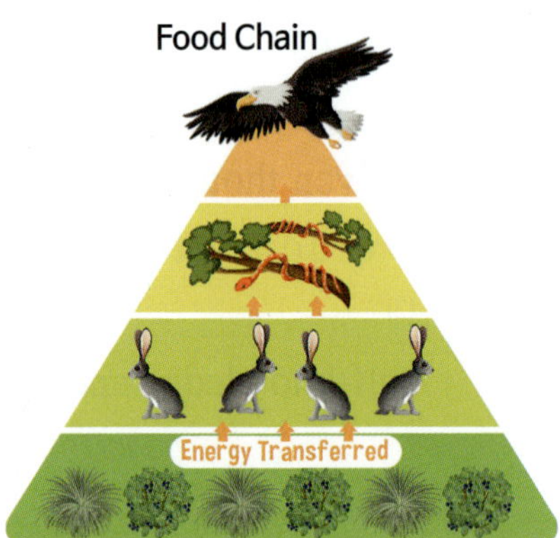

Reading 비법

글의 흐름을 이해하면서 내용상 흐름이 어색한 부분을 찾는다.

Reading Skill

글을 내용을 크게 두 부분으로 나눈 다음 표를 완성해 봅시다.

도입	먹이 사슬 설명	• 먹이 사슬은 __________가 에너지원으로부터 __________ 하는 것을 의미함 • 에너지의 이동은 __________ 반복되는 과정 동안 일련의 __________를 통해 이루어짐
전개	먹이 사슬 안에서의 에너지 효율 설명	• 먹이 사슬 과정에서 __________이 있음 • 먹이 사슬이 __________ 이용 가능한 에너지 섭취량이 더 커짐

1 글의 제목으로 가장 적절한 것은?

① Why We Should Eat Healthy Foods
② Be Careful When You Handle Foods
③ Threats to Humans in the Food Chain
④ The Transfer of Food Energy in Ecosystems
⑤ The Food Source We Get the Most Energy from

2 다음 빈칸에 공통으로 들어갈 단어를 글에서 찾아 쓰시오.

- She will _____________ her bag from one hand to the other.
- He will _____________ to UCLA after studying at Harvard.

Words

observation *n.* 관찰
transfer *n.* 이동 *v.* 옮기다, 이동하다
potential *a.* 잠재적인
source *n.* 원천, 근원
a series of 일련의
organism *n.* 유기체
repeated *a.* 반복되는
grassland *n.* 초원, 목초지
hence *ad.* 이런 이유로
limit *v.* 제한[한정]하다
available *a.* 이용 가능한
intake *n.* 섭취(량)

3 | Summary | 다음 표의 빈칸에 적절한 말을 글에서 찾아 쓰시오.

About the Food Chain	
Meaning	the (1)___________ of food energy from its source in plants, which is done through a series of organisms during the (2)___________ process of eating and being eaten
Example	grass eaten by rabbits and rabbits eaten by (3)___________
Energy Transfer	• food energy transfer from the (4)___________ to the (5)___________ or to a higher trophic level • a(n) (6)___________ food chain leads to a(n) (7)___________ available energy intake

직독직해 Skill 다음을 의미 단위로 끊어 읽고(/), 주어(S)와 동사(V)에 표시해 봅시다.

- According to observations, at each level of transfer, 80—90 percent of the potential energy is lost as heat.

____

READING 29

글의 핵심 어구를 찾아 두 단어
로 써 봅시다.

다음 글에서 전체 흐름과 관계 없는 문장은?

 I believe that the more you remember, the more you *can* remember. Memory, in many ways, is like a muscle. A muscle must be exercised and developed in order to give proper service and use: so must memory. ① The difference is that a muscle can be overtrained or become muscle-bound, while memory cannot. ② You can be taught to train your memory just as you can be taught anything else. ③ As a matter of fact, it is much easier to develop a trained memory than, say, to learn to play a musical instrument. ④ Memorization isn't practical for learning complex concepts and information. ⑤ Along with a trained memory you will probably acquire a greater power of concentration, a purer sense of observation, and perhaps, a stronger imagination.

*muscle-bound: 근육이 뻣뻣해진

Reading 비법

무관한 문장은 글의 주제에
서 벗어나 있는 경우가 많으
므로 무엇에 관한 글인지를
먼저 파악해야 한다.

Reading Skill 주제와 근거 문장을 찾아 다음 표를 완성해 봅시다.

주제	기억의 __________ 가능성과 훈련된 기억력의 장점
근거	• 기억은 __________ 과 같이 연습되고 발달될 수 있음 • __________ 를 배우는 것보다 훈련된 기억력을 발달시키는 것이 훨씬 더 쉬움 • 훈련된 기억력은 집중력, __________ , 상상력을 높여줌

1 글에 언급된 것은?

① benefits of a trained memory
② the danger of a trained memory
③ strategies for training your memory
④ side effects of an overtrained memory
⑤ characteristics of an overtrained memory

Words

muscle *n.* 근육
proper *a.* 적절한
overtrain *v.* 과도하게 훈련하다
musical instrument 악기
memorization *n.* 암기
practical *a.* 실용적인
complex *a.* 복잡한
concept *n.* 개념
along with ~와 함께
acquire *v.* 얻다, 획득하다
concentration *n.* 집중(력)
pure *a.* 순수한
observation *n.* 관찰(력)

2 글의 내용과 일치하지 <u>않는</u> 부분을 찾아 바르게 고쳐 쓰시오.

Learning to play a musical instrument is much easier than training your memory.

___________ → ___________

3 ꞁSummaryꞁ 빈칸에 적절한 단어를 글에서 찾아 요약문을 완성하시오.

> Like a muscle, memory must be (1)___________ and (2)___________ to give proper service and use. When you have a(n) (3)___________ memory, your power of (4)___________, sense of observation, and imagination will improve.

직독직해 Skill 다음을 의미 단위로 끊어 읽고(/), 주어(S)와 동사(V)에 표시해 봅시다.

· I believe that the more you remember. the more you *can* remember.

READING 30

다음 글에서 전체 흐름과 관계 <u>없는</u> 문장은? 　기출 응용

Health and the spread of disease are very closely linked to how we live and how our cities operate. The good news is that cities can recover more quickly than you might imagine. For example, many cities have experienced deadly diseases in the past. <u>After some period of pain and suffering, they not only survived, but also advanced.</u> ① In the nineteenth and early twentieth centuries, European cities saw destructive outbreaks of deadly diseases. ② Some famous doctors in Germany found the connection between poor living conditions and disease. ③ This led to the replanning and rebuilding of cities to stop the spread of deadly diseases. ④ In spite of the reconstruction efforts, cities declined in many areas and many people started to leave. ⑤ In the mid-nineteenth century, London's pioneering sewer system was built to stop the spread of cholera.

*sewer system: 하수도

Mini Quiz

글을 읽고 주제문을 찾아 밑줄을 그어 봅시다.

Reading 비법

앞문장 또는 뒷문장과의 흐름은 자연스러울지라도 전체 글의 주제와 반대되는 내용의 문장에 유의한다.

Reading Skill 글의 중심 내용에 맞게 다음 표를 완성해 봅시다.

주제문	건강 및 __________은 __________, __________ 운영과 밀접한 관련이 있다.
부연 설명	• 19세기와 20세기 초 유럽 도시들에서 치명적인 질병의 파괴적인 발생 • 독일의 의사들이 열악한 __________과 질병 사이의 연관성을 발견 • 치명적인 질병의 확산을 막기 위한 __________ 재계획과 재건 • 19세기 중반 콜레라 확산을 막기 위한 런던의 선구적인 __________ 건설

1 글에서 답을 찾을 수 <u>없는</u> 질문은?

① What are very closely linked to health and the spread of disease?
② What happened in Europe during the nineteenth and early twentieth centuries?
③ Who found the connection between poor living conditions and disease?
④ How many people died from cholera in London during the mid-nineteenth century?
⑤ When was London's pioneering sewer system built?

2 글의 밑줄 친 부분과 의미가 같도록 다음 문장의 빈칸에 적절한 말을 쓰시오.

> After some period of pain and suffering, they ______________ as well as ____________.

3 |Summary| 글의 흐름에 맞게 빈칸에 적절한 말을 넣어 다음 표를 완성하시오.

Destructive (1)______________ ____________ broke out.

↓

The connection between poor (2)____________ ____________ and disease was found.

↓

Cities were replanned and rebuilt.

↓

London's pioneering (3)______________ ____________ was built.

직독직해 Skill 다음을 의미 단위로 끊어 읽고(/), 주어(S)와 동사(V)에 표시해 봅시다.

· Health and the spread of disease are very closely linked to how we live and how our cities operate.

____

Words

spread *n.* 확산
disease *n.* 질병
operate *v.* 운영되다
advance *v.* 발전하다
century *n.* 세기
destructive *a.* 파괴적인
outbreak *n.* 발생, 발발
connection *n.* 연관성
replanning *n.* 재계획
rebuilding *n.* 재건
in spite of ~에도 불구하고
reconstruction *n.* 재건, 복원
effort *n.* 노력
decline *v.* 쇠퇴하다
pioneering *a.* 선구적인
cholera *n.* 콜레라

내용 추론하기

글의 내용을 단서로 추론하기

A 글에 빈칸이 있는 경우

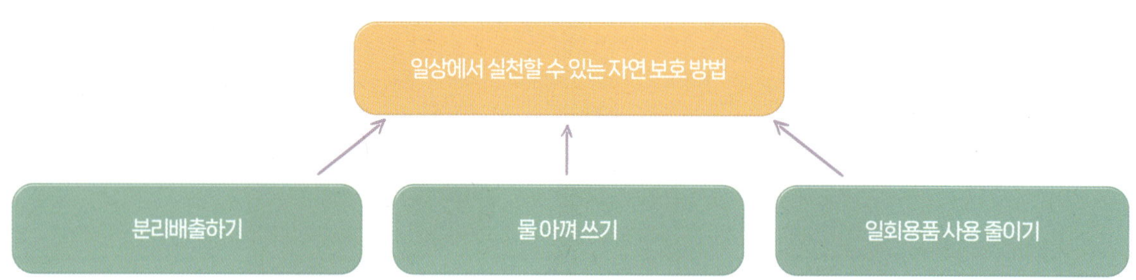

빈칸에 들어갈 말은 자신의 상식이나 생각에 따라 임의로 판단하면 절대 안 되고, 주제에 맞게, 즉 글의 내용을 단서로 추론해야 한다.

기출 예제

When you are motivated to achieve a goal, you will put in considerable ____________. For example, if you are motivated to buy a good car, you will research vehicles online, look at ads, visit dealerships, and so on. Likewise, if you are motivated to lose weight, you will buy low-fat foods, eat smaller portions, and exercise regularly.

＊ 윗글의 빈칸에 들어갈 알맞은 말은?

a. risk   b. effort   c. fortune

주제문	목표를 이루고자 하는 동기가 있으면 상당한 ________을 들인다.
근거문	예시1 좋은 차를 사고 싶으면 ________ 검색, 광고 읽기, 자동차 대리점 방문하기 등을 한다. 예시2 몸무게를 줄이고 싶으면 ________ 식품 구입, 더 적게 먹기, 규칙적인 ________ 등을 한다.

Words motivate *v.* 동기를 부여하다 achieve *v.* 이루다, 달성하다 goal *n.* 목적 considerable *a.* 상당한 vehicle *n.* 차량
dealership *n.* 대리점 low-fat *a.* 저지방의 portion *n.* 1인분(의 양)

B 추상적인 표현이 나온 경우

추상적인 표현이 나오는 글들이 있다. 상황에 동떨어진 표현을 갑자기 사용하는 경우는 없으므로, 글의 전체적인 내용과 흐름을 살피면, 추상적인 표현의 숨은 뜻을 추론해 낼 수 있다.

기출 예제

For almost all things in life, there can be too much of a good thing. Even the best things in life aren't so great in excess. Aristotle argued that being virtuous means finding a balance. For example, people should be brave, but if someone is too brave they become reckless. The best way is to live at the "sweet spot" that maximizes well-being. Aristotle suggests that virtue is a midpoint, where someone is neither too afraid nor recklessly brave.

아무리 좋은 것이라도 __________ 좋지 않으며, 미덕이란 __________ 을 찾는 것을 의미한다.

↓

최상의 방법은 행복을 극대화하는 'sweet spot'에 머무르는 것
sweet spot의 숨은 의미   넘치지도 모자라지도 않은 __________ 에 있는 것

Words in excess 과도하게   argue *v.* 주장하다   virtuous *a.* 미덕의, 도덕적인   reckless *a.* 무모한   maximize *v.* 최대화하다
midpoint *n.* 중간 지점   neither A nor B A도 B도 아닌

31

다음 빈칸에 들어갈 말로 가장 적절한 것은?

Reading fiction is one of the most loved hobbies of all time. Mysteries, science fiction, romance, and fantasy are all fiction. Reading fiction is exciting and, at the same time, very helpful. It is a well-known fact that it improves creativity. While you are reading fiction, you can get new ideas. And you can learn various ways of thinking about the world. Also, you can understand others better when you read fiction. Research indicates that fiction is more effective than nonfiction in changing our views about people who have different ideas. In addition, reading fiction can help you become better with people. It teaches you about how people may react to situations and challenges. Seeing the mistakes characters make in stories can help you gain wisdom to use in your own lives. With all these __________ in mind, how about setting aside your smartphone and reading some fiction today?

① benefits
② questions
③ limitations
④ challenges
⑤ differences

Mini Quiz

글을 읽으면서 주제문을 찾아 밑줄을 그어 봅시다.

Reading 비법

먼저 글의 주제를 파악한 후, 빈칸에 들어갈 말로는 주제 및 흐름에 잘 맞는 것을 골라야 한다.

Reading Skill

주제문과 근거문을 찾아 다음 표를 완성해 봅시다.

주제문	__________ 을 읽는 것은 큰 도움을 준다.
근거문	• __________ 을 향상시킨다. • 다른 사람들을 더 잘 __________ 수 있게 한다. • 사람들과 더 잘 __________ 돕는다.

1 글을 읽고 답할 수 <u>없는</u> 질문은?

① Why do people make mistakes?
② What are some examples of fiction?
③ What ability can be increased when you read fiction?
④ What can you learn from reading fiction?
⑤ How can reading fiction help you become better with people?

Words

fiction *n.* 소설, 허구
mystery *n.* 미스터리
fantasy *n.* 판타지
well-known *a.* 잘 알려진, 유명한
improve *v.* 향상시키다
creativity *n.* 창의성
research *n.* 연구
effective *a.* 효과적인
nonfiction *n.* 논픽션(소설이 아닌 산문)
react *v.* 반응하다
wisdom *n.* 지혜
set aside ~을 제쳐두다

2 글의 내용과 일치하도록 <u>틀린</u> 부분을 고쳐 문장을 다시 쓰시오.

When fiction is compared to nonfiction, it is less effective in changing our views about people different from ourselves.

→ ____

3 ǀ Summary ǀ 빈칸에 적절한 단어를 글에서 찾아 써서 요약문을 완성하시오.

> Reading fiction has many advantages. First, it improves your creativity by getting new (1)______________ and various ways of thinking. Second, it makes you understand others better by (2)______________ your views about others. Lastly, it helps you be better with people by gaining (3)______________ from reading about others' mistakes.

직독직해 Skill 다음을 의미 단위로 끊어 읽고(/), 주어(**S**)와 동사(**V**)에 표시해 봅시다.

· Seeing the mistakes characters make in stories can help you gain wisdom to use in your own lives.

____

32

READING

글을 읽으면서 필자의 주장이 가장 잘 드러난 문장에 밑줄을 그어 봅시다.

다음 빈칸에 들어갈 말로 가장 적절한 것은?   기출 응용

We want to provide good care for animals. To do that, an animal's needs should be met consistently and predictably all the time. Like humans, animals need a sense of control. So, an animal that doesn't know when food will appear may experience distress. We can provide a sense of control. We just need to ensure that our animal's environment is __________: that there is always water available and always in the same place. There is always food when we get up in the morning and after our evening walk. There will always be a time and place to eliminate without having to hold things in to the point of discomfort. Human companions can display consistent emotional support, rather than providing love one moment and withholding love the next. When animals know what to expect, they will feel more confident and calm.

*eliminate: 배설하다

① silent   ② natural   ③ isolated
④ dynamic   ⑤ predictable

Reading 비법

글에 제시된 다양한 예시가 무엇을 설명하기 위한 것인지를 파악하면 글의 주제 및 빈칸에 들어갈 말을 찾기 쉽다.

Reading Skill   주제문과 근거문을 찾아 다음 표를 완성해 봅시다.

주제문	동물의 돌봄은 __________이고 __________하게 이루어져야 한다.
근거문	• __________이 언제 나타날지를 알지 못하는 동물은 고통을 받는다. • 마실 수 있는 물이 항상 있고, 그것은 항상 __________ 곳에 있어야 한다. • __________ 할 수 있는 시간과 장소가 늘 있어야 한다.

1 글의 주제로 가장 적절한 것은?

① the relationship between humans and animals
② the influence of animals on their environment
③ the reason why animals need human companions
④ the necessity of protecting endangered animals in the wild
⑤ the importance of consistency and predictability in animal care

2 글의 내용과 일치하면 T, 일치하지 <u>않으면</u> F를 쓰시오.

(1) When animals know what to expect, they can feel more distressed. _____

(2) It is desirable for human companions to provide love one moment and withhold love the next. _____

3 |Summary| 빈칸에 적절한 단어를 |보기|에서 골라 넣어 표를 완성하시오.

| 보기 |

confident needs nervous control consistent belonging

Human Companions' Efforts	Results for an Animal
• Meeting an animal's (1)______________ consistently and predictably • Displaying (2)______________ emotional support	• Having a sense of (3)______________ • Feeling (4)______________ and calm

직독직해 Skill 다음을 의미 단위로 끊어 읽고(/), 주어(S)와 동사(V)에 표시해 봅시다.

· Human companions can display consistent emotional support. rather than providing love one moment and withholding love the next.

____

Words

consistently *ad.* 일관되게
predictably *ad.* 예측 가능하게
distress *n.* 고통, 괴로움
ensure *v.* 반드시 ~하게 하다, 보장하다
hold ~ in ~을 참다
discomfort *n.* 불편함
companion *n.* 친구, 동반자
display *v.* 보이다, 나타내다
emotional *a.* 정서적인
withhold *v.* (~을) 주지 않다
confident *a.* 자신감이 있는, 자신만만한

33

READING

다음 빈칸에 들어갈 말로 가장 적절한 것은?

Let's look back at famous individuals in history. Statements like "So and so was born to be a great leader" are often made. Well, those words are often not as true as they sound. Anyone at any time and in any place can become a leader. They can be so charismatic that the entire world will sit up and take notice. To understand this, one must first know the basic truth about what makes people great. That truth is that people don't make themselves great. Then what makes people great? It is ________________. When a person, no matter their background or environment, has a clear goal, belief, or something they want that they are willing to give up everything for, that faith will be the catalyst for their emotions, strength, and actions. When someone is wholly convinced of something, the world will watch in amazement.

*catalyst: 촉매

① creative ideas
② hard work and practice
③ the cause they believe in
④ their willingness to help others
⑤ the habit of learning from their mistakes

Mini Quiz

글의 핵심 소재를 찾아 밑줄을 그어 봅시다.

Reading 비법

글쓴이가 말하고자 하는 바를 가장 잘 나타내는 말이 무엇인지를 고려하며 빈칸에 들어갈 말을 골라야 한다.

Reading Skill 주제문과 세부 내용을 찾아 다음 표를 완성해 봅시다.

주제문	누구나 __________ 가 될 수 있으며 사람을 위대하게 만드는 기본적인 진리를 알아야 한다.
세부 내용	• 사람들이 __________ 를 위대하게 만들지는 않는다. • 사람들을 위대하게 만드는 것은 __________ 이다. • __________ 은 감정, 힘, 그리고 행동을 위한 촉매가 될 것이다.

1 글의 제목으로 가장 적절한 것은?

① Why Do Great Leaders Lie?
② Leadership for a Better World
③ Who Becomes a Great Leader?
④ Characteristics of a Born Leader
⑤ How Future Leaders Get Great Results

2 글의 내용과 일치하면 T, 일치하지 <u>않으면</u> F를 쓰시오.

(1) Statements like "So and so was born to be a great leader" are always true. ______

(2) The basic truth that makes people great is that people make themselves great. ______

3 |Summary| 빈칸에 적절한 단어를 글에서 찾아 넣어 표를 완성하시오.

All about Leaders	
What are leaders like?	They are so (1)______.
What makes people great?	Not themselves, but their (2)______.
What is the catalyst for a person's emotions, strength, and actions?	A clear goal, belief, or what they are willing to (3)______ ______ everything for.

직독직해 Skill 다음을 의미 단위로 끊어 읽고(/), 주어(S)와 동사(V)에 표시해 봅시다.

· They can be so charismatic that the entire world will sit up and take notice.

READING 34

다음 빈칸에 들어갈 말로 가장 적절한 것은?   기출 응용

Scientists believe that frogs' ancestors were water-dwelling, fishlike animals. The first frogs and their relatives gained the ability to come out onto land and enjoy the opportunities for food and shelter there. But they ___________________. A frog's lungs do not work very well, and they get part of their oxygen by breathing through their skin. But for this kind of "breathing" to work properly, the frog's skin must stay moist. And so, the frog must remain near the water. There, it can take a dip every now and then to keep its skin from drying out. Frogs must also lay their eggs in water, as their fishlike ancestors did. And eggs laid in the water must develop into water creatures if they are to survive. For frogs, metamorphosis thus provides the bridge between the water-dwelling young forms and the land-dwelling adults.

*metamorphosis: 탈바꿈

① still kept many ties to the water
② had almost all the necessary organs
③ had to develop an appetite for new foods
④ often competed with land-dwelling species
⑤ suffered from rapid changes in temperature

Mini Quiz

글을 읽으면서 핵심어 2개를 찾아 밑줄을 그어 봅시다.

Reading 비법

글의 주제문을 파악하면 이와 연결지어 빈칸이 있는 문장의 내용을 추론하기 쉽다.

Reading Skill 주제문과 세부 내용을 찾아 다음 표를 완성해 봅시다.

주제문	개구리는 __________ 에 있어야 한다.
세부 내용	• __________ 호흡을 해야 하므로 __________ 가 촉촉하게 유지되어야 한다. • 물속에 __________ 을 낳아야 한다. • 알이 __________ 에 사는 생물로 발달해야 한다.

1 개구리에 관한 글의 내용과 일치하는 것은?

① Its lungs work very well.
② It breathes through its skin.
③ Its skin must stay dry.
④ It must lay its eggs on land.
⑤ Its eggs don't have to become water creatures.

2 글의 내용을 가장 잘 나타내는 속담은?

① Still waters run deep.
② A watched pot never boils.
③ Blood is thicker than water.
④ You can't free a fish from water.
⑤ When in Rome, do as the Romans do.

3 | Summary | 빈칸에 적절한 단어를 글에서 찾아 넣어 개구리의 특징을 완성하시오.

Characteristics of Frogs		
Ancestors	**Breathing**	**Eggs**
· were probably (1) ________ · gained the ability to come out onto land	· use both lungs and (2) ________ · keep their skin (3) ________ · take a(n) (4) ________ every now and then	· laid in the (5) ________ · develop into water (6) ________

Words

ancestor *n.* 조상
water-dwelling 물에 사는
relative *n.* 동족, 동류
opportunity *n.* 기회, 가능성
shelter *n.* 거처, 은신처
lung *n.* 폐
take a dip (몸을) 잠깐 담그다, 잠깐 수영을 하다
dry out 건조해지다
lay *v.* (알을) 낳다
creature *n.* 생물
land-dwelling 육지에 사는
adult *n.* 성체

직독직해 Skill 다음을 의미 단위로 끊어 읽고(/), 주어(S)와 동사(V)에 표시해 봅시다.

· The first frogs and their relatives gained the ability to come out onto land and enjoy the opportunities for food and shelter there.

READING 35

밑줄 친 <u>remain within the box</u>가 다음 글에서 의미하는 바로 가장 적절한 것은?

Have you ever heard of "think outside the box"? When people try to think outside the box, the culture which they are a part of *is that box*. Like religion or other traditions, culture gives us a kind of mental comfort and protection. Wandering outside the box may be perceived as an act of creativity but only for a little while. People cannot live outside the box and still maintain all the rights and privileges that they can get when they stay inside it. The pressure to <u>remain within the box</u> is about internalizing our group beliefs and taking on group identities. Also, it is about acting as we are expected to act. People all do things without any sense that what they're doing could be questioned. Culture, therefore, defines what it means to be normal.

*privilege: 특권

Mini Quiz

글을 읽으면서 box로 비유된 것을 찾아 써 봅시다.

① make a creative decision
② break with long traditions
③ respect cultural differences
④ create something innovative
⑤ live within cultural expectations

Reading 비법

밑줄 친 부분에는 글의 핵심적인 내용이 비유되어 있는 경우가 많기 때문에 무엇이 비유된 것인지 파악하는 것이 중요하다.

Reading Skill 주제문과 근거문을 찾아 다음 표를 완성해 봅시다.

주제문	문화는 우리에게 일종의 __________과 __________를 제공한다.
근거문	• 상자 밖에서 살면서 상자 안에 있을 때 얻을 수 있는 모든 권리와 특권을 유지할 수는 없다. • 상자 안에 머물러야 한다는 압박은 우리의 __________을 내면화하고 __________을 취하는 것에 대한 것이다. • 문화는 __________이라는 것이 무엇을 의미하는지 정의한다.

1 글에서 의미하는 바가 나머지 넷과 <u>다른</u> 하나는?

① box   ② culture

③ creativity   ④ group belief

⑤ group identity

2 글의 내용과 일치하도록 <u>틀린</u> 부분을 고쳐 문장을 다시 쓰시오.

A person who wanders outside the box may be thought of as a typical person for a little while.

→ ____

3 ⌐ Summary ⌐ 빈칸에 적절한 단어를 ⌐보기⌐에서 골라 넣어 요약문을 완성하시오.

┌ 보기 ┐

acting   normal   miss   wandering   impossible   maintain

Culture provides us with a kind of mental comfort and protection. It is (1)__________ to live outside the culture and at the same time (2)__________ the rights and privileges of the culture. As culture is about our group beliefs, group identities, and ways of (3)__________, it defines what it means to be (4)__________.

직독직해 Skill 다음을 의미 단위로 끊어 읽고(/), 주어(**S**)와 동사(**V**)에 표시해 봅시다.

· When people try to think outside the box. the culture which they are a part of *is that box.*

____

Words

religion *n.* 종교

tradition *n.* 전통

wander *v.* 방황하다, 돌아다니다

perceive *v.* 인식하다

creativity *n.* 창의성

maintain *v.* 유지하다

pressure *n.* 압박

remain *v.* 머무르다

internalize *v.* 내면화하다

identity *n.* 정체성

define *v.* 정의하다

READING 36

밑줄 친 <u>want to use a hammer</u>가 다음 글에서 의미하는 바로 가장 적절한 것은?

기출 응용

We are likely to interpret events selectively. We want things to be "this way" or "that way". Then we can select, stack, or arrange evidence. And it is done most certainly in a way that supports our viewpoint. Selective perception is based on the things that seem to us to stand out. However, the things that seem to us to be standing out may very well be related to certain things. In other words, they are related to our goals, interests, expectations, past experiences, or current demands of the situation. It's like "with a hammer in hand, everything looks like a nail." This quote highlights the phenomenon of selective perception. If we <u>want to use a hammer,</u> then the world around us may begin to look as though it is full of nails!

① are unwilling to stand out
② make our effort meaningless
③ intend to do something in a certain way
④ hope others have a viewpoint similar to ours
⑤ have a way of thinking that is accepted by others

Mini Quiz

두 단어로 이루어진 글의 핵심 어구를 찾아 밑줄을 그어 봅시다.

Reading 비법

밑줄 친 비유적 표현은 글의 주제와도 밀접한 관련이 있다.

Reading Skill

주제문과 근거문을 찾아 다음 표를 완성해 봅시다.

주제문	우리는 __________으로 사건을 해석하는 경향이 있다.
근거문	• 우리의 __________을 뒷받침하는 방식으로 증거를 선택하고 쌓고 배열한다. • __________은 우리에게 두드러져 보이는 것에 기반을 둔다. • 우리에게 두드러져 보이는 것은 우리와 관련된 특정한 것들이다.

1 글의 내용을 가장 잘 나타내는 단어는?

① labor   ② control
③ mystery   ④ creativity
⑤ prejudice

2 글의 내용과 일치하면 T, 일치하지 <u>않으면</u> F를 쓰시오.

(1) We are likely to perceive events based on things related to ourselves. ______

(2) The quote "with a hammer in hand, everything looks like a nail" is related to perceiving selectively. ______

3 ┃Summary┃ 글의 내용을 토대로 selective perception의 과정을 다음과 같이 정리할 때 빈칸에 적절한 단어를 쓰시오. (단, 주어진 철자로 시작할 것)

The Process of Selective Perception

Being based on our goals, interests, (1)e__________, past experiences, or current demands of the situation

→ Selecting, stacking, or arranging (2)e__________

↙

Supporting our (3)v__________

→ Perceiving what we feel is right and completely ignoring the opposing viewpoints

직독직해 Skill   다음을 의미 단위로 끊어 읽고(/), 주어(S)와 동사(V)에 표시해 봅시다.

· If we want to use a hammer, then the world around us may begin to look as though it is full of nails!

____

긴 글 독해하기

Reading Key 긴 글의 구조 파악하기

A 주제와 부연 설명 구별하기

| 반려동물을 키우는 것은 쉽게 활용 가능한 저비용의 건강 대책이다. | 주제 부분은 자세히 읽기 |

- 반려동물 주인들이 더 낮은 혈압, 심장병 위험 감소, 더 낮은 수준의 스트레스를 나타냄
- 또한 직장에서도 동물은 이점이 될 수 있음
  - 직장인들의 스트레스 수치가 더 낮아짐
  - 직업 만족도와 직장 분위기에 긍정적인 영향을 미침

부연 설명/예시는 빠르게 읽기

긴 글일수록 예시나 부연 설명이 반드시 포함되므로 이에 유의하여 주제에 집중해야 한다. 모든 내용이 다 중요한 것이 아니기 때문에 부연 설명과 핵심을 구별하고, 중심 내용에 집중하며 읽는 것이 좋다.

기출 예제

Many high school students study and learn inefficiently because they try to do homework while watching TV or listening to music. These students also often interrupt their studying for phone calls, snacks, video games, and Internet browsing. Ironically, the students who need to focus the

most are often the ones surrounded by the most distractions. These teenagers believe that background noise can help them study *better*, and some experts agree. They think that many teenagers are used to hearing "background noise" since early childhood, so it might not hurt their learning. They think that asking students to turn off the TV or radio while doing homework may not always improve their academic performance. However, many teachers and learning experts disagree and believe from their experiences that students who study in a noisy environment usually learn less effectively.

주제문	많은 학생들이 TV를 보거나 음악을 들으며 _________으로 학습한다.
부연 설명	• 학생들은 _________이 공부를 더 잘할 수 있게 한다고 믿음 • 일부 전문가들은 학생들이 어릴 때부터 _________에 익숙해져 있으므로 학습을 해치지 않을 것이며 조용한 환경에서 학습하는 것이 항상 _________을 높이는 것은 아니라고 생각함
결론	_________ 환경에서 공부하는 학생들은 덜 _________으로 학습함

Words inefficiently *ad.* 비효율적으로   browsing *n.* 브라우징(인터넷에서 필요한 정보 찾기)   ironically *ad.* 모순적이게도
surround *v.* 둘러싸다   distraction *n.* 주의를 산만하게 하는 것   expert *n.* 전문가   be used to (-ing) ~에 익숙해지다
childhood *n.* 어린 시절   hurt *v.* 해치다, 다치게 하다   improve *v.* 높이다, 증가시키다   academic performance 학업 성적
noisy *a.* 시끄러운   effectively *ad.* 효과적으로

B 시간 순서에 따른 흐름 이해하기

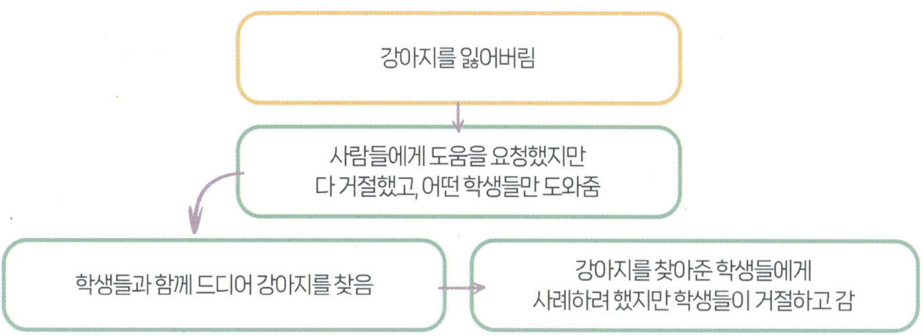

긴 글 중 시간 순서에 따라 전개되는 일화는 사건 전개 또는 시간 순서대로 흐름을 이해해야 한다. 이와 같은 글은 여러 단락이 섞여 있어도 시간/사건 전개 순서대로 단락의 순서를 쉽게 파악할 수 있을 정도로 그 흐름이 명확하다.

기출예제

(A) A boy lost his left arm in a car accident but decided to learn judo. The boy began lessons with an old Japanese judo master. In three months of training, his judo master only taught him one move.

(B) This time, his opponent was bigger, stronger, and more experienced. The referee called a timeout because he was concerned the boy might get hurt. However, the master insisted, "No, let him continue." Soon after the match resumed, his opponent made a critical mistake: he dropped his guard. Instantly, the boy used his move to pin him and win the tournament.

(C) Although the boy didn't understand his master, the boy kept training. Several months later, the master took the boy to his first tournament. To his surprise, the boy easily won his first two matches. In the third match, he skillfully used his one move to win. He was now in the finals.

(D) On the way home, he asked his master, "Master, how did I become the champion with only one move?" "You won for two reasons," the master answered. "First, you've mastered one of the most difficult throws in all of judo. And second, the only known defense for that move is for your opponent to grab your left arm." The boy's biggest weakness had become his biggest strength.

빈칸을 채운 후, 내용에 해당하는 문단의 기호를 쓰시오.

<table>
<tr><td rowspan="4">시간의
흐름에
따른 전개</td><td>(A) 자동차 사고로 __________을 잃은 소년이 세 달 동안 한 가지 유도 동작만 배웠음</td></tr>
<tr><td>☐ 소년이 첫 토너먼트에서 세 번의 경기를 이겨 __________에 갔음</td></tr>
<tr><td>☐ 대결 상대가 __________ 자세를 풀자 소년은 그의 동작을 사용해 상대를 꼼짝 못하게 만들었음</td></tr>
<tr><td>☐ 대결 상대가 소년의 __________을 잡지 못해 소년이 __________ 동작을 잘할 수 있었기 때문에 승리했음</td></tr>
</table>

Words master *n.* 숙련자, 스승   opponent *n.* (게임의) 상대   experienced *a.* 노련한, 경험 많은   referee *n.* 심판   insist *v.* 주장하다   resume *v.* 재개하다   critical *a.* 결정적인, 중대한   guard *n.* 방어 자세   instantly *ad.* 즉시, 곧바로   pin *v.* 꼼짝 못하게 하다   tournament *n.* 토너먼트   to one's surprise 놀랍게도   skillfully *ad.* 능숙하게, 노련하게   final *n.* 결승전   throw *n.* 던지기   defense *n.* 방어   weakness *n.* 약점   strength *n.* 강점

Mini Quiz

필자가 말하고자 하는 바가 가장
잘 드러난 문장을 찾아 밑줄을
그어 봅시다.

다음 글을 읽고, 물음에 답하시오.

By its nature, the exchange of products is actually the exchange of desires. All human beings have inherent physical and mental limitations. Therefore, any individual is usually only (a) <u>capable</u> of satisfying a limited number of personal desires independently. For instance, Thomas Edison may have had the brilliant mind to invent the electric light bulb, but he probably didn't have the right ability to be a farmer or a builder. He needed to find good food to eat and a place to live in. In order to satisfy those desires, he needed to (b) <u>offer</u> something that would satisfy the desires of other individuals in return. Therefore, trading becomes an effective means of (c) <u>decreasing</u> the various desires of individuals within a community. In the community, all kinds of commodities can be exchanged on the open market. Goods to be traded exist in the form of (d) <u>physical</u> objects, such as food, clothes, and cars. Or they exist in a more abstract or conceptual form, such as knowledge and music. Irrespective of the form, these commodities are traded. The reason is that they can satisfy the desires of other individuals. Those individuals are willingly and purposely (e) <u>participating</u> in the exchange. Therefore, the nature of trading is essentially the exchange of desires.

*abstract: 추상적인

1 글의 제목으로 가장 적절한 것은?

① Risk Management in an Open Market Economy
② A Secret of Success: When Others Sell, Buy More
③ Where There Are Human Desires, There Is Trading
④ Owning Things Doesn't Necessarily Make You Happier
⑤ The Desire to Have More Ways to Find Trading Opportunities

2 밑줄 친 (a) ~ (e) 중에서 문맥상 낱말의 쓰임이 적절하지 <u>않은</u> 것은?

① (a) ② (b) ③ (c) ④ (d) ⑤ (e)

3 글을 읽고 답할 수 있는 질문은?

① How do desires destroy human beings?
② What commodities do individuals prefer?
③ How can excessive demands be reduced?
④ Where can we buy abstract forms of commodities?
⑤ Where can commodities be exchanged in a community?

4 다음 영영풀이에 해당하는 단어를 각각 글에서 찾아 쓰시오.

(1) belonging to the basic nature of someone or something
(2) relating to the body of a person instead of to the mind
(3) extremely intelligent, much more intelligent than most people

5 |Summary| 빈칸에 적절한 단어를 글에서 찾아 알맞은 형태로 써서 요약문을 완성하시오.

> As humans can meet only a(n) (1)__________ number of desires independently, they need to satisfy their desires by (2)__________ something that can satisfy other people's desires. This is how (3)__________ came to appear.

Words

exchange *n.* 교환
inherent *a.* 타고난, 고유한
physical *a.* 신체적인, 물리적인
mental *a.* 정신적인
limitation *n.* 한계
independently *ad.* 독립적으로
brilliant *a.* 뛰어난, 훌륭한
satisfy *v.* 충족시키다
means *n.* 수단
community *n.* 공동체
commodity *n.* 상품
conceptual *a.* 개념적인
knowledge *n.* 지식
irrespective of ～에 상관없이
willingly *ad.* 기꺼이
purposely *ad.* 목적을 가지고
participate in ～에 참여하다
essentially *ad.* 본질적으로

Reading Skill 주제, 근거, 결론을 찾아 다음 표를 완성해 봅시다.

주제	상품의 교환은 __________의 교환
근거	• 인간에게는 타고난 신체적, 정신적 __________가 있어 제한된 수의 개인적 욕망만 충족 가능함 • 욕망 충족을 위해 __________을 충족시킬 무언가를 제공해야 함 • 거래되는 상품의 __________에 관계없이 사람들의 욕망을 충족시킬 수 있기 때문에 상품이 거래됨
결론	__________의 본질은 본질적으로 __________의 교환임

Reading 비법

긴 글일수록 예시나 부연 설명이 반드시 포함되므로 이에 유의하여 주제에 집중해야 한다.

직독직해 Skill 다음을 의미 단위로 끊어 읽고(/), 주어(S)와 동사(V)에 표시해 봅시다.

• Goods to be traded exist in the form of physical objects, such as food, clothes, and cars.

____

READING 38

다음 글을 읽고, 물음에 답하시오.   기출 응용

글을 읽으면서 핵심어를 찾아 밑줄을 그어 봅시다.

As kids, we worked hard at learning how to ride a bike; when we fell off, we got back on again, until it became second nature to us. But when we try something new in our adult lives we will usually make just one attempt before judging whether it (a) <u>worked</u>. If we don't succeed the first time, or if it feels a little awkward, we'll tell ourselves that it wasn't a success rather than giving it (b) <u>another</u> shot.

That's a shame, because repetition is central to the process of rewiring our brains. Consider the idea that your brain has a network of neurons. They will (c) <u>connect</u> with each other whenever you remember to use a brain-friendly feedback technique. Those connections aren't very (d) <u>reliable</u> at first, which may make your first efforts a little hit-or-miss. You might remember one of the steps involved, and not the others. But scientists have a saying: "neurons that fire together, wire together." In other words, repetition of an action (e) <u>blocks</u> the connections between the neurons involved in that action. That means the more times you try using that new feedback technique, the more easily it will come to you when you need it.

*hit-or-miss: 마구잡이의, 되는대로 하는

1 글의 제목으로 가장 적절한 것은?

① Repeat, and You Will Succeed
② Be More Curious, Be Smarter
③ Play Is What Makes Us Human
④ Stop and Think Before You Act
⑤ Growth Is All About Keeping Balanced

2 밑줄 친 (a) ~ (e) 중에서 문맥상 낱말의 쓰임이 적절하지 <u>않은</u> 것은?

① (a)   ② (b)   ③ (c)   ④ (d)   ⑤ (e)

3 글의 요지로 가장 적절한 것은?

① 뇌는 죽을 때까지 계속해서 성장한다.

② 뇌는 사회적으로 고립되면 기능이 떨어진다.

③ 꾸준한 운동과 독서는 뇌 건강에 도움을 준다.

④ 반복적인 성공의 경험은 긍정적인 뇌를 만든다.

⑤ 반복은 우리 뇌를 재연결하는 과정에 중요하다.

4 글의 내용과 일치하면 T, 일치하지 <u>않으면</u> F를 쓰시오.

(1) Whenever you remember to use a brain-friendly feedback technique, you might remember the steps involved all at once. _______

(2) Unlike kids, adults usually make just one attempt when they try something new. _______

5 | Summary | 빈칸에 알맞은 단어를 | 보기 | 에서 골라 다음 표를 완성하시오.

| 보기 |

repetition   practice   remember   frequency   connection

Learning to ride a bike		**Rewiring our brains**
We (1)_______ again and again until we become good at riding a bike.	(2)_______ is required.	As the (3)_______ of using new feedback techniques increases, they can be easily used when needed.

Reading Skill 주제와 근거를 찾아 다음 표를 완성해 봅시다.

주제	_______은 우리 뇌를 재연결하는 과정에 핵심적임
근거	• _______의 연결은 처음에는 그리 신뢰할 만하지 않을 수도 있음 • 함께 활성화되는 뉴런들은 함께 _______ • _______을 더 여러 차례 사용해 볼수록 그것은 필요할 때 더 쉽게 다가옴

Reading 비법

핵심어는 글의 중심 소재로 글쓴이가 말하고자 하는 바를 가장 잘 나타내는 말이므로 긴 글을 읽을 때는 반드시 핵심어를 찾아야 한다.

직독직해 Skill 다음을 의미 단위로 끊어 읽고(/), 주어(S)와 동사(V)에 표시해 봅시다.

• But when we try something new in our adult lives we will usually make just one attempt before judging whether it worked.

____

READING

39

글을 읽으면서 주요 등장인물을
찾아 밑줄을 그어 봅시다.

다음 글을 읽고, 물음에 답하시오.

(A) In the morning Gaby brought the bikes. Gaby and Nellie had lunches packed and were ready to pedal. Nellie was a bit worried. (a) <u>She</u> was still a novice on the bike. "Oh, you can do it, Nellie," she remembered Gaby saying to her. Sure. They pedaled side by side and were happy and laughed a lot.

(B) Gaby rushed to rescue Nellie. Nellie's nose and forehead were scraped but the bike was OK. Nellie felt so embarrassed and afraid that she would have to give up the trip and go back to the dorm and spend the beautiful day there alone. Gaby would not hear of it. (b) <u>She</u> would ride next to her friend. Nellie had nothing to fear. "You can do it, Nellie."

(C) With all that encouragement, who would not try again? So, Nellie got back on the bike and continued pedaling. (c) <u>Her</u> nose did not feel so good with the cool breeze blowing across her face. They had no further incidents for the rest of the trip and enjoyed a good day. Two tired girls pedaled back to the dorm, and there the housemother had a few words with Nellie about her swollen nose. (d) <u>She</u> had gotten on the bike, pedaled, and fell off. But she had done it.

(D) The road led them through the edge of town and there it forked. They stayed to the right. There was a home with a fence around it right at the Y in the road. All of a sudden, Nellie felt panic-stricken, and saw the wall coming right at her. Finally, (e) <u>she</u> ran into the wall. *novice: 초보자 **panic-stricken: 공황 상태에 빠진

1 주어진 글 (A)에 이어질 내용을 순서에 맞게 배열한 것으로 가장 적절한 것은?

① (B) − (D) − (C) ② (C) − (B) − (D)
③ (C) − (D) − (B) ④ (D) − (B) − (C)
⑤ (D) − (C) − (B)

2 밑줄 친 (a) ~ (e) 중에서 가리키는 대상이 나머지 넷과 <u>다른</u> 것은?

① (a)　　　② (b)　　　③ (c)　　　④ (d)　　　⑤ (e)

Words

pedal *v.* 페달을 밟다
side by side 나란히, 함께
rescue *v.* 구조하다
forehead *n.* 이마
scrape *v.* 긁다
embarrassed *a.* 당황한
give up 포기하다
dorm *n.* 기숙사
fear *v.* 두려워하다
encouragement *n.* 격려
breeze *n.* 산들바람
incident *n.* 사건
housemother *n.* 여자 사감
swollen *a.* 부은
edge *n.* 모퉁이
fork *v.* 갈라지다
run into ~와 충돌하다

3 글의 내용과 일치하지 <u>않는</u> 것은?

① 자전거 여행을 하기 전 Nellie는 약간 걱정이 되었다.
② 벽에 부딪쳐 Nellie의 코와 이마가 긁혔고 자전거가 망가졌다.
③ Nellie는 자전거에 다시 올라타서 계속 페달을 밟았다.
④ 지친 두 소녀는 기숙사로 자전거를 타고 갔다.
⑤ Y자형 길 바로 근처에서 Nellie는 공포에 질렸다.

4 글에서 언급되지 <u>않은</u> 것을 <u>모두</u> 고르면?

① Nellie가 다친 부위　　　② Nellie의 자전거 실력
③ Gaby의 자전거 상태　　　④ 기숙사로 돌아온 시각
⑤ Nellie가 다친 장소

5 글의 내용과 가장 어울리는 속담은?

① Honesty is the best policy.
② The early bird catches the worm.
③ The first step is always the hardest.
④ When in Rome, do as the Romans do.
⑤ A little knowledge is a dangerous thing.

6 |Summary| 빈칸에 적절한 단어를 |보기|에서 골라 요약문을 완성하시오.

|보기|

> proud   disappointed   novice   encouragement   injured

> As a(n) (1)__________ on the bike, Nellie went on a trip with Gaby. While riding her bike, Nellie ran into a wall and was (2)__________. With Gaby's (3)__________, Nellie continued the trip and enjoyed a good day. When Nellie got back to the dorm, she must have been (4)__________ of herself.

Reading 비법

복합 문단은 주제가 있는 글이 아니므로 등장인물 및 사건의 흐름을 중심으로 읽는다.

Reading Skill

소재와 중심 내용을 찾아 다음 표를 완성해 봅시다.

소재	Gaby와 Nellie의 자전거 여행
중심 내용	• 자전거 __________인 Nellie • __________의 좌절과 __________의 격려 • 자전거 여행 중 일어난 __________에도 불구하고 여행을 끝까지 마무리함

직독직해 Skill

다음을 의미 단위로 끊어 읽고(/), 주어(S)와 동사(V)에 표시해 봅시다.

• Nellie felt so embarrassed and afraid that she would have to give up the trip and go back to the dorm and spend the beautiful day there alone.

____

Wise English Sayings

> "The only way to do great work is to love what you do."
(훌륭한 일을 하는 유일한 방법은 당신이 하는 일을 사랑하는 것이다.)

Steve Jobs

> "I have not failed. I've just found 10,000 ways that won't work."
(나는 실패한 적이 없다. 나는 다만 효과가 없는 만 가지 방법을 찾았을 뿐이다.)

Thomas Edison

> "The biggest adventure you can ever take is to live the life of your dreams."
(당신이 할 수 있는 가장 큰 모험은 당신이 꿈꾸는 삶을 사는 것이다.)

Oprah Winfrey

> "All our dreams can come true if we have the courage to pursue them."
(우리가 그것들을 추구할 용기가 있다면 우리의 모든 꿈은 이루어질 수 있다.)

Walt Disney

> "Success is not final, failure is not fatal: it is the courage to continue that counts."
(성공은 최종적인 것이 아니며, 실패는 치명적이지 않다: 중요한 것은 계속하는 용기이다.)

Winston Churchill

READING 40

다음 글을 읽고, 물음에 답하시오.

기출 응용

(A) When I was 17, I discovered a wonderful thing. My father and I were sitting on the floor of his study. We were organizing his old papers. Across the carpet I saw a fat paper clip. Its rust dusted the cover sheet of a report of some kind. I picked it up. I started to read. Then I started to cry. 5

(B) "Daddy," I said, handing him the pages, "this speech—how did you ever get permission to give it? And weren't you scared?" "Well, honey," he said, "I didn't ask for permission. I just asked myself, 'What is the most important challenge facing my generation?' I knew immediately. Then (a) I asked myself, 'And 10 if I weren't afraid, what would I say about it in this speech?'"

(C) It was a speech he had written in 1920, in Tennessee. Then, only 17 himself and graduating from high school, he had called for equality for African-Americans. (b) I marvelled at his courage and wondered how, in 1920, so young, so white, 15 and in the deep South, where the law still separated black from white, (c) he had had the courage to deliver it. I asked him about it.

(D) "I wrote it. And I delivered it. About half way through I looked up to see the entire audience of teachers, students, and 20 parents stand up—and walk out. Left alone on the stage, (d) I thought to myself, 'Well, I guess I need to be sure to do only two things with my life: keep thinking for myself, and not get killed.'" He handed the speech back to me, and smiled. "(e) You seem to have done both," I said. 25

(B), (C), (D) 각각의 첫 문장에서 글의 순서를 파악하는 데 단서가 될 수 있는 바로 앞의 내용을 가리키는 말을 찾아 밑줄을 그어 봅시다.

1 주어진 글 (A)에 이어질 내용을 순서에 맞게 배열한 것으로 가장 적절한 것은?

① (B) – (D) – (C)　　② (C) – (B) – (D)
③ (C) – (D) – (B)　　④ (D) – (B) – (C)
⑤ (D) – (C) – (B)

● Answers p.42

2 밑줄 친 (a) ~ (e) 중에서 가리키는 대상이 나머지 넷과 <u>다른</u> 것은?

① (a)　　　② (b)　　　③ (c)　　　④ (d)　　　⑤ (e)

Words

organize *v.* 정리하다
paper clip 종이 클립[집게]
rust *n.* 녹 *v.* 녹슬다
dust *v.* 먼지투성이로 만들다
hand *v.* 건네주다
permission *n.* 허락, 허가
scared *a.* 겁먹은, 무서워하는
face *v.* 직면하다, 마주보다
generation *n.* 세대, (비슷한 연령의) 사람들
immediately *ad.* 즉시
equality *n.* 평등, 균등
marvel *v.* 놀라다, 경탄하다
separate *v.* 분리하다, 나누다
deliver *v.* (연설을) 하다
audience *n.* 청중

3 글의 내용과 일치하지 <u>않는</u> 것은?

① 아버지와 나는 서류를 정리하고 있었다.
② 나는 서재에서 발견한 것을 읽고 나서 울기 시작했다.
③ 아버지는 연설을 하기 위한 허락을 구하지 않았다.
④ 아버지가 연설문을 썼을 당시 17세였다.
⑤ 교사, 학생, 학부모 모두 아버지의 연설을 끝까지 경청했다.

4 글을 읽고 답할 수 있는 질문은?

① Why was my father killed?
② How long was my father's speech?
③ Why was my father's speech hidden?
④ What happened when my father made a speech?
⑤ How old was my father when I found his speech?

5 다음 영영풀이에 해당하는 단어를 각각 글에서 찾아 쓰시오.

(1) to cause two or more people or things to stop being together, joined, or connected
(2) to present a speech, statement, etc. to a group of people
(3) to arrange or order things so that they can be found or used easily and quickly

6 ｜Summary｜ 빈칸에 적절한 단어를 글에서 찾아 The speech에 대한 내용을 완성하시오.

The Speech	
The person who wrote it	My (1)__________
The purpose of writing it	To call for (2)__________ for African-Americans
The place where it was found	In my father's (3)__________
The year when it was written	In (4)__________

Reading 비법

복합 문단은 등장인물과 사건을 중심으로 서술되기 때문에 사건을 촉발하는 중심 소재가 있기 마련이므로 이를 반드시 확인해야 한다.

Reading Skill 소재와 중심 내용을 찾아 다음 표를 완성해 봅시다.

소재	아프리카계 미국인들을 위한 __________을 요구했던 아버지의 연설문
중심 내용	• 오래된 서류를 정리하다 두꺼운 __________을 발견함 • 아버지의 __________에 대해 놀라워하며 질문함 • 아버지에게서 __________에 대한 이야기를 들음

직독직해 Skill 다음을 의미 단위로 끊어 읽고(/), 주어(S)와 동사(V)에 표시해 봅시다.

• I marvelled at his courage and wondered how. in 1920. so young. so white. and in the deep South. where the law still separated black from white. he had had the courage to deliver it.

____

Wise English Sayings

“Believe you can and you're halfway there.”
(할 수 있다고 믿으면 절반은 간 것이다.)

Theodore Roosevelt

“You don't have to see the whole staircase, just take the first step.”
(계단 전체를 볼 필요는 없고, 첫걸음만 내딛으면 된다.)

Martin Luther King Jr.

“Success is not the key to happiness. Happiness is the key to success. If you love what you are doing, you will be successful.”
(성공이 행복의 열쇠는 아니다. 행복은 성공의 열쇠이다. 만약 여러분이 하고 있는 일을 사랑한다면, 여러분은 성공할 것이다.)

Albert Schweitzer

“The only limit to our realization of tomorrow will be our doubts of today.”
(우리가 내일을 실현하는 데 있어 유일한 한계는 오늘에 대한 의심일 것이다.)

Franklin D. Roosevelt

“The best way to predict your future is to create it.”
(미래를 예측하는 가장 좋은 방법은 그것을 창조하는 것이다.)

Abraham Lincoln

MEMO

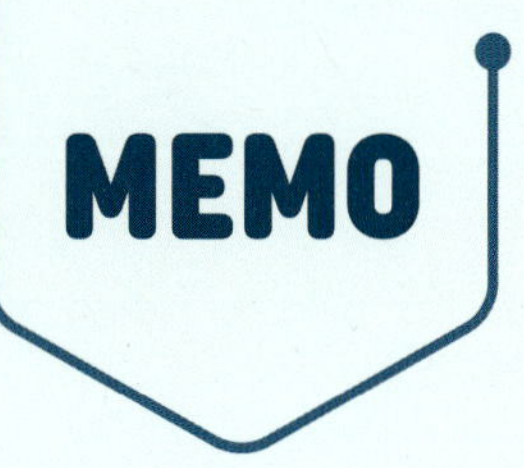

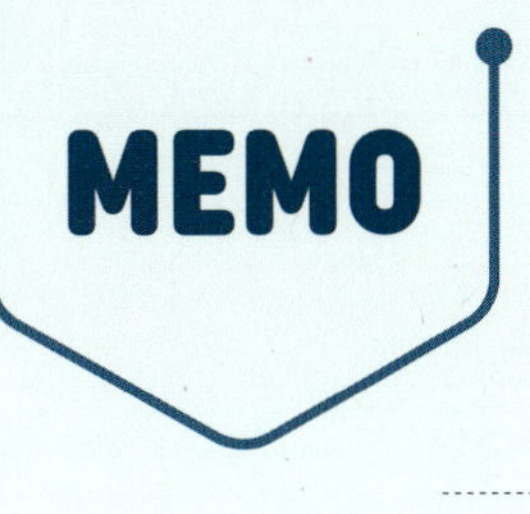

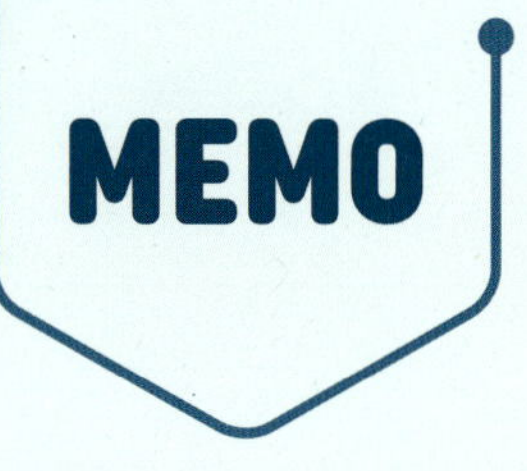

김선우 이해성 김해 의대관 학원
김성은 네오시스템영어전문학원
김소민 창원다올영어수학학원
김재원 창원 더케이영어학원
김주은 더큰샘학원
김준 가우스 SME전문학원
김태리 전문과외
김현우 창녕대성고등학교
김현주 삼성영어셀레나 프리미엄신명점
나현호 펜덕스 어학원 율하센터
박영하 네오시스템영어학원
박재형 인투잉글리쉬어학원
박정주 창원 타임영어전문학원
배송이 JS어학원
배승빈 에스영어전문학원
배현령 배선생영어
백민경 Michelle
손선영 이화멘토영어학원
신형섭 크림슨어학원
심정은 제시카영어교습소
안혜경 티오피에듀학원
양경화 봄영어
양기영 다니엘어학원
우지아 종로엠스쿨
윤지연 에이프릴어학원
이근호 레이첼 잉글리쉬
이수길 명성학원
이아현 다름학원
이연홍 Rhee's English Class
이원평 코치클래스 영어학원
이인아 인잉글리쉬
이지훈 엠베스트SE학원 신진주 캠퍼스
임나영 삼성영어셀레나 남양영어교습소
임진희 진해어썸영어학원
장은정 케이트어학원
장재훈 ASK 배움학원
장지영 잉글리시아이 명동사랑채점
정상락 비상잉글리시아이대운점영어교습소
정수정 지탑영어
최승관 창신고등학교
최지영 시퀀스영수학원
최환준 Jun English
최효정 인에이블영수학원
하동권 네오시스템영어학원
한지용 성민국영수학원
허민성 허달영어
황다영 헤럴드어학원
황은영 에이블어학원

경북

Kailey Pak 케일리 영어
강민표 현일고등학교
강유진 지니쌤영어
강은석 미래인재학원
강혜성 EiE 고려대 어학원
계지숙 Happy Helen English
김광현 그린빌
김도량 다이너마이트잉글리쉬
김도영 김도영어학원
김상호 전문과외
김주훈 아너스영어
김지훈 알앤비
김혜지 스카이 프라임 에듀
문상헌 안동 에이원영어
박경애 포항 대성초이스학원
박계민 영광중학교
박규정 베네치아 영어 교습소
박지은 능률주니어랩꿈터학원
배세왕 BK영수전문학원
변민준 한솔플러스영어수학학원 약목점
손누리 이든샘영수학원
유진욱 공부의힘 영어수학전문학원
윤재호 이상렬 일등단과학원
이강정 이룸단과학원
이상원 필즈학원
이지연 전문과외
이지은 Izzy English
장가은 앨리스영어학원
장미 잉글리시아이 원리학원
전영아 N&K영어학원
정보경 울진고등학교
정선린 포항항도중학교
최동희 전문과외
최미선 영천영어전문과외

광주

김도엽 스카이영어전문학원
김동익 이룸교육원
김병남 위즈덤 영어
김상연 공감영어학원
김서현 디엔영어
김수인 광주 모조잉글리쉬
김신 와이(Y) 아카데미
김영어 전문과외
김원경 전문과외
김유경 프라임아카데미
김유희 김유희 영어학원
김윤희 수프림 영어공부방
김인화 김인화영어학원
나혜영 윤선생우리집앞영어교실
문장엽 엠제이영어수학전문학원
박주형 봉선동 한수위 영어학원
봉병주 철수와영수
신지수 온에어영어학원
양신애 윤학당오름국어영어학원
오승리 이지스터디
오평안 상무 지산한길어학원
우진일 블루페스 영어학원
유현주 유즈영어교습소
윤상혁 하이엔드 영어 학원
이남주 장원학원
이민정 롱맨어학원
이현창 진월유앤아이어학원
임지상 외대어학원
전솔 서강고등학교
정지선 이지스터디
채성문 마하나임 영수학원
한기석 이(E)영어교습소
한방엽 베스트영수학원

대구

강정임 CanTalk English
고은진 헬렌영어
곽미경 조성애세움영어수학학원
구정모 대구여자상업고등학교
권보현 씨즈더데이어학원
권오길 공부를 디자인하다
권익재 제이슨영어교습소
권하련 아너스이엠에스학원
김근아 블루힐영어학원
김기목 목샘영어교습소
김나래 더베스트영어학원
김다영 헬렌영어학원
김미나 전문과외
김민재 열공열강 영수학원
김병훈 LU영어
김상완 YEP영어학원
김연정 유니티영어
김예지 헬렌 영어
김유환 잉글과한글
김정혜 제니퍼영어
김종석 에이블영수학원
김준석 크누KNU입시학원
김지영 김지영 영어
김진호 강성영어
김철우 메라키 영어 교습소
김하나 하나로운영어
김희정 이선생영어학원
노태경 전문과외
문창숙 지앤비(GnB)스페셜입시학원
민승규 민승규영어학원
박고은 스테듀입시학원
박라율 열공열강영어수학학원
박소현 공터영어 테크노폴리스센터
박연희 좀다른영어
박예빈 영재키움영어수학전문학원
박지환 전문과외
방성모 방성모영어학원
배정연 이앤하이공부방
백재민 에소테리카 영어학원
서정인 서울입시학원
신혜경 전문과외
심경아 Shim's English
심유진 대구유신학원
엄재경 하이엔드영어학원
오다인 헬렌영어 프리미어 1관,2관
원현지 원샘영어교습소
위은령 브릿지영어
유지연 에스피영어학원
윤이강 윤이강 영어
이근성 헬렌영어학원
이동현 쌤마스터입시학원
이미경 전문과외
이수혜 EAON 영어학원
이승민 KEREC
이승현 학문당입시학원
이지민 아이플러스 수학
이지현 아이플러스 수학
이진영 전문과외
이현욱 이현욱 영어학원
임지민 헬렌영어학원
임형주 사범대단과학원
장지연 이지영어
장현진 고려대EIE어학원(현풍)
전윤애 올링글리쉬
전윤영 뮤엠영어 경동초점
전지민 헬렌영어학원
정대운 유신학원
정소영 씨즈더데이윌암어학원

대전

Tony Park 전문과외
강은혜 노마드국어영어학원
고우리 영어의 꿈
권현이 디디샘영어
길민주 전문과외
김경이 영어서당학원
김근범 딱쌤학원
김기형 상승학원
김영철 빅뱅잉글리시캠퍼스
김유진 굿티쳐강남학원
김주리 위드제이영어
김하나 위드유학원
나규성 비전21학원
남영종 엠베스트SE 대전 전민점
노현서 앨리잉글리쉬아카데미
민지원 민쌤영어교습소
박난정 제일학원
박성희 청담프라임학원
박효진 박효진 영어
박효춘 수잔스튜터링
심효령 삼부가람학원
안수정 궁극의 사고
오봉주 새미래영수학원
유수민 제일학원
윤영숙 전문과외
이고은 고은영어
이길형 빌드업영어
이대희 청명대입학원
이보배 비비영어
이성구 청명대입학원
이수미 이수미어학원
이영란 일인주의 학원
이원성 파스칼베스티안학원
이재근 이재근영어수학학원
이홍원 홍T영어
임혜지 마이더스 손 영어학원
장유리 테스영어
정동현 대성외국어
정라라 영어문화원 정라라 영어교습소
정예슬 유레카원학원
정윤희 Alex's English
정혜수 쌜리영어
조재형 에듀플렉스
조현 퍼스트학원
채송은 위캔영어학원
최성호 에이스영어교습소
최현우 파스칼베스티안학원
한왕호 김태헌영어학원
한형식 서대전여자고등학교
황지현 공부자존감영어입시학원

부산

강민주 전문과외
강하늘 뉴스터디종합학원
고경원 JS 영수학원
김도담 도담한영어교실
김도윤 코어영어 교습소
김동혁 코어영어수학전문학원
김동휘 장정호 영어전문학원
김미혜 더멘토영어
김병택 탑으로가는 영어 교습소
김서영 대치명인학원(해운대)
김성미 다올영어
김소림 엘라영어학원
김소연 전문과외
김수정 리더스학원
김연주 링구아어학원
김은숙 강동초등학교
김재경 부산진구 탑클래스 영어학원
김지애 김지애영어연구소
김진규 의문을열다
김효은 김효은 영어전문학원
남재호 제니스학원
류미향 류미향입시영어
박미진 MJ영어학원
박수진 제이엔씨 영어학원
박영주 전문과외
박지우 영어를 ON하다
박지은 박지은영어전문과외방
박창헌 오늘도,영어그리고수학
배찬희 에이플러스 영어교습소
변혜련 전문과외
성장우 전문과외
손소희 호이겐스학원
손지안 정관 아슬란학원
송석준 비상아이비츠 해랑학원
송초롱 괴정최상위영어
심혜정 명품수학
안영실 개금국제어학원
안정희 GnB어학원양성캠퍼스
양희주 링구아어학원 해운대
오세창 범천반석단과학원
오정안 쏘트
오지은 이루다영어
윤경은 쌤드루
윤지영 잉글리쉬무무영어교습소
윤진희 전문과외
이기연 미네르바교제아카데미
이미정 탑에듀영어교습소
이상석 상석영어
이순실 종로엠스쿨(하단분원)
이윤호 메트로 영어
이재우 무한꿈터
이지현 Serena영어
이혜정 로엠어학원
임정연 침팬지영어학원 마린시티점
장민지 탑클래스영어학원
정승덕 성균관 영어
정영훈 J&C영어전문학원(제이엔씨)
조정훈 입시영어전문 THOUGHT
채지영 리드앤톡영어도서관학원
최승빈 다온학원
최우성 초이English&Pass

최이내 전문과외
최효선 해피트리어학원
탁아진 에이블영어·국어학원
한영희 미래탐구 해운대

서울
kimhyerim 아르테에비뉴
가혜림 벨쌤.com
강민정 네오 과학학원
강보겸 크라센어학원
강성호 대원고등학교
강정훈 더(the)상승학원
강준수 전문과외
강현숙 토피아어학원 중계캠퍼스
공리아 리더스 잠실
구나현 플러스잉글리쉬영어교습소
구대만 잇올 스파르타 독재학원
구민모 키움학원
구지은 DYB최선Mate 본사
권혜령 전문과외
김경수 탑킴입시앤영어
김나겸 레이쌤영어교습소
김남철 마이티마우스학원
김명원 대치명인학원
김미은 오늘도맑음 영어교습소
김미정 전문과외
김병준 iLO ENGLISH
김보경 클라우드캐슬영어교습소
김빛나 뮤엠영어피닉스영어교습소
김상회 스카이플러스학원
김선경 대치마크영어
김성근 배움자리학원
김성연 대치열린학원
김소정 브로드 영어
김승환 Arnold English Class
김연아 올리비아 영어교습소
김영삼 YS영어공부방
김은영 루시아 잉글리시
김은정 전문과외
김은진 에이스영어교습소
김정민 더블유 영어학원
김정수 토즈 스터디센터
김종현 김종현영어
김지헌 다원교육 목동
김태흥 이투스247학원 송파점
김하은 전문과외
김현영 대치웰영어학원
김현정 진심영어
김현지 전문과외
김혜림 대치 청담 어학원
김혜영 스터디원
김희정 스터디 코치
나선아 전문과외
노은경 이은재학원
노종주 전문과외
노진숙 최선어학원
노현희 전문과외
노혜정 최강학원
도선혜 중계동 영어 공부방
류하영 전문과외
맹혜선 휘경여자고등학교
명가은 명가은영어학원
문명기 문명기 영어학원

문민아 탄탄대로 입시컨설팅
문지현 반포헨리학원
박광운 영어교습소
박기철 한진연 입시전략연구소
박남규 알짜영어교습소
박미애 명문지혜학원
박미정 위드멘토학원
박병석 주영학원
박선경 씨투엠학원
박소영 JOY English
박소하 전문과외
박솔이 SOLE ENGLISH
박수정 YBM잉글루 박수정 영어학원
박숭규 이지수능교육
박은경 오늘영어교습소
박정미 드림영어하이수학학원
박정효 성북메가스터디
박준용 은평 G1230 학원
박지여 영어공부연구소
박진경 JAYz ENGLISH
박찬경 펜타곤영어학원
박현정 1등급학원
반향진 세레나영어수학
배수현 남다른이해
배현경 전문과외
변지예 북두칠성학원
서예은 스터디브릭스학원 내신관
서은조 방배중학교
손종민 미즈원어학원
신경훈 탑앤탑 수학영어 학원
신연우 목동 씨앤씨학원
신정애 당산점 와와학습코칭학원
신지혜 비욘드 어드밴스트
신호현 아로새김학원
신희경 신쌤 영어
심나현 성북메가스터디
안미영 스카이플러스학원
안웅희 이엔엠국영수전문학원
양세희 양세희수능영어 학원
양하나 목동 씨앤씨 바이올렛T
어홍주 이-베스트 영어학원
엄태열 대치차오름학원
오남숙 헬리오 오름 영어
오은경 전문과외
용혜영 SWEET ENGLISH 영어전문 공부방
우승희 우승희영어학원
유경미 무무&차(천광학원)
윤성 대치동 새움학원
윤은미 CnT 영어학원
윤지인 반포잉글리쉬튜터링
이계훈 이지영어학원
이광희 가온에듀 2관
이국재 공감학원
이남규 신정송현학원
이명순 Top Class English
이미나 위드미영어교습소
이미영 티엔하버드영어학원
이상수 넥서스학원
이석원 숭실중학교
이석호 한샘영재학원
이성택 엠아이씨영어학원
이수정 영샘영어

이승미 금천정상어학원
이아진 AJ INSTITUTE
이연주 Real_YJ English
이윤형 아만다영어학원
이은선 드림영어하이수학학원
이은영 DNA영어학원
이은정 전문과외
이은주 대치써미트영어학원
이자임 자몽영어교습소
이정인 프레임 학원
이정혜 수시이룸교육
이주희 윌링어학원
이지민 대치명인학원 은평캠퍼스
이지연 석률학원
이철웅 비상하는 또또학원
이혜숙 사당대성보습학원
이혜정 이루리학원
이희영 이샘영어 아카데미 교습소
이희진 목동씨앤씨
임서은 형설학원
임소례 윤선생영어교실 신내키움
임은희 전문과외
장서희 전문과외
장소담 최선어학원
전계령 신촌 메가스터디학원
전수진 절대영어학원
전지영 탑클래스영수학원
정가람 촘촘영어
정경록 미즈원어학원
정민혜 정민혜밀착영어학원
정성준 팁탑영어
정유하 YNS 열정과신념 영어학원
정재욱 씨알학원
정지희 대치하이영어전문학원
정해림 서울숭의초등학교 영어전담
조미영 튼튼영어 마스터클럽 구로학원
조민석 더원영수학원
조민재 정성학원
조봉현 조셉영어국어학원
조연아 연쌤 영어
조용수 EMC이승환영어전문학원
조용현 바른스터디학원
조은성 종로학원
조인희 가디언 어학원(본관)
진영민 브로든영어학원
채상우 클레어영어
채에스더 문래중학교
천수진 메리트영어
천예은 폴티스 영어학원
최가은 지엔영어
최민주 전문과외
최수린 목동 CNC 국제관
최안나 영어의완성 영어교습소
최유송 목동 씨앤씨학원(CNC)
최유정 강북청솔학원
최정문 한성학원
최형미 전문과외
최희재 SA학원
편선경 IGSE Academy
하다님 연세마스터스 학원
하제원 더블랙에듀
한인혜 레나잉글리쉬

한혜주 박홍학원
함규민 클레어영어교실
허미영 삼성영어 창일교실 학원
현승준 강남종로학원 교대점
홍대균 홍대균 영어
홍영민 성북상상학원
홍희진 이티영어학원
황상희 어나더레벨 영어전문학원
황선애 앤스영어학원
황혜진 이루다 영어

세종
김보경 더시에나
방종영 세움학원
백승희 백승희영어
손대령 강한영어학원
송지원 베이 교육컨설팅
안성주 더타임학원
안초롱 21세기학원
이지현 OEC 올리비아 영어 교습소
이현지 전문과외
허욱 전문과외

울산
강상배 전문과외
김경수 핀포인트영어학원
김경현 에린영어
김광규 EIE 온양어학원
김주희 하이디 영어교습소
김한중 스마트영어전문학원
서예원 해법멘토영어수학학원
송회철 꿈꾸는고래
양혜정 양혜정영어
엄여은 준쌤영어교습소
윤주이 인생영어학원
이서경 이서경영어
이수현 제이엘영어교습소
이윤미 제이앤에스 영어수학
임재희 임재희영어전문학원
정은선 한국esl어학원
조충일 YBM잉글루 울산언양 제1캠퍼스
최나비 더오름high-end학원
한건수 한스영어
허부배 비즈단과학원
황희정 장검 앵커어학원

인천
강재민 스터디위드제이쌤
고미경 쎄리영어학원
김갑현 카일쌤영어학원
김미경 전문과외
김선나 태풍영어학원
김영태 에듀터학원
김영호 조주석수학&영어클리닉학원
김옥경 잉글리쉬 베이
김지연 송도탑영어학원
김지이 Jenna's English
김현미 송도탑영어학원
김현이 에이플러스원영어수학학원
나일지 두드림하이학원
남미경 뮤엠구월서초영어교습소
문지현 고대학원
박민아 하이영어
박소연 링컨 영어

박정우 영수원칙학원
박주현 Ashley's English Corner
박진영 인천외국어고등학교
배이슬 비상영수학원
서유화 K&C American School
성하용 타이탄 영어
송현민 Kathy's Class
신나리 이루다교육학원
신은주 명문학원
신현경 전문과외
심현정 전문과외
오희정 엠베스트SE논현캐슬
원정연 공탑학원
윤선 밀턴 영어학원
윤효주 프렌잉글리시청라레이크블루
윤희영 세실영어
이가희 S&U영어
이동규 인천상아초등학교
이미선 고품격EM EDU
이수진 전문과외
이윤주 Triple One
이은정 인천 논현 고등학교
이주연 레이첼영어
이진희 이진희 영어
이하나 선한영수
장승혁 지엘학원
전혜원 제일고등학교
정도영 대신학원
정춘기 정상어학원 남동분원
조슈아 와이즈에듀학원
조윤정 원당중학교
최민지 빅뱅영어
최수련 업앤업영어교습소
최지유 J(제이)영수전문학원
최창영 학산에듀
한은경 호크마학원
황성현 인천외국어고등학교

전남
강용문 JK영수
강유미 정상어학원 목포남악분원
고경희 에이블 잉글리쉬
곽혜진 H&J ENGLISH
김미선 여수개인교습
김아름 전문과외
김은정 BestnBest
류성준 타임영어학원
박동규 정상학원
박민지 벨라영어
박현아 정상어학원 목포남악분원
서창현 목포백련초등학교
손빛나 프렌잉글리시 여수웅천학원
손성호 아름다운 11월학원
양명승 엠에스어학원
오은주 순천금당고등학교
이상호 스카이입시학원
이영주 재키리 영어학원
임동욱 문향고등학교
조소을 수잉글리쉬
차형진 상아탑학원
황상윤 K&H 중고등 영어 전문학원

전북
길지만 비상잉글리시아이영어학원

김대환 엠베스트SE 전주점
김설아 전주 에듀캠프학원
김수정 베이스탑영어
김예진 카일리영어학원
김주원 애플영어학원
박도희 전문과외
서명원 전북 군산 한림학원
안지은 안지은영어학원
유영목 유영목영어전문학원
은장원 의치약한수 학원
이경훈 리더스영수전문학원
이미정 토마토영어학원
이수정 씨에이엔 영어학원
이지원 탄탄영어수학학원
이진주 전문과외
이한결 DNA영어학원
이현준 준영어교습소
이효상 에임하이영수학원
임마지 조아잉글리쉬어학원
조예진 이란그마국영수김통한국사학원
조형진 대니아빠앤디영어교습소
최석원 전주에듀캠프학원
한주훈 알파스터디영어수학전문학원
한찬미 찬미쌤영수교실

제주

고보경 제주여자고등학교
고승용 제주알앤케이학원
김민정 제주낭만고등어학원
김평호 서이현 아카데미
김현정 유비고 영어학원
박시연 에임하이학원
배동환 뿌리와샘
이재철 함성소리학원
이호민 대정탑클래스학원
임정열 엑셀영어
정승현 J's English
조민수 함성소리연동학원

충남

강유안 전문과외
고유미 고유미영어
권선교 합덕토킹스타학원
김인영 더오름영어
김일환 김일환어학원
김창현 타임영어학원
김현우 프렌잉글리시로엘입시전문학원
남궁선 공부의 맵 학원
박서현 EiE고려대어학원 논산캠퍼스
박재영 로제타스톤 영어교실
박태혁 인디고학원
박희진 박쌤영어 과외
백일선 명사특강
설재윤 마스터입시교육원
우승직 제니스 영어 공부방
윤현미 비비안의 잉글리쉬 클래스
이규현 글로벌학원
이수진 이수진쌤영어
이종화 오름에듀
이호영 이플러스 학원
장성은 상승기류
장완기 장완기학원
장진아 종로엠스쿨 부여점
정래 (주)탑씨크리트교육

조남진 표선생영어학원
최용원 서일고등학교
허지수 전문과외

충북

마종수 새옴다옴학원
박광수 폴인어학원
박수열 팍스잉글리쉬학원
신유정 비타민영어클리닉
연수지 탑클랜영어수학학원
우선규 우선규영어교습소
윤홍석 대학가는길 학원
이경수 더에스에이티 영수단과 학원
이재욱 대학가는 길 학원
이재은 파머스영어와이즈톡학원
이혜인 위즈영어학원
임원용 KGI 의대학원
조현국 업클래스학원
최철우 최쌤영어
하선빈 어썸영어수학학원
홍병찬 서울학원

Reading∞ master 중등

Level 2

Reading∞ master 중등

수능 plus 내신

Level 2

PART 01 Review Test
PART 02 핵심 직독직해

다음 글을 읽고, 물음에 답해 봅시다.

Why don't we look as good in pictures as we do in the mirror? Here are some possible reasons. ___(A)___ , we see ourselves every day in the mirror. The most ⓐ familiar image of our faces is the reflection we see in the mirror. Since we are so used to the image in the mirror, when this image is reversed in pictures, it seems ⓑ natural. Our smiles could also be a reason. When we look at ourselves in the mirror, we're usually relaxed, ⓒ confident, and more likely to smile and act naturally. But when we have our pictures (B)take, we start to feel nervous and make an ⓓ awkward smile! Finally, pictures are a 2-D version of real life. They tend to make us look ⓔ strange or unnatural. These factors can lead us to feel uncomfortable with 우리가 사진에서 어떻게 보이는지.

1

윗글의 빈칸 (A)에 들어갈 말로 가장 적절한 것은?

① Besides
② In the end
③ First of all
④ As a result
⑤ In the same way

2

윗글의 밑줄 친 ⓐ~ⓔ 중, 문맥상 낱말의 쓰임이 적절하지 <u>않은</u> 것은?

① ⓐ　　② ⓑ　　③ ⓒ　　④ ⓓ　　⑤ ⓔ

3

윗글의 내용과 일치하는 것은?

① 거울보다 사진 속의 모습이 더 좋게 보인다.
② 대부분 거울에 비친 자신의 모습에 가장 친숙하다.
③ 우리는 거울을 볼 때보다 사진을 찍을 때 더 자신감이 넘친다.
④ 사진은 실제 삶의 2D 버전이어서 자연스럽게 보이게 한다.
⑤ 사진의 해상도가 종종 우리를 불편하게 느끼게 한다.

4 서술형

윗글의 밑줄 친 (B)take를 어법상 바르게 고쳐 쓰시오.

➡ _______________

5 서술형

윗글의 밑줄 친 우리말과 의미가 같도록 주어진 말을 바르게 배열하시오.

(we / in pictures / how / look)

➡ _______________

다음 글을 읽고, 물음에 답해 봅시다.

Have you ever seen milk in a can?

(A) Unfortunately, cans can make milk ⓐ <u>go</u> bad quickly because they conduct heat well. Furthermore, many canned foods are heated at high temperatures and ⓑ <u>expose</u> to high pressures. But when milk goes through this process, it can change the taste and properties of the milk due to browning.

(B) Additionally, cans are more expensive to produce than cartons or plastic bottles. Although milk producers could produce canned milk, the reasons mentioned above and a lack of proper packaging facilities make it a less ⓒ <u>attractive</u> option.

(C) While you may be familiar with milk in cartons or plastic bottles, you probably haven't seen it in cans. There ⓓ <u>are</u> interesting reasons for <u>this</u>. Milk is very sensitive to temperature and must ⓔ <u>be stored</u> at temperatures between 0 and 4 degrees Celsius.

1

주어진 글 다음에 이어질 글의 순서로 가장 적절한 것은?

① (A) − (C) − (B) ② (B) − (A) − (C)
③ (B) − (C) − (A) ④ (C) − (A) − (B)
⑤ (C) − (B) − (A)

2

윗글의 밑줄 친 ⓐ~ⓔ 중, 어법상 <u>틀린</u> 것은?

① ⓐ ② ⓑ ③ ⓒ ④ ⓓ ⑤ ⓔ

3

윗글의 내용과 일치하지 <u>않는</u> 것은?

① 캔은 열을 잘 전달한다.
② 캔 식품은 대개 높은 온도에서 가열되고 높은 압력에 노출된다.
③ 캔은 종이 팩보다 생산 비용이 적게 든다.
④ 우유는 온도에 매우 민감하다.
⑤ 우유의 적정 보관 온도는 섭씨 0도에서 4도 사이이다.

---

4 서술형

다음 영영풀이에 해당하는 단어를 윗글에서 찾아 알맞은 형태로 쓰시오.

the weight or force that is produced when something pushes against something else

---

5 서술형

윗글의 밑줄 친 this가 가리키는 내용을 우리말로 쓰시오.

→

다음 글을 읽고, 물음에 답해 봅시다.

Vegetarian eating is becoming more popular as more and more young adults say no to eating meat and fish. According to the American Dietetic Association, ⓐplanned vegetarian diets are healthful and nutritious. They also provide health benefits in ⓑpreventing and treating certain diseases.   (A)   , young adults don't decide to change their diets only out of concern for their health. Some make the choice out of concern for animal rights. Many statistics show that the majority of the animals raised for food ⓒis kept in small cages. So, many teens give up meat ⓓto protest those conditions. Others turn to vegetarianism to support the environment. Meat production uses large amounts of water, land, grain, and energy. (B)It also creates problems with animal waste resulting in pollution. These trends show ⓔthat today's youth are more aware of and sensitive to animal rights and environmental problems.

1

윗글의 밑줄 친 ⓐ~ⓔ 중, 어법상 <u>틀린</u> 것은?

① ⓐ　　② ⓑ　　③ ⓒ　　④ ⓓ　　⑤ ⓔ

2

윗글을 읽고 답할 수 <u>없는</u> 질문은?

① Is vegetarian eating becoming more popular?
② What are benefits of vegetarian diets?
③ Why do young adults decide to change their diets?
④ What's the side effect of vegetarianism?
⑤ What problems does meat production cause?

3

윗글의 빈칸 (A)에 들어갈 말로 가장 적절한 것은?

① However
② Above all
③ As a result
④ For example
⑤ Furthermore

4 서술형

다음 영영풀이에 해당하는 단어를 윗글에서 찾아 쓰시오.

> having substances that a person or animal needs to be healthy and grow properly

____

5 서술형

윗글의 밑줄 친 (B)It이 가리키는 내용을 글에서 찾아 쓰시오.

➡ _______________________

다음 글을 읽고, 물음에 답해 봅시다.

Stars start out as clouds of gas and dust. After millions of years, these clouds begin to _____ⓐ_____ because gravity forces the gas and dust together. As it (A) squeezes / is squeezed , the cloud heats up to form a young star. If this reaches 27 million degrees Fahrenheit, it is 핵융합을 시작할 만큼 충분히 뜨거운. This reaction is needed for a new star to form. The energy enables a star (B) keeping / to keep its shape and shine. What happens when the fuel runs out and the star dies? It depends on how much dust gathered in the first place. For example, stars with less than half the mass of the sun fade away very slowly. But most stars use up their fuel and finally (C) return / returning to _____ⓑ_____ of gas and dust after a series of steps.

1

윗글의 빈칸 ⓐ에 들어갈 말로 가장 적절한 것은?

① burst
② shrink
③ expand
④ increase
⑤ develop

2

(A), (B), (C)의 각 네모 안에서 어법에 맞는 표현으로 가장 적절한 것은?

	(A)		(B)		(C)
①	squeezes	·····	keeping	·····	returning
②	squeezes	·····	to keep	·····	return
③	is squeezed	·····	keeping	·····	returning
④	is squeezed	·····	to keep	·····	return
⑤	is squeezed	·····	to keep	·····	returning

3

윗글의 내용과 일치하지 <u>않는</u> 것은?

① 별의 최초의 형태는 가스와 먼지 구름이다.
② 핵융합을 하기 위해서는 화씨 2,700만 도에 도달해야 한다.
③ 가열된 별의 에너지로 별은 그 모양을 유지하고 빛이 난다.
④ 태양의 절반 이상의 질량을 가진 별들은 매우 천천히 사라진다.
⑤ 대부분의 별들은 일련의 단계를 거쳐 원래의 형태로 돌아간다.

4 서술형

윗글의 밑줄 친 우리말과 의미가 같도록 주어진 말을 바르게 배열하시오.

(start / enough / nuclear fusion / to / hot)

➡ _______________________________

5 서술형

윗글의 빈칸 ⓑ에 들어갈 말로 적절한 것을 글에서 찾아 쓰시오.

➡ _______________________________

다음 글을 읽고, 물음에 답해 봅시다.

In a movie, lighting does more than just allow us ⓐto see what is taking place. Brightly lit subjects naturally attract people's attention. ___(A)___, dimly lit subjects can create curiosity and fear. <u>How shadows are used is also an important part of lighting.</u> If a bright light is used ⓑto minimize shadows, it creates a bright and cheerful atmosphere. This effect is usually used in comedies and action movies. Light can also make dark shadows for a strong contrast between bright and dark scenes. This can emphasize the subject and create tension. So, it ⓒis used in horror movies or films with a dark atmosphere. The ___(B)___ of the light source can produce various dramatic effects as well. For example, a light ⓓshine directly down on the subject creates a feeling of holiness and mystery. Understanding these lighting techniques and their effects ⓔmakes watching movies even more exciting.

1

윗글의 빈칸 (A)에 들어갈 말로 가장 적절한 것은?

① Similarly
② Therefore
③ For instance
④ Consequently
⑤ On the other hand

2

윗글의 빈칸 (B)에 들어갈 말로 가장 적절한 것은?

① kind   ② color
③ weight   ④ position
⑤ brightness

3

윗글의 내용과 일치하지 <u>않는</u> 것은?

① 어둑하게 비춰지는 대상은 호기심과 두려움을 유발한다.
② 그림자를 최소화하기 위해 밝은 빛을 사용하면 쾌활한 분위기를 만들어 낸다.
③ 액션 영화에서는 주로 어두운 빛을 사용한다.
④ 빛을 이용한 어두운 그림자는 긴장감을 조성한다.
⑤ 대상을 아래로 직접 비추는 빛은 신비감을 만들어 낸다.

4 서술형

윗글의 밑줄 친 ⓐ~ⓔ 중, 어법상 틀린 것을 찾아 바르게 고쳐 쓰시오.

(　　　) ➡ _______________

5 서술형

윗글의 밑줄 친 문장을 우리말로 해석하시오.

➡ _______________

다음 글을 읽고, 물음에 답해 봅시다.

Think, for a moment, about when you bought something and you never ended up ⓐunderline{using} it.

(A) An item of clothing you never ended up wearing? A book you never read? Some piece of electronic equipment ⓑthat never even came out of the box? It is estimated that Australians alone spend on average $10.8 billion AUD (roughly $9.99 billion USD) every year on 그들이 사용하지 않는 물건.

(B) All the things we buy and then never use ⓒare waste — a waste of money, a waste of time, and waste in the sense of pure __________. As the author Clive Hamilton observes, 'The difference between the stuff we buy and what we use ⓓare waste.'

(C) That is ⓔmore than the total government spending on universities and roads. That is an average of $1,250 AUD (roughly $1,156 USD) for each household.

1

주어진 글 다음에 이어질 글의 순서로 가장 적절한 것은?

① (A) − (C) − (B)　　② (B) − (A) − (C)

③ (B) − (C) − (A)　　④ (C) − (A) − (B)

⑤ (C) − (B) − (A)

2

윗글의 밑줄 친 ⓐ~ⓔ 중, 어법상 **틀린** 것은?

① ⓐ　　② ⓑ　　③ ⓒ　　④ ⓓ　　⑤ ⓔ

3

윗글의 빈칸에 들어갈 말로 가장 적절한 것은?

① passion　　② range

③ heritage　　④ desire

⑤ rubbish

4 서술형

다음 영영풀이에 해당하는 단어를 윗글에서 찾아 쓰시오.

a number that is calculated by adding quantities together and then dividing the total by the number of quantities

____

5 서술형

윗글의 밑줄 친 우리말과 의미가 같도록 주어진 말을 바르게 배열하시오.

(do / use / they / goods / not)

➡ __________

다음 글을 읽고, 물음에 답해 봅시다.

To the Principal of Alcanse Middle School,

My name is Cathy Brown. My daughter, Amy, is a student at your school. I'm writing this email in ①response to the message I received from her homeroom teacher. He is suggesting that the school stop serving food (A) making / made with eggs. As the mother of a girl who needs a lot of nutrients, I strongly ②agree the suggestion. I understand that some students are ③allergic to eggs. However, ⓐhis suggestion is unfair to the other students. Our children need a ④well-balanced diet. Eggs have lots of nutrients such as protein and (B) is / are widely used in so many types of food. Removing them from the menu would ⑤limit our children's food choices and hinder their growth. Instead, the school could clearly label foods (C) that / what may contain eggs. ⓑIt is important students continue to have a wide choice of foods.

Sincerely,

Cathy Brown

1

윗글의 밑줄 친 ①~⑤ 중, 문맥상 낱말의 쓰임이 적절하지 <u>않은</u> 것은?

① ② ③ ④ ⑤

2

(A), (B), (C)의 각 네모 안에서 어법에 맞는 표현으로 가장 적절한 것은?

	(A)	(B)	(C)
①	making	is	what
②	making	are	that
③	made	is	what
④	made	is	that
⑤	made	are	that

3

윗글에서 필자가 주장하는 바로 가장 적절한 것은?

① 학생들이 스스로 자율 급식을 해야 한다.
② 고단백 음식 위주로 식단을 구성해야 한다.
③ 알레르기를 유발하는 식품을 사용하지 말아야 한다.
④ 학생들이 편식하지 않도록 음식 선택권을 제한해야 한다.
⑤ 달걀 사용을 제한하는 대신 달걀이 포함된 음식에 라벨을 붙여야 한다.

4 서술형

윗글의 밑줄 친 ⓐ his suggestion의 구체적인 내용을 우리말로 쓰시오.

➡ ______________________

5 서술형

윗글의 밑줄 친 ⓑ를 우리말로 해석하시오.

➡ ______________________

다음 글을 읽고, 물음에 답해 봅시다.

Some experts say that we communicate by ⓐ moving our bodies. This means we use 'body language'. Let's ① pay attention to the nonverbal 교사인 여러분이 여러분의 학생들에게 보내는 메시지. It can make a significant difference in your relationship with students. ② In general, most students are often very aware of their teacher's body language. ___________, when students first enter the classroom, they ③ look for their teacher. Imagine ⓑ that the teacher has a friendly greeting and a welcoming smile. It must be encouraging and ⓒ empowering for a student. The teacher smiles at students to let them ⓓ to know that he or she is glad to see them. It does not require ④ a great deal of time or effort. But it can make a significant difference in the classroom climate ⑤ right from the start of class. Teachers should remember that their body language ⓔ is always at work when they are with their students.

1

윗글의 밑줄 친 ⓐ~ⓔ 중, 어법상 틀린 것은?

① ⓐ　② ⓑ　③ ⓒ　④ ⓓ　⑤ ⓔ

2

윗글의 밑줄 친 ①~⑤의 우리말 풀이가 알맞지 <u>않은</u> 것은?

① ~에 주의를 기울이다
② 일반적으로
③ ~을 기대하다
④ 많은
⑤ ~의 시작부터 바로

3

윗글의 빈칸에 들어갈 말로 가장 적절한 것은?

① First of all
② In contrast
③ In addition
④ For example
⑤ Nevertheless

4 서술형

다음 영영풀이에 해당하는 단어를 윗글에서 찾아 쓰시오.

> not involving or using words

____

5 서술형

윗글의 밑줄 친 우리말과 의미가 같도록 주어진 말을 바르게 배열하시오.

(send / messages / your students / you teachers / to)

➡ ___________________________________

The Great Barrier Reef in Australia is one of the largest coral reef systems in the world. (①) It is home to ⓐ various marine species including over 1,500 different types of fish. (②) Global warming has caused an increase in ocean temperatures, resulting in coral bleaching. (③) (A) This causes the coral to lose its color and even die. (④) Furthermore, water pollution from water used for agriculture and industrial waste makes the water quality ⓑ better. (⑤) We must take ⓒ immediate action to protect the Great Barrier Reef and its marine life. (B) This requires a combination of efforts, such as reducing the amount of greenhouse gas emissions and improve water quality. The future of the Great Barrier Reef and the millions of species that call it home ⓓ depends on it. Without action, the future of this incredible ecosystem is ⓔ uncertain.

1

글의 흐름으로 보아, 주어진 문장이 들어가기에 가장 적절한 곳은?

> However, in recent years, it has been facing numerous environmental challenges.

①   ②   ③   ④   ⑤

2

윗글의 밑줄 친 ⓐ~ⓔ 중, 문맥상 낱말의 쓰임이 적절하지 <u>않은</u> 것은?

① ⓐ   ② ⓑ   ③ ⓒ   ④ ⓓ   ⑤ ⓔ

3

Great Barrier Reef에 관한 윗글의 내용과 일치하지 <u>않는</u> 것은?

① 세계에서 가장 큰 산호초 시스템 중 하나이다.
② 1,500종 이상의 물고기를 포함한 다양한 해양 종들의 서식지이다.
③ 해양 온도의 상승으로 산호의 색깔이 더 짙어졌다.
④ 농업용수와 산업 폐기물로 인해 수질이 악화되고 있다.
⑤ 보존을 위해 온실가스 배출량 감축과 수질 개선 등의 노력이 필요하다.

4   서술형

윗글의 밑줄 친 (A) This가 가리키는 것을 글에서 찾아 쓰시오.

➡ ______________________________________

5   서술형

윗글의 밑줄 친 문장 (B)에서 어법상 <u>틀린</u> 부분을 찾아 바르게 고쳐 쓰시오.

______________ ➡ ______________

다음 글을 읽고, 물음에 답해 봅시다.

You need to get comfortable with discomfort if you want to succeed. ___________, you should step out of your comfort zone. Trying new things outside of your comfort zone will greatly benefit you in many ways. First, you can 성장할 수 있는 귀중한 기회를 얻다. Challenging yourself provides opportunities for new experiences and unexpected changes, which can lead to personal growth. Furthermore, you will learn about (A) you / yourself. As you try new things, you will discover your talents, interests, strengths and weaknesses. Finally, you can also build new relationships. If you try something new, you can meet new people (B) who / whose you otherwise would never have had the chance to meet. It can make your life more exciting. And you will learn from them, too. The unfamiliarity will feel very (C) uncomfortable / uncomfortably. However, you will be able to expand your horizons and achieve success.

1

윗글의 빈칸에 들어갈 말로 가장 적절한 것은?

① Instead
② However
③ Moreover
④ In other words
⑤ On the other hand

2

(A), (B), (C)의 각 네모 안에서 어법에 맞는 표현으로 가장 적절한 것은?

	(A)	(B)	(C)
①	you	who	uncomfortable
②	you	whose	uncomfortably
③	yourself	who	uncomfortable
④	yourself	whose	uncomfortable
⑤	yourself	who	uncomfortably

3 　서술형

윗글의 내용을 다음과 같이 요약할 때, 빈칸 ⓐ와 ⓑ에 적절한 말을 글에서 찾아 쓰시오.

> Getting out of your ________ⓐ________ and trying something new can help you ______ⓑ______ your visions and achieve success.

ⓐ ➡ ________________________

ⓑ ➡ ________________

4 　서술형

윗글의 밑줄 친 우리말과 의미가 같도록 주어진 말을 바르게 배열하시오.

(opportunities / gain / to / valuable / grow)

➡ ________________________

다음 글을 읽고, 물음에 답해 봅시다.

ⓐIt is important for advertisements to grab people's attention. They need to reach people on a(n) ___(A)___ level. That is, the advertisement needs to show how the product can help them. Every good product or service can help people live, work, or enjoy their lives more. ___(B)___, imagine an advertisement for a new smartphone ①that just talks about its amazing features. That advertisement ②feels like an explanation. ___(C)___, it would not be a very effective advertisement. Now imagine an advertisement ③shown people taking beautiful photos in their daily lives or watching movies on their new smartphone. It would be ④far more memorable and people would be interested in it. Advertisements sell benefits, not features. Therefore, ⓑa successful advertisement must show people how its product can make their lives richer and ⑤more convenient.

1

윗글의 빈칸 (A)에 들어갈 말로 가장 적절한 것은?

① artistic   ② practical
③ technical   ④ emotional
⑤ intellectual

2

윗글의 빈칸 (B)와 (C)에 들어갈 말이 알맞게 짝지어진 것은?

	(B)		(C)
①	In short	·····	Suddenly
②	In short	·····	Accordingly
③	For example	·····	Similarly
④	For example	·····	Fortunately
⑤	For example	·····	Unfortunately

3

윗글의 밑줄 친 ⓑ를 가장 적절하게 설명한 것은?

① 제품의 기능을 상세하게 설명하는 광고
② 가상 인물을 이용한 새로운 콘셉트의 광고
③ 제품의 외관을 효과적으로 보여 주는 광고
④ 기억에 오래 남는 CM송을 사용한 광고
⑤ 제품이 삶을 더 풍부하게 만들 수 있는지 보여 주는 광고

4 〔서술형〕

윗글의 밑줄 친 ⓐ를 우리말로 해석하시오.

➡ _______________________________

5 〔서술형〕

윗글의 밑줄 친 ①~⑤ 중, 어법상 틀린 것을 찾아 바르게 고쳐 쓰시오.

(   ) ➡ _______________________

다음 글을 읽고, 물음에 답해 봅시다.

Artificial intelligence (AI) is rapidly changing the job market.

(A) But it is clear that AI is changing the nature of work. Workers in various industries will need to adapt to new technologies and ⓐ acquire new skills. For example, the use of AI in customer service requires workers ⓑ to improve their interpersonal skills. They also need to be familiar and comfortable with human-centered technology.

(B) In addition, AI will likely lead to the development of new job categories, such as AI ethics officers. Their job would be to make sure that AI systems ⓒ use in a responsible and ethical manner. As AI continues to have an impact on the job market, it is necessary for workers and organizations ⓓ to adapt to the changes.

(C) Some experts predict that AI will lead to job loss in certain industries by ⓔ automating many simple tasks. However, other experts believe that AI will create new job opportunities. <u>진실은 아마도 그 사이 어딘가에 있을 것이다.</u>

1

주어진 글 다음에 이어질 글의 순서로 가장 적절한 것은?

① (A) − (C) − (B)　　② (B) − (A) − (C)
③ (B) − (C) − (A)　　④ (C) − (A) − (B)
⑤ (C) − (B) − (A)

2

윗글의 밑줄 친 ⓐ~ⓔ 중, 어법상 **틀린** 것은?

① ⓐ　　② ⓑ　　③ ⓒ　　④ ⓓ　　⑤ ⓔ

3

윗글에서 필자가 주장하는 바로 가장 적절한 것은?

① AI를 활용한 일자리를 많이 만들어야 한다.
② 인간 중심적으로 AI 시스템을 개선해야 한다.
③ 특정 산업에서 AI의 일자리 잠식을 억제해야 한다.
④ AI에 의한 고용 시장 변화에 맞춰 근로자도 능력을 개발해야 한다.
⑤ AI가 윤리적인 방식으로 사용되는지 확인할 새로운 시스템이 필요하다.

4 〔서술형〕

다음 영영풀이에 해당하는 단어를 윗글에서 찾아 쓰시오.

moral principles that govern a person's behavior or the conducting of an activity

____

5 〔서술형〕

윗글의 밑줄 친 우리말과 의미가 같도록 주어진 말을 바르게 배열하시오.

(lies / in / somewhere / the truth / between / likely)

➡ _______________________

다음 글을 읽고, 물음에 답해 봅시다.

In one study, researchers asked pairs of strangers (A)<u>sit</u> down in a room and chat. (①) In half of the rooms, a cell phone was placed on a nearby table; in the other half, no phone was ⓐ<u>present</u>. (②) When a cell phone was present in the room, the participants reported the ⓑ<u>quality</u> of their relationship was worse than (B)<u>those who talked in a cell phone-free room</u>. (③) The pairs who talked in the rooms with cell phones thought their partners showed ⓒ<u>more</u> empathy. (④) Imagine you sit down to have lunch with a friend and set your phone on the table. (⑤) You might feel ⓓ<u>good</u> about yourself because you don't pick it up to check your messages. But your unchecked messages are still ⓔ<u>hurting</u> your connection with the person sitting across from you.

1

글의 흐름으로 보아, 주어진 문장이 들어가기에 가장 적절한 곳은?

> After the conversations ended, the researchers asked the participants what they thought of each other.

①   ②   ③   ④   ⑤

2

윗글의 밑줄 친 ⓐ~ⓔ 중, 문맥상 낱말의 쓰임이 적절하지 <u>않은</u> 것은?

① ⓐ   ② ⓑ   ③ ⓒ   ④ ⓓ   ⑤ ⓔ

3

윗글의 내용과 일치하는 것은?

① 휴대 전화 존재 유무와 대화의 질은 관계가 없다.
② 낯선 사람 사이에서는 휴대 전화가 대화에 도움이 된다.
③ 휴대 전화의 존재만으로도 마주앉은 사람과의 관계를 해칠 수 있다.
④ 휴대 전화가 있어도 메시지를 확인하지 않는 상대방에게 호감을 느끼게 된다.
⑤ 함께 식사를 하는 동안 휴대 전화를 사용하는 것은 무례하다는 인상을 줄 수 있다.

4 서술형

윗글의 밑줄 친 (A) sit을 어법에 맞게 고쳐 쓰시오.

➡ _______________________

5 서술형

윗글의 밑줄 친 (B)를 우리말로 해석하시오.

➡ _______________________

다음 글을 읽고, 물음에 답해 봅시다.

A Day with an Author

Amelia Tylor, the award-winning author of children's books, invites you to her new book, *Tommy's Adventure Under the Sea*. Join her at a special story time for kids!

■ When: Saturday, May 18th 11 a.m. ~ 1 p.m.

■ Where: Neilson Hall in the City Library

■ For whom: from 9 to 11-year-old kids

■ Event Includes:

· The author's reading session (*Tommy's Adventure Under the Sea*, Chapter 1)

· Acting performance of scenes in the book

· Book signing by the author

※ (A) <u>Please register at www.citylibrary.org/events to attend the event.</u>

※ Children should come with a parent/parents or guardian.

※ Please arrive on time. After the author's reading session begins, you cannot enter the hall ___(B)___ the session ends.

※ You can buy all of the author's books, including her new one, at a discount of 30% after the session.

1

윗글의 내용과 일치하는 것은?

① 행사는 3시간 동안 진행된다.

② 신청자는 바닷속 체험을 할 수 있다.

③ 참가 신청은 현장에서 할 수 있다.

④ 9살 이하의 어린이는 부모와 동반해야 한다.

⑤ Amelia Tylor의 모든 책을 할인된 가격에 살 수 있다.

2

윗글의 빈칸 (B)에 들어갈 말로 가장 적절한 것은?

① if　　　　② until

③ while　　　④ though

⑤ because

3 서술형

다음 영영풀이에 해당하는 단어를 윗글에서 찾아 쓰시오.

> a part of a play, movie, story, etc., in which a particular action or activity occurs

____

4 서술형

윗글의 밑줄 친 (A)를 우리말로 해석하시오.

➡ _______________________

다음 글을 읽고, 물음에 답해 봅시다.

Dream Company Cruise

<u>당신은 특별한 무언가를 찾고 있나요</u> for your family?

A Dream Company cruise creates memories ⓐ<u>that</u> bring families together.

Our ship, the Magic Dream, is your dream holiday ⓑ<u>itself</u>. This cruise ship is famous for ⓒ<u>its</u> classical design and modern facilities and ⓓ<u>have</u> the biggest pool of any cruise ship.

* Date of Departure: April 1-5 (4 nights sailing)
* Departing from / Returning to: Port of Miami, Florida
* Sailing to: Three islands in the Caribbean
* _______: 4 pools, 3 restaurants, 3 snack bars, 2 gyms
* Onboard Activities: magic shows, musicals, fireworks at night
* Meals: free breakfast, lunch, and dinner (additional charge for snacks and drinks)
* Room Description: 2 king beds, bathroom with shower, refrigerator, wireless Internet access, TV with recent movies
* Price: $4,500 ~ $5,000
● For more information and reservations, please ⓔ<u>call</u> (122) 341-1234.

1

윗글의 밑줄 친 ⓐ~ⓔ 중, 어법상 **틀린** 것은?

① ⓐ   ② ⓑ   ③ ⓒ   ④ ⓓ   ⑤ ⓔ

2

윗글의 빈칸에 들어갈 말로 가장 적절한 것은?

① Facilities
② Locations
③ Ingredients
④ Instruments
⑤ Entertainments

3 (서술형)

다음 영영풀이에 해당하는 단어를 윗글에서 찾아 쓰시오.

> an arrangement to have something (such as a room, table, or seat) held for your use at a later time

____

4 (서술형)

윗글의 밑줄 친 우리말과 의미가 같도록 주어진 말을 바르게 배열하시오.

(for / special / you / something / are / looking)

➡ ___________________

다음 글을 읽고, 물음에 답해 봅시다.

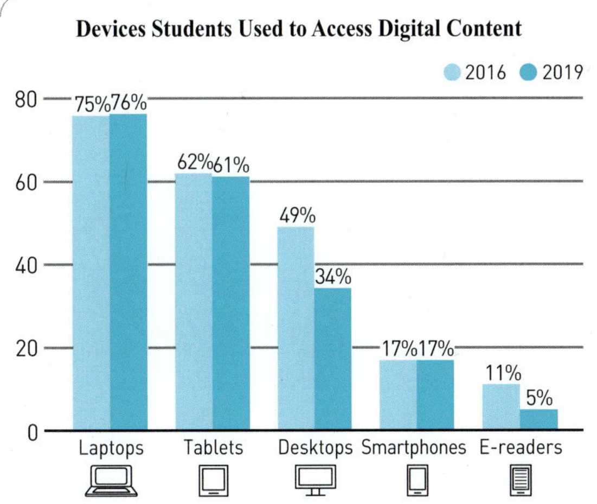

The above graph shows us (A)<u>what devices students used to access digital educational content</u>. The survey (B)<u>do</u> in both 2016 and 2019. Students from kindergarten to the 12th grade (C)<u>participate</u> in the survey, and they used many kinds of digital devices. Laptops were the ⓐ<u>most</u> popular device to access digital content in both years. Both in 2016 and in 2019, ⓑ<u>less</u> than 60 percent of the students used tablets for digital content. ⓒ<u>Less</u> than half the students used desktops for digital content in 2016, and ⓓ<u>more</u> than 30 percent used desktops for digital content in 2019. The percentage of students who used smartphones in 2016 was the same as (D)<u>that</u> in 2019. The percentages of students who used E-readers were the ⓔ<u>lowest</u> in both years.

1

윗글을 통해 알 수 <u>없는</u> 것은?

① 조사 주제 　② 조사 항목

③ 조사 시기 　④ 조사 주체

⑤ 조사 대상

2

윗글의 밑줄 친 (B), (C)를 어법상 알맞게 고친 것끼리 짝지어진 것은?

	(B)		(C)
①	did	……	participated
②	did	……	participating
③	was done	……	participated
④	was done	……	participating
⑤	was done	……	to participate

3

윗글의 밑줄 친 ⓐ~ⓔ 중, 도표의 내용상 낱말의 쓰임이 적절하지 <u>않은</u> 것은?

① ⓐ　② ⓑ　③ ⓒ　④ ⓓ　⑤ ⓔ

4 서술형

윗글의 밑줄 친 (A)를 우리말로 해석하시오.

➡ ________________________________

5 서술형

윗글의 밑줄 친 (D)that이 가리키는 내용을 글에서 찾아 쓰시오.

➡ ________________________________

다음 글을 읽고, 물음에 답해 봅시다.

June Almeida was born in 1930 in Scotland. Almeida excelled in school, and won the top science prize at her school. She wanted @to continue her studies in science after high school, but (A)there was no money for her college education. ____(B)____, at the age of 16, Almeida took a job as a lab technician. After that, she moved to London, then to Canada in 1954. There, she took a job detecting viruses and ⓑmade detailed pictures of them using a microscope. She became one of the best ⓒexperts in that job. Then, in London in 1964, she created a sharp, clear picture of a mysterious virus and ⓓnamed it coronavirus. It was the first identified human coronavirus. Due to her contributions in the field of biology, the University of London awarded her university degrees in 1970 and 1971. She finally received the degrees that she ⓔhad wanted since high school.

1

윗글을 통해 June Almeida에 대해 알 수 없는 것은?

① 출생 연도
② 출생지
③ 대학에서의 전공
④ 첫 직업
⑤ 학위 취득 연도

2

윗글의 밑줄 친 ⓐ~ⓔ 중, 어법상 틀린 것은?

① ⓐ　　② ⓑ　　③ ⓒ　　④ ⓓ　　⑤ ⓔ

3

윗글의 빈칸 (B)에 들어갈 말로 가장 적절한 것은?

① So
② Finally
③ Besides
④ However
⑤ Nonetheless

4 서술형

다음 영영풀이에 해당하는 단어를 윗글에서 찾아 쓰시오.

a course of study at a university, or the qualification that you get after completing the course

____

5 서술형

윗글의 밑줄 친 (A)를 우리말로 해석하시오.

➡ ______________________

다음 글을 읽고, 물음에 답해 봅시다.

The Secret: *A Treasure Hunt* is a book (A) created / creating by Byron Preiss in 1982. Before the book was published, Preiss buried 12 small treasure boxes across the United States and Canada. Each box had 교환될 수 있는 작은 열쇠 for one of 12 jewels in a safe deposit box in New York. The book has 12 mysterious paintings and poems. They contain the information that (B) indicate / indicates the location of the buried treasures. ____ⓐ____, a flower and a bell in one image stand for Bellflower Road in Cleveland. Up to the year of 2023, only three of the twelve boxes have been found. One was discovered in 1983 in Grant Park in Chicago, the next one in 2004 in the Greek Cultural Garden in Cleveland, and the most recent one (C) found / was found in 2019 in Langone Park in Boston. Preiss didn't leave any record of the treasures' exact ____ⓑ____ before his sudden death in a car accident in 2005. Many people are still out there looking for those treasures.

1

(A), (B), (C)의 각 네모 안에서 어법에 맞는 표현으로 가장 적절한 것은?

	(A)	(B)	(C)
①	created	indicates	found
②	created	indicate	was found
③	created	indicates	was found
④	creating	indicate	found
⑤	creating	indicates	was found

2

윗글의 빈칸 ⓐ에 들어갈 말로 가장 적절한 것은?

① Similarly
② Therefore
③ Otherwise
④ In addition
⑤ For example

3

윗글을 읽고 답할 수 <u>없는</u> 질문은?

① Who wrote the book *The Secret*: *A Treasure Hunt*?
② How many treasure boxes did Preiss bury?
③ What is in the treasure boxes buried by Preiss?
④ Who discovered the first treasure box in Chicago?
⑤ When did Byron Preiss die?

4 서술형

윗글의 빈칸 ⓑ에 들어갈 말을 글에서 찾아 쓰시오.

➡ _________________ s

5 서술형

윗글의 밑줄 친 우리말과 의미가 같도록 주어진 말을 바르게 배열하시오.

(could / that / exchanged / a small key / be)

➡ _________________________________

다음 글을 읽고, 물음에 답해 봅시다.

Ellen Church was born in Cresco, Iowa, in 1904. After ⓐgraduating from high school, she studied nursing. She worked ⓑas a nurse in San Francisco. One day Ellen stopped in at the Boeing office. She asked 그녀가 일자리를 얻을 수 있는지 as a nurse on their airplanes. Ellen suggested that nurses ⓒtook care of frightened passengers during flights. In 1930, she became the world's first female flight attendant. She worked on a Boeing 80A airplane, flying from Oakland to Chicago. Ellen, however, was forced ⓓto quit flying after eighteen months, __________ an injury from a car accident. She started her nursing career again at Milwaukee County Hospital. During World War II, Ellen joined the Army Nurse Corps. She helped evacuate wounded soldiers by airplane. She received an Air Medal for this. The Ellen Church Field Airport in Cresco ⓔwas named after her. She died in a horseback riding accident in 1965.

1

윗글의 밑줄 친 ⓐ~ⓔ 중, 어법상 틀린 것은?

① ⓐ   ② ⓑ   ③ ⓒ   ④ ⓓ   ⑤ ⓔ

2

윗글의 빈칸에 들어갈 말로 가장 적절한 것은?

① due to
② such as
③ in case of
④ in spite of
⑤ according to

3

윗글을 읽고 Ellen Church에 대해 답할 수 없는 질문은?

① Where was she born?
② What did she study after graduating from high school?
③ Was she the world's first female flight attendant?
④ Why did she quit working on a Boeing 80A airplane?
⑤ Who named the airport in Cresco after Ellen Church?

4 서술형

다음 영영풀이에 해당하는 단어를 윗글에서 찾아 쓰시오.

> a job or profession that someone does for a long time

____

5 서술형

윗글의 밑줄 친 우리말과 의미가 같도록 주어진 말을 바르게 배열하시오.

(she / a job / if / get / could)

➡ ________________________

다음 글을 읽고, 물음에 답해 봅시다.

Alex and Angie looked around <u>their new little house</u> and immediately felt at home. The kitchen was ⓐ<u>delightful</u>, with plenty of space for cooking. The family room had a large window and offered <u>휴식을 취할 수 있는 편안한 공간</u>. Upstairs, the bedrooms were ⓑ<u>cozy</u> and promised sweet dreams, while a family room downstairs awaited movie nights and games. They were ⓒ<u>disappointed</u> and went out to the small yard. The fenced-in yard was perfect for their needs and provided a sense of safety and privacy. Alex and Angie were ⓓ<u>excited</u> to start planting a garden in the coming spring and even discussed getting a small dog. Suddenly, children's laughter came from the neighborhood and created a warm and ⓔ<u>friendly</u> atmosphere. Great! Sarah, their daughter, would have many __________. This was the home of their dreams, and they knew they belonged here.

1

윗글의 밑줄 친 their new little house에 대한 설명으로 글의 내용과 일치하지 <u>않는</u> 것은?

① 부엌은 요리할 수 있는 공간이 충분하다.
② 거실과 침실은 2층에 있다.
③ 거실에서 영화를 보거나 게임을 할 수 있다.
④ 울타리가 쳐진 작은 마당이 있다.
⑤ 이웃에 어린아이들이 살고 있다.

2

윗글의 밑줄 친 ⓐ~ⓔ 중, 문맥상 낱말의 쓰임이 적절하지 <u>않은</u> 것은?

① ⓐ   ② ⓑ   ③ ⓒ   ④ ⓓ   ⑤ ⓔ

3

윗글의 빈칸에 들어갈 말로 가장 적절한 것은?

① toys   ② sisters
③ flowers   ④ puppies
⑤ playmates

4 서술형

다음 영영풀이에 해당하는 단어를 윗글에서 찾아 쓰시오.

> the mood or feeling that exists in a place and affects the people who are there

____

5 서술형

윗글의 밑줄 친 우리말과 의미가 같도록 주어진 말을 바르게 배열하시오.

(place / relax / a / to / comfortable)

➡ ______________________

다음 글을 읽고, 물음에 답해 봅시다.

Emily had a ⓐtough week at work, with long hours and tight deadlines. (①) The vibrant colors and delicate petals were ⓑrefreshing. (②) She could tell that her husband had put a lot of thought into the gift, and (A)it made her feel appreciated and loved. (③) As they stood there chatting and admiring the roses, Emily felt her stress and worries ⓒmelt away. (④) She thought that even on the toughest of days, (B)there are always reasons to smile and find joy in the world. (⑤) The roses served as a symbol of their love and partnership, and Emily felt ⓓunlucky to have such a wonderful person by her side. She hugged her husband and thanked him for the surprise. It was moments like this that made Emily feel truly ⓔblessed.

1

글의 흐름으로 보아, 주어진 문장이 들어가기에 가장 적절한 곳은?

> So, when her husband surprised her with beautiful roses after lunch, she was overjoyed.

①   ②   ③   ④   ⑤

2

윗글의 밑줄 친 ⓐ~ⓔ 중, 문맥상 낱말의 쓰임이 적절하지 <u>않은</u> 것은?

① ⓐ   ② ⓑ   ③ ⓒ   ④ ⓓ   ⑤ ⓔ

3

윗글을 읽고 답할 수 <u>없는</u> 질문은?

① How did Emily spend the week?
② What was the surprise gift of Emily's husband?
③ What did the surprise gift of Emily's husband symbolize?
④ Do Emily and her husband work for the same company?
⑤ How did Emily feel when she understood the meaning of her husband's gift?

4 서술형

윗글의 밑줄 친 (A)it이 가리키는 내용을 글에서 찾아 쓰시오.

➡ ________________

5 서술형

윗글의 밑줄 친 (B)를 우리말로 해석하시오.

➡ ________________

다음 글을 읽고, 물음에 답해 봅시다.

ⓐIt was Evelyn's first time exploring the Badlands of Alberta, famous across Canada for its numerous dinosaur fossils. As a young amateur bone-hunter, she was filled with anticipation. She ⓑhad not travelled this far for the bones of common dinosaur species. Her life-long dream to find rare fossils of dinosaurs ⓒwere about to come true. She began eagerly searching for them. After many hours of ⓓwandering throughout the deserted lands, however, she was __________. Now, the sun was beginning to set, and her goal was still far beyond her reach. She was looking at the slowly darkening ground before her. She sighed to ⓔherself, "I can't believe I came all this way for nothing. 정말 시간 낭비였네!"

1

윗글의 밑줄 친 ⓐ~ⓔ 중, 어법상 틀린 것은?

① ⓐ　　② ⓑ　　③ ⓒ　　④ ⓓ　　⑤ ⓔ

2

윗글의 빈칸에 들어갈 말로 가장 적절한 것은?

① satisfied　　② glorious
③ positive　　④ confident
⑤ unsuccessful

3

윗글의 내용과 일치하지 <u>않는</u> 것은?

① Evelyn은 이전에 Alberta의 Badlands에 가 본 적이 없었다.
② Alberta의 Badlands에는 많은 공룡 화석이 있다.
③ Evelyn은 직업적으로 화석을 발굴한다.
④ Evelyn의 오랜 꿈은 희귀한 공룡 화석을 발견하는 것이었다.
⑤ Evelyn은 해가 질 무렵까지 화석을 발견하지 못했다.

4 　서술형

다음 영영풀이에 해당하는 단어를 윗글에서 찾아 쓰시오.

> something that is from a plant or animal which lived in ancient times and that you can see in some rocks

____

5 　서술형

윗글의 밑줄 친 우리말과 의미가 같도록 주어진 말을 바르게 배열하시오.

(a / time / waste / what / of)

➡ ________________

다음 글을 읽고, 물음에 답해 봅시다.

Why do we so often fail to keep our resolutions? (①) Some psychologists suggest that most of us have _____(A)_____ expectations about our ability ⓐto change our behavior (in general, not only at New Year's). (②) This syndrome involves exaggerated feelings of control and overconfidence about our ability to change our behavior ⓑsuccessfully. (③) It often begins with an unrealistic goal (e.g., "I will exercise for two hours every day!"). (④) We also underestimate how difficult it will be to change our behavior (e.g., "I'll have no trouble ⓒstop my computer games!"). (⑤) Finally, we tend to expect dramatic, rapid results (e.g., "I'll probably lose about 10 pounds a week!"). ⓓBecause of these wrong expectations, we usually fail. (B)The new behavior proves to be more difficult than we expected. Visible results turn out to be ⓔslow. Then we often give up our attempts to change.

1

글의 흐름으로 보아, 주어진 문장이 들어가기에 가장 적절한 곳은?

> According to them, this produces the *false hope syndrome.*

①   ②   ③   ④   ⑤

2

윗글의 빈칸 (A)에 들어갈 말로 가장 적절한 것은?

① useless
② unrealistic
③ reasonable
④ meaningful
⑤ unimportant

3

윗글의 주제로 가장 적절한 것은?

① effective ways of losing weight
② advantages of false hope syndrome
③ how to change our behavior successfully
④ the reasons we fail to keep our resolutions
⑤ a huge gap between expectations and reality

4 서술형

윗글의 밑줄 친 (B)를 우리말로 해석하시오.

➡ ________________________________

5 서술형

윗글의 밑줄 친 ⓐ~ⓔ 중, 어법상 **틀린** 것을 찾아 바르게 고쳐 쓰시오.

(　　　) ➡ ________________________

다음 글을 읽고, 물음에 답해 봅시다.

Isaac Newton is 역사상 가장 위대한 과학자들 중 한 명. During his lifetime he made numerous contributions to science. But (A) few / little people realize that he was also a pet lover — or that sometimes many of his animal friends could drive him to distraction. ⓐ , he once suffered an emotional breakdown when a favorite dog knocked over a candle on his desk. The dog burned some of his important research notes. However, his dealings with an (B) annoying / annoyed cat led to a happier result. According to legend, a cat constantly interrupted Newton with its demands to be let in and out of the house. So, the scientist was annoyed and quickly came up with a solution — the pet ⓑ . The cat could come in and go out of Newton's house without disturbing him. Today, every cat with the ability to enter and leave a room without troubling their human friends (C) have / has Newton to thank.

1

(A), (B), (C)의 각 네모 안에서 어법에 맞는 표현으로 가장 적절한 것은?

	(A)	(B)	(C)
①	few	annoying	have
②	few	annoyed	has
③	few	annoying	has
④	little	annoyed	have
⑤	little	annoying	has

2

윗글의 빈칸 ⓐ에 들어갈 말로 가장 적절한 것은?

① Instead
② Moreover
③ For instance
④ In other words
⑤ On the other hand

3

윗글의 빈칸 ⓑ에 들어갈 말로 가장 적절한 것은?

① toy
② door
③ food
④ tower
⑤ owner

4 서술형

다음 영영풀이에 해당하는 단어를 윗글에서 찾아 쓰시오.

> something that gets your attention and prevents you from concentrating on something else

____

5 서술형

윗글의 밑줄 친 우리말과 의미가 같도록 주어진 말을 바르게 배열하시오.

(greatest / of / scientists / history's / one)

➡ _____________________

다음 글을 읽고, 물음에 답해 봅시다.

People spend much of their time ⓐ interact with media. But that does not mean that people have the critical skills to examine (A)it carefully and understand it. There's one well-known study from Stanford University in 2016. The study showed that young people are ⓑ easily fooled by misinformation, especially when (B)it comes through social media channels. This weakness ⓒ is not found only in youth, however. Research from New York University found that people over 65 shared (C)seven times as much misinformation as younger people. All of this raises a question: What's the ___________ to the misinformation problem? Governments and tech platforms certainly have a role ⓓ to play in blocking misinformation. However, every individual needs to become more information literate. And they should take responsibility for combating this threat by ⓔ becoming more information literate.

1

윗글의 밑줄 친 ⓐ~ⓔ 중, 어법상 틀린 것은?

① ⓐ ② ⓑ ③ ⓒ ④ ⓓ ⑤ ⓔ

2

윗글의 빈칸에 들어갈 말로 가장 적절한 것은?

① truth ② merit
③ cause ④ solution
⑤ side effect

3

윗글의 내용과 일치하는 것은?

① 사람들은 미디어를 주의 깊게 검토하는 데 많은 시간을 보낸다.
② 소셜 미디어 채널을 통해 잘못된 정보에 쉽게 속는 것은 젊은이들에게만 있는 현상이다.
③ 65세 이상의 노인들이 젊은이들보다 훨씬 더 많은 잘못된 정보를 공유한다.
④ 잘못된 정보를 막는 것은 전적으로 기술 플랫폼이 해야 할 일이다.
⑤ 개인은 정보 활용에 대한 책임을 질 필요가 없다.

4 〔서술형〕

윗글의 밑줄 친 (A), (B)의 it이 가리키는 것을 글에서 찾아 각각 한 단어로 쓰시오.

(A) ➡ _______________   (B) ➡ _______________

5 〔서술형〕

윗글의 밑줄 친 (C)를 우리말로 해석하시오.

➡ _______________________________________

다음 글을 읽고, 물음에 답해 봅시다.

Colors can help improve ___(A)___ . For example, some studies on Alzheimer's patients found that color cues ⓐ<u>helped</u> improve their recall of certain images. ___(B)___ , they could not remember black-and-white images, but could remember colored ⓑ<u>ones</u>. Another study found that red and blue were the best colors for improving brain function. Red came out on top ⓒ<u>because of</u> its role in society. Red is the color of stop signs and danger, and it is ⓓ<u>typically</u> the color of pens used by teachers. This means that red is an important color in learning and in the real world, and (C)<u>a person is more likely to remember something red</u>. Additionally, as the color red makes people cautious, they become more detail-oriented and pay better attention. This results in people ⓔ<u>recall</u> a red-colored object better later.

1

윗글의 빈칸 (A)에 들어갈 말로 가장 적절한 것은?

① memory
② patience
③ creativity
④ imagination
⑤ concentration

2

윗글의 빈칸 (B)에 들어갈 말로 가장 적절한 것은?

① However
② Otherwise
③ Furthermore
④ Nonetheless
⑤ Accordingly

3

윗글의 내용과 일치하는 것은?

① 알츠하이머 환자들은 컬러로 된 이미지보다 흑백 이미지를 더 잘 기억한다.
② 알츠하이머 환자들에게 색을 통한 심리 치료가 도움이 된다.
③ 뇌 기능을 향상시키는 데 가장 좋은 색은 파란색이다.
④ 사람들은 빨간색의 사물을 가장 잘 기억한다.
⑤ 사람들은 사회적 역할 때문에 빨간색을 부정적으로 인식한다.

4 서술형

윗글의 밑줄 친 (C)를 우리말로 해석하시오.

➡ ________________________________

5 서술형

윗글의 밑줄 친 ⓐ~ⓔ 중, 어법상 <u>틀린</u> 것을 찾아 바르게 고쳐 쓰시오.

(   ) ➡ ________________________

다음 글을 읽고, 물음에 답해 봅시다.

Despite the growing focus on EQ, a global lack in understanding and managing emotions still remains.

(A) But we are not yet skilled at spotting our emotions and ⓐ using them to our benefit. Emotional awareness and understanding are not taught in school. We enter the workforce after learning how to read, write, and report on bodies of knowledge.

(B) In a test, only 36 percent of the people who were tested ⓑ were able to accurately identify their emotions as they happened. What does this suggest? It means that two-thirds of us ⓒ is typically controlled by our emotions.

(C) Too often, __________, we lack the skills to manage our emotions in the heat of 우리가 직면하는 도전적인 문제들. Good decisions require ⓓ far more than factual knowledge. They are made by using our self-knowledge and emotional mastery when they ⓔ are needed most.

1

주어진 글 다음에 이어질 글의 순서로 가장 적절한 것은?

① (A) − (C) − (B)
② (B) − (A) − (C)
③ (B) − (C) − (A)
④ (C) − (A) − (B)
⑤ (C) − (B) − (A)

2

윗글의 밑줄 친 ⓐ~ⓔ 중, 어법상 <u>틀린</u> 것은?

① ⓐ   ② ⓑ   ③ ⓒ   ④ ⓓ   ⑤ ⓔ

3

윗글의 빈칸에 들어갈 말로 가장 적절한 것은?

① so   ② also
③ unless   ④ however
⑤ as a result

4 서술형

다음 영영풀이에 해당하는 단어를 윗글에서 찾아 쓰시오.

a feeling that you experience, for example, love, fear, or anger

____

5 서술형

윗글의 밑줄 친 우리말과 의미가 같도록 주어진 말을 바르게 배열하시오.

(that / face / challenging / we / the / problems)

➡ __________________

다음 글을 읽고, 물음에 답해 봅시다.

You may have heard of the food chain quite often in science class. What is a food chain? It means the transfer of food energy from its source in plants. The transfer is done through a series of organisms during the (A) repeating / repeated process of eating and being eaten. In a grassland, grass is eaten by rabbits, while rabbits in turn are eaten by foxes. This is a(n) ⓐ _______ of a simple food chain. In the course of following this food chain, food energy (B) transfers / is transferred from the plant to the animal or to a higher trophic level. According to observations, at each level of transfer, 80-90 percent of the potential energy is lost as heat. Hence the number of steps or links in a course (C) is / are limited, usually to four or five. ⓑThe shorter the food chain, the greater the available energy intake is.

1

(A), (B), (C)의 각 네모 안에서 어법에 맞는 표현으로 가장 적절한 것은?

	(A)	(B)	(C)
①	repeating	transfers	is
②	repeating	is transferred	are
③	repeated	is transferred	is
④	repeated	transfers	are
⑤	repeated	is transferred	are

2

윗글의 빈칸 ⓐ에 들어갈 말로 가장 적절한 것은?

① effect   ② origin
③ function   ④ example
⑤ definition

3

윗글의 내용과 일치하지 <u>않는</u> 것은?

① 먹이 사슬은 식품 에너지가 식물에 있는 에너지원으로부터 이동하는 것을 의미한다.
② 먹이 사슬 과정에서 식품 에너지는 더 높은 영양 수준으로 전달된다.
③ 각각의 먹이 사슬 이동 단계에서 많은 에너지가 열로 손실된다.
④ 먹이 사슬의 이동 단계는 무제한으로 일어날 수 있다.
⑤ 먹이 사슬의 단계가 많아지면 이용 가능한 에너지 섭취량이 줄어든다.

4 서술형

다음 영영풀이에 해당하는 단어를 윗글에서 찾아 쓰시오.

> an act or process of moving someone or something from one place to another

____

5 서술형

윗글의 밑줄 친 ⓑ를 우리말로 해석하시오.

➡ _______________

다음 글을 읽고, 물음에 답해 봅시다.

I believe that the more you remember, the ⓐ <u>much</u> you *can* remember. (①) Memory, in many ways, is like a muscle. (②) A muscle must be exercised and developed in order to give proper service and use: ⓑ <u>so must memory</u>. (③) You can be taught to train your memory just as you can be taught anything else. (④) ____________, it is much easier to develop a trained memory than, say, to learn to play a musical instrument. (⑤) Along with a trained memory you will probably acquire a greater power of concentration, a purer sense of observation, and perhaps, a stronger imagination.

1

글의 흐름으로 보아, 주어진 문장이 들어가기에 가장 적절한 곳은?

> The difference is that a muscle can be overtrained or become muscle-bound, while memory cannot.

①　　②　　③　　④　　⑤

2

윗글의 빈칸에 들어갈 말로 가장 적절한 것은?

① By the way
② Because of that
③ In the meantime
④ On the other hand
⑤ As a matter of fact

3

윗글에서 필자가 주장하는 바로 가장 적절한 것은?

① 무엇이든 지나친 것보다는 부족한 것이 낫다.
② 안 좋은 기억은 빨리 잊을수록 정신 건강에 좋다.
③ 기억을 잘 사용하기 위해서는 근육처럼 훈련시키고 발달시켜야 한다.
④ 악기 연주 또는 근력 운동이 기억력 향상에 도움이 된다.
⑤ 규칙적인 운동을 하면 집중력과 관찰력이 향상된다.

4 서술형

윗글의 밑줄 친 ⓐ를 어법상 알맞은 형태로 고쳐 쓰시오.

➡ ____________________

5 서술형

윗글의 밑줄 친 ⓑ가 의미하는 내용을 우리말로 쓰시오.

➡ ____________________

다음 글을 읽고, 물음에 답해 봅시다.

Health and the spread of disease ⓐ are very closely linked to how we live and how our cities operate. The good news is that cities can recover ⓑ more quickly than you might imagine. For example, many cities ⓒ have experienced deadly diseases in the past. After some period of pain and suffering, (A)they not only survived, but also advanced. In the nineteenth and early twentieth centuries, European cities saw destructive outbreaks of deadly diseases. Some famous doctors in Germany found the ___(B)___ between poor living conditions and disease. This led to the replanning and rebuilding of cities ⓓ to stop the spread of deadly diseases. In the mid-nineteenth century, London's pioneering sewer system ⓔ built to stop the spread of cholera.

1

윗글의 밑줄 친 ⓐ~ⓔ 중, 어법상 틀린 것은?

① ⓐ ② ⓑ ③ ⓒ ④ ⓓ ⑤ ⓔ

2

윗글의 빈칸 (B)에 들어갈 말로 가장 적절한 것은?

① solution
② difference
③ popularity
④ connection
⑤ competition

3

윗글의 내용과 일치하지 <u>않는</u> 것은?

① 건강과 질병의 확산은 생활 환경과 연관이 있다.
② 과거에 치명적인 질병을 경험한 대부분의 도시들이 사라졌다.
③ 19세기와 20세기 초에 유럽의 많은 도시에 치명적인 질병이 퍼졌다.
④ 치명적인 질병을 막기 위해 유럽의 도시들이 재건되었다.
⑤ 콜레라의 확산을 막기 위해 런던에 선구적인 하수도가 건설되었다.

4 서술형

다음 영영풀이에 해당하는 단어를 윗글에서 찾아 쓰시오.

> a sudden start or increase of fighting or disease

5 서술형

윗글의 밑줄 친 (A)를 우리말로 해석하시오.

➡

다음 글을 읽고, 물음에 답해 봅시다.

Reading fiction is one of the most loved ⓐhobbies of all time. Mysteries, science fiction, romance, and fantasy are all fiction. Reading fiction is exciting and, at the same time, very ⓑhelpful. It is a well-known fact that (A)it improves creativity. While you are reading fiction, you can get new ideas. And you can learn various ways of ⓒthinking about the world. Also, you can understand others better when you read fiction. Research indicates that fiction is more effective than nonfiction in changing our views about people who ⓓhas different ideas.   (B) , reading fiction can help you become better with people. It teaches you about how people may react to situations and challenges. 등장인물들이 저지르는 실수를 보는 것은 in stories can help you gain wisdom to use in your own lives. With all these benefits in mind, how about setting aside your smartphone and ⓔreading some fiction today?

1

윗글의 주제로 가장 적절한 것은?

① various genres of fiction
② advantages of reading fiction
③ how to read books effectively
④ popular hobbies with teenagers
⑤ differences between fiction and nonfiction

2

윗글의 밑줄 친 ⓐ~ⓔ 중, 어법상 틀린 것은?

① ⓐ   ② ⓑ   ③ ⓒ   ④ ⓓ   ⑤ ⓔ

3

윗글의 빈칸 (B)에 들어갈 말로 가장 적절한 것은?

① However
② Otherwise
③ In addition
④ For example
⑤ On the other hand

4 서술형

윗글의 밑줄 친 (A)it이 가리키는 내용을 글에서 찾아 쓰시오.

➡ ___________________

5 서술형

윗글의 밑줄 친 우리말과 의미가 같도록 주어진 말을 바르게 배열하시오.

(the mistakes / seeing / make / characters)

➡ ___________________

다음 글을 읽고, 물음에 답해 봅시다.

We want to provide good care for animals. To do that, an animal's needs should (A) meet / be met consistently and ___ⓐ___ all the time. Like humans, animals need a sense of control. So, ⓑan animal that doesn't know when food will appear may experience distress. We can provide a sense of control. We just need to ensure that our animal's environment is predictable: that there is always water available and always in the same place. There is always food when we get up in the morning and after our evening walk. There (B) always will / will always be a time and place to eliminate without having to hold things in to the point of discomfort. Human companions can display consistent emotional support, rather than providing love one moment and withholding love the next. When animals (C) know / will know what to expect, they will feel more confident and calm.

1

(A), (B), (C)의 각 네모 안에서 어법에 맞는 표현으로 가장 적절한 것은?

	(A)	(B)	(C)
①	meet	always will	know
②	meet	will always	will know
③	be met	will always	know
④	be met	always will	will know
⑤	be met	will always	will know

2

윗글에서 필자가 주장하는 바로 가장 적절한 것은?

① 동물들을 지나치게 통제하지 않도록 주의해야 한다.

② 동물들에게 과도한 애정을 주는 것은 동물들의 정서에 좋지 않다.

③ 동물들에게 강압적으로 배변 훈련을 시켜서는 안 된다.

④ 동물들이 섭취하는 물과 음식의 양을 적절하게 제한해야 한다.

⑤ 동물들의 생활 환경을 예측 가능하게 조성해야 한다.

3 서술형

윗글의 빈칸 ⓐ에 들어갈 말을 글에서 찾아 알맞은 형태로 고쳐 쓰시오.

→ _______________________

4 서술형

윗글의 밑줄 친 ⓑ를 우리말로 해석하시오.

→ _______________________

다음 글을 읽고, 물음에 답해 봅시다.

Let's look back at famous individuals in history. Statements like "So and so was born to be a great leader" are often made. Well, those words are often 그것들이 들리는 것만큼 사실이 아닌. Anyone at any time and in any place can become a leader. They can be (A) so / as charismatic that the entire world will sit up and take notice. To understand this, one must first know the basic truth about what makes people great. That truth is that people don't make themselves great. Then what makes people great? It is the cause they believe in. When a person, no matter their background or environment, (B) have / has a clear goal, belief, or something they want that they are willing to give up everything for, that faith will be the catalyst for their emotions, strength, and actions. When someone (C) is / will be wholly __________ of something, the world will watch in amazement.

1

(A), (B), (C)의 각 네모 안에서 어법에 맞는 표현으로 가장 적절한 것은?

	(A)	(B)	(C)
①	so	have	is
②	so	has	will be
③	so	has	is
④	as	have	will be
⑤	as	has	is

2

윗글의 밑줄 친 the basic truth를 바르게 설명한 것은?

① 뛰어난 리더는 타고나는 것이다.
② 사람들을 위대하게 만드는 것은 대의명분이다.
③ 카리스마가 없는 리더는 사람들을 이끌 수 없다.
④ 사람들은 누구나 스스로를 위대하게 만들 수 있다.
⑤ 강한 신념만으로는 리더가 될 수 없다.

3

윗글의 빈칸에 들어갈 말로 가장 적절한 것은?

① doubtful
② innocent
③ negative
④ convinced
⑤ indifferent

4 서술형

다음 영영풀이에 해당하는 단어를 윗글에서 찾아 쓰시오.

strong belief or trust in someone or something

____

5 서술형

윗글의 밑줄 친 우리말과 의미가 같도록 주어진 말을 바르게 배열하시오.

(true / sound / not / as / they / as)

➡ __________________

다음 글을 읽고, 물음에 답해 봅시다.

> Scientists believe that frogs' ancestors ① <u>were</u> water-dwelling, fishlike animals.

(A) Frogs must also lay their eggs in water, as their fishlike ancestors ② <u>were</u>. And eggs laid in the water must develop into water creatures ⓐ <u>if they are to survive</u>. For frogs, metamorphosis thus provides the bridge between the water-dwelling young forms and the land-dwelling adults.

(B) The first frogs and their relatives gained the ability to come out onto land and ③ <u>enjoy</u> the opportunities for food and shelter there. But they still kept many ties to the water.

(C) A frog's lungs do not work very well, and they get part of their oxygen by ④ <u>breathing</u> through their skin. But for this kind of "breathing" to work properly, the frog's skin must stay ______ ⓑ ______. And so, the frog must remain near the water. There, it can take a dip every now and then to keep ⑤ <u>its</u> skin from drying out.

1

주어진 글 다음에 이어질 글의 순서로 가장 적절한 것은?

① (A) − (C) − (B) 　② (B) − (A) − (C)
③ (B) − (C) − (A) 　④ (C) − (A) − (B)
⑤ (C) − (B) − (A)

2

윗글의 빈칸 ⓑ에 들어갈 말로 가장 적절한 것은?

① dry 　② soft
③ hard 　④ clean
⑤ moist

3

윗글의 주제로 가장 적절한 것은?

① some characteristics of frogs
② various animals' metamorphosis
③ the evolution of fishlike animals
④ how to breathe through one's skin
⑤ difference between water-dwelling animals and land-dwelling animals

4 서술형

윗글의 밑줄 친 ①~⑤ 중, 어법상 틀린 것을 찾아 바르게 고쳐 쓰시오.

(　) ➡ ________________

5 서술형

윗글의 밑줄 친 ⓐ를 우리말로 해석하시오.

➡ ________________

Have you ever ⓐ<u>heard</u> of "think outside the box"? When people try to think outside the box, the culture ⓑ<u>which</u> they are a part of *is that box*. Like religion or other traditions, culture gives us a kind of mental comfort and protection. ⓒ<u>Wandering</u> outside the box may be perceived as an act of creativity but only for a little while. People cannot live outside the box and still ⓓ<u>maintain</u> all the rights and privileges that they can get when they stay inside it. The pressure to remain within the box is about internalizing our group beliefs and ⓔ<u>takes</u> on group identities. ___________, it is about acting as we are expected to act. People all do things without any sense that what they're doing could be questioned. Culture, therefore, defines <u>정상적이라는 것이 무엇을 의미하는지</u>.

1

윗글의 밑줄 친 ⓐ~ⓔ 중, 어법상 틀린 것은?

① ⓐ ② ⓑ ③ ⓒ ④ ⓓ ⑤ ⓔ

2

윗글의 빈칸에 들어갈 말로 가장 적절한 것은?

① Also
② Then
③ However
④ In contrast
⑤ Nevertheless

3

윗글의 내용과 일치하지 <u>않는</u> 것은?

① 종교와 문화는 우리에게 정신적 편안함을 제공한다.
② 문화 밖에서 서성이는 것은 오랜 시간 동안 창의성의 행위로 인식될 수 있다.
③ 사람들은 문화 안에 존재할 때 권리와 특권을 유지할 수 있다.
④ 문화 안에 남아야 한다는 압박감은 집단 신념의 내면화와 관련된다.
⑤ 문화 안에서 사람들은 기대되는 정상적인 행동을 하게 된다.

4 서술형

다음 영영풀이에 해당하는 단어를 윗글에서 찾아 쓰시오.

> a right or benefit that is given to some people and not to others

____

5 서술형

윗글의 밑줄 친 우리말과 의미가 같도록 주어진 말을 바르게 배열하시오.

(to / normal / it / what / be / means)

➡ ___________

다음 글을 읽고, 물음에 답해 봅시다.

　　We are likely to interpret events ___(A)___. We want things ⓐ to be "this way" or "that way". Then we can select, stack, or arrange evidence. And it is done most certainly in a way that ⓑ supports our viewpoint. (①) Selective perception is based on the things that ⓒ seems to us to stand out. (②) However, the things that seem to us to be standing out may very well be related to certain things. (③) ___(B)___, they are related to our goals, interests, expectations, past experiences, or current demands of the situation. (④) This quote ⓓ highlights the phenomenon of selective perception. (⑤) If we want to use a hammer, then the world around us may begin ⓔ to look as though it is full of nails!

1

글의 흐름으로 보아, 주어진 문장이 들어가기에 가장 적절한 곳은?

> It's like "with a hammer in hand, everything looks like a nail."

①　　　②　　　③　　　④　　　⑤

2

윗글의 빈칸 (B)에 들어갈 말로 가장 적절한 것은?

① Hence
② However
③ Otherwise
④ In other words
⑤ On the other hand

3

윗글의 주제로 가장 적절한 것은?

① helpful quotes for our lives
② the way we interpret events
③ merits of selective perception
④ how to use a hammer correctly
⑤ the importance of various experiences

4　서술형

윗글의 빈칸 (A)에 들어갈 말을 글에서 찾아 알맞은 형태로 고쳐 쓰시오.

➡ _______________

5　서술형

윗글의 밑줄 친 ⓐ~ⓔ 중, 어법상 틀린 것을 찾아 바르게 고쳐 쓰시오.

(　　　) ➡ _______________

다음 글을 읽고, 물음에 답해 봅시다.

(A) By its nature, the exchange of products is actually the exchange of desires. All human beings have inherent physical and mental _____ⓐ_____. Therefore, any individual is usually only capable of ①satisfying a limited number of personal desires independently.

(B) Or they exist in a more abstract or conceptual form, such as knowledge and music. Irrespective of the form, these commodities ②are traded. The reason is that they can satisfy the desires of other individuals. Those individuals are ③willingly and purposely participating in the exchange. Therefore, the nature of trading is essentially the exchange of desires.

(C) For instance, Thomas Edison may have had ⓑthe brilliant mind to invent the electric light bulb, but he probably didn't have the right ability to be a farmer or a builder. He needed to find good food to eat and a place ④to live. In order to satisfy those desires, he needed to offer something ⑤that would satisfy the desires of other individuals in return.

(D) Therefore, trading becomes an effective means of satisfying the various desires of individuals within a community. In the community, all kinds of commodities can be exchanged on the open market. Goods to be traded exist in the form of physical objects, such as food, clothes, and cars.

1

주어진 글 (A)에 이어질 내용을 순서에 맞게 배열한 것으로 가장 적절한 것은?

① (B) – (D) – (C)　　② (C) – (B) – (D)
③ (C) – (D) – (B)　　④ (D) – (B) – (C)
⑤ (D) – (C) – (B)

2

윗글의 빈칸 ⓐ에 들어갈 말로 가장 적절한 것은?

① genes　　　　② senses
③ abilities　　　④ limitations
⑤ advantages

3 서술형

윗글의 밑줄 친 ①~⑤ 중, 어법상 틀린 것을 찾아 바르게 고쳐 쓰시오.

(　　) ➡ ________________

4 서술형

윗글의 밑줄 친 ⓑ를 우리말로 해석하시오.

➡ ________________

다음 글을 읽고, 물음에 답해 봅시다.

As kids, we worked hard at learning how to ride a bike; when we fell off, we got back on again, until it became second nature to us. But when we try something new in our adult lives we'll usually make just one attempt 그것이 잘됐는지를 판단하기 전에. If we don't succeed the first time, or if it (A) feels / will feel a little awkward, we'll tell ourselves that it wasn't a success rather than giving it another shot.

That's a shame, because repetition is central to the process of rewiring our brains. Consider the idea that your brain has a network of neurons. They will connect with each other whenever you remember (B) using / to use a brain-friendly feedback technique. Those connections aren't very reliable at first, which may make your first efforts a little hit-or-miss. You might remember one of the steps (C) involving / involved, and not the others. But scientists have a saying: "neurons that fire together, wire together." In other words, __________ of an action strengthens the connections between the neurons involved in that action. That means the more times you try using that new feedback technique, the more easily it will come to you when you need it.

1

(A), (B), (C)의 각 네모 안에서 어법에 맞는 표현으로 가장 적절한 것은?

	(A)	(B)	(C)
①	feels	using	involving
②	feels	to use	involved
③	feels	using	involved
④	will feel	to use	involving
⑤	will feel	using	involved

2

윗글의 빈칸에 들어갈 말로 가장 적절한 것은?

① plan
② result
③ subject
④ purpose
⑤ repetition

3 서술형

다음 영영풀이에 해당하는 단어를 윗글에서 찾아 쓰시오.

a feeling of guilt, regret, or sadness that you have because you know you have done something wrong

____

4 서술형

윗글의 밑줄 친 우리말과 의미가 같도록 주어진 말을 바르게 배열하시오.

(it / judging / worked / before / whether)

➡ _______________

다음 글을 읽고, 물음에 답해 봅시다.

In the morning Gaby brought the bikes. Gaby and Nellie had lunches packed and ⓐ were ready to pedal. Nellie was a bit worried. She was still a novice on the bike. "Oh, you can do it, Nellie," she remembered Gaby ① saying to her. Sure. They pedaled ⓑ side by side and were happy and laughed a lot.

The road led them through the edge of town and there it forked. They stayed to the right. There was a home with a fence around it right at the Y in the road. ⓒ All of a sudden, Nellie felt panic-stricken, and saw the wall ② to come right at her. Finally, she ran into the wall.

Gaby rushed to rescue Nellie. Nellie's nose and forehead were scraped but the bike was OK. Nellie (A) felt so embarrassed and afraid that she would have to give up the trip and go back to the dorm and ③ spend the beautiful day there alone. Gaby would not hear of it. She would ride ⓓ next to her friend. Nellie had nothing to fear. "You can do it, Nellie."

With all that ______(B)______, who would not try again? So, Nellie got back on the bike and continued pedaling. Her nose did not feel so good with the cool breeze ④ blowing across her face. They had no further incidents for the rest of the trip and enjoyed a good day. Two tired girls pedaled back to the dorm, and there the housemother had a few words with Nellie about her ⑤ swollen nose. She had gotten on the bike, pedaled, and ⓔ fell off. But she had done it.

1

윗글의 밑줄 친 ⓐ~ⓔ의 우리말 풀이가 알맞지 않은 것은?

① ⓐ: ~할 준비가 되었다
② ⓑ: 나란히
③ ⓒ: 갑자기
④ ⓓ: ~ 옆에
⑤ ⓔ: 포기했다

2

윗글의 빈칸 (B)에 들어갈 말로 가장 적절한 것은?

① criticism
② gratitude
③ challenge
④ responsibility
⑤ encouragement

3 서술형

윗글의 밑줄 친 ①~⑤ 중, 어법상 틀린 것을 찾아 바르게 고쳐 쓰시오.

(   ) ➡ ___________________

4 서술형

윗글의 밑줄 친 (A)를 우리말로 해석하시오.

➡ ___________________

다음 글을 읽고, 물음에 답해 봅시다.

When I was 17, I discovered a wonderful thing. My father and I were sitting on the floor of his study. We were organizing his old papers. Across the carpet I saw a fat paper clip. Its rust (A) dusting / dusted the cover sheet of a report of some kind. I picked it up. I started to read. Then I started to cry.

It was a speech he had written in 1920, in Tennessee. Then, only 17 himself and graduating from high school, he had called for equality for African-Americans. I marvelled at his courage and wondered how, in 1920, so young, so white, and in the deep South, where the law still separated black from white, he had had the courage to deliver it. I asked him about it.

"Daddy," I said, handing him the pages, "this speech — how did you ever get permission to give it? And weren't you scared?" "Well, honey," he said, "I didn't ask for permission. I just asked myself, 'What is 나의 세대가 직면한 가장 중요한 도전 과제?' I knew immediately. Then I asked myself, 'And if I (B) am not / weren't afraid, what would I say about it in this speech?'"

"I wrote it. And I delivered it. About half way through I looked up to see the entire audience of teachers, students, and parents (C) stand / to stand up — and walk out. Left alone on the stage, I thought to myself, 'Well, I guess I need to be sure to do only two things with my life: keep thinking for myself, and not get killed.'" He handed the speech back to me, and smiled. "You seem to have done both," I said.

1

(A), (B), (C)의 각 네모 안에서 어법에 맞는 표현으로 가장 적절한 것은?

	(A)	(B)	(C)
①	dusting	am not	stand
②	dusting	weren't	to stand
③	dusted	am not	stand
④	dusted	weren't	stand
⑤	dusted	am not	to stand

2

윗글의 밑줄 친 a speech에 관해 알 수 <u>없는</u> 것은?

① 작성자   ② 작성 시기
③ 작성 목적   ④ 작성 분량
⑤ 발견 장소

3 서술형

다음 영영풀이에 해당하는 단어를 윗글에서 찾아 쓰시오.

> the state of having the same rights, status, and opportunities

____

4 서술형

윗글의 밑줄 친 우리말과 의미가 같도록 주어진 말을 바르게 배열하시오.

(challenge / the / my generation / important / facing / most)

➡ ___________

READING 01

1 Here are some possible reasons.

2 First of all, we see ourselves every day in the mirror.

3 Since we are so used to the image in the mirror, when this image is reversed in pictures, it seems unnatural.

4 Our smiles could also be a reason.

5 When we look at ourselves in the mirror, we're usually relaxed, confident, and more likely to smile and act naturally.

READING 02

1 Milk is very sensitive to temperature and must be stored at temperatures between 0 and 4 degrees Celsius.

2 Furthermore, many canned foods are heated at high temperatures and exposed to high pressures.

3 But when milk goes through this process, it can change the taste and properties of the milk due to browning.

4 Additionally, cans are more expensive to produce than cartons or plastic bottles.

5 Although milk producers could produce canned milk, the reasons mentioned above and a lack of proper packaging facilities make it a less attractive option.

글을 의미 단위로 끊어 읽고 주어와 동사 에 표시하며 해석하시오.

READING 03

1 However, young adults don't decide to change their diets only out of concern for their health.

2 Some make the choice out of concern for animal rights.

3 So, many teens give up meat to protest those conditions.

4 It also creates problems with animal waste resulting in pollution.

5 These trends show that today's youth are more aware of and sensitive to animal rights and environmental problems.

READING 04

1 After millions of years, these clouds begin to shrink because gravity forces the gas and dust together.

2 As it is squeezed, the cloud heats up to form a young star.

3 What happens when the fuel runs out and the star dies?

4 For example, stars with less than half the mass of the sun fade away very slowly.

5 But most stars use up their fuel and finally return to clouds of gas and dust after a series of steps.

READING 05

1 In a movie, lighting does more than just allow us to see what is taking place.

2 If a bright light is used to minimize shadows, it creates a bright and cheerful atmosphere.

3 Light can also make dark shadows for a strong contrast between bright and dark scenes.

4 So, it is used in horror movies or films with a dark atmosphere.

5 Understanding these lighting techniques and their effects makes watching movies even more exciting.

READING 06

1 Think, for a moment, about when you bought something and you never ended up using it.

2 That is more than the total government spending on universities and roads.

3 That is an average of $1,250 AUD (roughly $1,156 USD) for each household.

4 All the things we buy and then never use are waste — a waste of money, a waste of time, and waste in the sense of pure rubbish.

5 As the author Clive Hamilton observes, 'The difference between the stuff we buy and what we use is waste.'

글을 의미 단위로 끊어 읽고 주어와 동사 에 표시하며 해석하시오.

READING **07**

1 I'm writing this email in response to the message I received from her homeroom teacher.

2 As the mother of a girl who needs a lot of nutrients, I strongly oppose the suggestion.

3 Removing them from the menu would limit our children's food choices and hinder their growth.

4 Instead, the school could clearly label foods that may contain eggs.

5 It is important students continue to have a wide choice of foods.

READING **08**

1 Some experts say that we communicate by moving our bodies.

2 It can make a significant difference in your relationship with students.

3 For example, when students first enter the classroom, they look for their teacher.

4 Imagine that the teacher has a friendly greeting and a welcoming smile.

5 Teachers should remember that their body language is always at work when they are with their students.

READING 09

1 The Great Barrier Reef in Australia is one of the largest coral reef systems in the world.

2 However, in recent years, it has been facing numerous environmental challenges.

3 Furthermore, water pollution from water used for agriculture and industrial waste makes the water quality poor.

4 We must take immediate action to protect the Great Barrier Reef and its marine life.

5 The future of the Great Barrier Reef and the millions of species that call it home depends on it.

READING 10

1 You need to get comfortable with discomfort if you want to succeed.

2 Trying new things outside of your comfort zone will greatly benefit you in many ways.

3 As you try new things, you will discover your talents, interests, strengths and weaknesses.

4 If you try something new, you can meet new people who you otherwise would never have had the chance to meet.

5 However, you will be able to expand your horizons and achieve success.

READING 11

1 That is, the advertisement needs to show how the product can help them.

____

2 For example, imagine an advertisement for a new smartphone that just talks about its amazing features.

____

3 Now imagine an advertisement showing people taking beautiful photos in their daily lives or watching movies on their new smartphone.

____

4 It would be far more memorable and people would be interested in it.

____

5 Therefore, a successful advertisement must show people how its product can make their lives richer and more convenient.

____

READING 12

1 Some experts predict that AI will lead to job loss in certain industries by automating many simple tasks.

____

2 However, other experts believe that AI will create new job opportunities.

____

3 For example, the use of AI in customer service requires workers to improve their interpersonal skills.

____

4 In addition, AI will likely lead to the development of new job categories, such as AI ethics officers.

____

5 As AI continues to have an impact on the job market, it is necessary for workers and organizations to adapt to the changes.

____

글을 의미 단위로 끊어 읽고 주어와 동사 에 표시하며 해석하시오.

READING 13

1 In one study, researchers asked pairs of strangers to sit down in a room and chat.

2 In half of the rooms, a cell phone was placed on a nearby table; in the other half, no phone was present.

3 Imagine you sit down to have lunch with a friend and set your phone on the table.

4 You might feel good about yourself because you don't pick it up to check your messages.

5 But your unchecked messages are still hurting your connection with the person sitting across from you.

READING 14

1 Join her at a special story time for kids!

2 Please register at www.citylibrary.org/events to attend the event.

3 Children should come with a parent/parents or guardian.

4 After the author's reading session begins, you cannot enter the hall until the session ends.

5 You can buy all of the author's books, including her new one, at a discount of 30% after the session.

READING 15

1 Are you looking for something special for your family?

2 A Dream Company cruise creates memories that bring families together.

3 Our ship, the Magic Dream, is your dream holiday itself.

4 This cruise ship is famous for its classical design and modern facilities.

5 It also has the biggest pool of any cruise ship.

READING 16

1 Students from kindergarten to the 12th grade participated in the survey, and they used many kinds of digital devices.

2 Laptops were the most popular device to access digital content in both years.

3 Both in 2016 and in 2019, more than 60 percent of the students used tablets for digital content.

4 More than half the students used desktops for digital content in 2016, and more than 30 percent used desktops for digital content in 2019.

5 The percentages of students who used E-readers were the lowest in both years.

READING **17**

1 Almeida excelled in school, and won the top science prize at her school.

____

2 She wanted to continue her studies in science after high school, but there was no money for her college education.

____

3 There, she took a job detecting viruses and making detailed pictures of them using a microscope.

____

4 Due to her contributions in the field of biology, the University of London awarded her university degrees in 1970 and 1971.

____

5 She finally received the degrees that she had wanted since high school.

____

READING **18**

1 Before the book was published, Preiss buried 12 small treasure boxes across the United States and Canada.

____

2 They contain the information that indicates the location of the buried treasures.

____

3 For example, a flower and a bell in one image stand for Bellflower Road in Cleveland.

____

4 Preiss didn't leave any record of the treasures' exact locations before his sudden death in a car accident in 2005.

____

5 Many people are still out there looking for those treasures.

____

글을 의미 단위로 끊어 읽고 주어와 동사 에 표시하며 해석하시오.

Answers p.61

READING 19

1 She asked if she could get a job as a nurse on their airplanes.

2 Ellen suggested that nurses take care of frightened passengers during flights.

3 In 1930, she became the world's first female flight attendant.

4 She worked on a Boeing 80A airplane, flying from Oakland to Chicago.

5 The Ellen Church Field Airport in Cresco was named after her.

READING 20

1 Alex and Angie looked around their new little house and immediately felt at home.

2 Upstairs, the bedrooms were cozy and promised sweet dreams, while a family room downstairs awaited movie nights and games.

3 The fenced-in yard was perfect for their needs and provided a sense of safety and privacy.

4 Suddenly, children's laughter came from the neighborhood and created a warm and friendly atmosphere.

5 This was the home of their dreams, and they knew they belonged here.

READING 21

1 Emily had a tough week at work, with long hours and tight deadlines.

2 So, when her husband surprised her with beautiful roses after lunch, she was overjoyed.

3 She could tell that her husband had put a lot of thought into the gift, and it made her feel appreciated and loved.

4 As they stood there chatting and admiring the roses, Emily felt her stress and worries melt away.

5 The roses served as a symbol of their love and partnership, and Emily felt lucky to have such a wonderful person by her side.

READING 22

1 It was Evelyn's first time exploring the Badlands of Alberta, famous across Canada for its numerous dinosaur fossils.

2 She had not travelled this far for the bones of common dinosaur species.

3 After many hours of wandering throughout the deserted lands, however, she was unsuccessful.

4 Now, the sun was beginning to set, and her goal was still far beyond her reach.

5 She was looking at the slowly darkening ground before her.

글을 의미 단위로 끊어 읽고 주어와 동사 에 표시하며 해석하시오.

READING 23

1 It often begins with an unrealistic goal (e.g., "I will exercise for two hours every day!").

2 Finally, we tend to expect dramatic, rapid results (e.g., "I'll probably lose about 10 pounds a week!").

3 This syndrome involves exaggerated feelings of control and overconfidence about our ability to change our behavior successfully.

4 Because of these wrong expectations, we usually fail.

5 Then we often give up our attempts to change.

READING 24

1 During his lifetime he made numerous contributions to science.

2 But few people realize that he was also a pet lover — or that sometimes many of his animal friends could drive him to distraction.

3 So, the scientist was annoyed and quickly came up with a solution — the pet door.

4 The cat could come in and go out of Newton's house without disturbing him.

5 However, his dealings with an annoying cat led to a happier result.

글을 의미 단위로 끊어 읽고 주어와 동사 에 표시하며 해석하시오.

● Answers p.63

READING 25

1 People spend much of their time interacting with media.

2 All of this raises a question: What's the solution to the misinformation problem?

3 Governments and tech platforms certainly have a role to play in blocking misinformation.

4 However, every individual needs to become more information literate.

5 And they should take responsibility for combating this threat by becoming more information literate.

READING 26

1 Red is the color of stop signs and danger, and it is typically the color of pens used by teachers.

2 Furthermore, they could not remember black-and-white images, but could remember colored ones.

3 Another study found that red and blue were the best colors for improving brain function.

4 Red came out on top because of its role in society.

5 Additionally, as the color red makes people cautious, they become more detail-oriented and pay better attention.

READING 27

1 Despite the growing focus on EQ, a global lack in understanding and managing emotions still remains.

2 In a test, only 36 percent of the people who were tested were able to accurately identify their emotions as they happened.

3 It means that two-thirds of us are typically controlled by our emotions.

4 But we are not yet skilled at spotting our emotions and using them to our benefit.

5 Too often, however, we lack the skills to manage our emotions in the heat of the challenging problems that we face.

READING 28

1 You may have heard of the food chain quite often in science class.

2 It means the transfer of food energy from its source in plants.

3 The transfer is done through a series of organisms during the repeated process of eating and being eaten.

4 In a grassland, grass is eaten by rabbits, while rabbits in turn are eaten by foxes.

5 Hence the number of steps or links in a course is limited, usually to four or five.

READING 29

1 A muscle must be exercised and developed in order to give proper service and use: so must memory.

2 The difference is that a muscle can be overtrained or become muscle-bound, while memory cannot.

3 You can be taught to train your memory just as you can be taught anything else.

4 Memorization isn't practical for learning complex concepts and information.

5 Along with a trained memory you will probably acquire a greater power of concentration, a purer sense of observation, and perhaps, a stronger imagination.

READING 30

1 The good news is that cities can recover more quickly than you might imagine.

2 In the nineteenth and early twentieth centuries, European cities saw destructive outbreaks of deadly diseases.

3 Some famous doctors in Germany found the connection between poor living conditions and disease.

4 This led to the replanning and rebuilding of cities to stop the spread of deadly diseases.

5 In spite of the reconstruction efforts, cities declined in many areas and many people started to leave.

READING 31

1 Reading fiction is one of the most loved hobbies of all time.

2 While you are reading fiction, you can get new ideas.

3 Also, you can understand others better when you read fiction.

4 In addition, reading fiction can help you become better with people.

5 It teaches you about how people may react to situations and challenges.

READING 32

1 To do that, an animal's needs should be met consistently and predictably all the time.

2 We just need to ensure that our animal's environment is predictable: that there is always water available and always in the same place.

3 There is always food when we get up in the morning and after our evening walk.

4 There will always be a time and place to eliminate without having to hold things in to the point of discomfort.

5 When animals know what to expect, they will feel more confident and calm.

글을 의미 단위로 끊어 읽고 주어와 동사 에 표시하며 해석하시오.

READING **33**

1 Statements like "So and so was born to be a great leader" are often made.

2 Well, those words are often not as true as they sound.

3 Anyone at any time and in any place can become a leader.

4 That truth is that people don't make themselves great.

5 When someone is wholly convinced of something, the world will watch in amazement.

READING **34**

1 Scientists believe that frogs' ancestors were water-dwelling, fishlike animals.

2 A frog's lungs do not work very well, and they get part of their oxygen by breathing through their skin.

3 There, it can take a dip every now and then to keep its skin from drying out.

4 And eggs laid in the water must develop into water creatures if they are to survive.

5 For frogs, metamorphosis thus provides the bridge between the water-dwelling young forms and the land-dwelling adults.

READING 35

1 Like religion or other traditions, culture gives us a kind of mental comfort and protection.

2 The pressure to remain within the box is about internalizing our group beliefs and taking on group identities.

3 Also, it is about acting as we are expected to act.

4 People all do things without any sense that what they're doing could be questioned.

5 Culture, therefore, defines what it means to be normal.

READING 36

1 We want things to be "this way" or "that way".

2 However, the things that seem to us to be standing out may very well be related to certain things.

3 In other words, they are related to our goals, interests, expectations, past experiences, or current demands of the situation.

4 It's like "with a hammer in hand, everything looks like a nail."

5 This quote highlights the phenomenon of selective perception.

READING 37

1 Therefore, any individual is usually only capable of satisfying a limited number of personal desires independently.

____

2 He needed to find good food to eat and a place to live in.

____

3 In the community, all kinds of commodities can be exchanged on the open market.

____

4 The reason is that they can satisfy the desires of other individuals.

____

5 Those individuals are willingly and purposely participating in the exchange.

____

READING 38

1 As kids, we worked hard at learning how to ride a bike; when we fell off, we got back on again, until it became second nature to us.

____

2 If we don't succeed the first time, or if it feels a little awkward, we'll tell ourselves that it wasn't a success rather than giving it another shot.

____

3 Consider the idea that your brain has a network of neurons.

____

4 Those connections aren't very reliable at first, which may make your first efforts a little hit-or-miss.

____

5 That means the more times you try using that new feedback technique, the more easily it will come to you when you need it.

____

READING **39**

1 Gaby and Nellie had lunches packed and were ready to pedal.

____

2 They pedaled side by side and were happy and laughed a lot.

____

3 Her nose did not feel so good with the cool breeze blowing across her face.

____

4 Two tired girls pedaled back to the dorm, and there the housemother had a few words with Nellie about her swollen nose.

____

5 The road led them through the edge of town and there it forked.

____

READING **40**

1 What is the most important challenge facing my generation?

____

2 Then I asked myself, 'And if I weren't afraid, what would I say about it in this speech?'

____

3 Then, only 17 himself and graduating from high school, he had called for equality for African-Americans.

____

4 Left alone on the stage, I thought to myself, 'Well, I guess I need to be sure to do only two things with my life: keep thinking for myself, and not get killed.'

____

5 He handed the speech back to me, and smiled.

____

MEMO

MEMO

800문장으로 강화하는 **고등 필수 구문**

C.O.R.E 구문 800

✓ 우선 순위 빈출 구문   ✓ 고득점 대비 주요 구문

❶ 필수 구문 포인트

도식화 설명으로
구문 패턴 학습 가능

PLUS코너를 통한
심화 내용 학습

❷ 대표&연습 문장

2~3개의 대표 문장으로
구문 패턴 연습 가능

직접 분석 및 해석 가능한
연습 문장 포함

❸ 고난도 문장

앞서 학습한 내용을
응용할 수 있는
고난도 문장 학습

Reading master ∞ 중등

수능 plus 내신

Level 2

ANSWERS

중심 내용 파악하기

Reading Key 영어 지문 구조 이해하기   pp.10~13

정답

A 주제문 공동, 목적
　　예시 자원봉사 집단

B 예시 빨리, 익숙해
　　주제문 행복, 익숙해

C 일반적인 이야기 실패, 미래
　　반론(주제문) 과거, 꿈

D 주제문 반려동물, 학생들
　　예시/근거 반려동물 치료, 혈압, 스트레스
　　주제문 반려동물 방문

해석

A 외로운 환자들이 공동의 목적을 가진 집단에 가입함으로써 친구를 사귈 수 있다. 예를 들어, 자원봉사 집단에 가입하는 사람들이 보통 더 행복하다. 자원봉사는 두 가지 방식으로 외로움을 감소시킬 수 있다. 우선, 다른 사람들을 도움으로써, 외로운 사람은 기분이 더 좋을지도 모른다. 또한 자원봉사 프로그램에 참여함으로써 그들은 자신들의 사회적 관계망을 형성할 수 있다.

B 만약 당신이 갓 구운 빵 냄새가 나는 방으로 걸어 들어간다면, 기분 좋은 그 냄새를 금방 알아차리게 된다. 하지만 당신이 몇 분 동안 그 방에 머무른 후에, 그 냄새는 사라지는 것 같다. 이것은 행복에서도 일어날 수 있다. 우리는 모두 다정한 동반자, 건강, 만족스러운 직업, 먹을 충분한 음식과 같이 우리를 행복하게 해 주는 것을 갖고 있다. 그러나 시간이 지남에 따라, 우리는 이러한 것들에 익숙해지고 우리가 얼마나 운이 좋은지 잊어버린다.

C 많은 사람들이 과거의 실패에 근거하여 미래에 일어날 수 있는 일들에 대해 생각하고 그것에 사로잡힌다. 예를 들어, 만약 여러분이 전에 어떤 것에 실패한 적이 있다면, 여러분은 다시 실패할까 봐 다시 시도하는 것을 두려워할지도 모른다. 그러나 여러분의 미래는 여러분의 과거가 아니고 여러분에게는 더 나은 미래가 있을 수 있다. 여러분은 실수에 대해 잊기로 결심해야 한다. 여러분의 과거가 여러분을 지배하게 둔다면, 여러분은 꿈을 이룰 수 없을 것이다.

D 미국과 다른 나라의 대학에서 반려동물들이 우울하고 불안해하는 학생들을 도와주는 데 이용되고 있다. 학생들이 스트

레스를 덜 느끼도록 돕기 위해 학교 관계자들은 특히 시험 기간 동안에 반려동물 치료 행사를 마련한다. 반려동물과 시간을 보내는 것이 혈압과 스트레스 수치는 낮추는 반면 행복감은 증가시킬 수 있다고 연구는 보여 준다. 대학 캠퍼스 내 반려동물 방문은 학생들을 도와주는 훌륭한 방법이 될 수 있다.

Unit 01 주제 파악하기

READING 01 ▸ 정답 ⑤   pp.14~15

Mini Quiz picture(s), mirror

1 ⑤　**2** (1) T (2) F (3) T
3 (1) reverse (2) relaxed

해석

왜 우리는 거울 속에서 보이는 것만큼 사진에서는 좋아 보이지 않을까? 여기 몇 가지 가능한 이유가 있다. 무엇보다도, 우리는 매일 거울 속에서 우리 자신을 본다. 우리 얼굴의 가장 친숙한 이미지는 거울에 비친 모습이다. 우리는 거울 속의 이미지에 너무 익숙하기에, 이 이미지가 사진 속에서 뒤바뀌면, 부자연스럽게 보인다. 우리의 미소도 이유가 될 수 있다. 우리가 거울 속의 우리 자신을 볼 때, 우리는 보통 편안하고, 자신감이 넘치며, 자연스럽게 미소 짓고 행동할 가능성이 더 크다. 하지만 우리가 사진을 찍을 때, 우리는 긴장하고 어색한 미소를 짓기 시작한다! 마지막으로, 사진은 실제 삶의 2D 버전이다. 그것들은 우리를 이상하거나 부자연스럽게 보이게 하는 경향이 있다. 이러한 요인들이 우리가 사진 속의 우리 모습에 대해 불편하게 느끼도록 만들 수 있다.

해설

p.14

우리가 거울과 달리 사진에서 더 익숙하지 않은 부자연스러운 모습으로 찍히는 이유를 설명하는 글이므로, 글의 주제로 가장 적절한 것은 ⑤ '우리가 사진보다 거울에서 더 낫게 보이는 이유'이다.
① 사진에서 좋게 보일 수 있는 방법
② 도시에서 관광객들에게 유명한 사진 촬영지
③ 사진에서 자연스럽게 보이는 것의 어려움
④ 우리 자신을 객관적으로 보는 것의 중요성

p.15

1 These factors(이러한 요인)는 거울 속 이미지와 사진 속 이미지의 차이를 만들어내는 요인이므로 글에서 언급되지 않은 ⑤가 These factors에 해당하지 않는다.

2 (1) 우리는 거울 속의 모습을 더 편안하게 느낀다고 했으므로 글의

내용과 일치한다.

(2) 우리는 사진을 찍을 때 긴장하고 어색한 미소를 짓는다고 했으므로 글의 내용과 일치하지 않는다.

(3) 사진의 특성상 우리는 사진 속 우리 모습을 불편하게 느낀다고 했으므로 글의 내용과 일치한다.

해석 (1) 우리는 사진에서보다 거울에서의 우리의 모습을 더 편하게 느낀다.

(2) 사진을 찍을 때, 우리는 자연스럽게 미소 짓고 행동한다.

(3) 우리는 종종 사진에서 우리가 이상하게 보인다고 생각한다.

3 **해석** 당신의 사진을 잘 찍는 방법

(1) '거울 모드'를 사용해라. 그것은 당신의 얼굴의 이미지를 뒤바꾸지 않을 것이다.

(2) 사진을 찍을 때 편안하게 느끼려고 노력해라.

구문 설명

· The most familiar image of our faces is the reflection [we see in the mirror].

[ ]는 목적격 관계대명사가 생략되어 있는 관계절로 선행사 the reflection을 부연 설명한다.

· They tend to **make us look** strange or unnatural.

「make+목적어+동사원형」은 '~가 …하게 만들다'의 의미이다.

Reading Skill

모범 답안

질문 제기	왜 우리의 모습이 거울보다 사진에서 더 좋지 않게 보일까?
이유 설명	· 우리가 매일 보는 거울 속의 모습이 더 익숙함 · 사진을 찍을 때 긴장해서 어색한 미소를 짓게 됨 · 사진은 우리의 모습을 이상하고 부자연스럽게 보이게 함

직독직해 Skill

· But / when we have / our pictures taken, / we (S) start (V) to feel nervous / and make an awkward smile!

그러나 / 우리가 ~할 때 / 사진을 찍는다 / 우리는 긴장감을 느끼기 시작한다 / 그리고 어색한 미소를 짓기

Mini Quiz Milk is very sensitive to temperature and

---

must be stored at temperatures between 0 and 4 degrees Celsius.

1 ② **2** Attractive[Proper]
3 B

해석

당신은 캔에 들어 있는 우유를 본 적이 있는가? 당신은 종이 팩이나 플라스틱 병에 들어 있는 우유에 익숙할 수 있지만, 아마도 캔에 들어 있는 우유를 본 적이 없을 것이다. 이것에 대한 흥미로운 이유들이 있다. 우유는 온도에 매우 민감하고 섭씨 0도에서 4도 사이의 온도에서 보관되어야 한다. 불행히도, 캔은 열을 잘 전달하기 때문에 우유를 빨리 상하게 만들 수 있다. 게다가, 많은 캔 식품들은 높은 온도에서 가열되고 높은 압력에 노출된다. 하지만 우유가 이 과정을 거치면, 갈변으로 인해 우유의 맛과 특성을 바꿀 수 있다. 게다가, 캔은 종이 팩이나 플라스틱 병보다 생산하는 것이 더 비싸다. 우유 생산자들이 캔 우유를 생산할 수는 있지만, 위에서 언급한 이유와 적절한 포장 시설의 부족은 그것을 덜 매력적인 선택으로 만든다.

해설

p.16

캔으로 된 우유를 생산하기 어려운 이유에 대한 글이므로, 글의 주제로 가장 적절한 것은 ① '캔 우유를 생산하는 데 있어서의 어려움'이다.

② 우리 건강을 향상하는 데 있어 우유의 역할

③ 우유에 중요한 요인으로서의 온도

④ 우유와 캔 음료 사이의 차이

⑤ 캔 우유를 매일 마시는 것의 단점

p.17

1 캔은 열을 잘 전달하기에 우유를 쉽게 상하게 만들 수 있다는 내용이 글에 제시되어 있으므로, 답할 수 있는 질문은 ② '왜 캔에 들어 있는 우유가 쉽게 상하는가?'이다.

① 하루에 얼마나 많은 우유가 생산되는가?

③ 왜 캔이 만들기에 더 비싼가?

④ 캔에 들어 있는 우유를 어디서 살 수 있는가?

⑤ 캔에 들어 있는 우유는 언제 인기 있어질까?

2 캔으로 된 우유를 생산하는 것은 여러 어려움이 있다는 내용의 글이므로, 빈칸에는 Attractive(매력적인) 또는 Proper(적절한)가 들어가야 한다.

해석 캔에 들어 있는 우유: 우유 생산에서 매력적이지[적절하지] 않은 선택

3 글에 제시된 캔의 특징과 캔 음료의 제조 과정을 살펴보면 캔을 포장재로 사용하기에 적합한 조건을 모두 갖춘 것은 B이다.

체크 사항	A	B	C	D
열에 매우 민감한가?	그렇다	아니다	아니다	아니다
고온에서 가열되고 높은 압력에 노출될 수 있는가?	그렇다	그렇다	그렇다	아니다
포장재 가격을 절감할 필요가 있는가?	아니다	아니다	그렇다	그렇다

구문 설명

- **While** you may be familiar with milk in cartons or plastic bottles, you probably **haven't seen** it in cans.

  while은 '~인 반면에'라는 뜻의 접속사이며 haven't seen은 현재완료로 〈경험〉의 의미를 나타낸다.

- **Although** milk producers could produce canned milk, the reasons [**mentioned** above] and a lack of proper packaging facilities **make it a less attractive option**.

  [ ]는 the reasons를 수식하는 과거분사구이며 「make+A(목적어)+B(명사구)」는 'A를 B로 만들다'의 의미이다.

Reading Skill

모범 답안

주제	우리가 캔으로 된 우유를 보지 못한 이유
근거	• 캔은 열을 잘 전달하여 우유를 쉽게 상하게 함 • 캔 제품이 되는 과정은 갈변으로 인해 우유의 맛과 특성을 변하게 함 • 캔이 다른 포장재에 비해 가격이 비쌈

직독직해 Skill

- Unfortunately, / cans (S) can make (V) / milk go bad quickly / because they conduct heat well.

  불행히도 / 캔은 만들 수 있다 / 우유를 빨리 상하게 / 그들이 열을 잘 전달하기 때문에

Mini Quiz However, young adults don't decide to change their diets only out of concern for their health.

1 ⑤ **2** Many teens choose vegetarian eating to protest the poor conditions of the animals raised for food.

3 (1) Health (2) Animals (3) Environment

해석

채식은 점점 더 많은 젊은 성인들이 고기와 생선을 먹는 것에 반대하면서 더 인기를 얻고 있다. 미국 영양학 협회에 따르면, 계획된 채식주의 식단은 건강에 좋고 영양가가 높다. 그것들은 또한 특정 질병을 예방하고 치료하는 데 건강상의 이점을 제공한다. 하지만, 젊은 성인들은 그들의 건강에 대한 염려 때문만으로 식단을 바꾸기로 결정하는 것은 아니다. 어떤 이들은 동물의 권리에 대한 관심 때문에 그 선택을 한다. 많은 통계는 식용으로 길러지는 대부분의 동물들이 작은 우리에 갇혀 있다는 것을 보여준다. 그래서, 많은 십 대들은 그러한 조건에 저항하기 위해 고기를 포기한다. 다른 사람들은 환경을 지지하기 위해 채식주의가 된다. 고기 생산은 많은 양의 물, 땅, 곡물과 에너지를 사용한다. 그것은 또한 오염을 일으키는 가축의 배설물 문제를 만들어 낸다. 이러한 경향은 오늘날 젊은이들이 동물의 권리와 환경 문제를 더 인식하고 그것에 더 민감하다는 것을 보여준다.

해설

p.18

많은 젊은이들이 채식을 선택하는 이유는 단지 건강상의 염려 때문이 아니라 동물의 권리나 환경에 대한 인식 때문이라는 내용의 글이므로, 글의 주제로 가장 적절한 것은 ① '젊은 사람들이 채식을 택하는 이유'이다.

② 십 대들이 건강에 좋은 식습관을 기르는 방법
③ 암의 위험을 낮추는 데 도움을 주는 채소
④ 균형잡힌 식단을 유지하는 것의 중요성
⑤ 식물 기반 식단의 단점

p.19

1 These trends 앞에는 젊은이들이 동물 권리와 환경 보호를 위해 채식을 선택한다는 내용이 제시되었고, 뒤에서 이는 요즘 젊은이들이 그러한 문제들을 더 인식하고 그것에 더 민감하다는 것을 보여준다고 언급되어 있으므로, 밑줄 친 These trends가 의미하는 것으로 ⑤가 가장 적절하다.

2 많은 통계가 식용으로 길러지는 대부분의 동물들이 작은 우리에 갇혀 있다는 것을 보여주며, 그러한 열악한 환경에 저항하기 위해 많은 십 대들이 채식을 선택한다는 내용이므로, support(지지하다)를 protest(저항하다)로 바꾸어야 한다.

 많은 십 대들은 식용으로 길러지는 동물들의 열악한 환경을 지지하기(→ 저항하기) 위해 채식을 선택한다.

3 계획된 채식주의 식단이 제공하는 다양한 건강상의 이점 때문만이 아니라 동물들이나 환경 문제를 생각하면서 젊은이들이 채식을 선택한다는 내용의 글이므로, 이를 바탕으로 포스터를 완성하면 빈칸에는 'Health(건강)', 'Animals(동물)', 'Environment(환경)'가 들어가는 것이 적절하다.

해석 채식주의자가 됩시다!

건강을 유지하세요

동물과 환경을 보호하세요

신선한 채소로 건강한 삶을 사세요

구문 설명

- They also provide health benefits in **preventing** and **treating** certain diseases.

  preventing과 treating은 전치사 in의 목적어로 쓰인 동명사로 and로 병렬 연결되었다.

- Many statistics show [that **the majority of the animals** {raised for food} **are kept** in small cages].

  [ ]는 명사절로 show의 목적어이다. 명사절의 주어는 the majority of the animals이며 동사는 are kept이다. { }는 the animals를 수식하는 과거분사구로 대부분의 동물들이 '길러진다'는 수동의 의미를 나타낸다.

Reading Skill

모범 답안

주제문	젊은이들은 단순히 건강을 신경 쓰기 때문에 식단을 바꾸는 것이 아니다.
근거문	• 식용으로 길러지는 동물들의 열악한 환경과 그들의 권리를 생각한다. • 고기를 생산하며 사용되는 수많은 양의 자원과 발생하는 오염을 고려한다.

직독직해 Skill

- Vegetarian eating (S) is becoming (V) / more popular / as more and more young adults say no / to eating meat and fish.

  채식은 ~이 되고 있다 / 더 인기 있는 / 점점 더 많은 젊은 성인들이 반대함에 따라 / 고기와 생선을 먹는 것에

Unit 02 제목 파악하기

READING 04 정답 ② pp.20~21

Mini Quiz star(s)

1 ④　**2** gravity

3 (1) shrink　(2) heat　(3) fusion　(4) shines　(5) returns

해석

별들은 가스와 먼지의 구름으로 시작한다. 수백만 년 후에, 중력이 가스와 먼지에 함께 힘을 가하기 때문에 이 구름들은 수축하기 시작한다. 그것이 압축되면서, 구름은 젊은 별을 형성하기 위해 가열된다. 만약 이것이 화씨 2,700만 도에 도달한다면, 핵융합을 시작할 만큼 충분히 뜨겁다. 이 반응은 새로운 별이 형성되기 위해 필요하다. 그 에너지는 별이 그것의 모양을 유지하고 빛날 수 있게 한다. 연료가 다 떨어지고 별이 죽을 때 무엇이 일어나는가? 그것은 처음에 얼마나 많은 먼지가 모였는가에 달려 있다. 예를 들어, 태양의 절반 이하의 질량을 가진 별들은 매우 천천히 사라진다. 그러나 대부분의 별들은 그들의 연료를 다 써버리고 일련의 단계를 거쳐 마침내 가스와 먼지의 구름으로 돌아간다.

해설

p.20

별들이 가스와 먼지의 구름으로 시작하여 별로서 빛나고 마침내 연료를 소진하고 다시 가스와 먼지의 구름으로 돌아가는 별의 일생에 대한 글로, 글의 제목으로 가장 적절한 것은 ② '별의 생명주기: 그것의 시작과 끝'이다.

① 별: 하늘에 빛나는 보석들

③ 밤이 더 어두울수록, 별은 더 밝다

④ 발을 내려다보지 말고 별을 올려다보라

⑤ 별의 성장 뒤의 마법 같은 힘

p.21

1 글에 태양의 질량이 정확히 얼마인지는 제시되지 않았으므로 답할 수 없는 질문은 ④ '태양의 질량은 얼마인가?'이다.

① 왜 가스와 먼지의 구름이 수축하기 시작하는가?

② 핵융합이 일어나기 위해 무엇이 필요한가?

③ 무엇이 별을 계속 빛나게 하는가?

⑤ 별은 언제 가스와 먼지의 구름으로 돌아가는가?

2 '물체를 지구의 중심을 향해 끌어당기는 힘'은 gravity(중력)이다.

3 **해석**

	별의 일생
별이 되기 전	• 가스와 먼지의 구름이 있다. • 그것들은 중력으로 인해 수축되기 시작하고, 이것은 열을 만들어낸다.
새로운 별	핵융합 후에, 새로운 별이 밝게 빛난다.
연료를 다 쓴 후	일련의 과정 후에 그것은 가스와 먼지의 구름으로 되돌아간다.

- **The energy enables a star to keep** its shape and **shine.**
  「enable+목적어+to부정사」는 '~가 …하는 것을 가능하게 하다'의 의미이다.

- **It depends on [how much dust gathered in the first place].**
  [ ]는 depends on의 목적어 역할을 하는 간접의문문으로, '얼마나 많은 ~이 …하는지'의 의미이다.

Reading Skill

모범 답안

주제	별의 생성부터 최후에 이르는 과정
세부 내용	· 별이 만들어지기 이전 초기의 상태 · 새로운 별이 탄생하기 위한 조건 · 별이 연료를 다 소진하고 겪는 소멸의 과정

직독직해 Skill

- If this reaches / 27 million degrees Fahrenheit, / it (S) is (V) hot enough / to start nuclear fusion.
  만약 이것이 도달한다면 / 화씨 2,700만 도에 / 그것은 충분히 뜨겁다 / 핵융합을 시작하기에

READING 05 · 정답 ② pp.22~23

Mini Quiz How shadows are used, The position of the light source

1 ⑤ 2 attention
3 (1) bright (2) atmosphere (3) comedies (4) contrast (5) emphasize (6) tension (7) horror (8) dark

해석

영화에서 조명은 우리가 무엇이 일어나고 있는지를 보게 해주는 것 이상의 역할을 한다. 밝게 비춰지는 대상은 자연스럽게 사람들의 관심을 끈다. 반면, 어둑하게 비춰지는 대상은 사람들의 호기심과 두려움을 유발할 수 있다. 그림자가 어떻게 사용되는지는 또한 조명의 중요한 한 부분이다. 그림자를 최소화하기 위해 밝은 빛이 사용되면 그것은 밝고 쾌활한 분위기를 만들어낸다. 이 효과는 코미디와 액션 영화에 주로 사용된다. 빛은 또한 밝은 장면과 어두운 장면 사이의 강한 대비를 위해 어두운 그림자를 만들 수도 있다. 이것은 피사체를 강조하고 긴장감을 조성한다. 그래서 공포 영화나 어두운 분위기의 영화에 사용된다. 광원의 위치는 또한 다양한 극적 효과를 만들어낼 수 있다. 예를 들어, 대상을 아래로 직접 비추는 빛은 신성함과 신비감을 만들어낸다. 이러한 조명 기술과 효과를 이해하는 것은 영화를 보는 것을 훨씬 더 흥미롭게 만든다.

해설

p.22

조명이 영화에서 만들어내는 효과와 역할에 대해 이야기하는 글이므로, 글의 제목으로 가장 적절한 것은 ② '영화에서의 조명: 그것의 역할과 효과'이다.
① 빛: 대상을 보여주는 가장 좋은 방법
③ 성공적인 영화는 창의성에서 나온다
④ 영화에 숨겨진 메시지를 찾는 방법
⑤ 조명이 밝을수록, 영화는 더 좋다

p.23

1 대상을 아래로 직접 비추는 빛은 신성함과 신비감을 느끼게 한다고 했으므로 글에서 언급된 것은 ⑤이다.

2 밝은 조명이 대상을 비출 때 사람들의 관심을 끈다고 했으므로 빈칸에는 'attention(관심, 주의, 이목)'이 들어가는 것이 적절하다.
해석 밝은 조명이 대상을 비출 때, 사람들은 자연스럽게 그것에 주의를 기울인다.

3 **해석**

	밝은/적은 그림자	어두운 그림자
무엇을 사용하는가?	밝은 조명	강한 대비
효과	밝고 쾌활한 분위기를 만들어 냄	피사체를 강조하고 긴장감을 조성함
장르	코미디와 액션 영화	공포 영화나 어두운 분위기의 영화

구문 설명

- **[How shadows are used]** is also an important part of lighting.
  [ ]는 문장의 주어로 쓰인 간접의문문이며 are used는 수동태(be동사+p.p.)이다.

- **For example, a light** [shining directly down on the subject] creates a feeling of holiness and mystery.
  문장의 주어는 a light이며 [ ]는 a light를 수식하는 현재분사구이다.

모범 답안

주제문	<u>조명</u>은 영화에서 대상을 <u>비추는</u> 것 이상의 것을 한다.
근거문	• 조명을 밝게 또는 <u>어둡게</u> 비춤에 따라 사람들의 <u>관심</u>을 끌거나 호기심과 두려움을 유발한다. • 어떻게 <u>그림자</u>를 활용하는지는 조명의 쓰임에서 중요하다. • 광원의 <u>위치</u>는 다양한 극적인 <u>효과</u>를 만들어낸다.

직독직해 Skill

• The position of the light source (S) / can produce (V) / various dramatic effects / as well.
광원의 위치는 / 만들어낼 수 있다 / 다양한 극적인 효과를 / 또한

READING 06 ▸ 정답 ③　　　pp.24~25

Mini Quiz ~ for each household. / All the things ~

1 ②, ④　2 (1) T (2) F
3 (1) Spend (2) Buy (3) Use (4) waste

해석

여러분이 무언가를 사고 결국은 한 번도 사용하지 않았던 때에 대해 잠시 생각해 보라. 결국에는 여러분이 한 번도 입지 않은 옷 한 점? 한 번도 읽지 않은 책 한 권? 심지어 상자에서 꺼내 본 적도 없는 어떤 전자기기? 호주인들만 보아도 사용하지 않는 물건에 매년 평균 108억 호주 달러(약 99억 9천 미국 달러)를 쓰는 것으로 추산된다. 그것은 대학과 도로에 사용하는 정부 지출 총액을 넘어서는 금액이다. 그 금액은 가구당 평균 1,250 호주 달러(약 1,156 미국 달러)이다. 우리가 구입하고 전혀 사용하지 않는 모든 물건은 낭비인데, 돈 낭비, 시간 낭비, 그리고 순전히 쓸모없는 물건이라는 의미에서 낭비이다. 작가 Clive Hamilton이 말하는 것처럼 '우리가 사는 물건에서 우리가 사용하는 것을 뺀 것은 낭비이다.'

해설

p.24

사 놓고 사용하지 않는 물건을 구입하는 데 많은 돈을 쓰는 것은 돈과 시간의 낭비라는 내용의 글이다. 따라서 글의 제목으로 가장 적절한 것은 ③ '사는 것은 그것을 사용하지 않으면 낭비이다'이다.
① 지출이 경제를 가능하게 한다
② 자금 관리: 해야 할 것과 하지 말아야 할 것
④ 지나친 쇼핑: 외로움의 신호
⑤ 쓰레기의 3R: 줄이라, 재사용하라, 그리고 재활용하라

---

p.25

1 글에서 무언가를 사고 한 번도 사용하지 않은 때에 대한 예시로 언급된 것은 clothing, book, electronic equipment로, 식료품과 가방은 언급되지 않았다.

2 (1) 사용하지 않는 물건에 호주인들만 해도 매년 108억 호주 달러를 쓴다고 글에 제시되어 있으므로, 글의 내용과 일치한다.
(2) 호주인들이 매년 사용하지 않는 물건에 쓰는 돈이 대학과 도로에 사용하는 정부 지출 총액을 넘어서는 금액이라고 글에 제시되어 있으므로, 글의 내용과 일치하지 않는다.
　해석 (1) 매년 호주인들은 한 번도 쓰지 않는 상품에 평균 100억 호주 달러 이상을 쓴다.
(2) 사용하지 않는 물건에 대한 호주인들의 연간 지출은 대학과 도로에 대한 총 정부 지출보다 적다.

3 　해석 당신의 돈을 현명하게 사용하는 방법
⑴ 정말로 필요로 하는 것을 <u>사라</u>.
⑵ 생활에서 그것을 <u>사용하라</u>.
그것은 쉽고 간단하다.
절대로 당신의 돈이나 시간을 <u>낭비하지</u> 마라.

구문 설명

• Some piece of electronic equipment [**that** never even came out of the box]?
that은 주격 관계대명사로, [　]가 선행사인 Some piece of electronic equipment를 수식한다.

• All the things [we buy and then never use] are waste — a waste of money, a waste of time, and waste in the sense of pure rubbish.
[　]는 All the things를 수식하며, we 앞에는 목적격 관계대명사 that이 생략되어 있다.

모범 답안

도입	우리는 <u>구매</u>하고 한 번도 <u>사용</u>하지 않는 경우가 많음
예시 품목	옷, 책, 전자기기
주제	우리가 구매 후 <u>사용</u>하지 않는 <u>물건</u>들은 시간과 돈의 낭비임

직독직해 Skill

• Think (V), / for a moment, / about when you bought something / and you never ended up using it.
생각해 보라 / 잠시 / 네가 무언가를 샀던 때에 대해 / 그리고 네가 한 번도 그것을 사용하지 않은

READING 07 · 정답 ③

Mini Quiz As the mother of a girl who needs a lot of nutrients, I strongly oppose the suggestion.

1 ①　**2** have lots of nutrients such as protein

3 (1) eggs (2) allergic (3) diet

해석

Alcanse 중학교 교장 선생님께,

제 이름은 Cathy Brown입니다. 제 딸 Amy는 당신의 학교 학생입니다. 저는 그녀의 담임 선생님으로부터 받은 메시지에 대한 답변으로 이 이메일을 쓰고 있습니다. 그는 학교가 달걀로 만든 음식을 제공하는 것을 중단할 것을 제안하고 있습니다. 많은 영양소를 필요로 하는 소녀의 어머니로서, 저는 그 제안에 강력히 반대합니다. 저는 몇몇 학생들이 달걀에 알레르기가 있다는 것을 이해합니다. 하지만, 그의 제안은 다른 학생들에게 불공평합니다. 우리 아이들은 균형 잡힌 식사가 필요합니다. 달걀은 단백질과 같은 많은 영양소를 가지고 있고 매우 많은 종류의 음식에 널리 사용됩니다. 달걀을 메뉴에서 제외하는 것은 우리 아이들의 음식 선택을 제한하고 그들의 성장을 방해할 것입니다. 대신에, 학교는 달걀을 포함할지도 모르는 음식에 명확하게 라벨을 붙일 수 있습니다. 학생들이 계속해서 다양한 음식을 선택하는 것이 중요합니다.

Cathy Brown 드림

해설

p.26

달걀이 들어간 음식을 제공하는 것을 중단하고자 하는 제안에 대한 답변으로 이를 반대한다는 내용의 글이므로, 글의 목적으로 가장 적절한 것은 ③이다.

p.27

1 글쓴이는 글의 후반부에 학교가 달걀을 포함할지도 모르는 음식에 명확하게 라벨을 붙일 수 있다고 했으므로 글쓴이가 제안한 방법은 ①이다.

2 글에 제시된 달걀이 많은 영양소를 가지고 있다는 내용을 그대로 활용하면 된다.

　해석 Q: 왜 달걀은 우리 건강에 좋은가?

　A: 그것들은 단백질과 같은 많은 영양소를 가지고 있다.

3 **해석** "안녕하세요, 학부모님. 저는 Alcanse 중학교의 Smith입니다. 저는 우리 학교에서 달걀이 들어간 음식을 제공하지 말아야 한다고 제안하고 싶었습니다. 여러분도 알다시피, 우리 학생들 중 몇몇은 그것들에 알레르기가 있습니다. 우리가 이 학생들이 안전하도록 지키고 그들에게 달걀이 없는 균형 잡힌 식단을 제공하는 것이 중요합니다. 우려되는 점이나 질문이 있으시면 언제든지 연락

주세요. 좋은 하루 보내세요."

구문 설명

- I'm writing this email in response to the message [I received from her homeroom teacher].

[ ]는 선행사 the message를 수식하는 관계절로, I 앞에 목적격 관계대명사가 생략되어 있다.

- Eggs **have** lots of nutrients (**such as** protein) and **are** widely **used** in so many types of food.

문장의 동사 have와 are used가 병렬구조로 이어져 있으며, are used는 수동태(be동사+p.p.)이다. ( )는 수식어구로, such as는 '~와 같은'의 뜻이다.

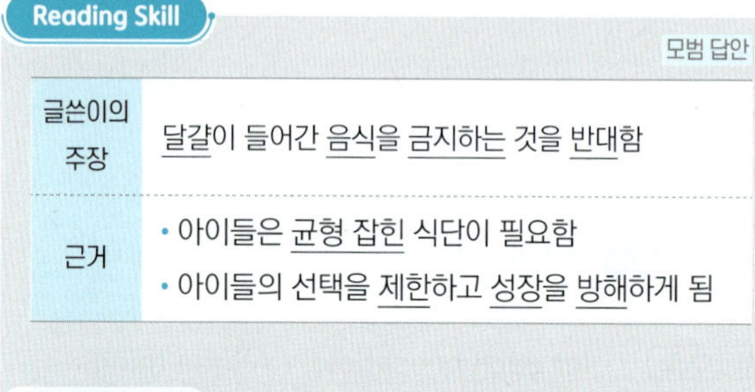

Reading Skill　　모범 답안

글쓴이의 주장	달걀이 들어간 음식을 금지하는 것을 반대함
근거	• 아이들은 균형 잡힌 식단이 필요함 • 아이들의 선택을 제한하고 성장을 방해하게 됨

직독직해 Skill

- He (S) is suggesting (V) / that the school stop serving / food made with eggs.

그는 제안하고 있다 / 학교가 제공하는 것을 멈춰야 한다고 / 달걀로 만들어진 음식을

READING 08 · 정답 ⑤

Mini Quiz body language[nonverbal messages]

1 ④　**2** Nonverbal

3 (1) relationship (2) friendly[welcoming] (3) significant

해석

일부 전문가들은 우리가 몸을 움직임으로써 의사소통을 한다고 말한다. 이것은 우리가 '몸짓 언어'를 사용한다는 것을 의미한다. 교사인 여러분이 여러분의 학생들에게 보내는 비언어적인 메시지에 주목해보자. 그것은 학생들과 여러분의 관계에 상당한 차이를 가져올 수 있다. 일반적으로 대부분의 학생들은 흔히 자신의 선생님의 몸짓 언어를 매우 인식한다. 예를 들어, 학생들이 처음 교실에 들어가면 그들은 자신의 선생님을 찾는다. 그 선생님이 친근한 인사를 하고 환영의 미소를 짓는다고 상상해보라. 그것은 학생에게 분명 격려가 되고 힘을 줄 것이다. 선생님은 학

생들에게 그 또는 그녀가 그들을 보게 되어 기쁘다는 것을 알리기 위해 미소를 짓는다. 그것은 많은 시간이나 노력을 요구하지 않는다. 하지만 그것은 수업 시작과 동시에 교실 분위기에 상당한 차이를 가져올 수 있다. 선생님은 그들이 학생들과 함께 있을 때, 그들의 몸짓 언어가 항상 작동하고 있다는 것을 기억해야 한다.

해설

p.28

교사가 학생에게 보내는 비언어적 메시지에 주목하는 것이 학생과의 관계에 차이를 가져올 수 있다고 설명하면서 그 예로 학생들에게 짓는 미소가 학생들에게 격려와 힘을 줄 수 있다고 했으므로, 필자가 주장하는 바로 가장 적절한 것은 ⑤이다.

p.29

1 교사가 수업에서 학생에게 보내는 비언어적 메시지에 주목하는 것이 중요하며 그것은 학생과의 관계에서 상당한 차이를 가져올 수 있다는 내용의 글이므로, 글의 제목으로 가장 적절한 것은 ④ '몸짓 언어: 수업에서 중요한 것'이다.
① 여러분의 학생들에게 솔직해라
② 교사 지침서: 해야 할 것과 하지 말아야 할 것
③ 친절: 가장 좋은 교수 방법
⑤ 더 나은 의사소통을 위해 우리가 필요한 것

2 비언어적 의사소통에 대한 설명이므로 빈칸에 들어갈 말은 Nonverbal(비언어적인)이다.
해석 비언어적인 의사소통은 말을 사용하지 않고 정보를 보내거나 받는 행동이다. 그것은 표정과 제스처를 사용하는 것을 포함한다.

3 **해석** 선생님들은 학생과의 좋은 관계를 형성하기 위해 그들의 몸짓 언어를 사용할 수 있다. 예를 들어, 만약 그들이 학생들에게 미소 짓는 것처럼 친근한[따스한] 제스처를 보여준다면, 그것은 그들의 수업에서 상당한 차이를 만들어낼 것이다.

구문 설명

- **Let's pay** attention to the nonverbal messages [you teachers send to your students].
「Let's+동사원형」은 '~하자'는 의미의 청유문이다. [ ]는 the nonverbal messages를 수식하는 관계절로, you 앞에 목적격 관계대명사 that[which]이 생략되어 있다.

- The teacher smiles at students to **let them know** [that he or she is glad to see them].
「let+목적어+동사원형」은 '~가 …하게 하다'라는 뜻이며, [ ]는 know의 목적어 역할을 하는 명사절이다.

모범 답안

주제	학생과의 관계에서 비언어적 표현의 중요성
근거	• 학생들은 교사의 몸짓 언어를 매우 인식하고 있음 • 학생들에게 미소 짓는 것이 교실 분위기에 큰 차이를 가져올 수 있음

직독직해 Skill

- In general, / most students (S) are (V) often very aware of / their teacher's body language.
일반적으로 / 대부분의 학생들은 흔히 매우 인식한다 / 그들의 선생님의 몸짓 언어를

Unit 04 요지 파악하기

READING 09 정답 ④ pp.30~31

Mini Quiz We must take immediate action to protect the Great Barrier Reef and its marine life.

1 ⑤ **2** (1) T (2) F
3 (1) threats (2) protect (3) efforts

해석

호주의 Great Barrier Reef는 세계에서 가장 큰 산호초 시스템 중 하나이다. 이곳은 1,500종이 넘는 다양한 종류의 물고기를 포함한 다양한 해양 종들의 서식지다. 그러나, 최근 몇 년 동안, 그것은 수많은 환경 문제에 직면해 왔다. 지구 온난화로 인해 해양 온도가 상승하여 산호 탈색을 초래했다. 이것은 산호가 색깔을 잃게 하고 심지어 죽게 만든다. 게다가, 농업에 사용되는 물과 산업 폐기물로 인한 수질 오염은 수질을 악화시킨다. 우리는 Great Barrier Reef와 그곳의 해양 생물을 보호하기 위해 즉각적인 조치를 취해야 한다. 이를 위해서는 온실가스 배출량을 줄이는 것과 수질을 개선하는 것과 같은 복합적인 노력이 필요하다. Great Barrier Reef와 그것을 집이라고 부르는(그곳에 서식하는) 수백만 종의 미래가 그것에 달려 있다. 조치가 없다면, 이 놀라운 생태계의 미래는 불확실하다.

해설

p.30

Great Barrier Reef가 지구 온난화를 포함한 환경 문제로 인해 위협받고 있으며 이를 해결하기 위한 노력과 행동이 필요하다는 내용의 글이므로, 글의 요지로 가장 적절한 것은 ④이다.

1 ⓐ~ⓓ는 모두 the Great Barrier Reef를 가리키며 ⓔ는 바로 앞 문장의 내용을 가리킨다.

2 (1) Great Barrier Reef는 다양한 해양 종들의 서식지라고 설명하므로 글의 내용과 일치한다.
(2) 지구 온난화로 인해 해양 온도가 올라갔다고 했으므로 글의 내용과 일치하지 않는다.
해석 (1) 많은 해양 종이 Great Barrier Reef에 산다.
(2) 최근 몇 년 동안 해양 온도가 내려갔다.

3 **해석** 호주의 Great Barrier Reef는 여러 가지 위협으로 인해 압박을 받고 있다. 그것의 해양 생태계를 보호하기 위해, 노력하고 즉시 조치를 취해야 할 때이다.

구문 설명

- Global warming **has caused** an increase in ocean temperatures, [**resulting** in coral bleaching].
has caused는 현재완료(have/has+과거분사) 형태이며, [ ]는 분사구문으로 '그래서 ~하다'의 의미로 주절에 대한 부수적 내용을 덧붙인다.

- This requires a combination of efforts, **such as** [**reducing** the amount of greenhouse gas emissions] and [**improving** water quality].
such as는 '~와 같은'이라는 뜻으로, 두 개의 동명사구 목적어인 [ ]가 병렬 구조로 이어져 있다.

Reading Skill

모범 답안

현 상황	환경 문제[위협]에 직면한 Great Barrier Reef
원인	• 지구 온난화로 인해 물의 온도 상승 • 농업 용수와 산업 폐기물로 인한 수질 오염
해결 방안	• 온실가스 배출량 줄이기 • 수질 개선하기

직독직해 Skill

- It (S) is (V) home / to various marine species / including over 1,500 different types of fish.
그것은 서식지이다 / 다양한 해양 종들의 / 1,500종이 넘는 다양한 물고기를 포함하여

 READING **10** · 정답 ④

Mini Quiz Trying new things outside of your comfort zone

1 ⑤ **2** Stepping out of your comfort zone means to be comfortable with trying to do new and uncomfortable things.
3 (1) grow (2) aware (3) establish

해석

성공하고 싶다면 불편함을 편안하게 받아들여야 한다. 다시 말해, 당신은 당신의 편안한 영역(안락지대)에서 벗어나야 한다. 당신의 편안한 영역 밖에서 새로운 것들을 시도하는 것은 많은 면에서 당신에게 큰 도움이 될 것이다. 첫째, 당신은 성장할 수 있는 귀중한 기회를 얻을 수 있다. 자신에게 도전하는 것은 새로운 경험과 예상치 못한 변화의 기회를 제공하며, 이는 개인의 성장으로 이어질 수 있다. 게다가, 당신은 자신에 대해 배우게 될 것이다. 당신이 새로운 것들을 시도하면서 자신의 재능, 관심사, 강점과 약점을 발견하게 될 것이다. 마지막으로, 당신은 또한 새로운 관계를 만들 수 있다. 만약 당신이 새로운 것을 시도한다면, 당신은 그렇지 않았으면 결코 만날 기회가 없었을 새로운 사람들을 만날 수 있다. 그것은 당신의 삶을 더 흥미롭게 만들 수 있다. 그리고 당신은 그들로부터 배울 것이다. 생소함은 매우 불편하게 느껴질 것이다. 하지만, 당신은 시야를 넓히고 성공을 이룰 수 있을 것이다.

해설

사람이 성공하기 위해서는 자신이 평소 느끼는 편안한 영역(안락지대)에서 벗어나 새로운 일을 시도해야 한다는 내용의 글이다. 따라서 글의 요지로 가장 적절한 것은 ④이다.

1 안락지대에서 벗어나 불편함을 감수하며 새로운 것에 도전해야 한다는 내용의 글로, 익숙한 것의 필요성에 대한 내용은 제시되어 있지 않으므로 답할 수 없는 질문은 ⑤ '왜 우리는 우리 삶에서 익숙한 것들이 필요한가?'이다.
① 우리는 성공하기 위해 무엇에 편안해져야 하는가?
② 우리의 안락지대에서 벗어나는 것의 이점들은 무엇인가?
③ 언제 우리가 우리 자신에 대해 배울 수 있는가?
④ 우리는 어떻게 그렇지 않았으면 만나지 않았을 새로운 사람들을 만날 수 있는가?

2 글의 내용에 따르면 안락지대 밖으로 넘어가는 것은 새롭고 불편한 것들을 하는 것에 편안해지는 것을 의미하므로 문장 뒷부분의 comfortable을 uncomfortable로 써야 한다.
해석 당신의 안락지대에서 벗어나는 것은 새롭고 편안한(→ 불편한) 것들을 시도하는 것에 편안해지는 것을 의미한다.

3

우리의 안락지대에서 벗어나기	
이점 1	그것은 우리에게 새로운 경험을 제공하고 우리가 더 나은 사람으로 성장하도록 도와줄 수 있다.
이점 2	그것은 우리가 우리를 더 잘 인식하도록 격려할 수 있다.
이점 3	그것은 우리가 새로운 사람들과 새로운 관계를 형성할 수 있도록 도와줄 수 있다.

구문 설명

- **Challenging yourself** provides opportunities for new experiences and unexpected changes, **which** can lead to personal growth.
  동명사구 Challenging yourself가 주어이며, which는 계속적 용법의 주격 관계대명사로 앞 문장 내용 전체를 가리킨다.

- If you try something new, you can meet new people [**who** you otherwise **would** never **have had** the chance to meet].
  관계절 [ ] 안의 who는 목적격 관계대명사로 new people을 가리킨다. 「would+have+과거분사(~했었을 텐데)」는 과거의 가정에 대한 추측을 나타내는 말이다.

Reading Skill

모범 답안

글쓴이의 주장	성공하기 위해서는 불편함을 받아들이는 것이 필요함
근거	안락지대에서 벗어나는 것은 다양한 이점을 제공함
결론	이를 통해 결국 우리의 시야를 넓히고 성공을 이룰 수 있음

직독직해 Skill

- It (S) can make (V) / your life / more exciting.
  그것은 만들 수 있다 / 당신의 삶을 / 더 흥미롭게

Unit 05 요약하기

READING **11** · 정답 ③ pp.34~35

Mini Quiz advertisements

---

1 ② 2 Effective advertisements will show consumers how the products make their lives convenient.
3 (B)

광고가 사람들의 관심을 끄는 것은 중요하다. 그들은 감정적인 차원에서 사람들에게 다가갈 필요가 있다. 즉, 광고는 제품이 어떻게 그들을 도울 수 있는지를 보여줄 필요가 있다. 모든 좋은 제품이나 서비스는 사람들이 그들의 삶을 더 많이 살고, 일하고, 즐기도록 도울 수 있다. 예를 들어, 새로운 스마트폰의 놀라운 기능에 대해서만 이야기하는 광고를 상상해보라. 그 광고는 설명처럼 느껴진다. 유감스럽게도, 그것은 그다지 효과적인 광고는 아닐 것이다. 이제 일상에서 아름다운 사진을 찍거나 새로운 스마트폰으로 영화를 보는 사람들을 보여주는 광고를 상상해보라. 그것은 훨씬 더 기억에 남을 것이고 사람들은 그것에 관심을 가질 것이다. 광고는 기능이 아닌 혜택을 판매한다. 그러므로, 성공적인 광고는 사람들에게 그것의 제품이 어떻게 그들의 삶을 더 풍부하고 편리하게 만들 수 있는지 보여주어야 한다.

➡ 효과적인 광고는 (사람들에게) 제품이 그들의 삶을 어떻게 개선하는지 보여줌으로써 사람들의 감정을 겨냥한다.

p.34
효과적인 광고를 만들기 위해서는 사람들의 감정에 호소하는 것이 중요하며, 광고하는 제품이 어떻게 그들의 삶을 더 좋게 만드는지 사람들에게 보여주어야 한다는 내용이다. 그러므로 빈칸 (A), (B)에 들어갈 말로 가장 적절한 것은 feelings(감정)와 improve(개선하다)이다.

p.35
1 효과적인 광고는 사람들의 감정에 호소하는 것임을 구체적인 예시를 들어 설명하며 그를 통해 사람들의 구매를 이끌어 낼 수 있다는 내용의 글이므로, 글의 주제로 가장 적절한 것은 ② '광고가 소비자들의 마음을 끌 수 있는 방법'이다.
① 새로운 아이템을 생각해 내는 것의 어려움
③ 제품을 판매하는 데 있어서 광고의 역할
④ 사람들이 새로운 제품에 관심을 가지지 않는 이유
⑤ 사람들의 지식이 광고에 미치는 영향

2 글의 내용에 따르면 효과적인 광고는 소비자들에게 어떻게 제품이 그들의 삶을 편리하게 만드는지를 보여주므로 inconvenient(불편한)를 convenient(편리한)로 써야 한다.
 효과적인 광고는 소비자들에게 어떻게 제품이 그들의 삶을 불편하게(→ 편리하게) 만드는지를 보여줄 것이다.

3 글쓴이는 광고하는 제품이 사람들의 삶을 좋게 만들 것이라고 보여주는 것이 중요하다고 말하며, 구체적으로 스마트폰을 광고할 때는 기능만 제시하고 설명하는 것이 아니라 사람들이 그것을 직접 활용하는 모습을 보여주는 것이 더 효과적일 것이라고 했으므로, 글쓴이가 생각하는 좋은 광고는 (B)이다.

- **Every** good product or service can **help people live**, **work**, or **enjoy** their lives more.

  Every는 '모든'이라는 뜻으로 뒤에 단수 명사가 온다. 「help+목적어+동사원형」은 '~가 …하는 것을 돕다'라는 뜻이다.

- Now imagine an advertisement [showing **people** {taking beautiful photos in their daily lives} **or** {watching movies on their new smartphone}].

  [ ]는 an advertisement를 부연 설명하는 현재분사구로 '~를 보여주는'의 의미이다. 두 개의 { }는 people을 수식하는 현재분사구로 or에 의해 병렬 연결되어 있다.

Reading Skill

모범 답안

주제문	사람들에게 제품이 어떻게 그들을 <u>돕는</u>지 <u>감정적인</u> 차원에서 설명하는 것이 중요하다.
예시문	새로운 <u>스마트폰</u>에 대한 두 가지 다른 광고를 <u>상상해</u> 봐라.
주제문	성공적인 광고는 어떻게 사람들의 삶을 더 <u>풍요롭</u>고 편리하게 만드는지를 보여줘야 한다.

직독직해 Skill

- It is (V) important / for advertisements / to grab people's attention (S).

  ~은 중요하다 / 광고가 / 사람들의 관심을 끄는 것은

READING **12** · 정답 ③   pp.36~37

Mini Quiz As AI continues to have an impact on the job market, it is necessary for workers and organizations to adapt to the changes.

1 ②   **2** Impact
3 (1) interact (2) human-centered

해석

인공지능(AI)이 고용 시장을 빠르게 변화시키고 있다. 일부 전문가들은 AI가 많은 단순 업무를 자동화함으로써 특정 산업의 일자리 감소를 초래할 것이라 예측한다. 하지만, 다른 전문가들은 AI가 새로운 일자리 기회를 창출할 것이라고 믿는다. 진실은 아마도 그 사이 어딘가에 있을 것이다. 하지만 AI가 업무의 본질을 바꾸고 있다는 것은 분명하다. 다양한 산업에 종사하는 근로자들은 새로운 기술에 적응하고 새로운 기량을 습득해야 할 것이다. 예를 들어, 고객 서비스에서 AI를 사용하는 것은 근로자들에게 그들의 대인 관계 기술을 향상시키는 것을 요구한다. 그들은 또한 인간 중심적인 기술에 익숙해지고 편안해질 필요가 있다. 게다가, AI는 아마 AI 윤리 책임자와 같은 새로운 직업 범주의 개발로 이어질 것이다. 그들의 임무는 AI 시스템이 책임감 있고 윤리적인 방식으로 사용되도록 하는 것일 것이다. AI가 계속해서 고용 시장에 영향을 미침에 따라, 근로자와 조직이 변화에 적응하는 것이 필요하다.

➡ 고용 시장이 AI에 의해 <u>변화되고</u> 있으므로, 우리는 성공적인 근로자가 되기 위해 우리의 능력을 <u>개발해야</u> 한다.

해설

p.36

인공지능이 업무의 본질을 바꿈에 따라 고용 시장이 변화하고 있기 때문에 사람들이 새로운 기술에 적응하고 새로운 기량을 익혀야 한다는 내용이므로, 빈칸 (A), (B)에 들어갈 말로 가장 적절한 것은 transformed(변화되다)와 develop(개발하다)이다.

p.37

1 인공지능이 고용 시장을 변화시킴에 따라 근로자들이 새로운 기술에 적응하고 새로운 능력을 익혀야 한다는 내용이므로, 답할 수 있는 질문은 ② 'AI가 근로자들에게 무엇을 하기를 요구하는가?'이다.
① 누가 AI를 처음으로 발명했는가?
③ AI가 절대 바뀌지 않을 직업은 무엇인가?
④ AI 기술을 어디서 배울 수 있는가?
⑤ 언제 AI가 고용 시장에 등장했는가?

2 인공지능으로 인해 업무의 본질이 바뀌고 일자리가 감소하거나 창출될 수도 있으니 사람들은 이러한 변화에 대비해야 한다는 내용의 글이므로, 빈칸에 들어갈 적절한 말은 Impact(영향)이다.
해석 인공지능: 고용 시장에 미치는 그것의 <u>영향</u>

3 **해석** **직책**: 고객 서비스 관리자
우리는 새로운 고객 서비스 관리자들을 찾고 있습니다. 합격자들은 우리 회사에서 고객들과 <u>상호작용하고</u> 그들의 문의사항에 대한 해결책을 제공하는 것과 같은 다양한 업무를 하게 될 것입니다.
책무: 전화, 이메일 및 채팅을 통해 고객의 질문에 응답합니다.
자격 요건: • <u>인간 중심적인</u> 기술에 익숙함
           • 탁월한 구두 및 서면 의사소통 기술

구문 설명

- But **it** is clear [**that** AI is changing the nature of work].

  it은 가주어이며 that이 이끄는 절 [ ]가 문장의 진주어이다.

- Their job would be to **make sure** [that AI systems **are used** in a responsible and ethical manner].

  make sure는 '~을 확실하게 하다'는 뜻으로 [ ]가 목적어로 쓰였다. are used는 수동태(be동사+과거분사)로 '사용된다'는 수동의 의미를 나타낸다.

모범 답안

주제	인공지능이 고용 시장에 미치는 영향
세부 내용	다양한 분야에서 사람들에게 새로운 기술과 능력을 갖추도록 요구함

직독직해 Skill

· Workers (S) / in various industries / will need (V) to adapt / to new technologies / and acquire new skills.
근로자들은 / 다양한 분야의 산업의 / 적응할 필요가 있을 것이다 / 새로운 기술에 / 그리고 새로운 기량을 습득할

READING **13** · 정답 ② pp.38~39

(Mini Quiz) In half of the rooms, a cell phone was placed on a nearby table; in the other half, no phone was present.

1 ④ **2** present
3 (1) strangers (2) chat (3) worse (4) empathy (5) hurt

해석

한 연구에서, 연구자들은 서로 모르는 사람끼리 짝을 이룬 사람들에게 한 방에 앉아서 이야기를 나누도록 요청했다. 절반의 방에는 근처의 탁자 위에 휴대전화가 놓여 있었고, 나머지 절반의 방에는 휴대전화가 없었다. 대화가 끝나고 나서, 연구자들은 참가자들에게 서로에 대해 어떻게 생각하는지 물었다. 방에 휴대전화가 있을 때 참가자들은 휴대전화가 없는 방에서 대화한 참가자들보다 그들의 관계의 질이 더 나빴다고 보고했다. 휴대전화가 있는 방에서 대화한 쌍들은 자신의 상대가 공감을 덜 보였다고 생각했다. 여러분이 친구와 점심을 먹으려고 자리에 앉아서 휴대전화를 탁자 위에 놓는다고 상상해 보라. 메시지를 확인하려고 휴대전화를 집어 들지 않기 때문에 자기 자신이 잘하고 있다고 느낄지 모른다. 그러나 여러분이 확인하지 않은 메시지도 여전히 맞은편에 앉아 있는 사람과의 관계를 해치고 있다.
➡ 휴대전화의 존재는 휴대전화가 무시되고 있을 때조차 대화에 참여하는 사람들의 관계를 약화시킨다.

해설

p.38
휴대전화가 있는 방에서 대화를 한 참가자들이 휴대전화가 없는 방에서 대화를 한 참가자들보다 관계의 질이 더 나빴다고 답한 실험 결과를 통해, 휴대전화의 존재만으로도 마주앉은 사람과의 관계를 해치고 있다는 것을 설명하는 글이다. 따라서 빈칸 (A), (B)에 들어갈 말로 가장 적절한 것은 weakens(약화시키다)와 ignored(무시되다)이다.

p.39
1 휴대전화의 존재만으로도 마주앉은 사람과의 관계를 해치고 있다는 내용의 글이므로, 글의 제목으로 가장 적절한 것은 ④ '휴대전화: 대화에 미치는 그것의 부정적인 영향'이다.
① 공감: 더 나은 대화를 만드는 것
② 놀라운 의사소통 도구로서의 휴대전화
③ 지나친 휴대전화 사용은 다른 사람들의 감정을 상하게 한다
⑤ 휴대전화가 다른 사람들과의 관계에 정말로 나쁜가?

2 present는 '선물, 현재의, 참석한' 등의 뜻을 가진다.
(해석) · 내가 너에게 특별한 선물을 줄게!
· 다른 것들을 시도하는 것은 현재 상황에서 쉽지 않다.
· 그 회의에는 300명의 사람들이 참석해 있었다.

3 (해석)

연구	연구자들은 모르는 사람끼리 짝이 된 쌍들에게 한 방에 앉아서 휴대전화가 있거나 없이 대화하도록 요청했다.
결과	참가자들은 휴대전화가 있었을 때 관계의 질이 더 나빴으며 상대로부터 더 적은 공감을 받았다고 보고했다.
예시	친구와의 점심 식사 동안에 탁자 위에 둔 전화는 관계를 해칠 수 있다.

구문 설명

· When a cell phone was present in the room, the participants reported [the quality of their relationship was worse than **those who** talked in a cell phone-free room].
[ ]는 reported의 목적어로 쓰인 명사절로 앞에 접속사 that이 생략되어 있다. those who는 '~한 사람들'이라는 뜻이다.

· The pairs [**who** talked in the rooms with cell phones] thought {their partners showed less empathy}.
who는 주격 관계대명사로 [ ]가 The pairs를 수식하며, { }는 thought의 목적어로 쓰인 명사절로 앞에 접속사 that이 생략되었다.

Reading Skill

모범 답안

주제	휴대전화의 존재 유무가 관계의 질에 영향을 미침
근거	실험 결과: 휴대전화의 존재 유무에 따라 참가자들이 서로에 대해 느끼는[생각하는] 점이 달라짐

직독직해 Skill

· After the conversations ended, / the researchers (S) asked (V) the participants / what they thought of each other.
대화가 끝난 후에 / 연구자들은 참가자들에게 물어봤다 / 그들이 서로에 대해 어떻게 생각하는지를

정보 파악하기

Chapter 02

Reading Key 필요한 정보 중심으로 빠르게 독해하기 pp.42~43

정답

A 체스, (경기) 장소, 연령 부문, 상

B James Van Der Zee, 둘째, 사진사, 스튜디오, 국제적, 인정

해석

A Waverly 고등학교 친선 체스 토너먼트
3월 23일 토요일 오전 10시
- 장소: Waverly 고등학교 강당
- 참가 신청 마감: 3월 22일 오후 4시
- 연령 부문: 7~12세, 13~15세, 16~18세
- 상: 각 부문별 금상, 은상, 동상
대회에 관심이 있다면, www.waverly.org에서 온라인으로 참가 신청하세요.

B James Van Der Zee는 1886년 6월 29일에 Massachusetts주 Lenox에서 태어났다. 여섯 명의 아이들 중 둘째였던 James는 창의적인 분위기의 집안에서 성장했다. 1907년에, 그는 Virginia주 Phoetus로 이사했고, 그곳의 Chamberlin 호텔 식당에서 일했다. 이 시기에 그는 또한 시간제 사진사로 일했다. 그는 1916년에 자신의 스튜디오를 열었다. 1969년에, 전시회 'Harlem On My Mind'로 그는 국제적인 인정을 받았다. 그는 1983년에 사망하였다.

Unit 06 안내문·도표 파악하기

READING **14** · 정답 ⑤ pp.44~45

Mini Quiz 모범 답안 작가와 만나는 행사 / 작가와의 만남

1 ④ **2** (1) T (2) F (3) T
3 (1) author (2) City Library (3) register (4) parent
(5) acting performance

해석

작가와의 하루
아동 도서상을 수상한 작가, Amelia Tylor가 여러분을 그녀의 새 책,

'Tommy의 해저 모험'으로 초대합니다. 아이들을 위한 특별한 이야기 시간을 그녀와 함께하세요!
- 언제: 5월 18일 토요일, 오전 11시 ~ 오후 1시
- 어디서: 시립 도서관의 넬슨 홀
- 누구를 위한: 9살부터 11살까지의 아이들
- 행사는 (아래 활동을) 포함합니다
  - 작가가 읽어주는 시간 ('Tommy의 해저 모험' 챕터 1)
  - 책의 장면을 연기하는 공연
  - 작가의 책 서명
※ 행사에 참석하기 위해 www.citylibrary.org/events에서 등록해주세요.
※ 아이들은 부모/부모들 또는 보호자와 함께해야 합니다.
※ 시간에 늦지 않게 와주세요. 작가의 책 읽기 시간이 시작한 후에는 그 시간이 끝날 때까지 홀에 들어갈 수 없습니다.
※ 그 시간 후 새 책을 포함한 작가의 모든 책을 30% 할인된 가격으로 구입할 수 있습니다.

해설

p.44

안내문에서 새 책을 포함하여 모든 책을 30% 할인된 가격으로 구입할 수 있다고 했으므로 ⑤가 안내문의 내용과 일치하지 않는다.

p.45

1 안내문에서 ① 소개할 책 제목(*Tommy's Adventure Under the Sea*), ② 행사 장소(Neilson Hall in the City Library), ③ 참여 등록 방법(register at www.citylibrary.org/events), ⑤ 보호자 동반 여부(Children should come with a parent/parents or guardian)는 언급되었지만, ④ '기념품 추첨 방법'은 언급되지 않았다.

2 (1) 아동도서상을 수상한 작가라는 언급이 있으므로 글의 내용과 일치한다.
(2) 행사에 참여하기 위해 사이트에서 등록하라고 했으므로 글의 내용과 일치하지 않는다.
(3) 작가의 책 읽기 시간이 시작한 후에는 그 시간이 끝날 때까지 홀에 들어가지 못하니 시간에 늦지 않게 와 달라는 내용이 있으므로 글의 내용과 일치한다.
해석 (1) Amelia Tylor는 그녀의 책으로 전에 상을 받았다.
(2) 예약 없이 행사를 방문할 수 있다.
(3) 만약 작가가 책 읽기를 시작한 후에 도착하면 그것이 끝날 때까지 홀에 들어갈 수 없다.

3 **해석** 'Tommy의 장난감 세계로의 모험'을 읽은 후, Amelia Tylor는 내가 가장 좋아하는 작가가 되었다. 운 좋게도, 시립 도서관이 그녀와 함께하는 작가의 독서 행사를 열었다. 나는 아버지께 도서관 사이트에서 우리를 등록해서 나를 그곳에 데려가 달라고 부탁드렸는데, 모든 아이가 부모나 보호자와 함께 와야 했기 때문이다. 그 행사에서, 나는 특히 Tommy가 돌고래와 수영하는 장면을

연기하는 <u>공연</u>을 즐겼다. 나는 정말 좋은 시간을 보냈다.

· Please register at www.citylibrary.org/events **to attend** the event.
to attend는 〈목적〉을 나타내는 부사적 용법의 to부정사로 '참석하기 위해서'의 의미를 나타낸다.

Reading Skill

모범 답안

일시	<u>5월 18일 토요일</u>
참가 대상	<u>9살</u>에서 <u>11살</u>까지의 아이들
포함된 활동	작가가 <u>책 읽어주기</u>, 책 장면으로 <u>연극하기</u>, 작가의 책 <u>서명</u>

직독직해 Skill

· Amelia Tylor (S), / the award-winning author of children's books, / invites (V) you / to her new book, / *Tommy's Adventure Under the Sea.*
Amelia Tylor가 / 아동 도서로 상을 수상한 작가인 / 여러분을 초대합니다 / 그녀의 새 책으로 / 'Tommy의 해저 모험'

READING **15** ▸ 정답 ④ — pp.46~47

Mini Quiz 모범 답안 ① 현대적인 디자인의 배로 유명하다.
→ This cruise ship is famous for its classical design and modern facilities.
② <u>4월 1일</u>에 출발하여 <u>5박</u>을 배에서 보낸다.
→ April 1 – 5 (4 nights sailing)
③ 출발지와 도착지가 다르다.
→ Departing from / Returning to: Port of Miami, Florida
④ 간식과 <u>음료수</u>는 추가 비용을 내야 한다.
→ additional charge for snacks and drinks
⑤ 추가 정보와 예약은 이메일로 가능하다.
→ For more information and reservations, please call ~.

1 ③ 2 ④
3 (1) special (2) April (3) port (4) free (5) fireworks (6) 4[four] (7) biggest

---

드림 컴퍼니 유람선 여행
여러분은 여러분의 가족을 위한 특별한 무언가를 찾고 있습니까?
드림 컴퍼니 유람선 여행은 가족을 함께 모으는 추억을 만듭니다.
우리의 배인 매직 드림은 여러분이 꿈꾸는 휴가 그 자체입니다. 이 유람선은 고전적인 디자인과 현대적인 시설로 유명합니다. 그것은 또한 어떤 유람선보다 가장 큰 수영장을 가지고 있습니다.
* 출발 날짜: 4월 1일 – 5일 (4박 항해)
* 출발하는 곳 / 도착하는 곳: 마이애미 항구, 플로리다
* 항해하는 곳: 카리브해의 세 곳의 섬
* 시설: 4개의 수영장, 3개의 레스토랑, 3개의 스낵바, 2개의 체육관
* 선상의 활동: 마술 쇼, 뮤지컬, 밤에 불꽃놀이
* 식사: 무료 아침, 점심, 저녁 식사
      (간식과 음료에는 추가 비용)
* 객실 설명: 2개의 킹사이즈 침대, 샤워 시설이 있는 화장실, 냉장고, 무선 인터넷 접속, 최신 영화가 있는 텔레비전
* 가격: $4,500 ~ $5,000
• 더 많은 정보와 예약을 위해서는, (122) 341-1234로 전화 주세요.

p.46
안내문 내용 중 free breakfast, lunch, and dinner (additional charge for snacks and drinks)로 보아 식사는 무료이지만 간식과 음료는 추가 비용을 내야 하므로, ④가 안내문의 내용과 일치한다.

p.47
1 ① 돌아오는 날짜(4월 5일), ② 방문하는 섬의 개수(3개), ④ 식사 비용(무료 아침, 점심, 저녁 식사), ⑤ 객실 내 인터넷 가능 여부(무선 인터넷 접속 가능)는 모두 제시되어 있으나, ③ '마술 쇼 시간'은 제시되어 있지 않다.

2 카리브해의 섬 방문을 말한 ①, 가장 큰 수영장을 거론한 ②, 3개의 레스토랑과 3개의 스낵바를 말한 ③, 객실에서 최신 영화 시청을 말한 ⑤는 모두 알맞으나, 안내문에 없는 오케스트라 공연을 거론한 ④는 알맞지 않다.
① 나는 언제나 카리브해의 섬을 방문하길 원했어.
② 나는 유람선 수영장 중 가장 큰 수영장에서 수영하는 게 너무 기대돼!
③ 나는 3개의 모든 레스토랑과 스낵바에서 음식을 즐길 거야!
④ 유람선 여행에 오케스트라 공연이 있다는 걸 알게 되어서 기뻐.
⑤ 나는 배의 내 방에서 최신 영화를 볼 거야.

3 **해석** 우리 엄마와 아빠는 가족 휴가를 위해 정말 <u>특별한</u> 것을 준비하셨다. 드림 컴퍼니 유람선 여행! 나는 커다란 유람선에서 시간을 보내는 것을 정말 원했었고 내 꿈이 실현되었다! <u>4월 1일</u>에 우리는 마이애미 <u>항구</u>에서 유람선에 탔다. 모든 것은 완벽했다. 나는 <u>공짜로</u> 너무나 많은 맛있는 음식을 즐겼다! 아무런 별도의 비용 없이 말이다! 나는 또한 바다 위에서 밤에 <u>불꽃놀이</u>를 보는 것을 즐겼다. 하지만 가장 멋졌던 것은 그 유람선이 <u>4개의</u> 수영장을 가지고

있고, 그것 중에 하나는 유람선 수영장 중에서 <u>가장 큰</u> 수영장이라는 것이었다! 나는 배 위에서의, 그리고 나의 유람선 여행에서의 모든 순간을 즐겼다.

· **Are you looking for something** [special for your family]?
[ ]는 something을 수식하는 형용사구이다.

· **This cruise ship is famous for** [its classical design] and [modern facilities].
be famous for는 '~로 유명하다'라는 뜻이다. 두 개의 [ ]가 and로 병렬 연결되어 for에 이어진다.

Reading Skill

모범 답안

선택지의 중요 단어	안내문 속 관련 내용
① 현대적 디자인의 배	<u>고전적인</u> 디자인으로 유명
② 4월 1일, 5박	4월 1일부터 <u>5일</u>까지 <u>4박</u>
③ 출발지와 도착지	출발지/도착지: <u>마이애미 항구, 플로리다</u>
④ 간식과 음료수	간식과 음료수는 <u>추가 비용</u> 지불
⑤ 정보, 예약, 이메일	정보와 예약을 위해 <u>전화</u>로 연락

직독직해 Skill

· A Dream Company cruise (S) / creates (V) memories / that bring families together.
드림 컴퍼니 유람선 여행은 / 추억을 만듭니다 / 가족을 함께 모으는

READING 16 ▸ 정답 ③　　　　　　　pp.48~49

Mini Quiz　제목: 디지털 콘텐츠에 접속하기 위해 학생들이 사용한 기기
가로축: 기기의 종류
세로축: 기기를 사용한 학생의 비율

1 ⑤　**2** less → more
3 (1) most　(2) twice　(3) down

위 그래프는 학생들이 교육용 디지털 콘텐츠에 접근하기 위해 무슨 기기를 사용했는지를 우리에게 보여준다. 조사는 2016년과 2019년 두 해에 수행되었다. 유치원에서 12학년까지의 학생들이 조사에 참여했으며, 그들은 많은 종류의 디지털 기기를 사용했다. 두 해 모두 노트북은 디지털 콘텐츠 접속을 위한 가장 인기 있는 기기였다. 2016년과 2019년 모두 60퍼센트 넘는 학생들이 디지털 콘텐츠를 위해 태블릿을 사용했다. <u>2016년에는 절반이 넘는 학생들이 디지털 콘텐츠를 위해 데스크톱을 사용했고, 2019년에는 30퍼센트 넘는 학생들이 디지털 콘텐츠를 위해 데스크톱을 사용했다.</u> 2016년에 스마트폰을 사용한 학생의 비율은 2019년에 스마트폰을 사용한 학생들의 비율과 같았다. 전자책 단말기를 사용한 학생들의 비율은 두 해 모두 가장 낮았다.

p.48
③ 2016년에 디지털 콘텐츠를 위해 데스크톱을 사용한 학생들의 수는 49%로 절반보다 적으므로 'More than half the students'라는 서술이 도표의 내용과 일치하지 않는다.

p.49
1 유치원부터 12학년까지의 학생 전체를 대상으로 한 조사로 고등학생만을 대상으로 한 결과는 알 수 없다. 따라서 ⑤ '2019년에 고등학생에게 가장 인기 있었던 기기는 무엇인가?'는 답할 수 없는 질문이다.
① 2019년에 몇 퍼센트의 학생들이 전자책 단말기를 사용했는가?
② 2016년보다 2019년에 학생들이 더 많이 사용한 기기는 무엇인가?
③ 2016년과 2019년 둘 다 같은 사용 비율을 보이는 기기는 몇 개인가?
④ 두 해 모두 50퍼센트 이상의 학생들이 사용한 기기들은 무엇인가?

2 2016년에 전자책 단말기를 사용한 학생들의 비율은 11퍼센트로 2019년의 5퍼센트의 2배보다 많으므로 less를 more로 고쳐야 한다.
　해석 2016년에 전자책 단말기를 사용한 학생들의 비율은 2019년의 그것(전자책 단말기를 사용한 학생들의 비율)의 두 배보다 <u>적다(→ 많다)</u>.

3 (1) 2016년과 2019년 모두 태블릿이 두 번째로 많이 쓰인 기기이므로 most가 알맞다.
(2) 2019년에 데스크톱을 사용한 학생들의 비율은 34퍼센트로, 그해에 스마트폰을 사용한 학생들의 비율인 17퍼센트의 2배이다. 따라서 twice가 빈칸에 알맞다.
(3) 2016년에서 2019년으로 가면서 데스크톱을 사용한 학생들의 비율은 49퍼센트에서 34퍼센트로 감소했으므로 down이 알맞다.
　해석 (1) 두 번째로 많이 쓰인 기기는 2016년과 2019년 모두 태블릿이었다.

(2) 2019년에 데스크톱을 사용한 학생들의 비율은 같은 해에 스마트폰을 사용한 학생들의 비율의 두 배였다.

(3) 데스크톱을 사용한 학생들의 비율은 2016년에서 2019년으로 시간이 지나면서 감소했다.

- The above graph **shows us** [what devices students used {**to access** digital educational content}].
  [ ]는 shows의 직접목적어 역할을 하는 간접의문문이다. { }는 '~하기 위하여〈목적〉'의 의미로 쓰인 부사적 용법의 to부정사구이다.

- **The percentages of students** [who used E-readers] **were** the lowest in both years.
  The percentages of students가 주어, were가 동사이며, [ ]는 주격 관계대명사절로 선행사 students를 꾸며준다.

Reading Skill

모범 답안

무엇을 조사한 도표인가?	디지털 콘텐츠에 접근하기 위해 학생들이 사용한 기기
조사한 시기는 언제인가?	2016년, 2019년
막대 그래프는 무엇을 나타내는가?	기기를 사용한 학생들의 비율

직독직해 Skill

- The percentage of students (S) / who used smartphones in 2016 / was (V) the same as / that in 2019.
  학생들의 비율은 / 2016년에 스마트폰을 사용한 / ~와 같았다 / 2019년의 그것

Unit 07 내용 일치 파악하기

READING 17 ▶ 정답 ⑤

pp.50~51

Mini Quiz Then, in London in 1964, she created a sharp, clear picture of a mysterious virus and named it coronavirus. It was the first identified human coronavirus.

1 ② **2** ③
3 (1) Scotland (2) science (3) university degrees
(4) lab technician (5) 16 (6) virus (7) coronavirus

June Almeida는 스코틀랜드에서 1930년에 태어났다. Almeida는 학교에서 뛰어났고 학교에서 과학 최고상을 받았다. 고등학교를 나온 후, 그녀는 과학 공부를 계속하기를 원했지만 대학 교육을 위한 돈이 없었다. 그래서, 16살의 나이에 Almeida는 실험실 기술자로 직업을 얻었다. 그 후, 그녀는 런던으로 이사했고, 그리고 나서 1954년에 캐나다로 이사했다. 그곳에서, 그녀는 현미경을 이용해서 바이러스를 찾고 바이러스의 자세한 사진을 만드는 직업을 얻었다. 그녀는 그 직업에서 최고 전문가 중 한 명이 되었다. 그 후, 1964년 런던에서 그녀는 알려지지 않은 바이러스의 선명하고 깨끗한 사진을 만들었고 그것을 코로나바이러스라고 이름 붙였다. 그것은 인간에게서 확인된 첫 번째 코로나바이러스였다. 생물학 분야에서 그녀가 한 기여 때문에, 런던 대학은 그녀에게 대학 학위를 1970년과 1971년에 수여했다. 그녀는 마침내 그녀가 고등학교 때부터 원했던 학위를 받았다.

p.50

글의 후반부 Due to her contributions in the field of biology, ~ since high school.에서 생물학 분야에서 그녀가 한 기여 때문에 런던 대학에서 학위를 수여했다고 했으므로 ⑤는 글의 내용과 일치하지 않는다.

p.51

1 그녀가 실험실 기술자로서 한 일의 종류는 명시되어 있지 않고 실험실 기술자로 일을 시작했다는 내용만 서술되어 있으므로, 답할 수 없는 질문은 ② '그녀가 실험실 기술자로서 한 일의 종류는 무엇인가?'이다.
① 그녀는 어디에서 태어났는가?
③ 그녀는 어떻게 바이러스의 상세한 사진을 만들었는가?
④ 그녀는 캐나다에서 어디로 이사했는가?
⑤ 그녀는 언제 런던 대학으로부터 학위를 받았는가?

2 ①, ②, ④, ⑤는 모두 본문에 언급된 내용을 기반으로 했으나, ③ '그녀가 바이러스 백신을 만드는 데 전문가가 됐다는 것이 인상적이었다.'는 본문에 언급되지 않은 내용이다.
① 그녀가 과학에서 최고상을 받았으므로 과학을 잘했음에 틀림없다.
② 그녀가 돈 때문에 대학을 가지 못해서 마음이 좋지 않았다.
④ 그녀가 코로나바이러스 이름을 지었다는 것을 알고 놀랐다.
⑤ 그녀가 원했던 학위를 받게 되어 행복했을 것이라고 생각한다.

3

	June Almeida	
출생	어디에서: <u>스코틀랜드</u>	
교육	• 학교에서, 특히 과학 과목에서 뛰어났다 • 런던 대학교에서 그녀에게 <u>대학 학위</u>를 수여했다	
직업	<u>16</u>살의 나이에 실험실 기술자로서 일을 시작했다	
성취	알려지지 않은 <u>바이러스</u>의 깨끗한 사진을 만들었고 그것을 <u>코로나 바이러스</u>라고 이름 붙였다	

구문 설명

• There, she took a job **detecting** viruses and **making** detailed pictures of them using a microscope.
detecting과 making은 and로 병렬 연결된 현재분사로 a job을 수식한다.

• She finally **received** the degrees [that she **had wanted** since high school].
대학 학위를 받은 때(received)와 비교했을 때, 학위를 원해 왔던 것(had wanted)은 그 이전부터 있었던 일이므로 과거보다 더 먼저의 일을 표현하기 위해 과거완료(had+p.p.)인 had wanted 형태를 사용했다. [ ]는 목적격 관계대명사절로 선행사 the degrees를 수식한다.

Reading Skill

모범 답안

인물 이름	June Almeida
시간 순서에 따른 인물 정보	출생년도 및 출생지 → <u>학업[학업 성취]</u> → <u>직업</u> → 업적

직독직해 Skill

• Then, in London in 1964, / she (S) created (V1) / a sharp, clear picture / of a mysterious virus / and named (V2) it / coronavirus.
그 후, 1964년 런던에서 / 그녀는 만들었다 / 선명하고 깨끗한 사진을 / 알려지지 않은 바이러스의 / 그리고 그것을 이름 지었다 / 코로나바이러스라고

READING **18** → 정답 ④   pp.52~53

Mini Quiz ①: *The Secret: A Treasure Hunt* is a book created by Byron Preiss

②: The book has 12 mysterious paintings and poems. They contain the information that indicates the location of the buried treasures.

③: Up to the year of 2023, only three of the twelve boxes have been found.

④: the most recent one was found in 2019 in Langone Park in Boston

⑤: before his sudden death in a car accident in 2005

1 ④ **2** exchanged
3 (1) Byron Preiss (2) United States (3) Canada
   (4) locations (5) 3[three]

'비밀: 보물 찾기'는 Byron Preiss에 의해 1982년에 창작된 책이다. 그 책이 출판되기 전에, Preiss는 12개의 작은 보물 상자를 미국과 캐나다 전역에 묻었다. 각각의 상자는 뉴욕의 안전 금고에 있는 12개의 보석 중 하나와 교환될 수 있는 작은 열쇠를 가지고 있었다. 그 책에는 12개의 신비한 그림과 시가 실려 있다. 그것들은 파묻힌 보물의 위치를 가리키는 정보를 담고 있다. 예를 들어, 한 그림의 꽃(flower)과 종(bell)은 Cleveland의 Bellflower 길을 상징한다. 2023년까지 12개의 상자 중 오직 3개만이 발견되었다. 하나는 시카고의 Grant Park에서 1983년에 발견되었고, 다음 것은 2004년에 Cleveland의 그리스 문화 정원에서, 가장 최근의 것은 보스턴의 Langone Park에서 2019년에 발견되었다. Preiss는 2005년 자동차 사고로 갑작스럽게 사망하기 전에 보물의 정확한 위치에 대한 어떠한 기록도 남겨놓지 않았다. 많은 사람들이 여전히 그 보물들을 찾고 있다.

해설

p.52
2023년까지 12개의 상자 중 3개만이 발견되었으며 가장 최근의 것은 보스턴의 Langone Park에서 2019년에 발견되었다. 따라서 ④는 글의 내용과 일치하지 않는다.

p.53
1 12개의 보물 상자가 뉴욕의 안전 금고에 있다고 했지만, ④ '안전 금고 안에 있는 보석의 종류'는 글에서 언급되지 않았다.
   ① 책을 쓴 작가
   ② 보물 상자가 묻힌 나라
   ③ 보물 상자 안에 있는 것
   ⑤ 두 번째 상자가 발견된 정원의 이름

2 두 문장 모두 '교환하다'는 의미의 exchange가 들어가는 것이 적절하며, 첫 번째 문장에는 과거분사형이, 두 번째 문장에는 과거형인 exchanged가 알맞다.
    • 이 쿠폰을 ABC 카페테리아에 가져가면, 그것은 무료 커피 한 잔으로 <u>교환</u>될 수 있다.

• 그 학생들은 서로 연락을 하기 위해 전화번호를 <u>교환했다</u>.

3 〔해석〕

> **여러분은 이 책을 살펴봐야 합니다!**
>
> 책 제목 '비밀: 보물 찾기'
> 작가 <u>Byron Preiss</u>
> 특징 작가는 12개의 보물 상자를 <u>미국과 캐나다</u>에 묻었고, 이 책은 그 상자들의 <u>위치</u>에 관한 단서를 담고 있습니다. 그 상자들 중에 오직 <u>3개</u>만이 발견되었습니다. 당신이 그 다음 것을 발견하는 사람이 될 수 있습니다!

〔구문 설명〕

• They contain the information [that indicates the location of the **buried** treasures].
[ ]는 주격 관계대명사절로 선행사 the information을 수식한다. buried는 treasures를 수식하는 분사인데, treasures가 '묻힌' 수동의 의미를 나타내므로 과거분사 형태로 쓰였다.

• Up to the year of 2023, only three of the twelve boxes **have been found**.
예전부터 2023년 현재까지의 상황을 나타내므로 현재완료 시제가 필요하며, 상자는 '발견되는' 것이므로 「have[has] been+p.p.」 형태의 현재완료 수동태인 have been found가 쓰였다.

Reading Skill

모범 답안

	The Secret: A Treasure Hunt
선택지 ①, ②	Byron Preiss에 의해 창작된 <u>책</u>으로, <u>그림과 시</u>가 실려 있음
선택지 ③, ④	최근까지도 상자들이 발견되고 있음
선택지 ⑤	저자의 사망 원인은 <u>자동차 사고</u>임

직독직해 Skill

• Each box (S) / has (V) a small key / that could be exchanged for one of 12 jewels / in a safe deposit box in New York.
각 상자는 / 작은 열쇠를 가지고 있다 / 12개의 보석 중 하나로 교환될 수 있는 / 뉴욕의 안전 금고에 있는

READING 19 ▸ 정답 ④   pp.54~55

Mini Quiz 〔모범 답안〕 In 1930, she became the world's

first female flight attendant.

1 ④ **2** female flight attendant
3 (1) nurse (2) attendant (3) first (4) evacuate
  (5) airplane

〔해석〕

Ellen Church는 1904년 아이오와 주 크레스코에서 태어났다. 고등학교를 졸업한 후 그녀는 간호학을 공부했다. 그녀는 샌프란시스코에서 간호사로 일했다. 어느 날 Ellen은 Boeing 사무실에 들렀다. 그녀는 비행기에서 간호사로서의 일자리를 얻을 수 있는지 물었다. Ellen은 비행 중 겁에 질린 승객을 간호사가 돌봐야 한다고 제안했다. 1930년에 그녀는 세계 최초의 여성 비행 승무원이 되었다. 그녀는 오클랜드에서 시카고까지 비행하면서 보잉 80A 비행기에서 근무했다. 그러나 Ellen은 교통사고 부상 때문에 18개월 후에 어쩔 수 없이 비행을 그만두어야 했다. 그녀는 밀워키 카운티 병원에서 다시 간호사 일을 시작했다. 제2차 세계대전 중 Ellen은 육군 간호 부대에 입대했다. 그녀는 부상당한 병사들을 비행기로 대피시키는 일을 도왔다. 그녀는 이 업적으로 항공 훈장을 받았다. 크레스코에 있는 Ellen Church Field 공항은 그녀의 이름을 따서 명명되었다. 그녀는 1965년에 승마 사고로 사망했다.

〔해설〕

p.54

Ellen은 세계 최초의 여성 승무원이 되었지만 교통사고 부상 때문에 18개월 후에 비행을 그만두어야 했다고 했으므로 ④는 글의 내용과 일치하지 않는다.

p.55

1 this는 바로 앞에 나온 During World War II, Ellen joined the Army Nurse Corps. She helped evacuate wounded soldiers by airplane.을 가리킨다.

2 1930년에 Ellen Church가 세계 최초의 여성 비행 승무원이 되었다고 했으므로 빈칸에는 female flight attendant가 적절하다.
〔해석〕 1930년 이전에는 세상에 <u>여성 비행 승무원</u>이 없었다.

3 〔해석〕 나는 특별한 한 여성에 관한 책을 읽었다. 그녀의 이름은 Ellen Church이다. 그녀는 간호사로서 또 비행 승무원으로서 일했다. 그녀는 세계 <u>최초의</u> 여성 비행 승무원으로 잘 알려져 있다. 또한, 그녀는 항공 훈장을 받은 것으로도 유명하다. 제2차 세계대전 동안 그녀는 육군 간호 부대에 입대하여 부상당한 병사들을 <u>비행기로 대피시키는</u> 것을 도왔다.

〔구문 설명〕

• Ellen **suggested** that nurses **take** care of frightened passengers during flights.
「suggest that 주어+(should+)동사원형」은 '~가 …할 것을 제안하다'의 의미를 나타내며 that절의 동사는 「(should+)동사원형」

의 형태로 쓴다.

- Ellen, however, was forced to **quit flying** after eighteen months, **due to** an injury from a car accident.

「quit -ing」는 '~ 하는 것을 그만두다'의 의미로 quit 뒤에 동명사가 목적어로 쓰인다. due to는 '~ 때문에'라는 의미로 원인이나 이유를 나타낸다.

- The Ellen Church Field Airport in Cresco **was named after** her.

name after는 '~의 이름을 따서 이름 짓다'의 의미이며 주어가 '이름 지어진' 것이므로 수동태로 쓰였다.

Reading Skill

모범 답안

인물	Ellen Church
정보	• 출생년도: <u>1904년</u> • 출생지: <u>Cresco, Iowa</u> • 직업: <u>간호사, 비행 승무원</u> • 업적: 세계 최초의 <u>여성 비행 승무원</u> 　<u>항공 훈장</u>을 받았음 　고향에 그녀의 이름을 따서 이름 붙인 <u>공항</u>이 　있음

직독직해 Skill

- Ellen, (S) / however, / was forced (V) to quit flying / after eighteen months, / due to an injury from a car accident.
  Ellen은 / 그러나 / 비행을 그만두어야 했다 / 18개월 뒤에 / 교통사고 부상 때문에

Chapter 03 묘사된 분위기나 심경 파악하기

Reading Key　인물과 사건 중심으로 빠르게 읽기　pp.58~59

정답

A	상황 묘사	꺼져, 움직임, 발목, 비명
	글 전반의 분위기	무서운 분위기
B	상황 묘사	난로, 나뭇조각, 소리침
	Norm의 심경	surprised and angry

해석

A 어느 날 밤, 나는 2층으로 가기 위해 문을 열었고, 복도 전등이 꺼진 것을 알아차렸다. 첫 칸에 발을 내디뎠을 때, 나는 계단 아래에서 어떤 움직임을 느꼈다. 일단 이상한 어떤 일이 일어나고 있다는 것을 깨닫자, 내 심장은 빠르게 뛰기 시작했다. 갑자기, 나는 손 하나가 계단 사이로부터 뻗어 나와서 내 발목을 잡는 것을 보았다. 나는 크게 비명을 질렀지만, 아무도 대답하지 않았다!

B Norm과 그의 친구 Jason이 겨울 캠프 여행을 갔다. 밤에 Norm은 잠에서 깼고 난로가 빨갛게 타고 있는 것을 보고 놀랐다! Norm이 Jason을 깨웠고 Jason이 난로에 나뭇조각을 너무 많이 넣었다는 것을 알았다. Norm은 오두막에 불이 날 것이라고 생각했다. 그는 Jason을 그의 침대에서 끌어냈다. Norm은 화가 나서 "네가 한 짓을 봐! 너 정말 부주의했어!"라고 소리쳤다.

Unit 08 분위기·심경 파악하기

READING 20 ▸ 정답 ④　　　　pp.60~61

Mini Quiz　모범 답안 felt at home, delightful, comfortable, satisfied, perfect, excited, warm and friendly

1 ④　2 (1) disappointed → satisfied　(2) large → small
3 (1) delightful　(2) space　(3) window　(4) cozy
　(5) perfect　(6) privacy

해석

Alex와 Angie는 그들의 새로운 작은 집을 둘러보았고 즉시 편안함을

느꼈다. 주방은 마음에 들었고 요리할 수 있는 공간이 많았다. 거실은 창문이 컸고 편안한 휴식 공간을 제공했다. 위층에서, 침실은 아늑했고 달콤한 꿈을 약속하는 한편, 아래층의 거실은 영화의 밤과 게임을 기다리고 있었다. 그들은 만족하며 작은 마당으로 나갔다. 울타리가 쳐진 그 마당은 그들의 필요에 완벽했고 안전감과 사생활 보호를 제공했다. Alex와 Angie는 다가오는 봄에 정원에 식물을 심기 시작할 것에 신이 났고 심지어 작은 개를 키우는 것에 대해서도 논의했다. 갑자기 이웃에서 아이들의 웃음소리가 들려오며 따뜻하고 친근한 분위기가 만들어졌다. 아주 좋았다! 그들의 딸인 Sarah에게는 많은 놀이 친구들이 있을 것이었다. 이곳은 그들이 꿈꾸던 집이었고, 그들은 자신들이 여기에 속한다는 것을 알았다.

p.60

Alex와 Angie는 편안함을 느끼게 하는 새집, 기분 좋은 주방, 편안한 휴식 공간을 제공하는 거실, 아늑한 침실 등에서 만족감을 느꼈고, 정원에는 봄에 식물을 심게 되어 신이 났으며 밖에서 들려오는 아이들의 웃음소리에 따뜻하고 친근한 분위기를 느꼈다고 했다. 따라서 글의 분위기로 가장 적절한 것은 ④ '따뜻하고 행복한'이다.
① 차분하고 조용한
② 슬프고 우울한
③ 시끄럽고 웃긴
⑤ 긴장되고 급박한

p.61

1 주방의 모습(마음에 들었고 요리할 수 있는 공간이 많았음), 위층 침실의 분위기(아늑함), 마당의 특징(그들의 필요에 완벽했고 안전감과 사생활 보호를 제공함), 동네의 분위기(따뜻하고 친근한 분위기)에 대해서는 언급되었으나 ④ '정원에 심은 꽃의 종류'에 대해서는 언급되지 않았다.

2 (1) 집을 보고 만족하여 마당으로 나갔다고 했으므로 disappointed를 satisfied로 고쳐야 한다.
  (2) 작은 개를 키우는 것에 대해서 논의했다고 했으므로 large를 small로 고쳐야 한다.
  해석 (1) Alex와 Angie는 그들의 새집에 불만족스러워했다.
  (2) Alex와 Angie는 큰 개를 키우는 것에 대해 논의했다.

3 **해석**

부엌	• 마음에 들어 보임 • 요리를 위한 많은 공간이 있음
거실	• 큰 창문이 있음 • 편안한 휴식 공간을 제공함
침실	• 아늑함 • 달콤한 꿈을 약속함
마당	• 울타리가 쳐져 있음 • 그들의 필요에 완벽함 • 안전감과 사생활 보호를 제공함

· Alex and Angie were **excited** [to start planting a garden in the coming spring] and even discussed getting a small dog.
주어가 감정을 느끼는 대상이므로 과거분사인 excited가 쓰였다. [ ]는 excited라는 감정의 원인을 나타내는 부사적 용법의 to부정사구이다.

· Suddenly, children's laughter **came** from the neighborhood and **created** a warm and friendly atmosphere.
두 개의 동사 came과 created가 and로 병렬 연결되어 있다.

모범 답안

주요 상황	Alex와 Angie가 새집을 둘러보는 상황
세부 내용	• 집을 둘러보고 편안함을 느낌 • 집안의 주방, 거실, 침실의 특징 묘사 • 작은 마당의 특징 묘사 • 밖에서 들려오는 아이들의 웃음소리

· The family room (S) / had (V1) a large window / and offered (V2) a comfortable place / to relax.
거실은 / 큰 창문을 가지고 있었다 / 그리고 편안한 공간을 제공했다 / 휴식할 수 있는

READING 21 · 정답 ⑤   pp.62~63

Mini Quiz 모범 답안 overjoyed, appreciated and loved, lucky, blessed

1 ⑤   2 (1) Roses. (2) She felt appreciated and loved.
3 (1) deadlines (2) petals (3) admiring (4) hugged

Emily는 장시간의 노동과 빠듯한 마감일로 직장에서 힘든 한 주를 보냈다. 그래서 그녀의 남편이 점심 식사 후에 아름다운 장미로 그녀를 놀라게 했을 때, 그녀는 매우 기뻐했다. 선명한 색과 섬세한 꽃잎이 상쾌했다. 그녀는 자신의 남편이 그 선물에 많은 생각을 기울였음을 알 수 있었고, 그것은 그녀가 감사함과 사랑을 느끼게 했다. 그들이 그곳에 서서 이야기를 나누며 장미를 감상하고 있을 때, Emily는 그녀의 스트레스와

걱정이 사라지는 것을 느꼈다. 그녀는 심지어 가장 힘든 날에도, 세상에는 항상 웃고 기쁨을 찾을 수 있는 이유가 있다고 생각했다. 장미는 그들의 사랑과 동반자 관계의 상징 역할을 했고, Emily는 그녀의 곁에 이렇게 멋진 사람이 있다는 것이 행운이라고 느꼈다. 그녀는 남편을 안고 그에게 깜짝 선물에 대한 감사를 전했다. 이런 순간들이 Emily를 진정으로 축복받은 것처럼 느끼게 했다.

p.62

직장에서 힘든 한 주를 보낸 Emily가 남편에게서 장미를 받아 기뻤고 스트레스와 걱정이 사라지는 것을 느꼈으며 축복받은 것처럼 느꼈다고 했으므로 Emily의 심경으로 가장 적절한 것은 ⑤ '즐겁고 만족한'이다.
① 안도하고 자랑스러운
② 무섭고 걱정되는
③ 불안하고 초조한
④ 화나고 좌절한

p.63

1 Emily는 그녀의 곁에 이렇게 멋진 사람이 있다는 것이 행운이라고 느꼈다고 했으므로 글의 내용과 일치하는 것은 ⑤ '그녀는 자신이 운이 좋은 사람이라고 느꼈다.'이다.
① 그녀는 직장에서 편안한 한 주를 보냈다.
② 그녀는 점심 전에 남편으로부터 장미꽃을 받았다.
③ 그녀는 남편과 이야기를 나누다가 스트레스를 받았다.
④ 그녀는 어떤 기쁨도 찾을 수 없어서 좌절했다.

2 (1) Emily와 그녀의 남편에게 사랑과 동반자 관계의 상징은 장미꽃이었다.
(2) 자신의 남편이 그 선물에 많은 생각을 기울였음을 이해할 수 있었을 때 Emily는 감사함과 사랑을 느꼈다고 했다.
해석 (1) Emily와 남편의 사랑과 동반자 관계의 상징은 무엇이었나?
(2) Emily는 남편의 사려 깊음을 이해했을 때 어떤 기분이 들었나?

3 해석

직장에서 그녀의 한 주	긴 노동 시간과 빠듯한 마감일로 힘듦
남편으로부터의 선물	색깔이 선명하고 섬세한 꽃잎을 가진 아름다운 장미꽃
Emily와 남편이 한 일들	이야기를 하고 장미를 감상하면서 서 있기
Emily가 남편을 위해 한 일들	안아 주고 감사했다

· She could tell [**that** her husband had put a lot of thought into the gift], and **it** made her feel appreciated and loved.

[ ]는 tell의 목적어 역할을 하는 명사절이고, that은 명사절을 이끄는 접속사이다. it은 [ ]를 가리킨다.

· **It** was moments like this **that** made Emily feel truly blessed.
「It ~ that ...」 강조구문으로 주어인 moments like this가 강조되고 있다.

모범 답안

주요 상황	남편에게서 장미꽃을 선물받은 Emily
세부 내용	· 점심 식사 후에 남편으로부터 아름다운 장미를 받아 놀랐음 · 장미는 Emily와 남편의 사랑과 동반자 관계의 상징 역할을 함 · Emily는 남편을 안고 뜻밖의 선물에 대해 감사함

· She (S) thought (V) / that even on the toughest of days, / there are always reasons / to smile and find joy / in the world.
그녀는 생각했다 / 심지어 가장 힘든 날에도 / 항상 이유가 있다고 / 웃고 기쁨을 찾을 수 있는 / 세상에는

READING **22** · 정답 ⑤　　pp.64~65

(Mini Quiz) 모범 답안 anticipation, eagerly, sighed, for nothing, What a waste of time

1 ⑤　2 (1) rare (2) wander
3 (1) find rare fossils of dinosaurs (2) the sun was beginning to set

해석

Evelyn이 캐나다 전역에서 수많은 공룡 화석으로 유명한 Alberta의 Badlands를 처음으로 탐험하던 때였다. 젊은 아마추어 뼈 발굴자로서 그녀는 기대감으로 가득 차 있었다. 그녀는 흔한 공룡 종의 뼈를 얻기 위해 이렇게 멀리까지 여행을 해본 적이 없었다. 희귀한 공룡 화석을 찾겠다는 그녀의 평생의 꿈이 막 이루어지려던 참이었다. 그녀는 그것을 열심히 찾기 시작했다. 그러나 몇 시간 동안 인적이 드문 땅을 헤매고 다녔지만, 그녀는 성공하지 못했다. 이제, 해가 지기 시작하고 있었고, 그

녀의 목표는 그녀의 손길이 닿는 곳 훨씬 너머에 있었다. 그녀는 자신 앞에서 서서히 어두워지는 땅을 바라보고 있었다. 그녀는 혼자 한숨지으며 "여기까지 와서 헛걸음을 했다니 믿을 수가 없네. 정말 시간 낭비였네!"라고 말했다.

해설

p.64

Evelyn은 희귀한 공룡 화석을 찾겠다는 평생의 꿈을 이루기 위해 Alberta의 Badlands에 가서 기대에 부풀어 있었지만, 해가 질 때까지 아무것도 찾지 못한 채 시간만 낭비했다는 내용의 글이다. 따라서 Evelyn의 심경 변화로 가장 적절한 것은 ⑤ '희망에 찬 → 실망한'이다.

① 혼란스러운 → 겁에 질린
② 낙담한 → 자신감 있는
③ 긴장을 푼 → 짜증이 난
④ 무관심한 → 우울한

p.65

1 Alberta의 Badlands가 무엇으로 유명한 곳인지(numerous dinosaur fossils), Evelyn의 평생의 꿈은 무엇이었는지(to find rare fossils of dinosaurs), Evelyn이 얼마나 오랫동안 인적이 드문 땅을 헤매고 다녔는지(many hours), 해가 지기 시작하고 있었을 때 Evelyn은 무엇을 보고 있었는지(the slowly darkening ground)를 묻는 질문에는 글에서 답을 찾을 수 있으나 ⑤ 'Evelyn이 공룡 화석을 몇 번 발견했는가?'에 대해서는 글에 제시되지 않았다.

① Alberta의 Badlands는 무엇으로 유명한가?
② Evelyn의 평생의 꿈은 무엇이었나?
③ Evelyn은 얼마나 오랫동안 인적이 드문 땅을 헤매고 다녔는가?
④ 해가 지기 시작하고 있었을 때 Evelyn은 무엇을 보고 있었는가?

2 (1) '그다지 자주 일어나지 않는'이라는 뜻을 갖는 단어는 rare(드문, 희귀한)이다.
(2) '고정된 경로, 목표, 혹은 목적 없이 이동해 다니다'라는 뜻을 갖는 단어는 wander((이리저리) 돌아다니다, 헤매다)이다.

3 **해석** 젊은 아마추어 뼈 발굴자인 Evelyn은 희귀한 공룡 화석을 찾기 위해서 Alberta의 Badlands를 탐험하고 있었다. 간절하게 공룡의 희귀 화석을 찾아다녔지만 그녀는 해가 지기 시작하기 전에 그것을 찾지 못했다.

구문 설명

• She sighed to herself, "I can't believe [I came all this way for nothing]. **What a waste of time!**"
[ ]는 목적어 역할을 하는 명사절로 앞에 접속사 that이 생략되어 있다. What a waste of time!은 감탄문이고 time 뒤에 「주어+동사」인 it was가 생략되어 있다고 볼 수 있다.

Reading Skill

모범 답안

주요 상황	희귀한 공룡 화석을 찾고 있는 Evelyn
세부 내용	• 공룡 화석으로 유명한 Alberta의 Badlands를 처음으로 탐험하는 중이었음 • Evelyn은 젊은 아마추어 뼈 발굴자임 • 희귀한 공룡 화석을 해가 저물 때까지 열심히 찾아다님

직독직해 Skill

• Her life-long dream (S) / to find rare fossils of dinosaurs / was (V) about to come true.
그녀의 평생의 꿈이 / 희귀한 공룡 화석을 찾겠다는 / 막 이루어지려던 참이었다

Reading Key 글의 흐름을 파악하고 이어질 내용 예측하기 *pp.68~69*

정답

A 보디빌딩 운동과 야구선수용 운동의 차이

B (A) 더 높이, 더 낮게 (B) 아래, 위
적절한 흐름 (B) – (A)의 순서

해석

A 야구를 위한 훈련과 몸만들기는 체력, 힘, 속도, 신속함, 유연성을 신장하는 데 초점을 둔다. 1980년대 이전에 근력 운동은 야구선수를 위한 몸만들기의 중요한 부분이 아니었다.

B (B) 어두운 색은 무거워 보이고, 밝은 색은 더 가벼워 보인다. 실내 디자이너들은 보는 사람들에게 진정 효과를 만들기 위해 종종 아래에 더 어두운 색을 사용하고 위에 더 밝은 색을 사용한다.
(A) 상품 전시도 같은 방식으로 작동한다. 밝은 색의 상품을 더 높이, 어두운 색의 상품을 더 낮게 배치하라. 이것은 더 안정적으로 보이고 고객이 편안하게 상품들을 훑어볼 수 있도록 해 준다.

Unit 09 글의 순서 파악하기

READING 23 정답 ② *pp.70~71*

Mini Quiz (A) – It (B) – them, this (C) – these

1 ④ **2** realistic → unrealistic
3 (1) unrealistic (2) overconfident (3) difficult (4) slow

해석

왜 우리는 종종 우리의 결심을 지키지 못하는가? 일부 심리학자들은 우리 대부분이 (일반적으로, 새해의 결심에 대해서뿐만 아니라) 우리의 행동을 바꿀 수 있는 능력에 대해 비현실적인 기대를 가지고 있다고 시사한다. (B) 그들에 따르면, 이것은 '거짓 희망 증후군'을 만들어낸다. 이 증후군은 우리의 행동을 성공적으로 바꿀 수 있는 우리의 능력에 대한 과장된 통제감과 지나친 자신감을 포함한다. (A) 그것은 종종 비현실적인 목표(예를 들어, "나는 매일 두 시간 동안 운동할 거야!")로 시작한다. 우리는 또한 우리의 행동을 바꾸는 것이 얼마나 어려울지 과소평가한다(예를 들어, "나는 컴퓨터 게임을 끊는 데 문제가 없을 것이다!"). 마지막으로, 우리는 극적이고 빠른 결과를 기대하는 경향이 있다(예를 들어, "나는 아마 일주일에 10파운드 정도를 뺄 것이다!"). (C) 이러한 잘못된 기대 때문에, 우리는 대개 실패한다. 새로운 행동은 우리가 예상했던 것보다 더 어려운 것으로 판명된다. 눈에 보이는 결과는 느린 것으로 판명된다. 그러고 나서 우리는 종종 변화하려는 시도를 포기한다.

해설

p.70
우리가 결심을 지키지 못하는 이유는 행동을 바꿀 수 있는 능력에 대해 비현실적인 기대를 가지고 있기 때문이라는 의견의 주어진 글에 이어, 이것을 가리키는 개념인 '거짓 희망 증후군'에 대한 내용으로 이어진 (B), 이 증후군에 대해 비현실적인 목표, 행동을 바꾸는 어려움에 대한 과소평가, 극적으로 빠른 결과에 대한 기대를 예를 들어 설명한 (A), 앞에서 제시된 잘못된 기대로 인해 실패한다는 내용의 (C)로 이어지는 것이 가장 자연스럽다.

p.71
1 결심을 지키지 못하는, 즉 변화하려는 시도를 포기하는 이유는 우리의 행동을 바꿀 수 있는 능력에 대해 비현실적인 기대를 가지고 있기 때문이라고 했으므로 글의 요지로 가장 적절한 것은 ④이다.

2 '거짓 희망 증후군'은 우리의 행동을 성공적으로 바꿀 수 있는 우리의 능력에 대한 과장된 통제감과 지나친 자신감을 포함한다고 했는데, 과장되거나 지나친 것은 현실적인 것이 아니라 비현실적인 것이므로 realistic을 unrealistic으로 고쳐야 한다.
해석 '거짓 희망 증후군'은 우리가 자신의 변화에 대한 현실적인 (→ 비현실적인) 기대를 갖고 있다는 것을 의미한다.

3 **해석** 우리는 왜 그렇게 자주 결심을 지키지 못하는가?

	기대	현실
목표	비현실적인	*언급되지 않음
우리의 행동을 성공적으로 변화시키는 능력	과장되고 자신감이 지나친	*언급되지 않음
어려움의 정도	과소평가된	예상되었던 것보다 더 어려운
결과를 보는 속도	극적인, 빠른	느린

구문 설명

· We also underestimate [how difficult **it** will be **to change** our behavior] (e.g., "I'll **have no trouble stopping** my computer games!").
[ ]는 underestimate의 목적어 역할을 하는 간접의문문으로 「의문사구+주어+동사」의 형식을 취하고 있는데, it은 가주어이고 to change our behavior가 진주어이다. 「have no trouble -ing」는 '~하는 데 어려움이 없다'를 의미한다.

· The new behavior **proves to be** *more* difficult *than*

we expected.

「prove+to부정사」는 '~로 판명되다'를 의미하며, more ~ than 의 비교급 비교 문장으로 '~보다 더 …한'의 의미를 나타낸다.

모범 답안

주제	결심을 지키지 못하는 이유
근거	• 행동을 바꿀 수 있는 능력에 대한 비현실적인 기대 • 비현실적인 목표, 행동을 변화시키는 것의 어려움에 대한 과소평가 • 극적이고 빠른 결과를 예상하는 경향 • 거짓 희망 증후군

• Some psychologists (S) suggest (V) / that most of us / have unrealistic expectations / about our ability / to change our behavior / (in general, not only at New Year's).
일부 심리학자들은 시사한다 / 우리 대부분이 / 비현실적인 기대를 가지고 있다고 / 우리의 능력에 대해 / 우리의 행동을 바꿀 수 있는 / (일반적으로, 새해의 결심에 대해서뿐만이 아니라)

READING 24 정답 ⑤   pp.72~73

Mini Quiz 모범 답안 고양이가 아니라 다른 동물의 예가 왔을 것이다.

1 ③ 2 (1) Because of the pet door, they can enter and leave a room without troubling their human friends. (2) Many of his animal friends (did).
3 (1) knocking (2) emotional (3) interrupted
  (4) annoyed

해석

아이작 뉴턴은 역사상 가장 위대한 과학자 중 한 명이다. 일생 동안 그는 과학에 수많은 공헌을 했다. 하지만 그가 또한 반려동물 애호가였다거나 때때로 그의 많은 동물 친구들이 그를 산만하게 만들 수 있었다는 것을 아는 사람은 거의 없다. (C) 예를 들어, 한번은 가장 좋아하는 개가 그의 책상 위에 있던 양초를 쳐서 넘어뜨렸을 때 그는 감정적인 신경쇠약을 겪었다. 그 개는 그의 중요한 연구 노트 중 일부를 태웠다. (B) 하지만, 짜증나게 하는 고양이에 대한 그의 대처는 더 행복한 결과로 이어졌다. 전해오는 이야기에 따르면, 고양이 한 마리가 끊임없이 뉴턴에게 집 안으로 들여보내 주고 집 밖으로 내보내 달라고 요구하며 방해했다

고 한다. (A) 그래서 그 과학자는 짜증이 났고 재빨리 해결책인 반려동물용 문을 생각해 냈다. 그 고양이는 뉴턴을 방해하지 않고 그의 집을 드나들 수 있었다. 오늘날, 인간 친구들을 괴롭히지 않고 방을 드나들 수 있는 능력을 가진 모든 고양이들은 뉴턴에게 감사해야 한다.

해설

p.72

뉴턴의 과학자로서의 공헌과 그가 또한 반려동물 애호가였고 동물 친구들 때문에 때때로 산만하게 되었다는 주어진 글에 이어, 이에 대한 예로서 개가 촛불을 넘어뜨려 괴로움을 겪었다는 내용의 (C)가 이어지고, 역접의 However로 시작하여 고양이의 경우는 개와는 달랐다는 상반된 내용의 (B)가 이어진 다음, 성가시게 하는 고양이를 위해 반려동물용 문을 생각해 냈다는 내용의 (A)가 마지막으로 이어지는 것이 가장 자연스럽다.

p.73

1 결국 고양이가 드나들 수 있도록 반려동물용 문을 생각해 낸 것을 의미하므로 a happier result가 의미하는 바로 가장 적절한 것은 ③ '반려동물용 문'이다.
 ① 양초
 ② 반려동물 애호가
 ④ 감정적인 신경쇠약
 ⑤ 과학에 대한 공헌

2 (1) 고양이들이 뉴턴에게 감사해야 하는 이유는 반려동물용 문을 뉴턴이 만들어 주어서 인간 친구들을 괴롭히지 않고 방을 드나들 수 있게 되었기 때문이다.
 (2) 때때로 그의 많은 동물 친구들이 그를 산만하게 만들 수 있었다고 했다.
 해석 (1) 왜 모든 고양이들이 뉴턴에게 고마워해야 하는가?
 (2) 무엇이 뉴턴을 산만하게 만들었는가?

3 해석

뉴턴의 동물 친구들로 인한 주의산만	
개	• 그의 책상 위에 있던 초를 쳐서 넘어뜨려 중요한 연구 노트 중 일부를 태웠다 • 그가 감정적인 신경쇠약을 겪게 했다
고양이	• 언제나 원할 때 집 안으로 들여보내 주고 집 밖으로 내보내 달라고 요구하며 그를 끊임없이 방해했다 • 그를 짜증 나게 했다

구문 설명

• Today, **every cat** [with the ability {to enter and leave a room *without troubling* their human friends}] **has** Newton to thank.
 [ ]는 문장의 주어인 every cat을 수식하며 그 안의 { }는 the ability를 수식하는 형용사적 용법의 to부정사구이다. 문장의 주어인 every cat이 단수이므로 동사도 단수형인 has가 쓰였다.

「without -ing」는 '~하지 않고'라는 뜻을 나타낸다.

- **For instance**, he once suffered an emotional breakdown [when a favorite dog knocked over a candle on his desk].
  For instance는 '예를 들어'를 의미하고 For example로 바꾸어 쓸 수 있다. [ ]는 시간을 나타내는 부사절로 '~할 때'라는 의미이다.

모범 답안

주제문	뉴턴은 반려동물 애호가였고 그들로 인해 산만해질 수 있었다.
부연 설명	• 반려동물용 문을 생각해 냈음 • 고양이의 끊임없는 방해를 받음 • 가장 좋아하는 개가 책상 위에 있던 양초를 쳐서 넘어뜨림 • 그 개가 중요한 연구 노트 중 일부를 태웠음

- According to legend, / a cat (S) constantly interrupted (V) Newton / with its demands / to be let in and out of the house.
  전해오는 이야기에 따르면 / 고양이 한 마리가 끊임없이 뉴턴을 방해했다 / 요구하며 / 집 안으로 들여보내 주고 집 밖으로 내보내 달라고

READING **25** → 정답 ②   pp.74~75

(Mini Quiz) But that does not mean that people have the critical skills to examine it carefully and understand it.

1 ⑤   2 ③
3 (1) more (2) fooled (3) social media

사람들은 많은 시간을 미디어와 상호 작용하는 데 보낸다. 하지만 그것은 사람들이 미디어를 주의 깊게 검토하여 이해하는 데 중요한 기술을 가지고 있다는 것을 의미하는 것은 아니다. (B) 2016년 스탠퍼드 대학교의 잘 알려진 한 연구가 있다. 그 연구는 젊은이들이 특히 소셜 미디어 채널을 통해 잘못된 정보에 쉽게 속는다는 것을 보여 주었다. 그러나 이러한 약점은 젊은이에게서만 발견되는 것은 아니다. (A) 뉴욕 대학교의 조사는 65세 이상의 사람들이 좀 더 젊은 사람들보다 7배나 더 많은 잘

못된 정보를 공유한다는 것을 알아냈다. 이 모든 것이 하나의 의문을 제기하는데, 즉 잘못된 정보 문제에 대한 해결책은 무엇인가? (C) 정부와 기술 플랫폼은 분명히 잘못된 정보를 막아내는 데 해야 할 역할이 있다. 그러나 모든 개인이 정보를 더 잘 이용하게 될 필요가 있다. 그리고 그들은 정보를 더 잘 이용하게 됨으로써 이러한 위협에 맞서 싸울 책임을 져야 한다.

p.74

사람들은 미디어와 상호 작용하는 데 많은 시간을 보내지만 그것이 그들이 미디어 분석과 이해에 중요한 기술을 가지고 있다는 것을 의미하지 않는다는 내용의 주어진 글 다음에는, 젊은이들이 소셜 미디어 채널을 통해 잘못된 정보에 쉽게 속는다는 연구 결과를 언급한 (B)가 오고, 또 다른 연구 결과로 65세 이상의 사람들이 젊은이들보다 7배나 많은 잘못된 정보를 공유한다는 것을 언급한 후, 이에 대한 해결책이 무엇인지 묻고 있는 (A)가 온 다음, 그 해결책으로 정부와 기술 플랫폼이 잘못된 정보를 막아내는 역할을 설명하는 (C)가 이어지는 것이 글의 흐름상 가장 자연스럽다.

p.75

1 모든 개인은 정보를 더 잘 이용하게 됨으로써 잘못된 정보의 위협에 맞서 싸울 책임을 져야 한다고 했으므로 글의 내용과 일치하지 않는 것은 ⑤ '개인은 잘못된 정보의 위협에 맞서 싸울 필요가 없다.'이다.
  ① 미디어와 상호 작용하는 것은 사람들이 그들의 많은 시간을 보내는 한 방식이다.
  ② 젊은이들은 잘못된 정보에 쉽게 속는 유일한 사람들이 아니다.
  ③ 정부와 기술 플랫폼은 잘못된 정보를 차단해야 한다.
  ④ 정보를 잘 활용할 수 있는 것은 모든 개인이 가져야 할 기술이다.

2 사람들이 미디어를 주의 깊게 검토하여 이해하는 데 중요한 기술을 가지고 있지 않다고 하면서 정부와 기술 플랫폼은 분명히 잘못된 정보를 막아내는 데 해야 할 역할이 있으나 모든 개인이 정보를 더 잘 이용하게 될 필요가 있고 잘못된 정보의 위협에 맞서 싸울 책임을 가져야 한다고 했으므로 필자가 주장하는 바로 가장 적절한 것은 ③이다.

3

	뉴욕 대학교	스탠퍼드 대학교
대상	65세 이상의 사람들과 좀 더 젊은 사람들	젊은이들
결과	65세 이상의 사람들이 더 젊은 사람들보다 훨씬 더 많은 잘못된 정보를 공유했다.	젊은이들은 소셜 미디어 채널을 통해 잘못된 정보에 쉽게 속는다.

- But that does not mean [**that** people have the critical skills {to examine it carefully and understand it}].

[ ]는 mean의 목적어 역할을 하는 명사절로 that은 접속사이다. 그 안의 { }는 the critical skills를 수식하는 형용사적 용법의 to부정사구이다.

· The study showed [**that** young people *are* easily *fooled by* misinformation, {especially when **it** comes through social media channels}].

[ ]는 showed의 목적어 역할을 하는 명사절로 that은 접속사이며 are fooled by ~는 수동태이다. 그 안의 { }는 시간을 나타내는 부사절로 '~할 때'를 의미하며 it은 misinformation을 가리킨다.

주제문	사람들은 <u>미디어</u>를 주의 깊게 검토하여 이해하는 데 중요한 기술을 가지고 있지 않다.
근거	· 잘못된 정보를 공유하는 것에 대해 연령별로 연구한 뉴욕 대학의 연구 결과 · 소셜 미디어의 잘못된 정보에 대해 <u>젊은이들</u>을 연구한 스탠퍼드 대학의 연구

· Research from New York University (S) found (V) / that people over 65 shared / seven times as much misinformation / as younger people.
뉴욕 대학의 조사는 알아냈다 / 65세 이상의 사람들이 공유한다는 것을 / 7배나 더 많은 잘못된 정보를 / 좀 더 젊은 사람들보다

Unit 10 주어진 문장 넣기

READING **26** · 정답 ③

pp.76~77

(Mini Quiz) Colors can help improve memory.

1 ③ 2 cautious
3 (1) colors (2) color cues (3) Black-and-white
  (4) colored (5) red (6) attention

색은 기억력 향상에 도움을 줄 수 있다. 예를 들어, 알츠하이머 환자들에 대한 일부 연구는 색 신호가 특정 이미지의 기억을 향상시키는 데 도움

이 된다는 것을 발견했다. 게다가, 그들은 흑백 이미지를 기억할 수 없었지만 컬러로 된 이미지를 기억할 수는 있었다. 또 다른 연구는 빨간색과 파란색이 뇌 기능을 향상시키는 데 가장 좋은 색이라는 것을 발견했다. 빨간색은 사회에서 그것의 역할 때문에 1위를 차지한다. <u>빨간색은 정지 신호와 위험의 색이고, 그것은 전형적으로 선생님들이 사용하는 펜의 색이다.</u> 이것은 빨간색이 학습과 현실 세계에서 중요한 색이고, 사람은 빨간색인 어떤 것을 기억할 가능성이 더 높다는 것을 의미한다. 게다가, 빨간색이 사람들을 주의 깊게 만들기 때문에, 그들은 세부적인 것을 더 많이 지향하게 되고 주의를 더 잘 기울인다. 이것은 사람들이 나중에 빨간색의 사물을 더 잘 기억하는 결과를 낳는다.

p.76

주어진 문장은 빨간색이 정지 신호와 위험의 색이면서 선생님들이 사용하는 펜의 색이라는 내용이다. ③ 다음의 문장에서 This가 학습과 현실 세계에서 중요한 색이며 기억할 가능성이 더 높은 것을 의미한다고 했는데 This가 가리키는 것이 주어진 문장의 내용이므로 주어진 문장이 들어가기에 가장 적절한 곳은 ③이다.

p.77

1 색이 기억력에 미치는 영향에 대해 몇 가지 예를 들어 설명하고 있으므로 글의 주제로 가장 적절한 것은 ③ '색이 기억력에 미치는 영향'이다.
① 여러분이 공부하는 데 도움을 줄 수 있는 색들
② 색채 교육의 필요성
④ 다채로운 기억들이 삶을 풍요롭게 하는 방식
⑤ 정말 잘 어울리는 두 가지 색

2 길을 건너거나 날카로운 도구를 사용할 때 느끼는 감정이나 상태를 나타내는 단어로 cautious(조심하는, 주의 깊은)가 적절하다.
(해석) · 나는 길을 건널 때 항상 <u>조심스럽다</u>.
· Mike는 날카로운 도구를 사용할 때 항상 <u>주의한다</u>.

3 (해석)

기억력은 색으로 향상될 수 있다.	
알츠하이머 환자들에 대한 연구	빨간색과 파란색에 대한 연구
· 특정 이미지의 기억이 색 신호의 도움으로 향상되었다. · 흑백 이미지는 기억될 수 없지만 컬러로 된 이미지는 기억될 수 있다.	· 학습과 현실 세계에서 중요한 색은 <u>빨간색</u>이다. · 빨간색은 사람들이 세부적인 것을 더 많이 지향하고 더 잘 <u>집중하게</u> 한다.

· This means [**that** {red is an important color in learning and in the real world}, and {a person is more likely to remember *something red*}].
[ ]는 means의 목적어 역할을 하는 명사절이고, that은 명사절을 이끄는 접속사이다. [ ] 안에는 두 개의 { }가 and로 병렬 연결

되어 있다. –thing으로 끝나는 명사는 뒤에서 형용사의 수식을 받아 something red와 같이 쓴다.

• This results in [**people** recalling a red-colored object better later].
[ ]는 전치사 in의 목적어 역할을 하는 동명사구이다. people은 동명사 recalling의 의미상 주어이다.

모범 답안

주제	색과 기억력 사이의 관계

근거	• 알츠하이머 환자들에 대한 실험: 컬러로 된 이미지를 기억함
	• 빨간색과 파란색에 대한 실험 결과: 빨간색인 사물을 더 잘 기억함
	  – 학습과 실제 세상에서 중요한 색임
	  – 사람들을 주의 깊게 만듦
	  – 사람들이 세부적인 것을 지향하게 하고 더 집중하게 함

• For example, / some studies on Alzheimer's patients (S) found (V) / that color cues helped / improve their recall of certain images.
예를 들어 / 알츠하이머 환자에 대한 일부 연구는 발견했다 / 색 신호가 도움이 된다는 것을 / 특정 이미지의 기억을 향상시키는 데

READING **27** 정답 ⑤ pp.78~79

(Mini Quiz) 모범 답안 감정을 이해하고 관리하는 것의 어려움(감정을 이해하고 관리하는 것이 부족함)

1 ⑤ 2 (1) F (2) F
3 (1) controlled (2) manage (3) required

해석

EQ에 대한 관심이 증가하고 있음에도 불구하고, 감정을 이해하고 관리하는 데 있어 전 세계적으로 부족한 부분이 여전히 남아 있다. 한 실험에서, 피실험자의 오직 36%만이 그들의 감정이 일어날 때 그것을 정확하게 식별할 수 있었다. 이것은 무엇을 시사하는가? 그것은 우리 중 3분의 2는 보통 우리의 감정에 의해 통제된다는 것을 의미한다. 하지만 우리는 아직 감정을 찾아내어 우리의 이익을 위해 그것들을 사용하는 데 능

숙하지 않다. 감정의 인식과 이해는 학교에서 가르치지 않는다. 우리는 지식의 본체를 읽고, 쓰고, 보고하는 방법을 배우고 나서 노동 시장에 들어간다. 하지만, 너무 자주, 우리가 직면한 도전적인 문제들의 열기 속에서 우리는 우리의 감정을 관리하는 기술이 부족하다. 훌륭한 결정은 사실적인 지식 훨씬 이상의 것을 필요로 한다. 그것들은 가장 필요할 때 우리의 자기 이해와 감정적 숙달을 사용하여 만들어진다.

해설

p.78

주어진 문장은 훌륭한 결정이 사실적인 지식 이상의 것을 필요로 한다는 내용이다. ⑤ 다음 문장의 They가 주어진 문장의 Good decisions를 가리켜, 자기 이해와 감정적 숙달이 훌륭한 결정을 위해 필요한 사실적인 지식 이상의 것이라는 문맥이 되어야 자연스러우므로, 주어진 문장이 들어가기에 가장 적절한 곳은 ⑤이다.

p.79

1 우리는 우리의 감정을 이해하고 찾아내어 그것을 사용하는 데 능숙하지 않고 우리의 감정을 관리하는 기술이 부족하다는 것이 글의 요지이다. 따라서 글의 제목으로 가장 적절한 것은 ⑤ '감정을 이해하고 관리하는 것에 있어 가야 할 길이 멀다'이다.
① 대화를 통해서 감정이 만들어지는 방식
② 우리 사이에: 문화가 어떻게 감정을 만들어 내는가
③ 마음의 울림: 숨겨진 감정 드러내기
④ 감정은 어떻게 만들어지는가: 뇌의 은밀한 생활

2 (1) 우리는 아직 감정을 찾아내어 우리의 이익을 위해 그것들을 사용하는 데 능숙하지 않다고 했으므로 글의 내용과 일치하지 않는다.
(2) 감정의 인식과 이해는 학교에서 가르치지 않는다고 했으므로 글의 내용과 일치하지 않는다.
(해석) (1) 감정을 찾아내어 이익을 위해 그것들을 사용하는 데 서툰 사람들은 거의 없다.
(2) 우리는 학교에서 감정의 인식과 이해를 배운다.

3 (해석) 우리는 대부분 감정에 의해 통제되지만, 감정을 완전히 이해하지 못하고 마음대로 관리할 수 없다. 하지만 훌륭한 결정을 내리기 위해서 자기 이해와 감정적 숙달이 요구된다.

구문 설명

• We enter the workforce after learning [**how to read, write, and report on bodies of knowledge**].
[ ]는 learning의 목적어 역할을 한다. 「how+to부정사」는 '~하는 방법'이라는 뜻이다.

• Too often, however, we lack the skills [**to manage our emotions**] in the heat of the challenging problems [**that** we face].
첫 번째 [ ]는 the skills를 수식하는 형용사적 용법의 to부정사구이다. 두 번째 [ ]는 the challenging problems를 수식하는 관계절이고, that은 목적격 관계대명사이다.

모범 답안

주제	감정에 대한 <u>이해</u>와 <u>관리</u>의 부족
근거	• 감정에 의해 통제되지만 감정을 찾아내어 <u>사용</u>하는 데 능숙하지 않음 • 감정의 인식과 이해는 <u>학교</u>에서 가르치지 않음 • 감정을 관리하는 기술이 <u>부족</u>함

직독직해 Skill

• They (S) are made (V) / by using our self-knowledge and emotional mastery / when they are needed most.

그것들은 만들어진다 / 우리의 자기 이해와 감정적 숙달을 사용함으로써 / 그것들이 가장 필요할 때

READING **28** ▸ 정답 ④ — pp.80~81

(Mini Quiz) food chain

1 ④ **2** transfer
3 (1) transfer (2) repeated (3) foxes (4) plant (5) animal
  (6) shorter (7) greater

해석

여러분은 과학 시간에 먹이 사슬에 대해 상당히 자주 들어본 적이 있을 것이다. 먹이 사슬은 무엇인가? 그것은 식품 에너지가 식물에 있는 에너지원으로부터 이동하는 것을 의미한다. 그 이동은 먹고 먹히는 반복되는 과정 동안 일련의 유기체를 통해 이루어진다. 초원에서는 풀이 토끼에게 먹히지만 결국 토끼는 여우에게 먹힌다. 이는 단순한 먹이 사슬의 사례이다. 이 먹이 사슬을 따르는 과정 속에서, 식품 에너지는 식물에서 동물로 또는 더 높은 영양 수준으로 전달된다. 관찰에 따르면, 각각의 이동 단계에서 잠재적 에너지의 80~90퍼센트가 열로 손실된다. 이런 이유로 하나의 과정 안에 있는 단계나 연결의 수는 보통 4~5개로 제한된다. 먹이 사슬이 짧을수록 이용 가능한 에너지 섭취량이 더 커진다.

해설

p.80
주어진 문장은 각 이동 단계에서 잠재적 에너지가 열로 손실된다는 내용이므로 '이런 이유로'라는 의미의 Hence로 시작하여 단계나 연결의 수가 4~5개로 제한된다는 내용 앞인 ④에 들어가는 것이 문맥상 가장 자연스럽다.

p.81
1 먹이 사슬에서 식품 에너지의 이동에 대한 글이므로 글의 제목으로

가장 적절한 것은 ④ '생태계에서 식품 에너지의 이동'이다.
① 왜 우리는 건강에 좋은 음식을 먹어야 하는가
② 음식을 다룰 때 조심하라
③ 먹이 사슬에서 인간에게 위협을 주는 것
⑤ 우리가 가장 많은 에너지를 얻는 식량원

2 빈칸에는 '옮기다, 이동하다' 등의 뜻을 갖는 transfer가 들어가야 한다.
  (해석) • 그녀는 자신의 가방을 한쪽 손에서 다른 쪽 손으로 <u>옮길</u> 것이다.
  • 그는 하버드에서 공부를 한 다음에 UCLA로 <u>옮길</u> 것이다.

3 (해석)

먹이 사슬에 대하여	
의미	식물에 있는 에너지원으로부터 식품 에너지의 <u>이동</u>, 이는 먹고 먹히는 <u>반복되는</u> 과정 동안 일련의 유기체를 통해 이루어짐
예	토끼에 의해 먹히는 풀과 여우에 의해 먹히는 토끼
에너지 이동	• 식물에서 동물 혹은 더 높은 영양 수준으로의 식품 에너지 이동 • 더 짧은 먹이 사슬이 더 <u>많이</u> 이용 가능한 에너지 섭취로 이어짐

구문 설명

• In the course of following this food chain, food energy **is transferred** [*from* the plant *to* the animal or *to* a higher trophic level].
is transferred는 수동태로 '전달된다'라는 뜻이다. [ ]에는 「from A to B」 구문이 쓰여 'A에서 B로'의 뜻을 나타낸다.

• **The shorter** the food chain, **the greater** the available energy intake is.
「the+비교급 ~, the+비교급 ...」은 '~하면 할수록 더 …하다'의 의미를 나타낸다.

Reading Skill

모범 답안

도입	먹이 사슬 설명	• 먹이 사슬은 식품 에너지가 에너지원으로부터 <u>이동</u>하는 것을 의미함 • 에너지의 이동은 먹고 먹히는 반복되는 과정 동안 일련의 <u>유기체</u>를 통해 이루어짐
전개	먹이 사슬 안에서의 에너지 효율 설명	• 먹이 사슬 과정에서 에너지 <u>손실</u>이 있음 • 먹이 사슬이 짧을수록 이용 가능한 에너지 섭취량이 더 커짐

• According to observations, / at each level of transfer, / 80 – 90 percent of the potential energy (S) / is lost (V) / as heat.
관찰에 따르면 / 각각의 이동 단계에서 / 잠재적 에너지의 80~90퍼센트가 / 손실된다 / 열로

Unit 11 무관한 문장 찾기

READING **29** · 정답 ④　　　　　　　　pp.82~83

(Mini Quiz) trained memory

1 ①　2 easier → harder[more difficult]
3 (1) exercised (2) developed (3) trained
　(4) concentration

해석

여러분이 더 많이 기억할수록 여러분은 더 많이 기억'할 수 있다'고 나는 믿는다. 기억은 많은 면에서 근육과 같다. 근육은 적절한 도움과 사용을 제공하기 위해 연습되고 발달되어야 하는데, 기억도 그래야만 한다. 다른 점은 근육이 과도하게 훈련되거나 근육이 뻣뻣해질 수 있는 반면 기억은 그럴 수 없다는 것이다. 여러분이 다른 어떤 것이든 배울 수 있는 것처럼 여러분의 기억력을 훈련하도록 배울 수 있다. 사실, 말하자면 악기를 연주하는 것을 배우는 것보다 훈련된 기억력을 발달시키는 것이 훨씬 더 쉽다. (암기는 복잡한 개념과 정보를 배우는 데 실용적이지 않다.) 훈련된 기억력과 함께 여러분은 아마도 더 큰 집중력, 더 순수한 관찰력, 그리고 아마도 더 강한 상상력을 얻게 될 것이다.

해설

p.82
기억은 근육과 같이 훈련될 수 있고 기억력이 훈련되면 집중력, 관찰력, 상상력이 좋아지는 효과를 얻게 될 것이라는 내용의 글로, '암기는 복잡한 개념과 정보를 배우는 데 실용적이지 않다'는 내용의 ④는 글의 흐름과 관계 없는 문장이다.

p.83
1 기억이 훈련되면 더 큰 집중력, 더 순수한 관찰력, 그리고 아마도 더 강한 상상력을 얻을 수 있다는 점이 언급되었으므로 글에 언급된 것은 ① '훈련된 기억의 혜택'이다.
② 훈련된 기억의 위험성
③ 여러분의 기억을 훈련하기 위한 전략
④ 지나치게 훈련된 기억의 부작용
⑤ 지나치게 훈련된 기억의 특징

2 훈련된 기억력을 발달시키는 것이 악기를 연주하는 것을 배우는 것보다 훨씬 더 쉽다고 했으므로 easier를 harder 또는 more difficult로 고쳐야 한다.
　해석 악기를 연주하는 것을 배우는 것이 기억력을 훈련시키는 것보다 훨씬 더 쉽다(→ 더 어렵다).

3 **해석** 근육처럼, 기억은 적절한 서비스와 사용을 제공하기 위해 연습되고 발달되어야 한다. 훈련된 기억력을 갖게 되면, 집중력, 관찰력, 상상력이 향상될 것이다.

구문 설명

• A muscle must be exercised and developed **in order to give** proper service and use: [so must memory].
「in order + to부정사」는 '~하기 위해서'라는 목적을 나타내고 「so as+to부정사」 혹은 'to부정사'로 바꾸어 표현할 수 있다. [ ]는 「so+동사+주어」의 도치구문으로 memory must be exercised and developed in order to give proper service and use, too를 의미한다.

• As a matter of fact, **it** is *much* easier [**to develop** a trained memory] than, say, [**to learn** to play a musical instrument].
it은 가주어이고 첫 번째 [ ]가 진주어이다. 「much easier ~ than ….」의 비교급 비교 구문이 사용되었는데, much는 비교급 강조 부사로 '훨씬'의 의미를 나타내며, 두 개의 [ ]가 서로 비교되었다.

　　　　　　　　　　　　　　　　　모범 답안

주제	기억의 <u>훈련</u> 가능성과 훈련된 기억력의 장점
근거	• 기억은 근육과 같이 연습되고 발달될 수 있음 • <u>악기 연주</u>를 배우는 것보다 훈련된 기억력을 발달시키는 것이 훨씬 더 쉬움 • 훈련된 기억력은 집중력, <u>관찰력</u>, 상상력을 높여줌

• I (S) believe (V) / that the more you remember, / the more you *can* remember.
나는 믿는다 / 여러분이 더 많이 기억할수록 / 여러분은 더 많이 기억'할 수 있다'고

READING 30 · 정답 ④

Mini Quiz Health and the spread of disease are very closely linked to how we live and how our cities operate.

1 ④ **2** advanced, survived
3 (1) deadly diseases (2) living conditions
    (3) sewer system

해석

건강과 질병의 확산은 우리가 어떻게 살고, 도시가 어떻게 운영되는지와 매우 밀접하게 연관되어 있다. 좋은 소식은 도시가 여러분이 상상할지도 모르는 것보다 더 빨리 회복될 수 있다는 것이다. 예를 들어, 많은 도시들이 지금까지 치명적인 질병을 경험해 왔다. 어느 정도 고통과 고난의 기간 후에 그들은 생존했을 뿐만 아니라 발전했다. 19세기와 20세기 초에 유럽의 도시들은 치명적인 질병의 파괴적인 발생을 보았다. 독일의 몇몇 유명한 의사들이 열악한 생활 환경과 질병 사이의 연관성을 발견했다. 이것은 치명적인 질병의 확산을 막기 위해 도시를 재계획하고 재건하는 것으로 이어졌다. (재건 노력에도 불구하고, 많은 지역의 도시들이 쇠퇴했고 많은 사람들이 떠나기 시작했다.) 19세기 중반, 콜레라의 확산을 막기 위해 런던의 선구적인 하수도가 건설되었다.

해설

p.84

건강과 질병 확산은 우리의 생활 환경 및 도시 기능과 밀접하게 연관되어 있다는 첫 문장이 주제문이다. 이어지는 문장에서는 많은 도시들이 치명적인 질병에서 살아남았고, 몇몇 의사들이 이런 연관성을 발견했으며, 질병 확산을 막기 위해 도시를 재건하는 노력을 해왔고, 그 예로 19세기 중반 런던의 하수 처리 시스템이 탄생했다고 언급하고 있다. 따라서 '재건의 노력에도 불구하고 도시들이 쇠퇴하고 사람들이 떠나기 시작했다'는 내용의 ④는 글의 흐름과 관계 없는 문장이다.

p.85

1 19세기 중반 런던에서 콜레라로 죽은 사람들의 숫자에 대해서는 언급되지 않았으므로 글에서 답을 찾을 수 없는 질문은 ④ '19세기 중반에 런던에서 얼마나 많은 사람들이 콜레라로 죽었는가?'이다.
① 무엇이 건강과 질병의 확산에 매우 밀접하게 연관되어 있는가?
② 19세기와 20세기 초에 유럽에서 무슨 일이 벌어졌는가?
③ 누가 열악한 생활 환경과 질병 사이의 연관성을 발견했는가?
⑤ 런던의 선구적인 하수도는 언제 만들어졌는가?

2 「not only A but also B」는 「B as well as A」로 바꾸어 쓸 수 있으므로 빈칸에는 차례로 advanced, survived가 들어가야 한다.

3 **해석** 파괴적인 치명적 질병이 발생했다. → 열악한 생활 환경과 질병 사이의 연관성이 발견되었다. → 도시가 재계획되고 재건되었다. → 런던의 선구적인 하수도가 건설되었다.

구문 설명

- After some period of pain and suffering, they **not only** survived, **but also** advanced.
  「not only A but (also) B」는 'A뿐만 아니라 B도'라는 의미를 나타내며 「B as well as A」로 바꿔 쓸 수 있다.

- In the mid-nineteenth century, London's pioneering sewer system **was built** [to stop the spread of cholera].
  was built는 수동태이며, [ ]는 목적을 나타내는 부사적 용법의 to부정사구로 '~하기 위해서'라는 뜻으로 해석된다.

Reading Skill

모범 답안

주제문	건강 및 질병의 확산은 생활 환경, 도시 운영과 밀접한 관련이 있다.
부연 설명	• 19세기와 20세기 초 유럽 도시들에서 치명적인 질병의 파괴적인 발생 • 독일의 의사들이 열악한 생활 환경과 질병 사이의 연관성을 발견 • 치명적인 질병의 확산을 막기 위한 도시 재계획과 재건 • 19세기 중반 콜레라 확산을 막기 위한 런던의 선구적인 하수도 건설

직독직해 Skill

- Health and the spread of disease (S) / are very closely linked (V) / to how we live / and how our cities operate.
  건강과 질병의 확산은 / 매우 밀접하게 연관되어 있다 / 우리가 어떻게 사는지에 / 그리고 도시가 어떻게 운영되는지에

Chapter 05

내용 추론하기

Reading Key 글의 내용을 단서로 추론하기 pp.88~89

정답

A b
주제문 노력
근거문 온라인, 저지방, 운동

B 지나치면, 균형, 중간 지점

해석

A 당신이 목표를 이루고자 하는 동기가 있으면, 당신은 상당한 노력을 들일 것이다. 예를 들면, 만약 좋은 차를 사고자 하는 동기가 있다면, 당신은 온라인으로 차들을 검색하고, 광고를 자세히 보며, 자동차 대리점들을 방문하는 것 등을 할 것이다. 마찬가지로, 몸무게를 줄이고자 하는 동기가 있다면, 당신은 저지방 식품을 사고, 더 적은 1인분의 양을 먹으며, 규칙적으로 운동을 할 것이다.

B 인생의 거의 모든 것에는, 좋은 것에도 지나침이 있을 수 있다. 심지어 인생에서 최상의 것도 지나치면 그리 좋지 않다. 아리스토텔레스는 미덕이 있다는 것은 균형을 찾는 것을 의미한다고 주장했다. 예를 들어, 사람들은 용감해져야 하지만, 만약 어떤 사람이 너무 용감하다면 그 사람은 무모해진다. 최상의 방법은 행복을 극대화하는 "sweet spot"에 머무르는 것이다. 아리스토텔레스는 미덕은 너무 두려워하지도 너무 무모하게 용감하지도 않은 중간 지점에 있다고 말한다.

Unit 12 빈칸 완성하기 1(단어)

READING **31** 정답 ① pp.90~91

Mini Quiz Reading fiction is exciting and, at the same time, very helpful.

1 ① **2** When fiction is compared to nonfiction, it is more effective in changing our views about people different from ourselves.
3 (1) ideas (2) changing (3) wisdom

해석

소설을 읽는 것은 역사상 가장 사랑받는 취미 중 하나이다. 미스터리, 공상 과학, 로맨스, 판타지는 모두 소설이다. 소설을 읽는 것은 흥미롭고 동시에 매우 도움이 된다. 그것이 창의성을 향상시킨다는 것은 잘 알려진 사실이다. 여러분이 소설을 읽는 동안, 여러분은 새로운 아이디어를 얻을 수 있다. 그리고 여러분은 세상에 대한 다양한 사고방식을 배울 수 있다. 또한, 소설을 읽을 때 여러분은 다른 사람들을 더 잘 이해할 수 있다. 연구는 다른 생각을 가지고 있는 사람들에 대한 우리의 견해를 바꾸는 데 소설이 논픽션보다 더 효과적이라는 것을 보여 준다. 게다가, 소설을 읽는 것은 여러분이 사람들과 더 잘 지내게 되는 데 도움을 줄 수 있다. 그것은 사람들이 상황과 도전에 어떻게 반응할 수 있는지에 대해 여러분에게 가르쳐준다. 등장인물들이 이야기에서 저지르는 실수를 보는 것은 여러분이 자신의 삶에서 사용할 수 있는 지혜를 얻는 것을 도울 수 있다. 이 모든 이점들을 염두에 두고, 오늘은 여러분의 스마트폰을 제쳐 두고 소설을 좀 읽는 것은 어떨까?

해설

p.90
글의 중심 내용은 소설이 여러 면에서 도움이 된다는 것이며 이를 뒷받침하기 위해 3가지 근거(창의성을 높여줌, 다른 사람들을 더 잘 이해할 수 있게 해줌, 사람들과 더 잘 지내도록 도와줌)를 들어 설명한 글이므로, 빈칸에는 앞에서 제시한 소설의 도움이 되는 면들을 종합할 수 있는 말이 들어가야 한다. 따라서 빈칸에 들어갈 말로 가장 적절한 것은 ① '이점들'이다.
② 질문들 ③ 한계들 ④ 도전들 ⑤ 차이점들

p.91

1 사람들이 실수를 하는 이유에 대해서는 언급되지 않았으므로, 답할 수 없는 질문은 ① '왜 사람들은 실수를 하는가?'이다.
② 소설의 몇 가지 예는 무엇인가?
③ 소설을 읽을 때 어떤 능력이 증가될 수 있는가?
④ 소설을 읽는 것으로부터 여러분은 무엇을 배울 수 있는가?
⑤ 소설을 읽는 것이 어떻게 여러분이 사람들과 더 잘 지내게 되는 것을 도울 수 있는가?

2 다른 사람들에 대한 우리의 견해를 바꾸는 데 소설이 논픽션보다 더 효과적이라고 했으므로 less를 more로 고쳐야 한다.
해석 소설을 논픽션과 비교할 때, 그것은 우리 자신과 다른 사람들에 대한 우리의 견해를 바꾸는 데 덜(→ 더) 효과적이다.

3 **해석** 소설을 읽는 것은 많은 이점이 있다. 첫째, 그것은 새로운 아이디어와 다양한 사고방식을 얻음으로써 창의력을 향상시킨다. 둘째, 그것은 다른 사람들에 대한 당신의 관점을 바꿈으로써 다른 사람들을 더 잘 이해할 수 있게 해 준다. 마지막으로, 그것은 다른 사람들의 실수에 대해 읽는 것으로부터 지혜를 얻음으로써 사람들과 더 잘 지낼 수 있도록 도와준다.

구문 설명

· **It is a well-known fact** [that it improves creativity].

It은 가주어이고 [　]가 진주어이다.

- Research indicates [that fiction is **more effective than** nonfiction in changing our views about people {who have different ideas}].
  [　]는 indicates의 목적어 역할을 하는 명사절이고, 이 절 내의 {　}는 주격 관계대명사절로 선행사 people을 수식한다. more effective than은 비교급 비교구문이다.

모범 답안

주제문	소설을 읽는 것은 큰 도움을 준다.
근거문	• 창의성을 향상시킨다. • 다른 사람들을 더 잘 이해할 수 있게 한다. • 사람들과 더 잘 지내도록 돕는다.

직독직해 Skill

- Seeing the mistakes (S) / characters make in stories / can help (V) you gain / wisdom to use / in your own lives.
  실수를 보는 것은 / 등장인물들이 이야기에서 저지르는 / 여러분이 얻는 것을 도울 수 있다 / 사용할 수 있는 지혜를 / 자신의 삶에서

READING 32 → 정답 ⑤　　　　pp.92~93

(Mini Quiz)　To do that, an animal's needs should be met consistently and predictably all the time.

1 ⑤　2 (1) F (2) F
3 (1) needs (2) consistent (3) control (4) confident

해석

우리는 동물에게 좋은 돌봄을 제공하고자 한다. 그렇게 하기 위해서는, 동물의 요구가 항상 일관적이고 예측 가능하게 충족되도록 해야 한다. 인간과 마찬가지로, 동물들은 통제감이 필요하다. 따라서 음식이 언제 나타날지를 알지 못하는 동물은 고통을 받을지도 모른다. 우리는 통제감을 줄 수 있다. 우리는 그저 우리 동물의 환경을 예측 가능하도록 확실히 해 주기만 하면 되는데, 그것은 마실 수 있는 물이 항상 있고, 그 물이 항상 같은 곳에 있는 것이다. 우리가 아침에 일어날 때와 저녁 산책을 한 후에는 늘 음식이 있다. 불편할 정도로 참을 필요 없이 배변할 수 있는 시간과 장소가 늘 있을 것이다. 반려인(사람 친구)은 한순간에 애정을 주다가 그다음에는 애정을 주지 않기보다는 일관된 정서적 지지를 보여 줄 수 있다. 무엇을 기대할 것인지를 알 때, 동물들은 더 자신감과 평온

함을 느낄 것이다.

해설

p.92

동물에게 좋은 보살핌을 주기 위해서는 동물의 요구를 일관성 있고 예측 가능하게 충족시켜야 한다는 내용의 글이고, 빈칸 다음에 우리가 동물에게 제공할 수 있는 환경의 사례를 들고 있으므로, 빈칸에 들어갈 말로 가장 적절한 것은 ⑤ '예측 가능하도록'이다.
① 조용하도록
② 자연적이도록
③ 고립되도록
④ 역동적이도록

p.93

1 글의 중심 내용은 동물에게 좋은 보살핌을 주기 위해서는 동물의 요구를 일관성 있고 예측 가능하게 충족시켜야 한다는 것이므로, 글의 주제로 가장 적절한 것은 ⑤ '동물의 보살핌에 있어서 지속성과 예측 가능성의 중요성'이다.
① 인간과 동물 사이의 관계
② 동물이 그들의 환경에 미치는 영향
③ 동물에게 반려인이 필요한 이유
④ 야생에서 멸종 위기에 처한 동물을 보호해야 할 필요성

2 (1) 무엇을 기대할 것인지를 알 때, 동물들은 더 자신감과 평온함을 느낄 수 있다고 했으므로 글의 내용과 일치하지 않는다.
　(2) 반려인이 한순간에 애정을 주다가 그다음에는 애정을 주지 않기보다는 일관된 정서적 지지를 보여줄 수 있다고 했으므로 글의 내용과 일치하지 않는다.
　해석 (1) 동물들이 무엇을 기대할지를 알 때, 그들은 더 고통을 느낄 수 있다.
　(2) 반려인이 한 번은 애정을 주고 그다음에는 애정을 주지 않는 것이 바람직하다.

3 **해석**

반려인의 노력	동물에 있어서의 결과
• 동물의 요구를 일관되고 예측 가능하게 충족시키기 • 일관된 정서적 지지 표시하기	• 통제감을 가짐 • 자신감과 평온함을 느낌

구문 설명

- So, an animal [**that** doesn't know when food will appear] may experience distress.
  [　]는 관계절로 an animal을 수식하며 that은 주격 관계대명사이다. 이 문장의 동사는 may experience이다.

- When animals know **what to expect**, they will feel more confident and calm.
  what to expect는 「의문사+to부정사」의 구조로 '무엇을 기대해야 할지'의 뜻이다.

모범 답안

주제문	동물의 돌봄은 일관적이고 예측 가능하게 이루어져야 한다.
근거문	• 음식이 언제 나타날지를 알지 못하는 동물은 고통을 받는다. • 마실 수 있는 물이 항상 있고, 그것은 항상 같은 곳에 있어야 한다. • 배변할 수 있는 시간과 장소가 늘 있어야 한다.

직독직해 Skill

· Human companions (S) can display (V) / consistent emotional support, / rather than / providing love one moment / and withholding love the next.
반려인은 보여줄 수 있다 / 일관된 정서적 지지를 / ~보다는 / 한순간에는 애정을 주다가 / 그다음에는 애정을 주지 않는 것

Unit 13 빈칸 완성하기2(구·절)

READING 33 · 정답 ③ pp.94~95

Mini Quiz 모범 답안 (great) leader, the basic truth about what makes people great

1 ③   2 (1) F (2) F
3 (1) charismatic (2) faith (3) give up

해석

역사상 유명한 사람들을 돌아보자. '아무개는 위대한 지도자가 될 운명으로 태어났다'는 식의 발언이 자주 나온다. 글쎄, 그 말은 종종 들리는 것만큼 사실은 아니다. 언제 어디서나 누구나 지도자가 될 수 있다. 그들은 너무나 카리스마가 있어서 전 세계가 주목할 것이다. 이것을 이해하기 위해서는 먼저 무엇이 사람을 위대하게 만드는가에 대한 기본적인 진리를 알아야 한다. 그 진리는 사람들이 스스로를 위대하게 만들지는 않는다는 것이다. 그렇다면 무엇이 사람들을 위대하게 만드는가? 그것은 그들이 믿는 대의이다. 배경이나 환경이 어떻든지 간에 어떤 사람에게 명확한 목표, 믿음, 또는 그들이 그것을 위해 모든 것을 기꺼이 포기할 원하는 어떤 것이 있을 때, 그 신념은 그의 감정, 힘, 그리고 행동을 위한 촉매가 될 것이다. 누군가가 어떤 것에 대해 전적으로 확신할 때, 세상은 놀라서 지켜볼 것이다.

해설

p.94

빈칸에는 사람을 위대하게 만드는 것이 무엇인지에 대한 답이 들어가야 하는데, 이에 대해 이어지는 문장에서 목표, 믿음, 원하는 것에 대한 신념이 이를 위한 촉매 역할을 한다고 설명하고 있다. 따라서 빈칸에 들어갈 말로 가장 적절한 것은 ③ '그들이 믿는 대의'이다.
① 창의적인 생각
② 노력과 연습
④ 기꺼이 다른 사람들을 도우려는 의지
⑤ 실수로부터 배우는 습관

p.95

1 지도자는 누구나 될 수 있고 훌륭한 지도자가 되게 하는 요인이 있다는 내용의 글이므로, 글의 제목으로 가장 적절한 것은 ③ '누가 위대한 지도자가 되는가?'이다.
① 왜 위대한 지도자들은 거짓말을 하는가?
② 더 나은 세상을 위한 리더십
④ 타고난 지도자의 특징
⑤ 미래의 지도자들이 위대한 결과를 얻는 방식

2 (1) '아무개는 위대한 지도자가 될 운명으로 태어났다'는 식의 발언은 종종 들리는 것만큼 사실은 아니라고 했으므로 글의 내용과 일치하지 않는다.
(2) 사람을 위대하게 만드는 기본적인 진리는 사람들이 스스로를 위대하게 만들지 않는 것이라고 했으므로 글의 내용과 일치하지 않는다.
해석 (1) '아무개는 위대한 지도자가 될 운명으로 태어났다'와 같은 발언은 항상 사실이다.
(2) 사람들을 위대하게 만드는 기본적인 진리는 사람들이 스스로를 위대하게 만든다는 것이다.

3 해석

지도자에 대한 모든 것	
지도자들은 어떠한가?	그들은 매우 카리스마 있다.
무엇이 사람들을 위대하게 만드는가?	그들 자신이 아니라, 그들의 신념.
어떤 사람의 감정, 힘, 그리고 행동을 위한 촉매가 되는 것은 무엇인가?	명확한 목표, 믿음, 또는 그것을 위해 모든 것을 기꺼이 포기할 어떤 것.

구문 설명

· [To understand this], one must first know the basic truth about [what makes people great].
첫 번째 [ ]는 to부정사의 부사적 용법으로 〈목적〉을 나타낸다. 두 번째 [ ]는 의문사 what이 이끄는 간접의문문으로 about의 목적어 역할을 한다.

· [When a person, no matter their background

or environment, has a clear goal, belief, or something {they want} {**that** they are willing to give up everything for}], that faith will be the catalyst for their emotions, strength, and actions.

[   ]는 시간의 부사절이고 '~할 때'를 의미한다. 그 안의 두 개의 목적격 관계대명사절인 {   }가 선행사 something을 수식하는 관계대명사의 이중한정 문장 구조로, 이중한정 문장에서 처음의 관계대명사는 생략되는 경우가 많다. 첫 번째 {   }의 they 앞에는 목적격 관계대명사 that이 생략되었다.

모범 답안

주제문	누구나 지도자가 될 수 있으며 사람을 위대하게 만드는 기본적인 진리를 알아야 한다.
세부 내용	• 사람들이 스스로를 위대하게 만들지는 않는다. • 사람들을 위대하게 만드는 것은 대의이다. • 신념은 감정, 힘, 그리고 행동을 위한 촉매가 될 것이다.

직독직해 Skill

• They (S) can be (V) / so charismatic / that the entire world will sit up and take notice.
그들은 ~일 수 있다 / 너무나 카리스마가 있는 / 그래서 전 세계가 주목할 것이다

READING 34 ▶ 정답 ①   pp.96~97

(Mini Quiz) frog(s), water

1 ②   **2** ④
3 (1) water-dwelling (2) skin (3) moist (4) dip
  (5) water (6) creatures

해석

과학자들은 개구리의 조상이 물에 사는, 물고기 같은 동물이었다고 믿는다. 최초의 개구리와 그들의 동족은 육지로 나와 그곳에서 먹이와 거처에 대한 기회를 누릴 수 있는 능력을 얻었다. 하지만 그들은 여전히 물과의 여러 인연을 유지했다. 개구리의 폐는 그다지 잘 기능하지 않고, 그것(개구리)은 피부를 통해 호흡함으로써 산소를 일부 얻는다. 하지만 이런 종류의 '호흡'이 제대로 이뤄지기 위해서는, 개구리의 피부가 촉촉하게 유지되어야 한다. 그래서 개구리는 물의 근처에 있어야 한다. 거기에서 그것은 피부가 건조해지는 것을 막기 위해 이따금 물에 몸을 잠깐 담

글 수 있다. 물고기 같은 조상이 그랬던 것처럼, 개구리 역시 물속에 알을 낳아야 한다. 그리고 물속에 낳은 알이 살아남으려면, 물에 사는 생물로 발달해야 한다. 따라서, 개구리에게 있어서 탈바꿈은 물에 사는 어린 형체와 육지에 사는 성체를 이어주는 다리를 제공한다.

해설

p.96

개구리가 물고기 같은 조상에서 시작해 점차 육지에서 사는 능력을 얻었지만 여전히 호흡이나 번식 등의 이유로 물을 필요로 한다는 내용이 빈칸 뒤에 이어지고 있으므로, 빈칸에 들어갈 말로 가장 적절한 것은 ① '여전히 물과의 여러 인연을 유지했다'이다.
② 필요한 기관을 거의 모두 가지고 있었다
③ 새로운 먹이에 대한 식욕을 키워야 했다
④ 종종 육지에 사는 종들과 경쟁했다
⑤ 급격한 온도 변화에 고통받았다

p.97

1 피부를 통해 호흡함으로써 산소를 일부 얻는다고 했으므로, 글의 내용과 일치하는 것은 ② '그것은 피부를 통해 호흡한다.'이다.
① 그것의 폐는 매우 잘 기능한다.
③ 그것의 피부는 건조하게 유지되어야 한다.
④ 그것은 육지에 알을 낳아야 한다.
⑤ 그것의 알은 물에 사는 생물이 되어야 할 필요가 없다.

2 개구리와 물은 서로 밀접한 관계가 있어 개구리가 물을 떠나 살 수 없다는 내용이므로, 글의 내용을 가장 잘 나타내는 속담은 ④ '물고기를 물에서 자유롭게 할 수 없다.'이다.
① 잔잔한 물이 깊다(잔잔한 물이 깊이 흐른다).
② 지켜보는 냄비는 끓지 않는다.
③ 피는 물보다 진하다.
⑤ 로마에서는 로마법을 따르라.

3 **해석**

개구리의 특징		
조상	호흡	알
• 아마도 물에 살았을 것이다 • 육지로 나오는 능력을 얻었다	• 폐와 피부를 둘 다 사용한다 • 피부를 촉촉하게 유지한다 • 이따금 몸을 잠깐 담근다	• 물에 낳는다 • 물에 사는 생물로 발달한다

구문 설명

• But **for this kind of "breathing"** [to work properly], the frog's skin **must** stay moist.
[   ]는 〈목적〉을 나타내는 부사적 용법의 to부정사구이고 for this kind of "breathing"은 to부정사구의 의미상 주어이다. must는 조동사로 '~해야 한다'의 뜻이며 뒤에 동사원형이 와야 한다.

- Frogs must also lay their eggs in water, as their fishlike ancestors **did**.

did는 laid their eggs in water를 대신하는 대동사이다.

모범 답안

주제문	개구리는 물가에 있어야 한다.
세부 내용	• 피부 호흡을 해야 하므로 피부가 촉촉하게 유지되어야 한다. • 물속에 알을 낳아야 한다. • 알이 물에 사는 생물로 발달해야 한다.

직독직해 Skill

- The first frogs and their relatives (S) / gained (V) the ability / to come out onto land / and enjoy the opportunities / for food and shelter there.

최초의 개구리와 그들의 동족은 / 능력을 얻었다 / 육지로 나와 / 기회를 누릴 수 있는 / 그곳에서 먹이와 거처에 대한

Unit 14 밑줄 친 부분 파악하기

READING **35** · 정답 ⑤

pp.98~99

Mini Quiz culture

1 ③

2 A person who wanders outside the box may be thought of as a creative person for a little while.

3 (1) impossible (2) maintain (3) acting (4) normal

해석

"상자 밖에서 생각하다"라는 말을 들어본 적이 있는가? 사람들이 상자 밖에서 생각하려고 할 때, 그들이 속한 문화가 바로 '그 상자이다.' 종교나 다른 전통들처럼, 문화는 우리에게 일종의 정신적인 위안과 보호를 제공한다. 상자 밖에서 방황하는 것은 창의성의 행위로 인식될 수 있지만, 잠시 동안만이다. 사람들은 상자 밖에서 살면서 상자 안에 있을 때 얻을 수 있는 모든 권리와 특권을 유지할 수는 없다. 그 상자 안에 남아야 한다는 압박감은 우리의 집단 신념을 내면화하고 집단 정체성을 취하는 것에 대한 것이다. 또한, 그것은 우리가 행동할 것으로 기대되는 대로 행동하는 것에 관한 것이다. 사람들은 모두 자신들이 하고 있는 일에

의문이 제기될 수 있다는 것을 전혀 의식하지 않고 일을 한다. 그러므로 문화는 정상적이라는 것이 무엇을 의미하는지를 정의한다.

해설

p.98

상자는 문화를 의미하므로 상자 안에 머물러야 한다는 것은 문화를 벗어나서는 안 된다는 것을 의미하며 이것은 집단 신념의 내면화, 집단 정체성, 기대되는 대로 행동하는 것에 관한 것이라고 했으므로, 밑줄 친 부분이 의미하는 바로 가장 적절한 것은 ⑤ '문화적 기대 속에 살아야'이다.
① 창의적인 결정을 해야
② 오랜 전통을 깨야
③ 문화적인 차이를 존중해야
④ 혁신적인 어떤 것을 만들어 내야

p.99

1 글에서 문화는 상자로 비유되어 있고, 문화를 집단의 신념과 정체성에 관한 것으로 설명하고 있으므로, 글에서 의미하는 바가 나머지 넷과 다른 하나는 ③ '창의성'이다.
① 상자
② 문화
④ 집단 신념
⑤ 집단 정체성

2 문화 밖에서 방황하는 사람은 잠시 동안 창의적인 사람이라고 인식될 수도 있다고 했으므로 typical(일반적인, 전형적인)을 creative(창의적인)로 고쳐야 한다.
해석 상자 밖에서 방황하는 사람은 잠시 동안 전형적인(→ 창의적인) 사람으로 인식될 수도 있다.

3 **해석** 문화는 우리에게 일종의 정신적 위안과 보호를 제공한다. 그 문화 밖에서 살면서 동시에 문화의 권리와 특권을 유지하는 것은 불가능하다. 문화는 우리의 집단 신념, 집단 정체성, 그리고 행동 방식에 관한 것이기 때문에, 그것은 정상적이라는 것이 무엇을 의미하는지 정의한다.

구문 설명

- [Wandering outside the box] **may be perceived** as an act of creativity but [only for a little while].

첫 번째 [ ]는 문장의 주어 역할을 하는 동명사구이다. may be perceived는 조동사가 있는 수동태 형태로 문장의 동사 역할을 한다. 두 번째 [ ]는 it may be perceived as an act of creativity only for a little while의 의미이다.

- People cannot [live outside the box] and [still maintain all the rights and privileges {**that** they can get when they stay inside it}].

두 개의 [ ]가 and로 연결되어 cannot에 이어져 있다. 두 번째 [ ] 안의 { }는 선행사 all the rights and privileges를 수식하는 관계절이고 that은 목적격 관계대명사이다.

모범 답안

주제문	문화는 우리에게 일종의 <u>정신적 안정</u>과 <u>보호</u>를 제공한다.
근거문	• 상자 밖에서 살면서 상자 안에 있을 때 얻을 수 있는 모든 권리와 특권을 유지할 수는 없다. • 상자 안에 머물러야 한다는 압박은 우리의 <u>집단 신념</u>을 내면화하고 <u>집단 정체성</u>을 취하는 것에 대한 것이다. • 문화는 <u>정상적</u>이라는 것이 무엇을 의미하는지 정의한다.

• When people try / to think outside the box, / the culture (S) / which they are a part of / is (V) *that box.*
사람들이 노력할 때 / 상자 밖에서 생각하려고 / 문화가 / 그들이 속한 / '그 상자이다'

READING **36** → 정답 ③   pp.100~101

Mini Quiz   Selective perception

1 ⑤   2 (1) T (2) T
3 (1) (e)xpectations (2) (e)vidence (3) (v)iewpoint

해석

우리는 선택적으로 사건을 해석하는 경향이 있다. 우리는 일이 '이런 방식' 또는 '저런 방식'이기를 원한다. 그러면 우리는 증거를 선택하거나 쌓거나 배열할 수 있다. 그리고 그것은 가장 확실히 우리의 관점을 뒷받침하는 방식으로 이루어진다. 선택적 지각은 우리에게 두드러져 보이는 것에 기반을 둔다. 그러나 우리에게 두드러져 보이고 있는 것은 특정한 것들과 매우 관련 있을지도 모른다. 즉, 그것은 우리의 목표, 관심사, 기대, 과거의 경험 또는 상황에 대한 현재의 요구와 관련되어 있다. 그것은 "망치를 손에 들고 있으면, 모든 것이 못처럼 보인다"와 같다. 이 인용문은 선택적 지각의 현상을 강조한다. 만약 우리가 <u>망치를 사용하기를 원</u>한다면, 그러면 우리 주변의 세상은 마치 못으로 가득 찬 것처럼 보이기 시작할지도 모른다!

해설

p.100

우리는 사건을 선택적으로 해석하는 경향이 있고, 선택적 지각이 우리에게 두드러져 보이는 것은 우리의 경험, 관심사, 기대 등과 관련 있

다는 내용의 글이다. 인용문의 '망치를 든다'는 것은 선택적 지각의 비유이고, 있는 그대로가 아닌 보고 싶은 대로 이해한다는 뜻이므로, 밑줄 친 부분이 의미하는 바로 가장 적절한 것은 ③ '특정 방식으로 무언가를 하고자 하다'이다.
① 돋보이는 것을 꺼리다
② 우리의 노력을 헛되게 만들다
④ 다른 사람들이 우리와 비슷한 관점을 갖기를 바라다
⑤ 다른 사람들에게 받아들여지는 사고방식을 가지다

p.101

1 망치를 손에 들고 있으면, 모든 것이 못처럼 보인다는 표현과 선택적 지각은 모두 자기 중심적인 사고, 즉 편견과 관련이 있으므로, 글의 내용을 가장 잘 나타내는 단어는 ⑤ '편견'이다.
① 노동 ② 통제 ③ 미스터리 ④ 창의력

2 (1) 우리는 우리 자신과 관련된 것들을 기반으로 사건을 인식하는 경향이 있다고 했으므로 글의 내용과 일치한다.
(2) "망치를 손에 들고 있으면, 모든 것이 못처럼 보인다"는 인용문은 선택적 지각의 현상을 강조한다고 했으므로 글의 내용과 일치한다.
해석 (1) 우리는 우리 자신과 관련된 것들을 기반으로 사건을 인식하는 경향이 있다.
(2) "망치를 손에 들고 있으면, 모든 것이 못처럼 보인다"는 인용문은 선택적으로 인식하는 것과 관련이 있다.

3 **해석**   선택적 지각의 과정

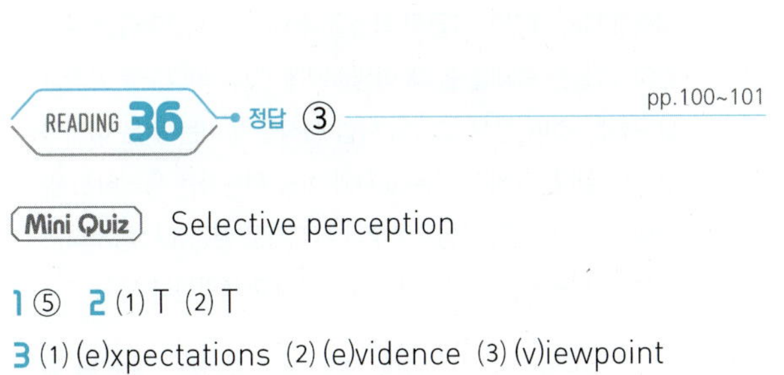

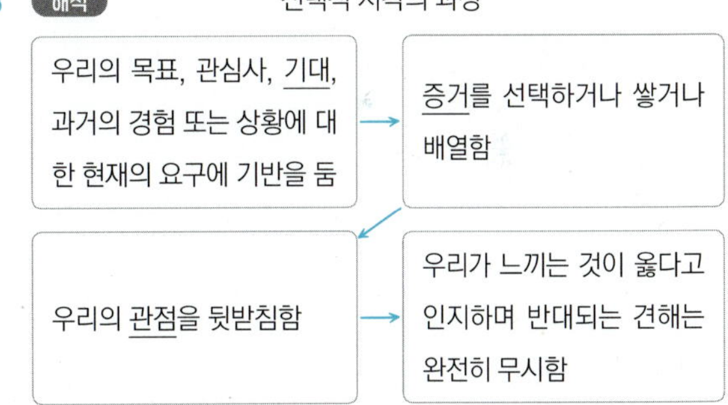

구문 설명

• And it is done most certainly in a way [that supports our viewpoint].
[ ]는 주격 관계대명사 that이 이끄는 관계절로 선행사 a way를 수식한다.

• However, the things [that seem to us to be standing out] may very well **be related** to certain things.
[ ]는 주격 관계대명사 that이 이끄는 관계절로 선행사 the things를 수식한다. be related는 「be+과거분사」 형태의 수동태이다.

모범 답안

주제문	우리는 <u>선택적으로</u> 사건을 해석하는 경향이 있다.
근거문	• 우리의 <u>관점</u>을 뒷받침하는 방식으로 증거를 선택하고 쌓고 배열한다. • <u>선택적 지각</u>은 우리에게 두드러져 보이는 것에 기반을 둔다. • 우리에게 두드러져 보이는 것은 우리와 관련된 특정한 것들이다.

직독직해 Skill

• If we want / to use a hammer, / then the world around us (S) / may begin (V) to look / as though it is full of nails!
만약 우리가 원한다면 / 망치를 사용하기를 / 그러면 우리 주변의 세상은 / 보이기 시작할지도 모른다 / 마치 그것이 못으로 가득 찬 것처럼

Chapter 06 긴 글 독해하기

Reading Key 긴 글의 구조 파악하기 pp.104~107

정답

A 주제문 비효율적
부연 설명 배경 소음, 배경 소음, 학업 성적
결론 시끄러운, 효과적

B 왼팔, (C), 결승전, (B), 방어, (D), 왼팔, 던지기

해석

A 많은 고등학생들이 TV를 보거나 음악을 들으면서 숙제를 하려고 하기 때문에 비효율적으로 공부하고 학습한다. 이 학생들은 또한 전화 통화, 간식, 비디오 게임, 인터넷 브라우징 때문에 공부하는 것을 방해받는다. 모순적이게도, 가장 집중을 해야 하는 학생들이 흔히 주의를 산만하게 하는 가장 많은 것들로 에워싸이게 되는 사람들이다. 이런 십 대들은 배경 소음이 공부를 '더 잘' 할 수 있게 한다고 믿으며, 일부 전문가들은 동의한다. 그들은 많은 십 대들이 어린 시절부터 '배경 소음'에 익숙해져서 그것이 그들의 학습을 해치지 않을 것이라고 주장한다. 그들은 숙제를 할 때 학생들에게 TV나 라디오를 끄라고 요구하는 것이 항상 그들의 학업 성적을 높이는 것은 아니라고 생각한다. 그러나 많은 교사와 학습 전문가는 동의하지 않으며, 그들 자신의 경험으로부터 시끄러운 환경에서 공부하는 학생들이 보통 덜 효과적으로 학습한다고 생각한다.

B (A) 한 소년이 자동차 사고로 왼쪽 팔을 잃었지만 유도를 배우기로 결심했다. 소년은 어느 나이 지긋한 일본 유도 숙련자와 레슨을 시작했다. 3개월간의 훈련 동안 유도 스승은 그에게 한 가지 동작만을 가르쳤다.

(C) 소년은 스승을 이해할 수 없었지만 훈련을 계속했다. 몇 달 후 스승은 소년을 첫 번째 토너먼트에 데려갔다. 놀랍게도 소년은 처음 두 경기를 쉽게 승리했다. 세 번째 경기에서는 자신의 한 가지 동작을 능숙하게 사용하여 승리했다. 그는 이제 결승전에 서게 되었다.

(B) 이번에는 상대가 더 컸고, 더 강했고, 더 노련했다. 그가 다칠 것을 염려했기 때문에 심판은 타임아웃을 선언했다. 그러나 스승은 "안 돼요, 경기를 계속하게 하세요." 라고 주장했다. 경기가 재개되고 얼마 되지 않아, 상대는 결정적 실수를 저질렀다. 그가 방어 자세를 풀었던 것이다. 그 즉시 소년은 자신의 동작을 사용해 그를 꼼짝 못하게 만들어 토너먼트에서 승리했다.

(D) 집으로 돌아오는 길에 그는 그의 스승에게 물었다. "스승님, 동작 하나만 가지고 어떻게 제가 챔피언이 되었나요?"

"너는 두 가지 이유 때문에 이겼다." 스승이 대답했다. "첫 번째, 너는 유도에서 가장 어려운 던지기 동작 중 하나에 통달했다. 그리고 두 번째로, 그 동작에 대한 유일하게 알려진 방어는 너의 상대가 너의 왼팔을 잡는 것이다." 소년의 가장 큰 약점이 그의 최고의 강점이 된 것이다.

Unit 15 장문 독해하기

READING **37** • 정답　　　pp.108~109

Mini Quiz　Therefore, the nature of trading is essentially the exchange of desires.

1 ③　**2** ③　**3** ⑤
4 (1) inherent (2) physical (3) brilliant
5 (1) limited (2) offering (3) trade

해석

본질적으로, 상품의 교환은 사실상 욕망의 교환이다. 모든 인간에게는 타고난 신체적, 정신적 한계가 있다. 그러므로 어떤 개인이든 대개 제한된 수의 개인적인 욕망만을 독립적으로 충족시킬 수 있을 뿐이다. 예를 들어, 토마스 에디슨은 전구를 발명할 수 있는 뛰어난 지성을 가지고 있었을지 모르지만, 아마도 농부나 건축가가 될 수 있는 적절한 능력을 가지고 있지는 않았을 것이다. 그는 먹을 만한 좋은 음식과 살 곳을 찾아야 했다. 그런 욕망을 충족시키기 위해서, 그는 그 대가로 다른 사람들의 욕망을 충족시킬 무언가를 제공할 필요가 있었다. 따라서 거래는 공동체 내에서 개인의 다양한 욕구를 줄이는(→ 충족시키는) 효과적인 수단이 된다. 그 공동체 내에서 모든 종류의 상품은 공개 시장에서 교환될 수 있다. 거래되는 상품은 음식, 옷, 자동차와 같은 물리적인 물건의 형태로 존재한다. 그렇지 않으면 지식과 음악처럼 더 추상적이거나 개념적인 형태로 존재한다. 형태에 관계없이, 이러한 상품들은 거래된다. 그 이유는 그것이 다른 사람들의 욕망을 충족시킬 수 있기 때문이다. 그러한 개인들은 기꺼이 그리고 목적을 가지고 그 거래에 참여하고 있다. 그러므로 거래의 본질은 본질적으로 욕망의 교환이다.

해설

p.108

1 거래는 인간의 욕구 충족을 위해 생겨났다는 것이 글의 요지이므로 글의 제목으로 가장 적절한 것은 ③ '인간의 욕망이 있는 곳에 거래가 있다'이다.
① 개방형 시장경제에서의 위기 관리
② 성공의 비결: 다른 사람들이 팔면 더 많이 사라
④ 물건을 소유한다고 해서 반드시 더 행복해지는 것은 아니다

⑤ 거래의 기회를 찾는 더 많은 방법을 가지려는 욕구

2 인간은 제한된 양의 욕구만을 독립적으로 충족시킬 수 있으므로 다른 사람의 욕망을 충족시킬 수 있는 무언가를 제공함으로써 자신의 욕망을 충족시키고 이렇게 하여 거래가 생겨나게 되었다는 내용이다. 따라서 거래는 공동체 내에서 개인의 다양한 욕구를 줄이는 수단이 아니라 충족시키는 수단이라고 볼 수 있으므로 (c) decreasing은 satisfying과 같은 단어로 바꾸는 것이 문맥상 자연스럽다.

p.109

3 공동체 내에서 모든 종류의 상품은 공개 시장에서 교환될 수 있다고 했으므로 글을 읽고 답할 수 있는 질문은 ⑤ '상품은 공동체의 어디에서 거래될 수 있는가?'이다.
① 욕망은 어떻게 인간을 파괴하는가?
② 개인이 선호하는 상품은 무엇인가?
③ 어떻게 하면 과도한 요구를 줄일 수 있는가?
④ 추상적인 형태의 상품을 어디서 살 수 있는가?

4 (1) '어떤 사람 혹은 어떤 것의 기본적인 성질에 속하는'의 뜻을 갖는 단어는 inherent이다.
(2) '마음이 아니라 사람의 신체와 관련된'이라는 뜻을 갖는 단어는 physical이다.
(3) '매우 지능이 높은, 대부분의 사람들보다 훨씬 더 지능이 높은'이라는 뜻을 갖는 단어는 brilliant이다.

5 **해석** 인간은 제한된 수의 욕망만을 독립적으로 충족시킬 수 있기 때문에, 다른 사람들의 욕망을 충족시킬 수 있는 무언가를 제공함으로써 그들의 욕망을 충족시킬 필요가 있다. 이렇게 해서 거래가 등장하게 되었다.

구문 설명

• For instance, Thomas Edison **may have had** the brilliant mind [**to invent** the electric light bulb], but he probably didn't have the right ability [**to be** a farmer or a builder].
may have had는 「may have+p.p.」의 형태로 과거의 일에 대한 추측(~했을지도 모른다)을 나타낸다. 두 개의 [ ]는 형용사적 용법의 to부정사구로 각각 the brilliant mind와 the right ability를 수식한다.

• [**In order to** satisfy those desires], he needed to offer something [that would satisfy the desires of other individuals in return].
첫 번째 [ ]에서 in order to는 '~하기 위해서'라는 의미로 목적을 나타내며 so as to로 바꾸어 쓸 수 있다. 두 번째 [ ]는 주격 관계대명사절로 something을 수식한다.

모범 답안

주제	상품의 교환은 욕망의 교환
근거	• 인간에게는 타고난 신체적, 정신적 한계가 있어 제한된 수의 개인적 욕망만 충족 가능함 • 욕망 충족을 위해 다른 사람들의 욕망을 충족시킬 무언가를 제공해야 함 • 거래되는 상품의 형태에 관계없이 사람들의 욕망을 충족시킬 수 있기 때문에 상품이 거래됨
결론	거래의 본질은 본질적으로 욕망의 교환임

직독직해 Skill

• Goods to be traded (S) exist (V) / in the form of physical objects, / such as food, clothes, and cars.
거래되는 상품은 존재한다 / 물리적인 물건의 형태로 / 음식, 옷, 자동차와 같은

READING 38 ▸ 정답

pp.110~111

Mini Quiz repetition

1 ① 2 ⑤ 3 ⑤ 4 (1) F (2) T
5 (1) practice (2) Repetition (3) frequency

해석

아이였을 때, 우리는 자전거 타는 법을 열심히 배웠다. 넘어지면 우리는 다시 올라탔는데, 그것이 우리에게 습관이 될 때까지 그렇게 했다. 그러나 어른으로 살면서 새로운 것을 시도해 볼 때 우리는 대개 단 한 번만 시도해 보고 나서 그것이 잘되었는지 판단하려 한다. 만일 우리가 처음에 성공하지 못하거나 혹은 약간 어색한 느낌이 들면, 또 다른 시도를 해 보기보다는 스스로에게 그것이 성공이 아니었다고 말할 것이다.
그것은 애석한 일인데, 반복이 우리 뇌를 재연결하는 과정에 핵심적이기 때문이다. 여러분의 뇌가 뉴런의 연결망을 가지고 있다는 개념을 생각해 보라. 여러분이 뇌 친화적인 피드백 기술을 잊지 않고 사용할 때마다 그것들은 서로 연결될 것이다. 그 연결은 처음에는 그리 신뢰할 만하지 않고, 여러분의 첫 번째 시도를 다소 마구잡이가 되도록 할 수도 있다. 여러분은 연관된 단계 중 하나는 기억하고, 다른 것들은 기억하지 못할 수도 있다. 그러나 과학자들은 "함께 활성화되는 뉴런들은 함께 연결된다."라고 말한다. 다시 말해서, 어떤 행동의 반복은 그 행동에 연관된 뉴런들 사이의 연결을 차단한다(→ 강화한다). 그것은 여러분이 그 새로운 피드백 기술을 더 여러 차례 사용해 볼수록, 여러분이 그것을 필요로 할 때 그것이 더 쉽게 여러분에게 다가올 것임을 의미한다.

해설

p.110

1 자전거 타는 법을 배울 때 넘어지면 다시 올라타서 습관이 될 때까지 반복하는 것처럼, 반복이 우리 뇌를 재연결하는 과정에 핵심적이며 어떤 행동의 반복은 그 행동에 연관된 뉴런들 사이의 연결을 강화한다는 내용의 글이다. 따라서 글의 제목으로 가장 적절한 것은 ① '반복하라, 그러면 여러분은 성공할 것이다'이다.
② 더 호기심을 갖고, 더 영리해져라
③ 놀이는 우리를 인간답게 만드는 것이다
④ 행동하기 전에 멈추고 생각하라
⑤ 성장은 균형을 유지하는 것이 전부다

2 반복이 우리 뇌를 재연결하는 과정에 핵심적이며, '함께 활성화되는 뉴런들은 함께 연결된다'고 했으므로, 어떤 행동의 반복은 그 행동에 연관된 뉴런들 사이의 연결을 강화한다고 볼 수 있다. 따라서 (e) blocks를 strengthens와 같은 단어로 바꾸는 것이 문맥상 자연스럽다.

p.111

3 자전거 타는 법을 배울 때와 비교하면서 우리 뇌를 재연결할 때 반복이 중요하다는 점을 말하고자 하므로 글의 요지로 가장 적절한 것은 ⑤이다.

4 (1) 뇌 친화적인 피드백 기술을 잊지 않고 사용할 때마다 그것들은 서로 연결될 것인데 연관된 단계 중 하나는 기억하고, 다른 것들은 기억하지 못할 수도 있다고 했으므로 글의 내용과 일치하지 않는다.
(2) 아이였을 때는 실패하더라도 습관이 될 때까지 반복해서 배웠지만 어른으로 살면서는 새로운 것을 시도해 볼 때 우리는 대개 단 한 번만 시도해 본다고 했으므로 글의 내용과 일치한다.
해석 (1) 뇌 친화적인 피드백 기술을 사용하는 것을 기억할 때마다 연관된 단계들을 동시에 기억할 것이다.
(2) 아이들과는 달리 어른들은 새로운 것을 시도할 때 대개 단 한 번만 시도한다.

5 **해석**

자전거 타는 법 배우기		우리의 뇌를 재연결하기
우리가 자전거를 잘 타게 될 때까지 우리는 반복해서 연습한다.	반복이 필요하다.	새로운 피드백 기술 사용 빈도가 증가함에 따라, 그것들은 필요할 때 쉽게 사용될 수 있다.

구문 설명

• They will connect with each other [**whenever** you *remember to use* a brain-friendly feedback technique].
[ ]는 시간의 부사절로 whenever는 '~할 때마다'라는 의미의 접속사이다. remember 다음에 to부정사가 목적어로 쓰일 때는 '~할 것을 기억하다'의 의미이다.

· You might remember one of the steps **involved**, and [not the others].

involved는 the steps를 수식하는 과거분사이다. 단계는 주체적으로 포함하는 행위자가 아니라 포함이 되는 대상이므로 수동의 의미를 갖는 과거분사로 수식을 받아야 한다. [   ]는 you might not remember the others를 의미한다.

모범 답안

주제	<u>반복</u>은 우리 뇌를 재연결하는 과정에 핵심적임
근거	· <u>뉴런</u>의 연결은 처음에는 그리 신뢰할 만하지 않을 수도 있음 · 함께 활성화되는 뉴런들은 함께 <u>연결됨</u> · 새로운 피드백 기술을 더 여러 차례 사용해 볼수록 그것은 필요할 때 더 쉽게 다가옴

· But / when we try something new / in our adult lives / we (S) will usually make (V) just one attempt / before judging / whether it worked.
그러나 / 새로운 것을 시도해 볼 때 / 어른으로 살면서 / 우리는 대개 단 한 번만 시도해 볼 것이다 / 판단하기 전에 / 그것이 잘 되었는지를

Unit 16 복합 문단 독해하기

READING 39 · 정답

pp.112~114

Mini Quiz Gaby, Nellie

1 ④ 2 ② 3 ② 4 ③, ④ 5 ③
6 (1) novice (2) injured (3) encouragement (4) proud

해석

(A) 아침에 Gaby는 자전거를 가져왔다. Gaby와 Nellie는 도시락을 쌌고 페달을 밟을 준비가 되었다. Nellie는 약간 걱정이 되었다. (a) <u>그녀</u>는 여전히 자전거 초보자였다. 그녀는 "오, 넌 할 수 있어, Nellie."라고 Gaby가 그녀에게 말했던 것을 기억한다. 물론이다. 그들은 나란히 페달을 밟았고 행복했으며 많이 웃었다.

(D) 길은 그들이 도시의 가장자리를 통과하게 이어졌고 거기서 갈림길이 되었다. 그들은 오른쪽으로 계속해서 갔다. Y자형 길 바로 근처에 울타리가 있는 집이 있었다. 갑자기, Nellie는 공포에 질렸고, 벽이 자신에게 바로 다가오는 것을 보았다. 마침내, (e) <u>그녀</u>는 벽에 부딪쳤다.

(B) Gaby는 Nellie를 구하러 달려갔다. Nellie의 코와 이마는 긁혔지만 자전거는 멀쩡했다. Nellie는 너무나 당황스럽고 두려워서 여행을 포기하고 기숙사로 돌아가 거기에서 혼자 아름다운 하루를 보내야 할 것 같았다. Gaby는 그 말을 듣지 않으려고 했다. (b) <u>그녀</u>는 자기 친구 옆에서 (자전거를) 타려고 했다. Nellie는 두려울 것이 없었다. "Nellie, 넌 할 수 있어."

(C) 그런 격려를 받고, 누가 다시 시도하지 않을 것인가? 그래서 Nellie는 자전거에 다시 올라타서 계속 페달을 밟았다. 시원한 바람이 얼굴을 스쳐 불면서 (c) <u>그녀</u>의 코는 느낌이 별로 좋지 않았다. 그들에게는 남은 여행 동안 더 이상의 사건이 없었고 좋은 하루를 즐겼다. 지친 두 소녀가 기숙사로 페달을 밟아 돌아왔고, 그곳에서 여자 사감은 Nellie의 부은 코에 대해 그녀와 몇 마디 이야기를 나누었다. (d) <u>그녀</u>는 자전거에 올라 페달을 밟다가 떨어졌다. 하지만 그녀는 해냈다.

해설

<u>p.112</u>

1 (A)에서 Gaby가 가져온 자전거를 타고 두 사람이 여행을 시작했다는 내용으로 시작하여, 갈림길에서 울타리가 있는 집의 벽에 Nellie가 부딪쳤다는 내용의 (D), Nellie를 구하기 위해서 Gaby가 달려왔고 Nellie가 자전거 여행을 포기하지 않도록 Gaby가 Nellie를 응원했다는 내용의 (B), 마침내 자전거 여행을 해내고 두 사람이 기숙사로 돌아왔다는 내용의 (C)로 이어지는 것이 글의 흐름상 가장 적절하다.

<u>p.113</u>

2 (b)의 She는 Gaby를 가리키고, 나머지는 모두 Nellie를 가리킨다.

3 (B)에서 Nellie의 코와 이마는 긁혔지만 자전거는 멀쩡했다 (Nellie's nose and forehead were scraped but the bike was OK.)고 했으므로 글의 내용과 일치하지 않는 것은 ② 이다.

4 Nellie가 다친 부위(코와 이마), Nellie의 자전거 실력(초보자), Nellie가 다친 장소(Y자형 길의 울타리가 있는 집 앞)에 대해서는 언급되었지만, Gaby의 자전거 상태와 기숙사로 돌아온 시각에 대해서는 언급되지 않았다.

5 자전거 초보자인 Nellie가 넘어지는 시련을 겪으면서 자전거 타기에 힘겹게 성공한 내용이므로 글의 내용과 가장 어울리는 속담은 ③ '첫걸음을 떼는 것이 항상 가장 어렵다.(시작이 반이다.)'이다.
① 정직이 최상의 방책이다.
② 일찍 일어나는 새가 벌레를 잡는다.
④ 로마에서는 로마 사람들이 하는 대로 해라.(로마에서는 로마법을 따라야 한다.)
⑤ 조금 아는 것이 위험하다.(선무당이 사람 잡는다.)

6 　**해석**　자전거 초보자로서 Nellie는 Gaby와 함께 여행을 갔다. 자전거를 타는 동안, Nellie는 벽에 부딪쳐서 다쳤다. Gaby의 격려로 Nellie는 여행을 계속했고 좋은 하루를 즐겼다. Nellie가 기숙사로 돌아왔을 때, 그녀는 스스로가 자랑스러웠을 것이다.

구문 설명

· "Oh, you can do it, Nellie," she **remembered Gaby saying** to her.
「remember+동명사」는 '~했던 것을 기억하다'라는 뜻이다. Gaby는 동명사 saying의 의미상 주어이다.

· All of a sudden, Nellie felt panic-stricken, and [**saw** the wall **coming** right at her].
[　]는 「지각동사 see+목적어+목적격보어」 구문으로 지각동사의 목적격보어로 동사원형 또는 분사가 올 수 있다.

Reading Skill

모범 답안

소재	Gaby와 Nellie의 자전거 여행
중심 내용	· 자전거 초보자인 Nellie · Nellie의 좌절과 Gaby의 격려 · 자전거 여행 중 일어난 사고에도 불구하고 여행을 끝까지 마무리함

직독직해 Skill

· Nellie (S) felt (V) so embarrassed and afraid / that she would have to give up the trip / and go back to the dorm / and spend the beautiful day there alone.
Nellie는 너무나 당황스럽고 두려워서 / 여행을 포기해야 할 것 같았다 / 그리고 기숙사로 돌아가 / 거기에서 혼자 아름다운 하루를 보내야 (할 것 같았다)

READING **40** · 정답　　　　　　　　　pp.116~118

Mini Quiz　모범 답안　(B) the pages(= (C)의 a speech)
(C) It(= (A)의 a fat paper clip)
(D) it(= (B)의 this speech)

1 ②　**2** ②　**3** ⑤　**4** ④
5 (1) separate　(2) deliver　(3) organize

---

6 (1) father　(2) equality　(3) study　(4) 1920

해석

(A) 내가 17살이었을 때, 나는 놀라운 물건 하나를 발견했다. 아버지와 나는 그의 서재 바닥에 앉아 있었다. 우리는 그의 오래된 서류들을 정리하고 있었다. 나는 카펫 건너에 있는 두꺼운 종이 클립을 보았다. 그것의 녹이 일종의 보고서의 표지 겉장 부분을 더럽혔다. 나는 그것을 집어 들었다. 나는 읽기 시작했다. 그러고 나서 나는 울기 시작했다.

(C) 그것은 아버지가 Tennessee주에서 1920년에 썼던 연설문이었다. 당시 (아버지는) 겨우 17살이었고 고등학교를 졸업했을 때인데, 그는 아프리카계 미국인들을 위한 평등을 요구했다. (b) 나는 그의 용기에 놀라워했고 1920년에 법으로 흑인과 백인을 여전히 분리시켰던 최남부 지역에서, 그렇게 어리고 백인이었던 (c) 그가 어떻게 그것(연설)을 할 용기가 있었는지 궁금했다. 나는 그에게 그것에 대해 물었다.

(B) "아빠," 나는 그에게 연설문을 넘겨주며 말했다. "이 연설문이요, 어떻게 그것(연설)을 할 허락을 받았어요? 그리고 두렵지 않았어요?" "음, 얘야," 그가 말했다. "나는 허락을 구하지 않았어. 나는 그저 나 자신에게 물었어. '우리 세대가 직면한 가장 중요한 도전 과제는 무엇인가?' 나는 바로 알았지. 그러고 나서 (a) 나는 스스로에게 물었어. '내가 두려워하지 않는다면, 내가 이 연설에서 그것에 대해 무엇을 말할까?'"

(D) "나는 그것(연설문)을 썼어. 그리고 연설을 했지. 나는 (연설) 중간쯤 교사, 학생, 학부모인 전체 청중이 일어나서 나가 버리는 것을 바라보았어. 무대에 홀로 남아서 (d) 나는 마음속으로 생각했어, '그럼, 내 인생에서 두 가지만 확실히 하면 되겠어. 계속 스스로를 생각할 것과 죽임을 당하지 않는 것.'" 그는 연설문을 내게 돌려주며 미소 지었다. "(e) 아빠는 그 두 가지를 모두 해낸 것 같아요."라고 나는 말했다.

해설

1 17살의 필자와 그의 아버지가 함께 서류 정리를 하다가 필자가 발견한 보고서 같은 것을 읽기 시작했다는 내용의 (A) 뒤에, 읽고 있는 그것이 아버지가 쓴 연설문임을 알게 되는 (C)가 오고, 아버지가 한 연설에 대해 궁금한 필자가 그것에 대해 질문하는 (B)로 이어진 후, 아버지가 평등을 요구하는 연설을 했을 때의 상황을 설명한 (D)가 마지막으로 오는 것이 글의 흐름상 가장 적절하다.

2 (b)의 I는 필자를 가리키고 나머지는 모두 필자의 아버지를 가리킨다.

3 (D)에서 연설 중간쯤 청중이 일어나 나가 버리는 것을 보았다(About half way through I looked up to see the entire audience of teachers, students, and parents stand up—and walk out.)고 했으므로 글의 내용과 일치하지 않는 것은 ⑤이다.

4 아버지가 연설을 했을 때 교사, 학생, 학부모인 전체 청중이 일어나서 나가 버렸다고 했으므로 글을 읽고 답할 수 있는 질문은 ④ '나의 아버지가 연설을 했을 때 무슨 일이 벌어졌는가?'이다.
① 왜 나의 아버지는 죽임을 당했는가?
② 나의 아버지의 연설은 얼마나 길었는가?
③ 왜 나의 아버지의 연설은 숨겨졌는가?
⑤ 내가 아버지의 연설문을 찾았을 때 아버지는 몇 살이었는가?

5 (1) '둘 이상의 사람 또는 사물이 함께 있는 것, 결합되는 것, 연결되는 것을 그만두게 하다'의 뜻을 갖는 단어는 separate이다.
(2) '한 무리의 사람들에게 연설, 성명 등을 발표하다'라는 뜻을 갖는 단어는 deliver이다.
(3) '물건을 쉽고 빠르게 찾거나 사용할 수 있도록 정리하거나 정돈하다'라는 뜻을 갖는 단어는 organize이다.

p.118

6 해석

	연설문
그것을 쓴 사람	나의 아버지
그것을 쓴 목적	아프리카계 미국인들을 위한 평등을 요구하기 위해서
그것이 발견된 장소	나의 아버지의 서재에서
그것이 작성된 해	1920년에

구문 설명

· It was **a speech** [he had written in 1920, in Tennessee].
[　]는 a speech를 수식하는 관계절로, 목적격 관계대명사 which[that]가 생략되어 있다.

· About half way through I looked up [**to see** the entire audience of teachers, students, and parents {**stand up — and walk out**}].
[　]는 〈결과〉의 의미를 나타내는 부사적 용법의 to부정사구이다.
{　}는 「지각동사 see+목적어+목적격보어」 구문에서 목적격보어에 해당한다.

모범 답안

소재	아프리카계 미국인들을 위한 평등을 요구했던 아버지의 연설문
중심 내용	• 오래된 서류를 정리하다 두꺼운 종이 클립을 발견함 • 아버지의 용기에 대해 놀라워하며 질문함 • 아버지에게서 연설문에 대한 이야기를 들음

직독직해 Skill

· I (S) marvelled (V1) / at his courage / and wondered (V2) / how, / in 1920, / so young, so white, / and in the deep South, / where the law still separated black from white, / he had had the courage / to deliver it.
나는 놀라워했고 / 그의 용기에 / 그리고 궁금했다 / 어떻게 / 1920년에 / 그렇게 어리고 백인이었던 / 그리고 최남부 지역에서 / 법으로 흑인과 백인을 여전히 분리시켰던 / 그에게 용기가 있었는지 / 그것(연설)을 할

Unit 01 주제 파악하기

READING **01**　　　　　　　　　　　Workbook p.2

1 ③　　2 ②　　3 ②　　4 taken
5 how we look in pictures

해설

1 거울만큼 사진에서 좋게 보이지 않는 몇 가지 이유에 대해 설명하는 글로, 가장 중요한 첫 번째 이유를 들고 있는 문장 앞이므로 '무엇보다도'의 의미를 나타내는 ③이 적절하다.
① 게다가　　② 결국　　④ 결과적으로　　⑤ 마찬가지로

2 우리는 거울 속의 이미지에 너무 익숙해서 이 이미지가 사진 속에서 뒤바뀌면 부자연스럽게 보일 것이므로, ⓑ natural(자연스러운)을 unnatural(부자연스러운)과 같은 말로 바꿔 써야 한다.

3 매일 보는 거울 속의 이미지가 가장 친숙하기 때문에 사진 속의 이미지보다 자연스럽고 좋게 보인다고 했으므로 ②가 글의 내용과 일치한다.

4 사역동사 have의 목적어(our pictures)와 목적격보어가 수동의 관계이므로 과거분사인 taken으로 고쳐 써야 한다.

5 전치사 with의 목적어 역할을 하는 간접의문문의 형태가 되어야 하므로 「의문사+주어+동사」의 순으로 배열한다.

READING **02**　　　　　　　　　　　Workbook p.3

1 ④　　2 ②　　3 ③　　4 pressure
5 캔에 든 우유를 본 적이 없는 것

해설

1 캔에 든 우유를 본 적이 있는지를 물어보는 주어진 글 뒤에, 캔에 든 우유를 볼 수 없는 이유로 온도에 민감한 우유의 특성을 언급한 (C)가 먼저 오고, 높은 온도와 압력에 노출되는 캔 식품 제조 과정이 우유에 미칠 수 있는 영향을 설명한 (A) 다음에 비용 문제까지 추가적으로 이유를 드는 (B)가 이어지는 것이 글의 순서로 적절하다.

2 등위접속사 and에 의해 두 개의 동사가 are 뒤에 이어져서 수동의 의미를 나타내므로 ⓑ를 과거분사인 exposed로 고쳐 써야 한다.

3 캔은 종이 팩이나 플라스틱보다 생산하는 비용이 더 비싸다고 했

으므로 ③은 글의 내용과 일치하지 않는다.

4 '어떤 것이 다른 무언가를 밀 때 발생되는 무게 또는 힘'의 의미를 나타내는 단어는 pressure(압력)이다.

5 밑줄 친 this는 바로 앞 문장의 내용으로 '캔에 든 우유를 본 적이 없는 것'을 의미한다.

READING **03**　　　　　　　　　　　Workbook p.4

1 ③　　2 ④　　3 ①　　4 nutritious
5 Meat production

해설

1 that절의 핵심 주어는 the majority of the animals로 복수이므로 ⓒ를 복수 동사인 are로 고쳐 써야 한다.

2 채식주의의 부작용에 대한 언급은 없으므로 글을 읽고 답할 수 없는 질문은 ④ '채식주의의 부작용은 무엇인가?'이다.
① 채식이 점점 인기를 끌고 있는가?
② 채식주의 식단의 이점은 무엇인가?
③ 젊은 성인들이 왜 자신들의 식단을 바꾸기로 결심하는가?
⑤ 고기 생산은 어떤 문제들을 야기하는가?

3 빈칸 앞에서는 채식주의 식단이 건강에 이롭다는 내용이 나오고 뒤에서는 건강에 대한 우려 때문으로만 식단을 바꾸기로 결정한 것은 아니라는 내용이 이어지므로 역접의 연결어인 ① '그러나'가 적절하다.
② 무엇보다도　　③ 결과적으로　　④ 예를 들어　　⑤ 게다가

4 '사람이나 동물이 건강하고 적절하게 성장하기 위해 필요한 물질들을 갖고 있는'의 의미를 나타내는 단어는 nutritious(영양가 있는)이다.

5 밑줄 친 It은 바로 앞 문장의 주어인 Meat production을 가리킨다.

Unit 02 제목 파악하기

READING **04**　　　　　　　　　　　Workbook p.5

1 ②　　2 ④　　3 ④　　4 hot enough to start nuclear fusion　5 clouds

1 중력이 가스와 먼지에 함께 힘을 가하고 뒤 문장에서 구름들이 압축된다고 했으므로 빈칸에 들어갈 말로 가장 적절한 것은 ② '수축하다'이다.
① 터지다   ③ 팽창하다   ④ 증가하다   ⑤ 발달하다

2 (A) 주어인 it이 the cloud를 가리키므로 수동형인 is squeezed가 적절하다. (B) enables의 목적격보어로 to부정사 to keep이 적절하다. (C) 동사 use와 등위접속사 and에 의해 병렬 연결되므로 return이 적절하다.

3 태양의 절반 이하의 질량을 가진 별들은 매우 천천히 사라진다고 했으므로 ④는 글의 내용과 일치하지 않는다.

4 '~할 만큼 충분히 …한'의 의미는 「형용사+enough+to부정사」의 형태로 나타낸다.

5 결국 원래의 형태인 가스와 먼지의 구름으로 되돌아간다는 의미가 되어야 하므로 clouds가 적절하다.

READING 05

Workbook p.6

1 ⑤   **2** ④   **3** ③   **4** ⓓ → shining
5 그림자가 어떻게 사용되는지는 또한 조명의 중요한 한 부분이다.

1 앞 문장의 내용은 밝게 비춰지는 대상에 대한 설명이고, 빈칸 뒤의 내용은 어둡게 비춰지는 대상에 대한 설명이므로 대조의 의미를 나타내는 ⑤ '반면에'가 적절하다.
① 유사하게   ② 그러므로   ③ 예를 들어   ④ 결과적으로

2 뒤 문장에서 앞 문장에 대한 예로 대상을 아래로 직접 비추는 빛에 대해 설명하고 있으므로 빈칸에 들어갈 가장 적절한 것은 ④ '위치'이다.
① 종류   ② 색깔   ③ 무게   ⑤ 밝기

3 그림자를 최소화하기 위해 밝은 빛을 사용하면 쾌활한 분위기를 만들어 내어 코미디와 액션 영화에 주로 사용된다고 했으므로 ③은 글의 내용과 일치하지 않는다.

4 문장의 주어는 a light이고 동사는 creates이므로 ⓓ는 a light를 수식하는 분사 형태가 적절하다. 수식을 받는 말과의 관계가 능동이므로 현재분사인 shining으로 고쳐 써야 한다.

5 간접의문문인 How shadows are used가 문장의 주어이고 is가 동사, 그 이하가 주격보어이므로 이에 알맞게 해석한다.

READING 06

Workbook p.7

1 ①   **2** ④   **3** ⑤   **4** average
5 goods they do not use

1 무언가를 사고 결국은 한 번도 사용하지 않은 때에 대해 생각해 보라는 주어진 글 뒤에, 그런 물건들에 대한 설명과 사용하지 않는 물건에 호주인들이 소비하는 금액을 설명하는 내용의 (A)가 먼저 오고, (C)의 That은 (A)에서 설명한 사용하지 않는 물건에 호주인들이 소비하는 금액을 나타내므로 (A) 바로 뒤에 (C)가 이어지며, 글의 전체적인 결론에 해당하는 (B)가 마지막에 오는 것이 적절하다.

2 주어의 핵심은 단수인 The difference이므로 ⓓ는 단수 동사 is로 고쳐 써야 한다.

3 앞에서 언급한 돈 낭비, 시간 낭비와 유사한 개념이어야 하므로, 빈칸에 들어갈 말로 가장 적절한 것은 ⑤ '쓰레기 (같은 것), 쓸모없는 것'이다.
① 열정   ② 범위   ③ 유산   ④ 욕망

4 '숫자를 모두 더하고 그 총 합계를 수량으로 나누어 계산된 수'의 의미를 나타내는 단어는 average(평균)이다.

5 목적격 관계대명사가 생략된 형태로, 선행사에 해당하는 goods 뒤에 주어와 동사의 순으로 배열한다.

Unit 03 목적·주장 파악하기

READING 07

Workbook p.8

1 ②   **2** ⑤   **3** ⑤
4 학교에서 달걀로 만든 음식을 제공하는 것을 중단해야 한다.
5 학생들이 계속해서 다양한 음식을 선택하는 것이 중요하다.

1 글쓴이는 딸의 담임 교사의 주장에 대해 반대하는 입장이므로, ② agree(동의하다)를 oppose(반대하다)와 같은 말로 바꿔 써야 한다.

2 (A) 수식을 받는 명사인 food와 분사구의 관계가 수동이므로 과거분사 made가 적절하다. (B) 주어가 복수인 Eggs이고, have와 be동사가 등위접속사 and에 의해 병렬 연결되므로 복수 동사인 are가 적절하다. (C) 앞에 선행사 foods가 있으므로

주격 관계대명사 that이 적절하다.

3 달걀이 알레르기를 유발해서 사용을 제한해야 한다는 주장에 대해 반대하면서 영양분이 풍부한 달걀을 제한하는 대신 달걀에 알레르기가 있는 학생들을 위해 라벨을 붙일 수 있다고 했으므로, 필자가 주장하는 바로 가장 적절한 것은 ⑤이다.

4 밑줄 친 his suggestion은 딸의 담임 교사의 주장으로, '학교에서 달걀로 만든 음식을 제공하는 것을 중단해야 한다.'는 것이다.

5 It은 가주어이고, students 앞에 접속사 that이 생략된 형태로, students 이하의 명사절이 진주어이다.

READING **08** ● Workbook p.9

1 ④　**2** ③　**3** ④　**4** nonverbal
5 messages you teachers send to your students

해설

1 사역동사 let의 목적격보어로 동사원형이 오므로 ⓓ to know를 know로 고쳐 써야 한다.

2 look for는 '~을 찾다'의 의미이다.

3 빈칸 앞 문장에서 대부분의 학생들은 흔히 자신의 선생님의 몸짓 언어를 매우 인식한다는 내용이 나오고 빈칸 뒤에 그것의 예를 보여 주는 문장이 이어지므로 ④ '예를 들면'이 적절하다.
① 무엇보다도　② 반대로　③ 게다가　⑤ 그럼에도 불구하고

4 '말을 포함하거나 사용하지 않는'의 의미를 나타내는 단어는 nonverbal(비언어적인)이다.

5 목적격 관계대명사가 생략된 형태로, 선행사 messages 뒤에 주어와 동사의 순서로 배열한다.

Unit 04 요지 파악하기

READING **09** ● Workbook p.10

1 ②　**2** ②　**3** ③　**4** coral bleaching
5 improve → improving

해설

1 '하지만 그것은 최근에 수많은 환경 문제에 직면해 왔다'는 내용의

주어진 문장은 글의 흐름이 바뀌며 여러 환경 문제를 언급하기 전인 ②에 들어가는 것이 적절하다.

2 농업용수와 산업 폐기물로 인한 수질 오염은 수질을 악화시키므로 ⓑ better를 poor와 같은 말로 바꿔 써야 한다.

3 해양 온도의 상승이 산호 탈색을 초래해서 산호가 색깔을 잃고 심지어 죽게 된다고 했으므로 ③은 글의 내용과 일치하지 않는다.

4 밑줄 친 This는 바로 앞 문장에 나오는 coral bleaching(산호 탈색)을 가리킨다.

5 improve는 such as의 목적어 역할을 하는 앞의 reducing과 병렬 연결되므로 improving으로 고쳐 써야 한다.

READING **10** ● Workbook p.11

1 ④　**2** ③　**3** ⓐ comfort zone ⓑ expand
4 gain valuable opportunities to grow

해설

1 성공하고 싶다면 불편함을 감수해야 한다는 앞 문장의 말을 풀어서 다른 말로 표현하고 있으므로 ④ '다시 말해서'가 적절하다.
① 대신에　② 하지만　③ 게다가　⑤ 반면에

2 (A) 전치사 about의 목적어로 주어와 동일한 대상을 가리키므로 재귀대명사 yourself가 적절하다. (B) 선행사 new people을 수식하는 목적격 관계대명사 who 또는 whom이 적절하다. (C) feel의 주격보어로 형용사인 uncomfortable이 적절하다.

3 '여러분의 ⓐ 편안한 영역(안락지대)을 벗어나서 새로운 무언가를 시도하는 것은 여러분의 시야를 ⓑ 확장하고 성공을 이루도록 도울 수 있다.'와 같이 요약하는 것이 적절하므로, 빈칸 ⓐ, ⓑ에 각각 comfort zone과 expand가 적절하다.

4 형용사적 용법의 to부정사는 명사 뒤에 오므로 「형용사+명사+to부정사」의 순으로 배열한다.

Unit 05 요약하기

READING **11** ● Workbook p.12

1 ④　**2** ⑤　**3** ⑤
4 광고가 사람들의 관심을 끄는 것은 중요하다.
5 ③ → showing

---

1 효과적인 광고는 사람들에게 상품이 그들의 삶을 어떻게 개선하는지 보여 줌으로써 사람들의 감정을 겨냥한다는 것이 글의 요지이므로 빈칸에 들어갈 말로 가장 적절한 것은 ④ '감정적인'이다.
① 예술적인　② 실용적인　③ 기술적인　⑤ 지적인

2 (B) 빈칸 앞 문장에서 모든 좋은 제품이나 서비스는 사람들이 자신들의 삶을 더 많이 살고, 일하고, 즐기도록 도울 수 있다는 내용이 나오고, 빈칸 뒤에서 스마트폰 광고를 예로 들어 설명하고 있으므로 '예를 들면'이라는 뜻의 For example이 적절하다.
(C) 빈칸 앞에서 기능을 이야기하는 광고는 설명처럼 느껴진다고 했고 빈칸 뒤에서 그것은 그다지 효과적인 광고는 아니라고 했으므로 '불행하게도'의 의미를 나타내는 Unfortunately가 적절하다.
① 요약하면 – 갑자기　② 요약하면 – 그래서　③ 예를 들면 – 유사하게　④ 예를 들면 – 다행히도

3 성공적인 광고는 사람들에게 제품이 삶을 더 풍부하고 편리하게 만들 수 있는지를 보여 주는 광고라고 했으므로 ⑤가 적절하다.

4 It이 가주어, to grab 이하가 진주어, advertisements가 to부정사의 의미상 주어이다.

5 분사구의 수식을 받는 명사인 advertisement와 분사가 능동의 관계이므로 ③을 현재분사인 showing으로 고쳐 써야 한다.

<hr>

READING **12**　Workbook p.13

1 ④　2 ③　3 ④　4 ethics
5 The truth likely lies somewhere in between.

1 인공지능(AI)이 고용 시장을 빠르게 변화시키고 있다는 주어진 글 뒤에, 이에 관련된 전문가들의 두 가지 의견을 말하고 있는 (C)가 먼저 오고, 인공지능에 의한 변화에 대한 근로자들의 대응 필요성과 방법을 설명하는 (A)가 이어지며, In addition으로 시작하여 추가적인 내용과 결론을 말하고 있는 (B)가 마지막에 오는 것이 적절하다.

2 that절의 주어인 AI systems가 '사용된다'는 의미가 되어야 하므로 ⓒ use를 수동태인 are used로 고쳐 써야 한다.

3 고용 시장이 AI에 의해 변화되고 있기 때문에 성공적인 근로자가 되기 위해 우리의 능력을 개발해야 한다는 요지의 글이므로, 필자가 주장하는 바로 가장 적절한 것은 ④이다.

4 '인간의 행동 또는 활동의 수행을 지배하는 도덕적 원칙'의 의미를 나타내는 단어는 ethics(윤리)이다.

5 주어(The truth)와 동사(lies)를 먼저 확인하고 동사 앞에 '아마도 ~할 것 같은'의 의미를 갖는 부사 likely가 오도록 쓰고, somewhere 뒤에 이를 수식하는 in between이 오도록 배열한다.

<hr>

READING **13**　Workbook p.14

1 ②　2 ③　3 ③　4 to sit
5 휴대 전화가 없는 방에서 대화한 사람들

1 주어진 문장은 '대화가 끝나고 나서, 연구자들은 참가자들에게 서로에 대해 어떻게 생각하는지 물었다.'는 내용이므로 실험 조건을 설명한 부분과 실험 결과를 설명한 부분 사이인 ②에 들어가는 것이 적절하다.

2 바로 앞 문장에서 방에 휴대 전화가 있을 때 참가자들의 관계의 질은 휴대 전화가 없는 방에서 대화한 참가자들보다 더 나빴다고 말했으므로 휴대 전화가 있는 방에서 대화한 쌍들은 자신의 상대가 공감을 덜 보였다고 생각했다는 흐름이 알맞다. 따라서 ⓒ more를 less로 써야 적절하다.

3 휴대 전화의 존재는 심지어 휴대 전화가 무시되고 있을 때조차 대화에 참여하는 사람들의 관계를 악화시킬 수 있다는 것이 글의 요지이므로 ③이 글의 내용과 일치한다.

4 동사 ask의 목적격보어로 to부정사가 오므로 to sit으로 고쳐 써야 한다.

5 who는 주격 관계대명사이며 those who는 '~한 사람들'의 의미를 나타낸다.

Unit 06 안내문·도표 파악하기

READING **14**　Workbook p.15

1 ⑤　2 ②　3 scene
4 행사에 참여하려면 www.citylibrary.org/events에서 등록하세요.

해설

1 행사는 2시간 동안 진행되고, 바닷속 체험과 관련된 내용은 언급되지 않았으며, 참가 신청은 웹사이트에서 해야 하고, 9살부터 11살 사이의 어린이만 행사에 참여할 수 있다고 했다.

2 문맥상 '~할 때까지'의 의미를 나타내는 접속사 until이 적절하다.
① 만약 ~라면　③ ~하는 동안　④ ~에도 불구하고
⑤ ~ 때문에

3 '특정한 행동이나 활동이 일어나는 연극, 영화, 이야기 등의 한 부분'의 의미를 나타내는 단어는 scene(장면)이다.

4 to attend는 목적을 나타내는 부사적 용법의 to부정사이므로 '참여하기 위해서'의 의미로 해석한다.

2 (B) 조사는 '수행되는' 것이므로 수동태로 써야 하며 과거시제이므로 was done이 적절하다. (C) 주어가 Students이고, participate는 동사이므로 과거 시제에 맞게 participated로 써야 한다.

3 2016년에는 62%, 2019년에는 61%의 학생들이 디지털 콘텐츠를 위해 태블릿을 사용했으므로 ⓑ less를 more로 고쳐 써야 한다.

4 밑줄 친 부분은 shows의 직접목적어로 쓰인 간접의문문이고, to access는 목적을 나타내는 부사적 용법의 to부정사로 쓰였다.

5 밑줄 친 that은 문장의 주어인 The percentage of students who used smartphones를 대신하는 대명사로 쓰였다.

READING 15　　　　　　　　　● Workbook p.16

1 ④　**2** ①　**3** reservation
4 Are you looking for something special

해설

1 단수 주어인 This cruise ship에 대한 동사로 is와 and에 의해 병렬 연결되므로 ⓓ는 단수 동사 has로 고쳐 써야 한다.

2 유람선에 있는 시설들에 대한 항목이므로 빈칸에 들어갈 말로 가장 적절한 것은 ① '시설'이다.
② 위치　③ 재료　④ 기구　⑤ 오락거리

3 '나중에 사용하기 위해 (방, 식탁, 자리와 같은) 어떤 것을 잡아 두는 준비'의 의미를 나타내는 단어는 reservation(예약)이다.

4 -thing으로 끝나는 대명사는 형용사가 뒤에서 수식하므로 something special의 순으로 배열해야 한다.

READING 16　　　　　　　　　● Workbook p.17

1 ④　**2** ③　**3** ②
4 학생들이 교육용 디지털 콘텐츠에 접근하기 위해 무슨 기기를 사용했는지를
5 The percentage of students who used smartphones

해설

1 조사를 진행한 주체에 대해서는 언급되어 있지 않다.

Unit 07 내용 일치 파악하기

READING 17　　　　　　　　　● Workbook p.18

1 ③　**2** ②　**3** ①　**4** degree
5 그녀의 대학 교육을 위한 돈이 없었다

해설

1 돈이 없어서 대학을 가지 못했으므로 대학에서의 전공에 대해서는 알 수 없다.

2 a job을 수식하는 현재분사 detecting과 and로 병렬 연결되므로 ⓑ는 현재분사 형태인 making으로 고쳐 써야 한다.

3 빈칸 앞 문장에 대한 결과가 이어지고 있으므로 ① '그래서'가 적절하다.
② 마침내　③ 게다가　④ 하지만　⑤ 그럼에도 불구하고

4 '대학에서 공부하는 과정 또는 그 과정을 완료한 후에 받는 자격'의 의미를 나타내는 단어는 degree(학위)이다.

5 「there was no+단수 명사」는 '~이 없었다'의 의미이다.

READING 18　　　　　　　　　● Workbook p.19

1 ③　**2** ⑤　**3** ④　**4** location
5 a small key that could be exchanged

---

1   (A) Byron Preiss에 의해 만들어진 책이므로 수동의 의미를 나타내는 과거분사 created가 적절하다. (B) that은 주격 관계대명사로 선행사가 단수인 information이므로 단수 동사 indicates가 적절하다. (C) 주어인 the most recent one의 one은 a treasure box를 가리키므로 수동태인 was found가 적절하다.

2   빈칸 앞에서 책에 12개의 신비한 그림과 시가 있는데 그것들은 파묻힌 보물의 위치를 가리키는 정보를 담고 있다고 했고, 빈칸 뒤에서 그림과 시가 가리키는 구체적인 내용을 예를 들어 설명하고 있으므로 ⑤ '예를 들어'가 적절하다.
   ① 유사하게   ② 그러므로   ③ 그렇지 않으면   ④ 게다가

3   보물 상자를 발견한 사람이 누구인지에 대해서는 언급되어 있지 않으므로, 글을 읽고 답할 수 없는 질문은 ④ '누가 시카고에서 첫 번째 보물 상자를 발견했는가?'이다.
   ① 책 '비밀: 보물 찾기'는 누가 썼는가?
   ② Preiss는 얼마나 많은 보물 상자를 묻었는가?
   ③ Preiss에 의해 묻힌 보물 상자에는 무엇이 들어 있는가?
   ⑤ Byron Preiss는 언제 사망했는가?

4   글의 내용상 보물들의 정확한 '위치'가 되어야 하므로 locations가 적절하다.

5   주격 관계대명사 that이 이끄는 절이 선행사인 a small key를 수식하고, 조동사가 있는 수동태는 「조동사+be+과거분사」의 형태로 쓰므로 이에 맞게 배열한다.

READING **19**   ● Workbook p.20

1 ③   2 ①   3 ⑤   4 career
5 if she could get a job

1   제안을 나타내는 동사 suggest가 쓰이면 「suggest that+주어+(should+)동사원형」의 형태로 써서 '~에게 …할 것을 제안하다'의 의미를 나타내며 that절의 동사 형태는 「(should+)동사원형」으로 쓰므로, took를 (should) take로 고쳐 써야 한다.

2   빈칸 뒤는 일을 그만둔 이유에 해당하므로 ① '~ 때문에'가 적절하다.
   ② ~와 같은   ③ ~의 경우   ④ ~에도 불구하고   ⑤ ~에 따르면

3   Ellen Church의 이름을 따서 공항의 이름이 지어졌다고 했지만 누가 공항 이름을 그녀의 이름을 따서 지었는지는 언급되지 않았으므로, 글을 읽고 답할 수 없는 질문은 ⑤ '누가 Cresco에 있는 공항을 Ellen Church의 이름을 따서 이름 지었는가?'이다.

① 그녀는 어디에서 태어났는가?
② 그녀는 고등학교를 졸업한 후에 무엇을 공부했는가?
③ 그녀는 세계 최초의 여성 승무원이었는가?
④ 그녀는 왜 Boeing 80A 비행기에서 일하는 것을 그만두었는가?

4   '누군가가 오랫동안 하는 일이나 직업'의 의미를 나타내는 단어는 career(경력, 이력)이다.

5   asked의 목적어 역할을 하는 명사절로, 접속사 if 뒤에 주어와 동사의 순으로 배열한다.

Unit 08 분위기·심경 파악하기

READING **20**   ● Workbook p.21

1 ②   2 ③   3 ⑤   4 atmosphere
5 a comfortable place to relax

1   침실은 2층에 있고, 거실은 1층에 있다고 했으므로 ②는 글의 내용과 일치하지 않는다.

2   새로운 집의 내부를 둘러보며 만족한 심정으로 집 밖의 마당으로 나가고 있는 상황이므로 ⓒ disappointed(실망한)를 satisfied(만족한)와 같은 말로 바꿔 써야 한다.

3   이웃에서 어린아이들의 웃음소리가 들렸다는 앞 문장의 내용과 연관되어 그들의 딸이 갖게 될 대상이어야 하므로, 빈칸에 들어갈 말로 가장 적절한 것은 ⑤ '놀이 친구들'이다.
   ① 장난감   ② 여자 형제들   ③ 꽃   ④ 강아지들

4   '어떤 장소에 존재하고 그곳에 있는 사람들에게 영향을 끼치는 분위기나 느낌'의 의미를 나타내는 단어는 atmosphere(분위기)이다.

5   형용사적 용법으로 쓰인 to부정사는 명사 뒤에서 명사를 꾸미므로 명사 뒤에 to부정사의 순으로 배열한다.

READING **21**   ● Workbook p.22

1 ①   2 ④   3 ④
4 (that) her husband had put a lot of thought into the gift

5 세상에는 항상 웃고 기쁨을 찾을 수 있는 이유가 있다

해설

1 주어진 문장은 '그래서 남편이 점심 식사 후에 아름다운 장미로 그녀를 놀라게 했을 때 매우 기뻤다'는 내용으로, Emily가 힘든 한 주를 보냈다는 내용과 선명한 색과 섬세한 꽃잎이 상쾌했다는 내용 사이인 ①에 들어가는 것이 적절하다.

2 글의 흐름상 그녀의 곁에 남편 같이 멋진 사람이 있다는 것을 행운이라고 느끼는 것이 자연스러우므로 ⓓ unlucky를 lucky로 바꿔 써야 한다.

3 Emily와 그녀의 남편이 같은 회사에서 일하는지에 대해서는 글에 언급되지 않았으므로, 글을 읽고 답할 수 없는 질문은 ④ 'Emily와 그녀의 남편은 같은 회사에서 일하는가?'이다.
① Emily는 그 주를 어떻게 보냈는가?
② Emily 남편의 깜짝 선물은 무엇이었는가?
③ Emily 남편의 깜짝 선물은 무엇을 상징했는가?
⑤ Emily는 남편의 선물의 의미를 이해했을 때 기분이 어땠는가?

4 it은 바로 앞 문장의 목적어 역할을 하는 that절의 내용을 가리킨다.

5 to smile 이하가 앞의 명사 reasons를 꾸며 주는 형용사적 용법의 to부정사구이다.

READING 22 • Workbook p.23

1 ③ **2** ⑤ **3** ③ **4** fossil
5 What a waste of time

해설

1 주어의 핵심은 단수 명사인 dream이므로 ⓒ를 단수 동사 was로 고쳐 써야 한다.

2 뒤에 이어지는 내용으로 보아 결국 화석을 찾지 못한 것이므로 빈칸에 들어갈 말로 가장 적절한 것은 ⑤ '성공하지 못한'이다.
① 만족한 ② 영광스러운 ③ 긍정적인 ④ 자신감 있는

3 두 번째 문장에서 Evelyn은 아마추어 뼈 발굴자라고 했으므로 ③은 글의 내용과 일치하지 않는다.

4 '고대에 살았던 식물이나 동물에서 온 것으로, 일부 암석에서 볼 수 있는 것'의 의미를 나타내는 단어는 fossil(화석)이다.

5 뒤에 주어와 동사가 생략된 what 감탄문이므로 「what+a+(형용사)+명사」의 순으로 배열한다.

Unit 09 글의 순서 파악하기

READING 23 • Workbook p.24

1 ② **2** ② **3** ④
4 새로운 행동은 우리가 예상했던 것보다 더 어려운 것으로 판명된다.
5 ⓒ → stopping

해설

1 주어진 문장의 them은 Some psychologists를 가리키며 the *false hope syndrome*을 ②의 뒤 문장에서 This syndrome으로 받아 설명하므로 주어진 문장은 ②에 들어가는 것이 적절하다.

2 이어지는 내용의 '과장된 통제감', '지나친 자신감' 등과 유사한 개념이 되어야 하므로, 빈칸에 들어갈 말로 가장 적절한 것은 ② '비현실적인'이다.
① 쓸모없는 ③ 합리적인 ④ 의미 있는 ⑤ 중요하지 않은

3 결심을 지키지 못하는 이유에 대해 설명하는 글이므로, 글의 주제로 가장 적절한 것은 ④ '우리가 결심을 지키지 못하는 이유'이다.
① 체중을 줄이는 효과적인 방법들
② 거짓 희망 증후군의 이점
③ 성공적으로 우리의 행동을 변화시키는 방법
⑤ 기대와 현실 사이의 큰 차이

4 비교급 문장이므로 '~보다 더 …한'으로 해석한다.

5 '~하는 데 어려움이 없다'라는 의미의 「have no trouble -ing」 구문이므로 ⓒ를 동명사 형태인 stopping으로 고쳐 써야 한다.

READING 24 • Workbook p.25

1 ③ **2** ③ **3** ② **4** distraction
5 one of history's greatest scientists

해설

1 (A) 셀 수 있는 명사의 복수형 앞이므로 few가 적절하다. (B) 수식을 받는 명사와의 관계가 능동이므로 현재분사 annoying이 적절하다. (C) with ~ friends는 주어인 every cat을 수식하는 전치사구이므로 단수 동사 has가 적절하다.

2 앞 문장에서 동물 친구들이 그를 산만하게 만들었다는 내용이 나오고 빈칸 뒤의 문장에서 그런 예들이 나오고 있으므로 ③ '예를 들어'가 적절하다.

① 대신에　　② 게다가　　④ 다시 말해서　　⑤ 반면에

3 고양이 한 마리가 끊임없이 뉴턴에게 집 안으로 들여보내 주고 집 밖으로 내보내 달라고 요구하며 방해하는 데 대한 해결책이므로, 빈칸에 들어갈 말로 가장 적절한 것은 ② '(반려동물용) 문'이다.
① 장난감　　③ 음식　　④ 탑　　⑤ 주인

4 '주의를 빼앗고 다른 무언가에 집중하지 못하게 하는 것'의 의미를 나타내는 단어는 distraction(집중을 방해하는 것, 산만)이다.

5 '가장 ~한 것들 중의 하나'의 의미는 「one of the+최상급+복수 명사」의 형태로 쓴다. 여기서는 최상급 앞에 history's를 써서 '역사상'의 의미를 덧붙였다.

READING 25

Workbook p.26

1 ①　　**2** ④　　**3** ③
4 (A) media (B) misinformation
5 더 젊은 사람들보다 7배 더 많은 잘못된 정보

해설

1 「spend+시간+동명사」의 형태로 써서 '~하는 데 시간을 쓰다'의 의미를 나타내므로 ⓐ interact를 interacting으로 고쳐 써야 한다.

2 뒤에 이어지는 문장들에서 잘못된 정보에 대한 여러 가지 해결책을 말하고 있으므로 빈칸에 들어갈 말로 가장 적절한 것은 ④ '해결책'이다.
① 진실　　② 장점　　③ 원인　　⑤ 부작용

3 뉴욕 대학교의 조사에서 65세 이상의 사람들이 더 젊은 사람들보다 7배나 더 많이 잘못된 정보를 공유한다는 것을 알아냈다고 했으므로 ③이 글의 내용과 일치한다.

4 (A)는 앞 문장에 나온 media를, (B)는 앞에 언급된 젊은이들을 속이는 행위자인 misinformation을 가리킨다.

5 「배수사+as+원급+명사+as」의 형태로 써서 '~보다 −배만큼 더 …한 명사'의 의미를 나타낸다.

Unit 10 주어진 문장 넣기

READING 26

Workbook p.27

1 ①　　**2** ③　　**3** ④
4 사람은 빨간색인 어떤 것을 기억할 가능성이 더 높다
5 ⓔ → recalling

해설

1 뒤에 이어지는 내용에서 색이 기억력 향상에 도움을 준다는 몇 가지 연구 결과를 언급하고 있으므로 빈칸에 들어갈 말로 가장 적절한 것은 ① '기억력'이다.
② 인내심　　③ 창의성　　④ 상상력　　⑤ 집중력

2 알츠하이머 환자에 대한 일부 연구는 색 신호가 특정 이미지의 기억을 향상시키는 데 도움이 된다는 것을 발견했다는 문장 뒤에, 추가적으로 알츠하이머 환자들이 흑백 이미지는 기억할 수 없었지만 컬러로 된 이미지는 기억할 수 있었다는 내용이 이어지고 있으므로 추가의 의미를 나타내는 ③ '게다가'가 적절하다.
① 하지만　　② 그렇지 않으면　　④ 그럼에도 불구하고
⑤ 따라서

3 빨간색이 학습과 현실 세계에서 중요한 색이라서 빨간색의 사물을 더 잘 기억하게 된다고 했으므로 ④가 글의 내용과 일치한다.

4 「be likely to+동사원형」은 '~할 가능성이 있다, ~하기 쉽다'의 의미이다.

5 전치사 in의 목적어 역할을 하는 동명사 형태로 써야 하므로 ⓔ를 recalling으로 고쳐 써야 한다.

READING 27

Workbook p.28

1 ②　　**2** ③　　**3** ④　　**4** emotion
5 the challenging problems that we face

해설

1 EQ에 대한 관심이 증가하고 있음에도 불구하고, 감정을 이해하고 관리하는 데 있어 부족한 부분이 남아 있다는 주어진 글 뒤에, 실험 결과를 근거로 우리들 중 3분의 2는 감정에 의해 통제된다는 내용의 (B)가 먼저 오고, 감정의 인식과 이해가 학교에서 학습되지 않은 상태에서 노동자가 된다는 내용의 (A)가 이어지고, 그 결과 직면한 도전적인 문제에서 감정을 관리하는 기술이 부족하게 된다는 내용의 (C)가 마지막에 오는 것이 자연스럽다.

2 「분수+of+복수 명사」는 복수 취급하므로 ⓒ is를 are로 고쳐 써야 한다.

3 빈칸 앞 (A)의 마지막 문장에서 우리는 읽고, 쓰고, 지식 체계를 전하는 방법을 배운 후에 직장에 들어간다고 했고 빈칸에 있는 문장에서는 우리가 너무 자주 직면하는 문제에 대한 감정 관리 기술이 부족하다고 했으므로, 빈칸에는 반대되는 내용을 이어 주는 연결어 ④ '그러나'가 적절하다.
① 그래서   ② 또한   ③ 만약 ~이 아니라면   ⑤ 그 결과

4 '사랑, 두려움, 또는 분노와 같은 우리가 경험하는 느낌'의 의미를 나타내는 단어는 emotion(감정)이다.

5 선행사 the challenging problems 뒤에 목적격 관계대명사 that과 「주어+동사」의 순으로 배열한다.

READING 28
Workbook p.29

1 ③   **2** ④   **3** ④   **4** transfer
5 먹이 사슬이 짧을수록 이용 가능한 에너지 섭취량이 더 커진다.

해설

1 (A) 수식을 받는 명사인 process와의 관계가 수동이므로 과거분사인 repeated가 적절하다. (B) 식품 에너지가 '전달되는' 것이므로 수동태인 is transferred가 적절하다. (C) 「the number of+복수 명사」는 '~의 수'의 의미로 단수 취급하므로 단수 동사 is가 적절하다.

2 앞 문장에서 먹이 사슬의 예로 초원에서는 풀이 토끼에게 먹히지만 결국 토끼는 여우에게 먹힌다는 내용이 나오므로 빈칸에 들어갈 말로 가장 적절한 것은 ④ '사례'이다.
① 효과   ② 기원   ③ 기능   ⑤ 정의

3 먹이 사슬의 이동 단계에서 잠재적 에너지의 80~90퍼센트가 열로 손실되어서 하나의 과정 안에 있는 단계나 연결의 수는 보통 네다섯 개로 제한된다고 했으므로 ④는 글의 내용과 일치하지 않는다.

4 '누군가 또는 무언가를 한 곳에서 다른 곳으로 옮기는 행위 또는 과정'의 의미를 나타내는 단어는 transfer(이동)이다.

5 「the+비교급 (+주어+동사), the+비교급 (+주어+동사)」는 '~할수록 더 …하다'의 의미를 나타낸다.

READING 29
Workbook p.30

1 ③   **2** ⑤   **3** ③   **4** more
5 기억도 적절한 도움과 사용을 제공하기 위해 연습되고 발달되어야 한다

해설

1 주어진 문장은 근육과 기억의 차이점에 대한 내용이므로, 기억과 근육이 비슷하다는 내용 뒤인 ③에 들어가는 것이 가장 적절하다.

2 빈칸 앞 문장에서는 다른 어떤 것이든 배울 수 있는 것처럼 기억력을 훈련하도록 배울 수 있다는 내용이 나오고, 빈칸 뒤에는 악기를 연주하는 것을 배우는 것보다 훈련된 기억력을 발달시키는 것이 훨씬 더 쉽다는 내용이 나오므로 주장을 뒷받침하는 내용을 덧붙이는 ⑤ '사실'이 적절하다.
① 그런데   ② 그 때문에   ③ 그 사이에   ④ 반면에

3 기억도 근육처럼 훈련될 수 있다고 주장하며 훈련된 기억력의 여러 이점에 대해 설명하는 글이므로, 필자가 주장하는 바로 가장 적절한 것은 ③이다.

4 「the+비교급+주어+동사, the+비교급+주어+동사」의 형태로 '~할수록 더 …하다'의 의미를 나타내므로 much의 비교급인 more로 고쳐 써야 한다.

5 「so+조동사+주어」의 형태로 써서 '주어도 그렇다[마찬가지이다]'의 의미를 나타내므로 ⓑ는 memory must be exercised and developed ~, too의 의미이다.

READING 30
Workbook p.31

1 ⑤   **2** ④   **3** ②   **4** outbreak
5 그들은 생존했을 뿐만 아니라 발전했다

해설

1 선구적인 하수도가 '건설된' 것이므로 ⓔ는 수동태인 was built로 고쳐 써야 한다.

2 열악한 생활 환경을 개선하여 치명적인 질병의 확산을 막으려 했다는 인과 관계에 대한 내용이 이어지므로 빈칸에 들어갈 말로 가장 적절한 것은 ④ '연관성'이다.
① 해결책   ② 차이점   ③ 평판   ⑤ 경쟁

3 치명적인 질병을 경험한 후에 생존했을 뿐만 아니라 발전했다고

했으므로 ②는 글의 내용과 일치하지 않는다.

4 '전쟁이나 질병의 갑작스러운 시작이나 증가'의 의미를 나타내는 단어는 outbreak(발생, 발발)이다.

5 「not only A but also B」는 'A뿐만 아니라 B도'의 의미를 나타낸다.

Unit 12 빈칸 완성하기 1 (단어)

READING **31**
Workbook p.32

1 ② 2 ④ 3 ③ 4 Reading fiction
5 Seeing the mistakes characters make

해설

1 소설을 읽는 것의 여러 장점에 대한 글이므로, 글의 주제로 가장 적절한 것은 ② '소설 읽기의 장점'이다.
① 소설의 다양한 장르
③ 책을 효과적으로 읽는 방법
④ 10대들에게 인기 있는 취미
⑤ 소설과 논픽션의 차이

2 선행사가 복수 명사 people이므로 ⓓ는 복수 동사인 have로 고쳐 써야 한다.

3 빈칸 앞에서 소설 읽기의 여러 장점을 언급했고, 빈칸 뒤에서 소설 읽기의 추가적인 장점을 언급하고 있으므로 첨가의 의미를 나타내는 ③ '게다가'가 적절하다.
① 하지만   ② 그렇지 않으면   ④ 예를 들면   ⑤ 반면에

4 밑줄 친 it은 앞 문장의 주어인 Reading fiction을 가리킨다.

5 문장의 주어인 동명사구로 동명사 Seeing 뒤에 Seeing의 목적어 the mistakes를 쓰고, 목적격 관계대명사가 생략된 관계대명사절이 이 선행사를 수식하도록 주어와 동사의 순으로 배열한다.

READING **32**
Workbook p.33

1 ③ 2 ⑤ 3 predictably
4 음식이 언제 나타날지를 알지 못하는 동물은 고통을 받을지 모른다

해설

1 (A) 욕구가 '충족되어야' 하는 것이므로 수동태로 나타내며, 조동사가 있는 수동태는 「조동사+be+과거분사」의 형태로 쓴다. (B) always와 같은 빈도부사는 조동사 뒤에 쓴다. (C) 시간의 부사절에서 현재 시제가 미래를 대신하므로 현재 시제인 know가 적절하다.

2 동물에게 좋은 돌봄을 주기 위해서는 동물의 욕구가 일관적이고 예측 가능하게 충족되도록 해야 한다는 내용의 글이므로, 필자가 주장하는 바로 가장 적절한 것은 ⑤이다.

3 뒤에 이어지는 문맥으로 보아 동물의 욕구가 일관적이고 '예측 가능하게' 충족되어야 한다는 것이 적절하고, 동사를 꾸미는 부사가 와야 하므로 본문에 나오는 형용사 predictable의 부사형인 predictably로 써야 한다.

4 that ~ will appear는 주격 관계대명사절로 주어인 an animal을 꾸며 주며, 문장의 동사는 may experience이다.

Unit 13 빈칸 완성하기 2 (구·절)

READING **33**
Workbook p.34

1 ③ 2 ② 3 ④ 4 faith
5 not as true as they sound

해설

1 (A) 「so+형용사+that ~」의 형태로, '매우 …해서 ~하다'의 의미를 나타내므로 so가 적절하다. (B) when절의 주어는 단수인 a person이므로 단수 동사 has가 적절하다. (C) 시간의 부사절에서 현재 시제가 미래를 대신하므로 is가 적절하다.

2 뒤에 이어지는 문장들에서 사람들은 스스로를 위대하게 만들 수 없고, 사람들을 위대하게 만드는 것은 그들이 믿는 대의라고 했으므로 ②가 정답이다.

3 빈칸 앞에서 신념은 감정, 힘, 그리고 행동을 위한 촉매가 된다고 했으므로 빈칸에 들어갈 말로 가장 적절한 것은 ④ '확신하는'이다.
① 의심을 품는   ② 결백한   ③ 부정적인   ⑤ 무관심한

4 '누군가 혹은 무언가에 대한 강한 믿음이나 신뢰'의 의미를 나타내는 단어는 faith(믿음, 신뢰)이다.

5 「not+as+원급+as」의 형태로 써서 '~만큼 …하지 않은'의 의미를 나타낸다.

READING 34 ────────────● Workbook p.35

1 ③   **2** ⑤   **3** ①   **4** ② → did
5 그것들이 살아남으려면

해설

1 과학자들은 개구리의 조상이 물에 살며 물고기 같은 동물이었다고 믿는다는 주어진 글 뒤에, 개구리가 육지에서 살 수 있는 능력을 얻었음에도 여전히 물과 인연을 유지했다는 내용의 (B)가 이어지고, 그에 대한 근거로 피부를 통해 호흡해야 해서 물가 근처에 있어야 한다는 내용의 (C)가 오고, 또 다른 근거인 물속에 낳은 알이 살아남기 위해서는 물에 사는 생물로 자라야 한다는 내용의 (A)가 이어지는 것이 적절하다.

2 뒤의 문장에서 건조해지는 것을 막기 위해 물에 몸을 담글 수 있도록 물 근처에 살아야 한다고 했으므로 빈칸에 들어갈 말로 가장 적절한 것은 ⑤ '촉촉한, 물기 있는'이다.
① 건조한   ② 부드러운   ③ 딱딱한   ④ 깨끗한

3 개구리의 여러 특징에 대해 설명한 글이므로, 글의 주제로 가장 적절한 것은 ① '개구리의 몇몇 특징'이다.
② 다양한 동물들의 탈바꿈
③ 물고기 같은 동물들의 진화
④ 피부를 통해 호흡하는 방법
⑤ 물에 사는 동물들과 땅에 사는 동물들의 차이점

4 앞 문장의 lay를 대신하는 대동사가 필요하므로 ② were를 do의 과거형인 did로 고쳐 써야 한다.

5 to survive는 의도를 나타내는 be to 용법으로 쓰였으므로 '~하려면'으로 해석한다.

Unit 14 밑줄 친 부분 파악하기

READING 35 ────────────● Workbook p.36

1 ⑤   **2** ①   **3** ②   **4** privilege
5 what it means to be normal

해석

1 전치사 about의 목적어로 internalizing과 접속사 and로 병렬 연결된 것이므로 ⓔ를 taking으로 고쳐 써야 한다.

2 빈칸 뒤의 it은 앞 문장의 The pressure to remain within the box를 가리키며, 상자 안에 남아야 한다는 압박감의 의미를

덧붙여 말하고 있으므로 추가의 의미를 나타내는 ① '또한'이 적절하다.
② 그다음에   ③ 하지만   ④ 그에 반해서
⑤ 그럼에도 불구하고

3 문화 밖에서 서성이는 것은 창의성의 행위로 인식될 수 있지만 잠시 동안만이라고 했으므로 ②는 글의 내용과 일치하지 않는다.

4 '일부 사람들에게 주어지고 다른 사람들에게는 그렇지 않은 권리나 이익'의 의미를 나타내는 단어는 privilege(특권)이다.

5 defines의 목적어로 쓰인 간접의문문으로, it이 가주어, to부정사가 진주어 역할을 하도록 「의문사(what)+가주어(it)+동사(means)+진주어(to be normal)」의 순으로 배열한다.

READING 36 ────────────● Workbook p.37

1 ④   **2** ④   **3** ②   **4** selectively
5 ⓒ → seem

해설

1 ④ 뒤의 This quote가 주어진 문장의 인용구인 "with a hammer in hand, everything looks like a nail"을 가리키므로 주어진 문장은 ④에 들어가는 것이 적절하다.

2 앞 문장의 내용을 한 번 더 풀어서 설명하고 있으므로 ④ '즉, 다시 말해서'가 적절하다.
① 그래서   ② 그렇지만   ③ 그렇지 않으면   ⑤ 반면에

3 우리는 사건을 선택적으로 해석하는 경향이 있다는 내용의 글이므로, 글의 주제로 가장 적절한 것은 ② '우리가 사건을 해석하는 방식'이다.
① 우리의 인생에 도움이 되는 인용구
③ 선택적 지각의 장점
④ 망치를 올바르게 사용하는 법
⑤ 다양한 경험의 중요성

4 이어지는 문장에서 우리의 선택적 지각에 대해 설명하고 있으며, 동사를 수식해야 하므로 본문에 나오는 형용사 selective의 부사형인 selectively로 써야 한다.

5 주격 관계대명사 that 앞의 선행사가 복수인 the things이므로 ⓒ seems를 seem으로 고쳐 써야 한다.

READING 37
Workbook p.38

1 ③   2 ④   3 ④ → to live in
4 전구를 발명할 수 있는 뛰어난 지성

해설

1 상품의 교환은 사실상 욕망의 교환이며 어떤 개인이든 대개 제한된 수의 개인적인 욕구만을 독립적으로 충족시킬 수 있을 뿐이라는 내용의 주어진 글 (A) 뒤에, 구체적인 예로 에디슨을 들어 다른 사람들과의 상호 교환의 필요성을 설명하는 (C)가 오고, 따라서 거래는 공동체 내에서 개인의 다양한 욕구를 충족시키는 효과적인 수단이 된다는 내용의 (D) 다음에 거래되는 상품이 물리적 형태 말고도 지식과 음악처럼 더 추상적이거나 개념적인 형태로 존재할 수 있다는 내용인 (B)가 이어지는 것이 적절하다.

2 바로 뒤의 문장에서 '그러므로 어떤 개인이든 대개 제한된 수의 개인적인 욕구만을 독립적으로 충족시킬 수 있을 뿐이다'라고 했으므로 빈칸에 들어갈 말로 가장 적절한 것은 ④ '한계'이다.
① 유전자   ② 감각   ③ 능력   ⑤ 장점

3 a place를 수식하는 형용사적 용법의 to부정사로 live in a place의 의미가 되어야 하므로 to live 뒤에 전치사 in을 넣어 to live in으로 써야 한다.

4 to invent 이하가 the brilliant mind를 수식하는 형용사적 용법의 to부정사로 쓰였다.

READING 38
Workbook p.39

1 ②   2 ⑤   3 shame
4 before judging whether it worked

해설

1 (A) 조건의 부사절에서 현재 시제가 미래를 대신하므로 feels가 적절하다. (B) remember 뒤에 to부정사가 오면 '~할 것을 기억하다'의 의미이고, 동명사가 오면 '~한 것을 기억하다'의 의미이므로 to use가 적절하다. (C) 수식하는 명사구 the steps와의 관계가 수동이므로 과거분사인 involved가 적절하다.

2 반복이 뇌를 재연결하는 과정에 핵심적이며 뇌 친화적인 피드백 기술을 계속 사용할 때마다 뉴런들은 서로 연결된다고 했으므로, 빈칸에 들어갈 말로 가장 적절한 것은 ⑤ '반복'이다.
① 계획   ② 결과   ③ 주체   ④ 목적

3 '자신이 잘못된 무언가를 했다는 것을 알기 때문에 가지게 되는 죄책감, 후회, 또는 슬픔과 같은 감정'의 의미를 나타내는 단어는 shame(수치(심), 부끄러운 생각)이다.

4 전치사 before 뒤에 judging을 쓰고, judging의 목적어 역할을 하는 간접의문문인 whether it worked의 순으로 배열한다.

READING 39
Workbook p.40

1 ⑤   2 ⑤   3 ② → coming[come]
4 너무 당황스럽고 두려워서 여행을 포기해야 할 것 같았다

해설

1 fall off는 '넘어지다'의 의미이다.

2 Gaby가 Nellie에게 계속 할 수 있다고 격려했고, 그런 격려에 용기를 얻어 포기하지 않고 다시 자전거 여행을 한 것이므로, 빈칸에 들어갈 말로 가장 적절한 것은 ⑤ '격려'이다.
① 비판   ② 감사   ③ 도전   ④ 책임감

3 지각동사 saw의 목적격보어로 동사원형이나 현재분사가 적절하다.

4 「so+형용사+that+주어+동사 ~」의 형태로 써서 '너무 …해서 ~하다'의 의미를 나타낸다.

READING 40
Workbook p.41

1 ④   2 ④   3 equality
4 the most important challenge facing my generation

해설

1 (A) 문장의 동사가 필요하므로 과거형인 dusted가 적절하다. (B) 주절의 시제로 보아 가정법 과거 문장이므로 조건절에 be동사의 과거형인 weren't가 적절하다. (C) 지각동사 see의 목적격보어이므로 동사원형인 stand가 적절하다.

2 연설문의 작성 분량에 대해서는 언급되지 않았다.

3 '같은 권리, 지위, 기회를 가지는 상태'의 의미를 나타내는 단어는 equality(평등)이다.

4 현재분사구인 facing my generation이 최상급의 수식을 받는 명사 challenge를 뒤에서 꾸며 주는 형태로 배열한다.

Unit 01 주제 파악하기

READING 01 ● Workbook p.42

1 Here are / some possible reasons.
여기 있다 / 몇 가지 가능한 이유가

2 First of all, / we see ourselves / every day / in the mirror.
무엇보다도 / 우리는 우리 자신을 본다 / 매일 / 거울 속에서

3 Since we are / so used to the image / in the mirror, / when this image is reversed / in pictures, / it seems / unnatural.
우리는 ~하기 때문에 / 이미지에 너무 익숙하기 / 거울 속의 / 이 이미지가 뒤바뀌면 / 사진 속에서 / 그것은 보인다 / 부자연스럽게

4 Our smiles / could also be / a reason.
우리의 미소가 / 또한 ~일 수 있다 / 이유

5 When we look at ourselves / in the mirror, / we're usually relaxed, confident, / and more likely to / smile and act naturally.
우리가 우리 자신을 볼 때 / 거울 속의 / 우리는 보통 편안하고 자신감이 넘치며 / 가능성이 더 크다 / 미소 짓고 자연스럽게 행동할

READING 02 ● Workbook p.42

1 Milk is very sensitive / to temperature / and must be stored / at temperatures / between 0 and 4 degrees Celsius.
우유는 매우 민감하다 / 온도에 / 그리고 보관되어야 한다 / 온도에서 / 섭씨 0도에서 4도 사이의

2 Furthermore, / many canned foods are heated / at high temperatures / and exposed to high pressures.
게다가 / 많은 캔 식품들은 가열된다 / 높은 온도에서 / 그리고 높은 압력에 노출된다

3 But / when milk goes through / this process, / it can change / the taste and properties of the milk / due to browning.
하지만 / 우유가 ~을 거치면 / 이 과정을 / 그것은 바꿀 수 있다 / 우유의 맛과 특성을 / 갈변으로 인해

4 Additionally, / cans are more expensive / to produce / than cartons or plastic bottles.
게다가 / 캔은 더 비싸다 / 생산하기에 / 종이 팩이나 플라스틱 병보다

5 Although milk producers could produce / canned milk, / the reasons mentioned above / and a lack of proper packaging facilities / make it / a less attractive option.
우유 생산자들이 생산할 수 있지만 / 캔 우유를 / 위에서 언급한 이유 / 그리고 적절한 포장 시설의 부족은 / 그것을 만든다 / 덜 매력적인 선택으로

READING 03 ● Workbook p.43

1 However, / young adults don't decide / to change their diets / only out of concern / for their health.
하지만 / 젊은 성인들은 결정하는 것은 아니다 / 식단을 바꾸기로 / 우려 때문만으로 / 그들의 건강에 대한

2 Some make the choice / out of concern / for animal rights.
어떤 이들은 그 선택을 한다 / 관심 때문에 / 동물의 권리에 대한

3 So, / many teens give up meat / to protest those conditions.
그래서 / 많은 십 대들은 고기를 포기한다 / 그러한 조건에 저항하기 위해

4 It also creates / problems with animal waste / resulting in pollution.
그것은 또한 만들어 낸다 / 가축의 배설물 문제를 / 오염을 일으키는

5 These trends show / that today's youth are / more aware of / and sensitive to / animal rights and environmental problems.
이러한 경향은 보여준다 / 오늘날의 젊은이들이 ~하다는 것을 / 더 인식하는 / 그리고 ~에 더 민감한 / 동물의 권리와 환경 문제

Unit 02 제목 파악하기

READING 04 ● Workbook p.43

1 After millions of years, / these clouds begin to shrink / because gravity forces / the gas and dust

together.
수백만 년 후에 / 이 구름은 수축하기 시작한다 / 중력이 힘을 가하기 때문에 / 가스와 먼지에 함께

2 As it is squeezed, / the cloud heats up / to form / a young star.
그것이 압축되면서 / 구름은 가열된다 / 형성하기 위해 / 젊은 별을

3 What happens / when / the fuel runs out / and the star dies?
무엇이 일어나는가 / ~일 때 / 연료가 다 떨어진다 / 그리고 별이 죽는다

4 For example, / stars / with less than half the mass of the sun / fade away very slowly.
예를 들어 / 별들은 / 태양의 절반 이하의 질량을 가진 / 매우 천천히 사라진다

5 But / most stars / use up their fuel / and finally return to / clouds of gas and dust / after a series of steps.
그러나 / 대부분의 별들은 / 그들의 연료를 다 써버린다 / 그리고 마침내 ~으로 돌아간다 / 가스와 먼지의 구름 / 일련의 단계를 거쳐

1 In a movie, / lighting does / more than / just allow us to see / what is taking place.
영화에서 / 조명은 역할을 한다 / ~ 이상의 / 단지 우리가 보게 해준다 / 무엇이 일어나고 있는지를

2 If a bright light is used / to minimize shadows, / it creates / a bright and cheerful atmosphere.
만약 밝은 빛이 사용되면 / 그림자를 최소화하기 위해 / 그것은 만들어 낸다 / 밝고 쾌활한 분위기를

3 Light can also make / dark shadows / for a strong contrast / between bright and dark scenes.
빛은 또한 만들 수도 있다 / 어두운 그림자를 / 강한 대비를 위해 / 밝은 장면과 어두운 장면 사이의

4 So, / it is used / in horror movies / or films with a dark atmosphere.
그래서 / 그것은 사용된다 / 공포영화에서 / 또는 어두운 분위기의 영화(에서)

5 Understanding / these lighting techniques / and their effects / makes watching movies / even more exciting.
이해하는 것은 / 이러한 조명 기술을 / 그리고 그것의 효과를 / 영화를 보는 것을 만든다 / 훨씬 더 흥미롭게

1 Think, / for a moment, / about when / you bought something / and you never ended up using it.
생각해보라 / 잠시 / ~한 때에 대해 / 여러분이 무언가를 샀다 / 그리고 결국은 한 번도 사용하지 않았다

2 That is / more than / the total government spending / on universities and roads.
그것은 ~이다 / 넘어서는 / 정부 지출 총액을 / 대학과 도로에 대한 (지출)

3 That is / an average of $1,250 AUD (roughly $1,156 USD) / for each household.
그것은 ~이다 / 평균 1,250 호주 달러(약 1,156 미국 달러) / 가구당

4 All the things / we buy / and then never use / are waste / — a waste of money, / a waste of time, / and waste / in the sense of / pure rubbish.
모든 물건은 / 우리가 구입하는 / 그리고 전혀 사용하지 않는 / 낭비이다 / 즉 돈 낭비 / 시간 낭비 / 그리고 낭비(이다) / ~이라는 의미에서 / 순전히 쓸모없는 물건

5 As the author Clive Hamilton observes, / 'The difference / between / the stuff we buy / and / what we use / is waste.'
작가 Clive Hamilton이 말한 것처럼 / '그 차이는 / 사이의 / 우리가 사는 물건 / 그리고 / 우리가 사용하는 것 / 낭비이다'

Unit 03 목적·주장 파악하기

1 I'm writing / this email / in response / to the message / I received / from her homeroom teacher.

저는 쓰고 있습니다 / 이 이메일을 / 답변으로 / 메시지에 대한 / 제가 받은 / 그녀의 담임 선생님으로부터

2 As the mother / of a girl / who needs / a lot of nutrients, / I strongly oppose / the suggestion.
어머니로서 / 소녀의 / 필요로 하는 / 많은 영양소를 / 저는 강력히 반대합니다 / 그 제안에

3 Removing them / from the menu / would limit / our children's food choices / and hinder / their growth.
그것들을 제외하는 것은 / 메뉴에서 / 제한할 것입니다 / 우리 아이들의 음식 선택을 / 그리고 방해할 것입니다 / 그들의 성장을

4 Instead, / the school could clearly label / foods that may contain eggs.
대신에 / 학교는 명확하게 라벨을 붙일 수 있습니다 / 음식에 / 달걀을 포함할지도 모르는

5 It is important / students continue / to have a wide choice / of foods.
중요합니다 / 학생들이 계속하는 것 / 다양한 선택을 하는 것을 / 음식의

READING **08** • Workbook p.45

1 Some experts say / that we communicate / by moving / our bodies.
일부 전문가들은 말한다 / 우리가 의사소통을 한다고 / 움직임으로써 / 우리의 몸을

2 It can make / a significant difference / in your relationship / with students.
그것은 가져올 수 있다 / 상당한 차이를 / 여러분의 관계에 / 학생들과

3 For example, / when students first enter / the classroom, / they look for / their teacher.
예를 들어 / 학생들이 처음 들어가면 / 교실에 / 그들은 찾는다 / 자신의 선생님을

4 Imagine / that the teacher has a friendly greeting / and a welcoming smile.
상상해 보라 / 그 선생님이 친근한 인사를 한다고 / 그리고 환영의 미소를 (짓는다고)

5 Teachers should remember / that / their body language / is always at work / when they are /

with their students.
선생님은 기억할 필요가 있다 / ~이라는 것을 / 그들의 몸짓 언어는 / 항상 작동하고 있다 / 그들이 있을 때 / 자신의 학생들과 함께

Unit 04 요지 파악하기

READING **09** • Workbook p.46

1 The Great Barrier Reef / in Australia / is one of / the largest coral reef systems / in the world.
Great Barrier Reef는 / 호주의 / ~ 중 하나이다 / 가장 큰 산호초 시스템들 / 세계에서

2 However, / in recent years, / it has been facing / numerous environmental challenges.
그러나 / 최근 몇 년 동안 / 그것은 직면해 왔다 / 수많은 환경 문제에

3 Furthermore, / water pollution / from water used for agriculture / and industrial waste / makes the water quality poor.
게다가 / 수질 오염은 / 농업에 사용되는 물로 인한 / 그리고 산업 폐기물(로 인한) / 수질을 악화시킨다

4 We must take immediate action / to protect / the Great Barrier Reef / and its marine life.
우리는 즉각적인 조치를 취해야 한다 / 보호하기 위해 / Great Barrier Reef를 / 그리고 그곳의 해양 생물을

5 The future of / the Great Barrier Reef / and the millions of species / that call it home / depends on it.
~의 미래가 / Great Barrier Reef / 그리고 수백만 종 / 그것을 집이라고 부르는(그곳에 서식하는) / 그것에 달려 있다

READING **10** • Workbook p.46

1 You need to get comfortable / with discomfort / if you want / to succeed.
당신은 편안해져야 한다 / 불편함에 / 당신이 원한다면 / 성공하기를

2 Trying new things / outside of / your comfort

zone / will greatly benefit you / in many ways.
새로운 것들을 시도하는 것은 / ~ 밖에서 / 당신의 편안한 영역 /
당신에게 큰 도움이 될 것이다 / 많은 면에서

3 As you try / new things, / you will discover / your
talents, interests, strengths / and weaknesses.
당신이 시도하면서 / 새로운 것들을 / 당신은 발견하게 될 것이다
/ 자신의 재능, 관심사, 강점 / 그리고 약점을

4 If you try / something new, / you can meet / new
people / who you otherwise would never have
had / the chance to meet.
만약 당신이 시도한다면 / 새로운 것을 / 당신은 만날 수 있다 / 새
로운 사람들을 / 그렇지 않았으면 결코 없었을 / 만날 기회가

5 However, / you will be able to expand / your
horizons / and achieve / success.
하지만 / 당신은 넓힐 수 있을 것이다 / 당신의 시야를 / 그리고 이
룰 수 있을 것이다 / 성공을

Unit 05 요약하기

READING **11** ● Workbook p.47

1 That is, / the advertisement needs to show / how
the product / can help them.
즉 / 광고는 보여줄 필요가 있다 / 제품이 어떻게 / 그들을 도울 수
있는지를

2 For example, / imagine an advertisement / for
a new smartphone / that just talks about / its
amazing features.
예를 들어 / 광고를 상상해 보라 / 새로운 스마트폰의 / ~에 대해
서만 이야기하는 / 그것의 놀라운 기능

3 Now imagine an advertisement / showing people
/ taking beautiful photos / in their daily lives / or
watching movies / on their new smartphone.
이제 광고를 상상해 보라 / 사람들을 보여주는 / 아름다운 사진을
찍는 / 그들의 일상에서 / 또는 영화를 보는 / 그들의 새로운 스마
트폰으로

4 It would be / far more memorable / and people
would be / interested in it.
그것은 ~일 것이다 / 훨씬 더 기억에 남는 / 그리고 사람들은 ~일
것이다 / 그것에 관심을 갖는

5 Therefore, / a successful advertisement / must
show people / how its product / can make their
lives / richer and more convenient.
그러므로 / 성공적인 광고는 / 사람들에게 보여주어야 한다 / 그것
의 제품이 어떻게 / 그들의 삶을 만들 수 있는지 / 더 풍부하고 더
편리하게

READING **12** ● Workbook p.47

1 Some experts predict / that AI will lead to / job
loss / in certain industries / by automating /
many simple tasks.
일부 전문가들은 예측한다 / AI가 초래할 것이라고 / 일자리 감소
를 / 특정 산업의 / 자동화함으로써 / 많은 단순 업무를

2 However, / other experts believe / that AI will
create / new job opportunities.
하지만 / 다른 전문가들은 믿는다 / AI가 창출할 것이라고 / 새로
운 일자리 기회를

3 For example, / the use of AI / in customer
service / requires workers / to improve / their
interpersonal skills.
예를 들어 / AI를 사용하는 것은 / 고객 서비스에서 / 근로자들에
게 요구한다 / 향상시키는 것을 / 그들의 대인 관계 기술을

4 In addition, / AI will likely lead to / the
development of new job categories, / such as AI
ethics officers.
게다가 / AI는 아마 이어질 것이다 / 새로운 직업 범주의 개발로 /
AI 윤리 책임자와 같은

5 As AI continues to have an impact / on the job
market, / it is necessary / for workers and
organizations / to adapt to the changes.
가주어   진주어
AI가 계속해서 영향을 미침에 따라 / 고용 시장에 / 필요하다 / 근
로자와 조직이 / 변화에 적응하는 것이

READING **13** ● Workbook p.48

1 In one study, / researchers asked / pairs of
strangers / to sit down in a room / and chat.
한 연구에서 / 연구자들은 요청했다 / 모르는 사람끼리 짝을 이룬

사람들에게 / 한 방에 앉도록 / 그리고 이야기를 나누도록

2 In half of the rooms, / a cell phone was placed / on a nearby table; / in the other half, / no phone was present.
절반의 방에는 / 휴대전화가 놓여 있었다 / 근처의 탁자 위에 / 나머지 절반의 방에는 / 휴대전화가 없었다

3 Imagine / you sit down / to have lunch / with a friend / and set your phone / on the table.
상상해 보라 / 여러분이 자리에 앉는다 / 점심을 먹으려고 / 친구와 / 그리고 여러분의 휴대전화를 놓는다 / 탁자 위에

4 You might feel good / about yourself / because you don't pick it up / to check your messages.
여러분은 잘하고 있다고 느낄지 모른다 / 자기 자신에 대해 / 휴대전화를 집어 들지 않기 때문에 / 메시지를 확인하려고

5 But / your unchecked messages / are still hurting / your connection / with the person / sitting across from you.
그러나 / 여러분이 확인하지 않은 메시지도 / 여전히 해치고 있다 / 여러분의 관계를 / 그 사람과의 / 맞은편에 앉아 있는

Unit 06 안내문·도표 파악하기

READING 14
Workbook p.48

1 Join her / at a special story time / for kids!
그녀와 함께하세요 / 특별한 이야기 시간에 / 아이들을 위한

2 Please register / at www.citylibrary.org/events / to attend the event.
등록해 주세요 / www.citylibrary.org/events에 / 행사에 참석하기 위해서

3 Children should come / with a parent/parents or guardian.
아이들은 와야 합니다 / 부모(중 한 명) 또는 보호자와 함께

4 After the author's reading session begins, / you cannot enter / the hall / until the session ends.
작가의 책 읽기 시간이 시작한 후에는 / 여러분은 들어갈 수 없습니다 / 홀에 / 그 시간이 끝날 때까지

5 You can buy / all of the author's books, /

including her new one, / at a discount of 30% / after the session.
여러분은 구입할 수 있습니다 / 작가의 모든 책을 / 새 책을 포함하여 / 30% 할인된 가격으로 / 그 시간이 끝난 후에

READING 15
Workbook p.49

1 Are you looking for / something special / for your family?
여러분은 찾고 있습니까 / 특별한 무언가를 / 여러분의 가족을 위한

2 A Dream Company cruise / creates memories / that bring families together.
드림 컴퍼니 유람선 여행은 / 추억을 만듭니다 / 가족을 함께 모으는

3 Our ship, / the Magic Dream, / is your dream holiday itself.
우리의 배인 / 매직 드림은 / 여러분의 꿈의 휴가 그 자체입니다

4 This cruise ship / is famous for / its classical design / and modern facilities.
이 유람선은 / ~으로 유명합니다 / 그것의 고전적인 디자인 / 그리고 현대적인 시설

5 It also has / the biggest pool / of any cruise ship.
그것은 또한 가지고 있습니다 / 가장 큰 수영장을 / 유람선 중에서

READING 16
Workbook p.49

1 Students / from kindergarten to the 12th grade / participated in the survey, / and they used / many kinds of digital devices.
학생들이 / 유치원에서 12학년까지의 / 조사에 참여했다 / 그리고 그들은 사용했다 / 많은 종류의 디지털 기기를

2 Laptops were / the most popular device / to access / digital content / in both years.
노트북은 ~였다 / 가장 인기 있는 기기 / 접속하는 / 디지털 콘텐츠에 / 두 해 모두

3 Both in 2016 and in 2019, / more than 60 percent of the students / used tablets / for digital content.

2016년과 2019년 모두 / 60퍼센트가 넘는 학생들이 / 태블릿을 사용했다 / 디지털 콘텐츠를 위해

4 More than half the students / used desktops / for digital content / in 2016, / and more than 30 percent / used desktops / for digital content / in 2019.
절반이 넘는 학생들이 / 데스크톱을 사용했다 / 디지털 콘텐츠를 위해 / 2016년에는 / 그리고 30퍼센트 넘는 학생들이 / 데스크톱을 사용했다 / 디지털 콘텐츠를 위해 / 2019년에는

5 The percentages of students / who used E-readers / were the lowest / in both years.
학생들의 비율은 / 전자책 단말기를 사용한 / 가장 낮았다 / 두 해 모두

Unit 07 내용 일치 파악하기

1 Almeida excelled / in school, / and won the top science prize / at her school.
Almeida는 뛰어났다 / 학교에서 / 그리고 과학 최고상을 받았다 / 그녀의 학교에서

2 She wanted / to continue / her studies in science / after high school, / but there was no money / for her college education.
그녀는 원했다 / 계속하기를 / 과학 공부를 / 고등학교를 나온 후 / 그러나 돈이 없었다 / 대학 교육을 위한

3 There, / she took a job / detecting viruses / and making detailed pictures of them / using a microscope.
그곳에서 / 그녀는 직업을 얻었다 / 바이러스를 찾는 / 그리고 바이러스의 자세한 사진을 만드는 / 현미경을 이용해서

4 Due to her contributions / in the field of biology, / the University of London / awarded her university degrees / in 1970 and 1971.
그녀가 한 기여 때문에 / 생물학 분야에서 / 런던 대학은 / 그녀에게 대학 학위를 수여했다 / 1970년과 1971년에

5 She finally received / the degrees / that she had wanted / since high school.
그녀는 마침내 받았다 / 학위를 / 그녀가 원했던 / 고등학교 때부터

1 Before the book was published, / Preiss buried / 12 small treasure boxes / across the United States and Canada.
그 책이 출판되기 전에 / Preiss는 묻었다 / 12개의 작은 보물 상자를 / 미국과 캐나다 전역에

2 They contain / the information / that indicates / the location of / the buried treasures.
그것들은 담고 있다 / 정보를 / 가리키는 / ~의 위치를 / 파묻힌 보물

3 For example, / a flower and a bell / in one image / stand for / Bellflower Road in Cleveland.
예를 들어 / 꽃(flower)과 종(bell)은 / 한 그림의 / 상징한다 / Cleveland의 Bellflower 길을

4 Preiss didn't leave / any record of / the treasures' exact locations / before his sudden death / in a car accident / in 2005.
Preiss는 남겨놓지 않았다 / ~에 대한 어떠한 기록도 / 보물의 정확한 위치 / 그의 갑작스러운 사망 전에 / 자동차 사고로 / 2005년에

5 Many people / are still out there looking for / those treasures.
많은 사람들이 / 여전히 찾고 있다 / 그 보물들을

1 She asked / if she could get a job / as a nurse / on their airplanes.
그녀는 물었다 / 그녀가 일자리를 얻을 수 있는지 / 간호사로서 / 비행기에서

2 Ellen suggested / that nurses take care of / frightened passengers / during flights.
Ellen은 제안했다 / 간호사가 돌봐야 한다고 / 겁에 질린 승객을 / 비행 중에

3 In 1930, / she became / the world's first female flight attendant.
1930년에 / 그녀는 되었다 / 세계 최초의 여성 비행 승무원이

4 She worked / on a Boeing 80A airplane, / flying / from Oakland to Chicago.
그녀는 근무했다 / 보잉 80A 비행기에서 / 비행하면서 / 오클랜

드에서 시카고까지

5 The Ellen Church Field Airport / in Cresco / was named after her.
Ellen Church Field 공항은 / 크레스코에 있는 / 그녀의 이름을 따서 명명되었다

Unit 08 분위기·심경 파악하기

READING 20
Workbook p.51

1 Alex and Angie / looked around / their new little house / and immediately felt at home.
Alex와 Angie는 / 둘러보았다 / 그들의 새로운 작은 집을 / 그리고 즉시 편안함을 느꼈다

2 Upstairs, / the bedrooms were cozy / and promised sweet dreams, / while a family room downstairs awaited / movie nights and games.
위층에서 / 침실은 아늑했다 / 그리고 달콤한 꿈을 약속했다 / 한편 아래층의 거실은 기다리고 있었다 / 영화의 밤과 게임을

3 The fenced-in yard / was perfect / for their needs / and provided a sense of / safety and privacy.
울타리가 쳐진 그 마당은 / 완벽했다 / 그들의 필요에 / 그리고 ~에 대한 느낌을 제공했다 / 안전과 사생활

4 Suddenly, / children's laughter / came from the neighborhood / and created / a warm and friendly atmosphere.
갑자기 / 아이들의 웃음소리가 / 이웃에서 들려왔다 / 그리고 만들었다 / 따뜻하고 친근한 분위기를

5 This was the home / of their dreams, / and they knew / they belonged here.
이곳은 집이었다 / 그들이 꿈꾸던 / 그리고 그들은 알았다 / 자신들이 여기에 속한다는 것을

READING 21
Workbook p.52

1 Emily had a tough week / at work, / with long hours / and tight deadlines.
Emily는 힘든 한 주를 보냈다 / 직장에서 / 장시간(의 노동) / 그

리고 빠듯한 마감일로

2 So, / when her husband surprised her / with beautiful roses / after lunch, / she was overjoyed.
그래서 / 그녀의 남편이 그녀를 놀라게 했을 때 / 아름다운 장미로 / 점심 식사 후에 / 그녀는 매우 기뻐했다

3 She could tell / that her husband had put / a lot of thought / into the gift, / and it made her feel / appreciated and loved.
그녀는 알 수 있었다 / 자신의 남편이 기울였다는 것을 / 많은 생각을 / 그 선물에 / 그리고 그것은 그녀가 느끼게 했다 / 감사함과 사랑을

4 As they stood there / chatting and admiring the roses, / Emily felt / her stress and worries / melt away.
그들이 그곳에 서 있었을 때 / 이야기를 나누고 장미를 감상하면서 / Emily는 느꼈다 / 그녀의 스트레스와 걱정이 / 사라지는 것을

5 The roses served / as a symbol / of their love and partnership, / and Emily felt lucky / to have / such a wonderful person / by her side.
장미는 역할을 했다 / 상징으로 / 그들의 사랑과 동반자 관계의 / 그리고 Emily는 행운이라고 느꼈다 / 가지고 있다는 것이 / 이렇게 멋진 사람을 / 그녀의 곁에

READING 22
Workbook p.52

1 It was Evelyn's first time / exploring the Badlands of Alberta, / famous across Canada / for its numerous dinosaur fossils.
그것은 Evelyn이 처음 하는 것이었다 / Alberta의 Badlands를 탐험하는 / 캐나다 전역에서 유명한 / 수많은 공룡 화석으로

2 She had not travelled / this far / for the bones / of common dinosaur species.
그녀는 여행을 해 본 적이 없었다 / 이렇게 멀리까지 / 뼈를 얻기 위해 / 흔한 공룡 종의

3 After many hours of wandering / throughout the deserted lands, / however, / she was unsuccessful.
몇 시간 동안 헤매고 다닌 후에 / 인적이 드문 땅을 / 그러나 / 그녀는 성공하지 못했다

4 Now, / the sun was beginning to set, / and her

goal / was still far / beyond her reach.
이제 / 해가 지기 시작하고 있었다 / 그리고 그녀의 목표는 / 여전히 멀리 있었다 / 그녀의 손길이 닿는 곳 너머

5 She was looking at / the slowly darkening ground / before her.
그녀는 바라보고 있었다 / 서서히 어두워지는 땅을 / 자신 앞에서

Unit 09 글의 순서 파악하기

READING 23
Workbook p.53

1 It often begins / with an unrealistic goal / (e.g., / "I will exercise / for two hours / every day!").
그것은 종종 시작한다 / 비현실적인 목표로 / (예를 들어 / "나는 운동할 거야 / 두 시간 동안 / 매일")

2 Finally, / we tend / to expect dramatic, rapid results / (e.g., / "I'll probably lose / about 10 pounds / a week!").
마지막으로 / 우리는 경향이 있다 / 극적이고 빠른 결과를 기대하는 / (예를 들어 / "나는 아마 뺄 것이다 / 10파운드 정도를 / 일주일에")

3 This syndrome involves / exaggerated feelings of control / and overconfidence / about our ability / to change our behavior successfully.
이 증후군은 포함한다 / 과장된 통제감 / 그리고 지나친 자신감을 / 우리의 능력에 대한 / 우리의 행동을 성공적으로 바꿀 수 있는

4 Because of / these wrong expectations, / we usually fail.
~ 때문에 / 이러한 잘못된 기대 / 우리는 대개 실패한다

5 Then / we often give up / our attempts / to change.
그러고 나서 / 우리는 종종 포기한다 / 우리의 시도를 / 변화하려는

READING 24
Workbook p.53

1 During his lifetime / he made / numerous contributions / to science.
그의 일생 동안 / 그는 했다 / 수많은 공헌을 / 과학에

2 But / few people realize / that he was / also a pet lover — / or that sometimes many of his animal friends / could drive him / to distraction.
하지만 / 아는 사람은 거의 없다 / 그가 ~이었다는 것을 / 또한 반려동물 애호가 / 또는 때때로 그의 많은 동물 친구들이 / 그를 만들 수 있었다(는 것을) / 산만하게

3 So, / the scientist was annoyed / and quickly came up with / a solution — / the pet door.
그래서 / 그 과학자는 짜증이 났다 / 그리고 재빨리 생각해 냈다 / 해결책을 / 반려동물용 문이라는

4 The cat / could come in and go out of / Newton's house / without disturbing him.
그 고양이는 / 드나들 수 있었다 / 뉴턴의 집을 / 그를 방해하지 않고

5 However, / his dealings / with an annoying cat / led to / a happier result.
하지만 / 그의 대처는 / 짜증나게 하는 고양이에 대한 / ~로 이어졌다 / 더 행복한 결과

READING 25
Workbook p.54

1 People spend / much of their time / interacting with media.
사람들은 보낸다 / 그들의 많은 시간을 / 미디어와 상호 작용하면서

2 All of this raises / a question: / What's the solution / to the misinformation problem?
이 모든 것이 제기한다 / 하나의 의문을 / 무엇이 해결책인가 / 잘못된 정보 문제에 대한

3 Governments and tech platforms / certainly have / a role / to play / in blocking misinformation.
정부와 기술 플랫폼은 / 분명히 ~을 가지고 있다 / 역할을 / 해야 할 / 잘못된 정보를 막아내는 데

4 However, / every individual needs / to become more information literate.
그러나 / 모든 개인은 필요가 있다 / 정보를 더 잘 이용하게 될

5 And / they should take responsibility / for combating this threat / by becoming more information literate.
그리고 / 그들은 책임을 져야 한다 / 이러한 위협에 맞서 싸울 / 정

보를 더 잘 이용하게 됨으로써

Unit 10 주어진 문장 넣기

READING 26   Workbook p.54

1 Red is / the color of stop signs and danger, / and it is / typically the color of pens / used / by teachers.
빨간색은 ~이다 / 정지 신호와 위험의 색 / 그리고 그것은 ~이다 / 전형적으로 펜의 색 / 사용되는 / 선생님들에 의해

2 Furthermore, / they could not remember / black-and-white images, / but could remember / colored ones.
게다가 / 그들은 기억할 수 없었다 / 흑백 이미지를 / 그러나 기억할 수는 있었다 / 컬러로 된 이미지를

3 Another study found / that red and blue were / the best colors / for improving brain function.
또 다른 연구는 발견했다 / 빨간색과 파란색이 ~이었다는 것을 / 가장 좋은 색 / 뇌 기능을 향상시키는 데

4 Red came out / on top / because of its role / in society.
빨간색은 차지한다 / 1위를 / 그것의 역할 때문에 / 사회에서

5 Additionally, / as the color red makes / people cautious, / they become more detail-oriented / and pay better attention.
게다가 / 빨간색이 만들기 때문에 / 사람들을 주의 깊게 / 그들은 더 많이 세부적인 것을 지향하게 된다 / 그리고 주의를 더 잘 기울인다

READING 27   Workbook p.55

1 Despite the growing focus / on EQ, / a global lack / in understanding and managing emotions / still remains.
증가하는 주목에도 불구하고 / EQ에 대한 / 전 세계적인 부족이 / 감정을 이해하고 관리하는 데 있어 / 여전히 남아 있다

2 In a test, / only 36 percent of the people / who

were tested / were able to accurately identify / their emotions / as they happened.
한 실험에서 / 오직 36%의 사람들만이 / 실험을 받은 / 정확하게 식별할 수 있었다 / 그들의 감정을 / 그것들이 일어났을 때

3 It means / that two-thirds of us are typically controlled / by our emotions.
그것은 의미한다 / 우리 중 3분의 2는 보통 통제된다는 것을 / 우리의 감정에 의해

4 But / we are not yet skilled / at spotting our emotions / and using them / to our benefit.
하지만 / 우리는 아직 능숙하지 않다 / 감정을 찾아내는 것에 / 그리고 그것들을 사용하는 것에 / 우리의 이익을 위해

5 Too often, / however, / we lack the skills / to manage our emotions / in the heat of the challenging problems / that we face.
너무 자주 / 하지만 / 우리는 기술이 부족하다 / 우리의 감정을 관리하는 / 도전적인 문제들의 열기 속에서 / 우리가 직면한

READING 28   Workbook p.55

1 You may have heard / of the food chain / quite often / in science class.
여러분은 들어 본 적이 있을 것이다 / 먹이 사슬에 대해 / 상당히 자주 / 과학 시간에

2 It means / the transfer of food energy / from its source / in plants.
그것은 의미한다 / 식품 에너지가 이동하는 것을 / 에너지원으로부터 / 식물에 있는

3 The transfer is done / through a series of organisms / during the repeated process / of eating and being eaten.
그 이동은 이루어진다 / 일련의 유기체를 통해 / 반복되는 과정 동안 / 먹고 먹히는

4 In a grassland, / grass is eaten / by rabbits, / while rabbits in turn / are eaten / by foxes.
초원에서는 / 풀이 먹힌다 / 토끼에게 / 한편 토끼는 결국 / 먹힌다 / 여우에게

5 Hence / the number of steps or links / in a course / is limited, / usually to four or five.
이런 이유로 / 단계나 연결의 수는 / 하나의 과정 안에 있는 / 제한

된다 / 보통 4~5개로

Unit 11 무관한 문장 찾기

READING 29
Workbook p.56

1 A muscle must be exercised and developed / in order to give / proper service and use: / so must memory.
근육은 연습되고 발달되어야 한다 / 제공하기 위해 / 적절한 도움과 사용을 / 기억도 그래야만 한다

2 The difference is / that a muscle can be overtrained / or become muscle-bound, / while memory cannot.
다른 점은 ~이다 / 근육이 과도하게 훈련되거나 / 근육이 뻣뻣해질 수 있다 / 반면 기억은 그럴 수 없다

3 You can be taught / to train your memory / just as you can be taught / anything else.
여러분이 배울 수 있다 / 여러분의 기억력을 훈련하도록 / 여러분이 배울 수 있는 것처럼 / 다른 어떤 것이든

4 Memorization isn't practical / for learning / complex concepts and information.
암기는 실용적이지 않다 / 배우는 데 / 복잡한 개념과 정보를

5 Along with a trained memory / you will probably acquire / a greater power of concentration, a purer sense of observation, / and perhaps, a stronger imagination.
훈련된 기억력과 함께 / 여러분은 아마도 얻게 될 것이다 / 더 큰 집중력, 더 순수한 관찰력 / 그리고 아마도 더 강한 상상력을

READING 30
Workbook p.56

1 The good news is / that cities can recover / more quickly / than you might imagine.
좋은 소식은 ~이다 / 도시가 회복될 수 있다는 것 / 더 빨리 / 여러분이 상상할지도 모르는 것보다

2 In the nineteenth and early twentieth centuries, / European cities saw / destructive outbreaks / of deadly diseases.
19세기와 20세기 초에 / 유럽의 도시들은 보았다 / 파괴적인 발생을 / 치명적인 질병의

3 Some famous doctors in Germany found / the connection / between poor living conditions and disease.
독일의 몇몇 유명한 의사들이 발견했다 / 연관성을 / 열악한 생활 환경과 질병 사이의

4 This led to / the replanning and rebuilding / of cities / to stop the spread / of deadly diseases.
이것은 ~으로 이어졌다 / 재계획과 재건 / 도시의 / 확산을 막기 위해 / 치명적인 질병의

5 In spite of the reconstruction efforts, / cities declined / in many areas / and many people started / to leave.
재건 노력에도 불구하고 / 도시들이 쇠퇴했다 / 많은 지역에서 / 그리고 많은 사람들이 시작했다 / 떠나기를

Unit 12 빈칸 완성하기 1 (단어)

READING 31
Workbook p.57

1 Reading fiction is / one of the most loved hobbies / of all time.
소설을 읽는 것은 ~이다 / 가장 사랑받는 취미 중 하나 / 역사상

2 While you are reading / fiction, / you can get / new ideas.
여러분이 읽는 동안 / 소설을 / 여러분은 얻을 수 있다 / 새로운 아이디어를

3 Also, / you can understand / others better / when you read fiction.
또한 / 여러분은 이해할 수 있다 / 다른 사람들을 더 잘 / 여러분이 소설을 읽을 때

4 In addition, / reading fiction can help you / become better with people.
게다가 / 소설을 읽는 것은 여러분을 도울 수 있다 / 사람들과 더 잘 지내게 되도록

5 It teaches / you / about how people may react /

to situations and challenges.
그것은 가르쳐준다 / 여러분에게 / 사람들이 어떻게 반응할 수 있는지에 대해 / 상황과 도전에

READING **32** ──────────● Workbook p.57

1 To do that, / an animal's needs / should be met / consistently and predictably / all the time.
그렇게 하기 위해서는 / 동물의 요구가 / 충족되도록 해야 한다 / 일관적이고 예측 가능하게 / 항상

2 We just need to ensure / that our animal's environment / is predictable: / that there is / always water available / and always in the same place.
우리는 그저 확실히 해 주기만 하면 된다 / 우리 동물의 환경이 / 예측 가능하다는 것을 / 그것은 ~이다 / 마실 수 있는 물이 항상 있다는 것 / 그리고 항상 같은 곳에 있다는 것

3 There is always food / when we get up / in the morning / and after our evening walk.
늘 음식이 있다 / 우리가 일어날 때 / 아침에 / 그리고 저녁 산책을 한 후에

4 There will always be / a time and place / to eliminate / without having to hold things in / to the point of discomfort.
늘 있을 것이다 / 시간과 장소가 / 배변할 수 있는 / 참을 필요 없이 / 불편할 정도로

5 When animals know / what to expect, / they will feel / more confident and calm.
동물들이 알 때 / 무엇을 기대할 것인지를 / 동물들은 느낄 것이다 / 더 자신감과 평온함을

Unit 13 빈칸 완성하기 2 (구·절)

READING **33** ──────────● Workbook p.58

1 Statements like / "So and so was born / to be a great leader" / are often made.
~라는 식의 발언이 / '아무개는 태어났다 / 위대한 지도자가 될 운명으로' / 자주 나온다

2 Well, / those words are / often not as true / as they sound.
글쎄 / 그 말은 ~이다 종종 사실은 아닌 / 그것들이 들리는 것만큼

3 Anyone / at any time / and in any place / can become a leader.
누구나 / 언제나 / 그리고 어디서나 / 지도자가 될 수 있다

4 That truth is / that people don't make / themselves great.
그 진리는 ~이다 / 사람들이 만들지 않는다는 것 / 스스로를 위대하게

5 When someone is wholly convinced / of something, / the world will watch / in amazement.
누군가가 전적으로 확신할 때 / 어떤 것에 대해 / 세상은 지켜볼 것이다 / 놀라서

READING **34** ──────────● Workbook p.58

1 Scientists believe / that frogs' ancestors were / water-dwelling, fishlike animals.
과학자들은 믿는다 / 개구리의 조상이 ~이었다고 / 물에 사는, 물고기 같은 동물

2 A frog's lungs / do not work / very well, / and they get / part of their oxygen / by breathing / through their skin.
개구리의 폐는 / 기능하지 않는다 / 그다지 잘 / 그리고 그것(개구리)은 얻는다 / 산소의 일부를 / 호흡함으로써 / 피부를 통해

3 There, / it can take a dip / every now and then / to keep its skin / from drying out.
거기에서 / 그것은 물에 잠깐 담글 수 있다 / 이따금 / 자신의 피부를 지키기 위해 / 건조해지는 것으로부터

4 And / eggs laid in the water / must develop / into water creatures / if they are to survive.
그리고 / 물속에 낳은 알이 / 발달해야 한다 / 물에 사는 생물로 / 그것들이 살아남으려면

5 For frogs, / metamorphosis thus provides / the bridge / between the water-dwelling young forms / and the land-dwelling adults.
개구리에게 있어서 / 탈바꿈은 따라서 제공한다 / 이어주는 다리를 / 물에 사는 어린 형체와 / 육지에 사는 성체 (사이에)

READING 35 Workbook p.59

1 Like religion or other traditions, / culture gives us / a kind of mental comfort and protection.
종교나 다른 전통들처럼 / 문화는 우리에게 제공한다 / 일종의 정신적인 위안과 보호를

2 The pressure / to remain within the box / is about / internalizing our group beliefs / and taking on group identities.
압박감은 / 그 상자 안에 남아야 한다는 / ~에 대한 것이다 / 우리의 집단 신념을 내면화하는 것 / 그리고 집단 정체성을 취하는 것

3 Also, / it is about / acting / as we are expected / to act.
또한 / 그것은 ~에 대한 것이다 / 행동하는 것 / 우리가 기대되는 대로 / 행동할 것으로

4 People all do things / without any sense / that what they're doing / could be questioned.
사람들은 모두 일을 한다 / 전혀 의식하지 않고 / 자신들이 하고 있는 일이 / 의문이 제기될 수 있다는 것을

5 Culture, therefore, defines / what it means / to be normal.
그러므로 문화는 정의한다 / 무엇을 의미하는지를 / 정상적이라는 것이

READING 36 Workbook p.59

1 We want / things / to be "this way" / or "that way".
우리는 원한다 / 일이 / '이런 방식'이기를 / 또는 '저런 방식'(이기를)

2 However, / the things / that seem to us to be standing out / may very well be related / to certain things.
그러나 / 것들은 / 우리에게 두드러져 보이고 있는 / 매우 관련 있을지도 모른다 / 특정한 것들과

3 In other words, / they are related / to our goals, interests, expectations, past experiences, / or current demands of the situation.
즉 / 그것들은 관련되어 있다 / 우리의 목표, 관심사, 기대, 과거의

경험과 / 또는 상황에 대한 현재의 요구와

4 It's like / "with a hammer in hand, / everything looks like a nail."
그것은 ~와 같다 / "망치를 손에 들고 있으면 / 모든 것이 못처럼 보인다"

5 This quote highlights / the phenomenon / of selective perception.
이 인용문은 강조한다 / 현상을 / 선택적 지각의

READING 37 Workbook p.60

1 Therefore, / any individual is / usually only capable of satisfying / a limited number of personal desires / independently.
그러므로 / 어떤 개인이든 ~이다 / 대개 충족시킬 수 있을 뿐 / 제한된 수의 개인적인 욕망만을 / 독립적으로

2 He needed to find / good food / to eat / and a place / to live in.
그는 찾아야 했다 / 좋은 음식을 / 먹을 만한 / 그리고 장소를 / 살

3 In the community, / all kinds of commodities can be exchanged / on the open market.
그 공동체 내에서 / 모든 종류의 상품은 교환될 수 있다 / 공개 시장에서

4 The reason is / that they can satisfy / the desires of other individuals.
그 이유는 ~이다 / 그것이 충족시킬 수 있기 때문이라는 것 / 다른 사람들의 욕망을

5 Those individuals / are willingly and purposely participating / in the exchange.
그러한 개인들은 / 기꺼이 그리고 목적을 가지고 참여하고 있다 / 그 거래에

READING 38 Workbook p.60

1 As kids, / we worked hard at learning / how to ride a bike; / when we fell off, / we got back on

again, / until it became / second nature / to us.
아이였을 때 / 우리는 열심히 배웠다 / 자전거 타는 법을 / 우리가 넘어지면 / 우리는 다시 올라탔다 / 그것이 될 때까지 / 습관이 우리에게

2 If we don't succeed / the first time, / or if it feels / a little awkward, / we'll tell / ourselves / that it wasn't a success / rather than giving it another shot.
만일 우리가 성공하지 못하면 / 처음에 / 혹은 느낌이 들면 / 약간 어색한 / 우리는 말할 것이다 / 스스로에게 / 그것이 성공이 아니었다고 / 또 다른 시도를 해 보기보다는

3 Consider / the idea / that your brain has / a network of neurons.
생각해 보라 / 개념을 / 여러분의 뇌가 가지고 있다는 / 뉴런의 연결망을

4 Those connections aren't / very reliable / at first, / which may make / your first efforts / a little hit-or-miss.
그 연결은 ~이지 않다 / 그리 신뢰할 만한 / 처음에는 / 그것은 만들 수도 있다 / 여러분의 첫 번째 시도를 / 다소 마구잡이로

5 That means / the more times you try using / that new feedback technique, / the more easily it will come / to you / when you need it.
그것은 의미한다 / 여러분이 더 여러 차례 사용해 볼수록 / 그 새로운 피드백 기술을 / 그것이 더 쉽게 다가올 것임을 / 여러분에게 / 여러분이 그것을 필요로 할 때

Unit 16 복합 문단 독해하기

READING 39　　　　　　　Workbook p.61

1 Gaby and Nellie / had lunches packed / and were ready to pedal.
Gaby와 Nellie는 / 도시락을 쌌다 / 그리고 페달을 밟을 준비가 되었다

2 They pedaled / side by side / and were happy / and laughed a lot.
그들은 페달을 밟았다 / 나란히 / 그리고 행복했다 / 그리고 많이 웃었다

3 Her nose did not feel so good / with the cool

breeze blowing / across her face.
그녀의 코는 느낌이 별로 좋지 않았다 / 시원한 바람이 불면서 / 얼굴을 스쳐

4 Two tired girls pedaled back / to the dorm, / and there / the housemother had a few words / with Nellie / about her swollen nose.
지친 두 소녀가 페달을 밟아 돌아왔다 / 기숙사로 / 그리고 그곳에서 / 여자 사감은 몇 마디 이야기를 나누었다 / Nellie와 / 그녀의 부은 코에 대해

5 The road led them / through the edge of town / and there / it forked.
그 길은 그들을 이끌었다 / 도시의 가장자리를 지나가게 / 그리고 거기서 / 그것은 갈라졌다

READING 40　　　　　　　Workbook p.61

1 What is / the most important challenge / facing my generation?
무엇이 ~인가 / 가장 중요한 도전 과제 / 우리 세대가 직면한

2 Then / I asked myself, / 'And if I weren't afraid, / what would I say / about it / in this speech?'
그러고 나서 / 나는 스스로에게 물었어 / '그리고 내가 두려워하지 않는다면 / 내가 무엇을 말할까 / 그것에 대해 / 이 연설에서'

3 Then, / only 17 himself / and graduating from high school, / he had called for equality / for African-Americans.
당시 / (아버지는) 겨우 17살에 / 고등학교를 졸업한 / 그는 평등을 요구했다 / 아프리카계 미국인들을 위한

4 Left alone on the stage, / I thought to myself, / 'Well, I guess / I need to be sure to do / only two things / with my life: / keep thinking for myself, / and not get killed.'
무대에 홀로 남아서 / 나는 마음속으로 생각했어 / '그럼, 나는 생각해 / 나는 확실히 하면 되겠어 / 두 가지만 / 내 인생에서 / 계속 스스로를 생각하는 것 / 그리고 죽임을 당하지 않는 것'

5 He handed / the speech / back to me, / and smiled.
그는 주었다 / 연설문을 / 다시 내게 / 그리고 미소 지었다

MEMO

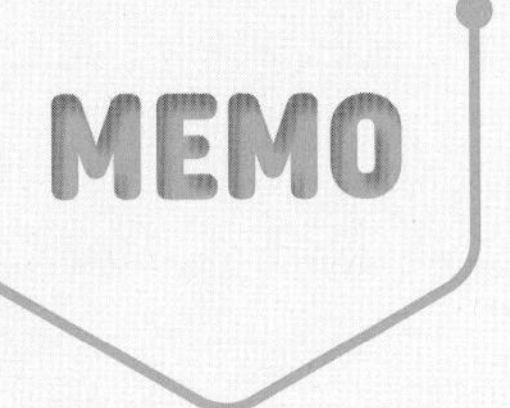